XUANZANG

A Buddhist Pilgrim on the Silk Road

XUANZANG

A Buddhist Pilgrim on the Silk Road

SALLY HOVEY WRIGGINS

with a foreword by Frederick W. Mote

Taylor & Francis Group
NEW YORK AND LONDON

First published 1996 by Westview Press, Inc.

Published 2021 by Routledge
605 Third Avenue, New York, NY 10017
2 Park Square, Milton Park, Abingdon, Oxon OX14 4RN

Routledge is an imprint of the Taylor & Francis Group, an informa business

Copyright © 1996 by Taylor & Francis

All rights reserved. No part of this book may be reprinted or reproduced or utilised in any form or by any electronic, mechanical, or other means, now known or hereafter invented, including photocopying and recording, or in any information storage or retrieval system, without permission in writing from the publishers.

Notice:
Product or corporate names may be trademarks or registered trademarks, and are used only for identification and explanation without intent to infringe.

Library of Congress Cataloging-in-Publication Data
Wriggins, Sally Hovey.
    Xuanzang : a Buddhist pilgrim on the Silk Road / Sally Hovey Wriggins.
        p.   cm.
    Includes bibliographical references and index.
    ISBN 0-8133-2801-2 (HC)
    1. Hsüan-tsang, ca. 596–664.   2. Priests, Buddhist—China—
Biography.   I. Title.
BQ8149.H787W75   1996
294.3′92—dc20
[B]
                                                                            95-46702
                                                                                CIP

ISBN 13: 978-0-3672-1386-2 (hbk)
ISBN 13: 978-0-3672-1667-2 (pbk)

TO HOWARD,
source of wisdom and fun

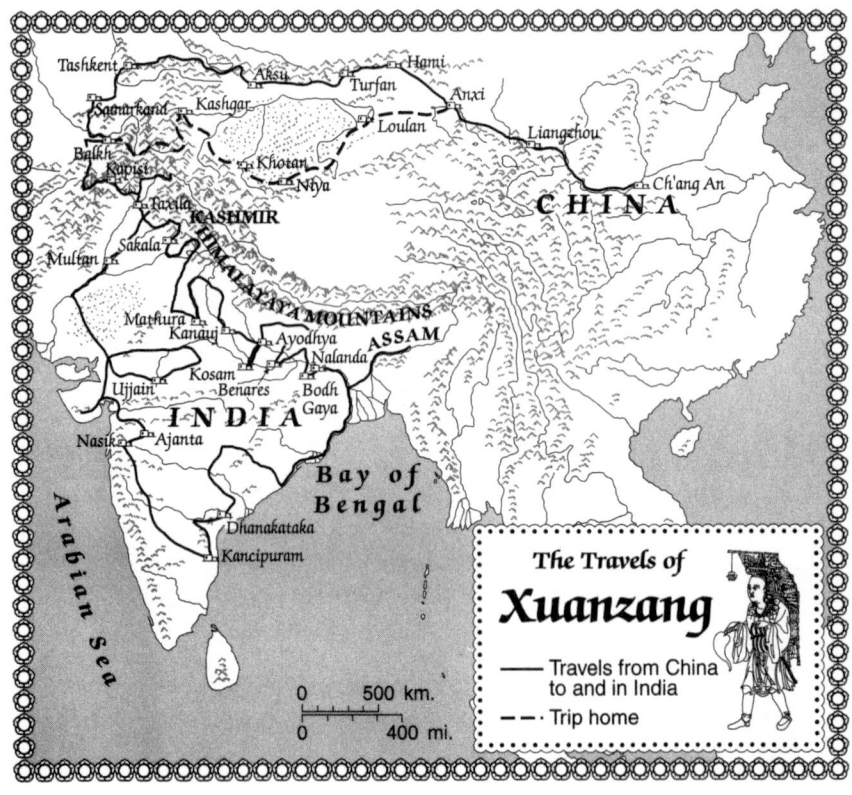

Contents

List of Maps	x
Foreword FREDERICK W. MOTE	xi
Preface	xv
Acknowledgments	xxi
Notes on Spelling and Pronunciation	xxiii

1 THE PILGRIM & THE EMPEROR — 1
Studying in Monasteries — 7
Preparing Himself in Chang'an — 10
Beginning His Journey — 12
Being Lost in the Desert — 14

2 THE OASES OF THE NORTHERN SILK ROAD — 19
Staying at the Hami Oasis — 21
Opposing the King of Turfan — 22
Visiting the Monasteries at Kucha (Kuqa) — 26
Crossing the Tian Shan Mountains — 29
Meeting the Great Khan — 30

3 THE CROSSROADS OF ASIA — 35
Winning Over the King of Samarkand — 37
Poisoning at Kunduz — 39
Visiting Stupas in Balkh — 39
Seeing the Famous Buddhas at Bamiyan — 43
Finding Hidden Treasures in Kapisa — 45

4 THE LAND OF INDIA — 51
Praying in the Shadow Cave at Jalalabad — 54
Pursuing King Kanishka Around Peshawar — 56

Seeking the Four Great Stupas and the Visvantara Site   58
Collecting Healing Sutras and Trekking in the Swat Valley   63
Exploring Monuments at Taxila   65
Studying the Law in Kashmir   69

5 PHILOSOPHERS & PIRATES IN NORTHERN INDIA   73

Fleeing from Robbers in the Punjab   75
Reaching Mathura, the Heartland of India   77
Seeing the Sacred Ganges River   81
Paying Reverence at the Heavenly Staircase   81
Visiting King Harsha's Kingdom   83
Pursuing Philosophy and Escaping from Pirates in Ayodhya   85
Finding the Sandalwood Image at Kausambi   87

6 THE BUDDHIST HOLY LAND   91

Beholding the Site of the Great Miracle at Sravasti   94
Seeking the Sacred Traces at Kapilavastu and Lumbini   95
Paying Reverence at Kusinagara, Where the Buddha Died   98
Paying Reverence at the Deer Park, in Sarnath   100
Visiting Holy Places at Vaisali   105
Worshipping at the Bo Tree, in Bodh Gaya   106

7 NALANDA MONASTERY & ENVIRONS   113

Meeting the Venerable One   115
Riding an Elephant to Rajagriha (Rajgir)   120
Climbing Vulture Peak   121
Attending Lectures at Nalanda   124
Lecturing and Writing at Nalanda   126

8 PHILOSOPHERS, ROCK-CUT CAVES & A FORTUNE-TELLER   129

Traveling Around the East Coast   132
Exploring a Rock-Cut Cave in South Kosala   134

Visiting Andhra and the South	136
Imagining Simhala (Sri Lanka)	137
Touring the West Coast	137
Staying at Nalanda Monastery Again	144
Meeting with a Fortune-Teller	146

9 THE JOURNEY HOME TO CHINA   149

Meeting King Harsha	151
Debating in the Grand Tournament	153
Starting His Journey Back to China	155
Losing Scriptures in the Indus River	155
Crossing the Hindu Kush and Pamir Ranges	157
Stopping at the Kashgar Oasis	160
Waiting at the Khotan Oasis	162
Entering the Desert	166

10 BACK IN CHINA   169

Resting at the Dunhuang Oasis	172
Triumphant Return to Chang'an	176
Being Interviewed by the Emperor	177
Writing the Record of the Western Regions	180
The Death of the Emperor and the Big Wild Goose Pagoda	181

AFTERWORD: THE LEGACY OF XUANZANG   185

Archaeological Legacy	185
Among Art Historians	187
Literary Heritage	190
Translation Legacy	191

Glossary	195
Notes on Illustrations	208
Notes	224
Selected Bibliography	249
About the Book and Author	257
Index	258

Maps

	The travels of Xuanzang	VI
1.1	Itinerary of Xuanzang on the Silk Road in China (from Chang'an to Hami)	2
2.1	Itinerary of Xuanzang on the Northern Silk Road (from Hami to Samarkand)	20
2.2	Archaeological sites at Turfan oasis	23
3.1	Itinerary of Xuanzang in Afghanistan (from Samarkand to Jalalabad)	36
4.1	Itinerary of Xuanzang in Gandharan Pakistan (from Jalalabad to Kashmir)	52
5.1	Itinerary of Xuanzang through northern India (from Kashmir to Kausambi)	74
6.1	Itinerary of Xuanzang in the Buddhist holy land (from Kausambi to Bodh Gaya)	92
8.1	Itinerary of Xuanzang around the Indian continent (from Nalanda to Parvata)	130
8.2	Archaeological Survey of India map of trade routes and sites of major rock-cut caves	141
9.1	Itinerary of Xuanzang from India to western China (Nalanda to Jalandhara)	150
9.2	Itinerary of Xuanzang from India to western China (Jalandhara to Kashgar)	156
9.3	Itinerary of Xuanzang from India to western China (Kashgar to Loulan)	164
10.1	Itinerary of Xuanzang from western China back home (Loulan to Chang'an)	170

Foreword

The story of the seventh-century Chinese Buddhist monk Xuanzang (in older writings spelled Hsuan-tsang, Yuan Chwang, Hiuen Tsiang, and other ways), who made a sixteen-year pilgrimage to the India of the great King Harsha in order to learn about Buddhist teachings at the source, is one of the great sagas in human history. It illuminates a phase of cultural interchange that had the most profound effect on the maturing of Chinese civilization. It is also a chapter in the larger history of Mahayana Buddhism, depicting its transmission via China through East and Inner Asia. Most immediately, as we encounter Xuanzang here, we learn about Buddhist belief and its concrete expression in the lives of this monk-pilgrim and the people he encountered in China and along the way in Central Asia and India. As such, it is a warmly human account of a remarkable personality, brought to life with sympathy and narrative skill. Xuanzang's story touches the reader, as it has touched the life of the author, Sally Hovey Wriggins, a person who, although not committed to Buddhist belief in any specific sense, nonetheless has been deeply stirred to understand the inescapable attraction of this great personality. All this is deftly and memorably communicated to the reader; the book is an important achievement.

Several aspects of Wriggins's technique in writing this book deserve special mention. One is that she has assembled a striking portfolio of illustrations, ranging from photos taken on the ground by herself and others to maps and photos of major works of art and architecture, all linked directly to her narrative. Another is her imaginative use of observations on the scenes in China, Central Asia, Afghanistan, and India as she followed the route of Xuanzang's travels; by describing for the reader the features of the life and of the physical setting that made the most vivid impressions on her, she re-creates what Xuanzang had seen in those places fourteen hundred years ago. Often they are seemingly insignificant vignettes of ordinary life. She uses them to remind the reader of the human dimensions of her subject's truly heroic undertaking.

As she takes the reader into that intimate encounter with the setting, she also has drawn very intelligently on the relevant secondary scholarship, thus introducing the reader to the state of the field and to the importance that scholars have always seen in the story. She has not, to be sure, pursued all the scholarly details exhaustively or exhaustingly, in the manner of a specialist's monograph. Instead, in this charmingly accessible book, she has drawn on the best of the literature to remind us of the essential points of fact and interpretation, in the mode of the best popular scholarly writing. I find her way of meeting her responsibilities to her predecessors in the field very satisfying. In fact, however, her predecessors did not give us a fully rounded picture of Xuanzang; the image of the Prince of Pilgrims that we gain from these pages bears us to a new level of that understanding and appreciation.

When we meet a figure of such immense personal achievement, and hence of importance to a phase of human cultural history, we may well ask how history would be different had he not lived. Although history is about "what really happened," asking such a nonhistorical question can help us to appreciate better what really happened. Without Xuanzang, Buddhism of some kind would nonetheless have come to play a central role in Chinese civilization. That cannot be doubted, for the process of full-scale adaptation to the Indian religion was long under way in China by the time of Xuanzang's birth about 596 of the common era. He was born a little more than twenty years before the founding of the glorious Tang dynasty (618–907 C.E.), during which Buddhism reached the height of its flowering in China. When the dynasty was founded, Buddhism had already been present on Chinese soil for six centuries, and from its beginnings there as a religion of the common people, often confused with its native Chinese counterpart, popular Daoism, it had gradually come to be recognized as a great system of religion and thought that had originated a thousand years earlier in northern India.

Over several centuries other Chinese had preceded Xuanzang to India or into Indian-dominated areas of Central Asia and maritime Southeast Asia, going as pilgrim monks who were seeking direct knowledge of the Buddha's teachings. Many Indians and others from those regions had come to China, bringing texts and knowledge of religious practice, to introduce them to the Chinese. Chinese and other merchants traveling the trade routes between eastern and western or southern Asia, especially those who followed the various sources of the Silk Road overland from northwest China into northern India, had become ardent Buddhists. They had long patronized the growing institutions, the temples, shrines, and monasteries, that sustained the religious community. The young Xuanzang could conceive of the notion of traveling to the source because so much had already been accomplished in making the Buddha's truths known within the sphere of Chinese life.

Yet even given this history, one must admit that without Xuanzang the character of Chinese Buddhism would have been quite different. The consequences of his pilgrimage, and of his entire life as a teacher-translator-scholar, which best reveal his historical importance, include the following:

1. It was his personal achievement to bring the emperor of China, Tang Taizong (who reigned 626–649), to wholehearted acceptance of Buddhism as a component of Chinese life. Because of him, the emperor began the patronage of Buddhist institutions, starting with his extraordinary favor toward Xuanzang himself; he founded a teaching and study monastery at the capital and agreed to Xuanzang's call for increased licensing of Chinese monks throughout the realm. Because of that, patronage of Buddhism by the Chinese elite greatly increased. This patronage occurred at the beginning of a stable and rich cultural era that lasted two centuries, during which the fullest flowering of Chinese Buddhism took place within a highly cosmopolitan phase of Chinese civilization.

2. Buddhism's transmission into China and from China through East Asia had an authoritative quality because of the depth of Xuanzang's mastery of the sacred texts and teachings he brought back from India. He greatly expanded the corpus of authentic texts available for study in China, and his life work of translating and commenting on those texts purified and expanded Buddhist doctrines. He was completely at home in both Sanskrit and Chinese; his translations greatly exceed in precision and in intelligibility those produced in earlier periods.

3. Xuanzang offered the Chinese intellectual world a greatly enhanced understanding of the highest intellectual attainment of the Indian Buddhist mind. Recognized in India as a person of powerful intellect, Xuanzang was able to penetrate the esoteric logic and philosophy at the highest levels current there. He succeeded in giving this rarefied level of Indian thought a full and accurate Chinese cultural expression for the first time, especially in translating the basic texts of and commentary on the profound school of radical idealism called the School of Mere Ideation, the most subtle and philosophical of Buddhist traditions. This philosophical current within Indian Buddhism is also known as the doctrines of the Consciousness Only school, which, though too difficult for many to follow, nonetheless left an imperishable mark on Chinese intellectual development.

4. Xuanzang became a powerful human image that intrigued all manner of Chinese who knew him, an image that lived through the centuries thereafter. He was portrayed in popular storytelling, in drama, and in several fictional guises; he was painted in temple wall decorations and was the subject of popular wood-block prints. As a Chinese folk hero, he was a devoted believer under the protection of

his Buddhist guardians, one who struggled to attain enlightenment and to bring religion to the masses of suffering humans. This image is at many points fanciful, but it was powerfully projected and undoubtedly touched more human lives than did his intellectual feats. It may be the most important aspect of Xuanzang's legacy, the most influential—if unanticipated—consequence of his daring pilgrimage in search of wisdom and truth.

Sally Hovey Wriggins, whether or not with such purpose in mind, has in this book recounted her own pilgrimage, driven by a necessity quite as real as that of Xuanzang fourteen centuries before. On one level, thus, this book records the spiritual odyssey of a twentieth-century pilgrim; that, however, is never made overt, for her genuine concern in writing lies in understanding her subject, not in revealing herself. Yet that quality of personal involvement is nonetheless latent throughout, and it adds richly to the satisfaction that the reader takes from her book. The immediacy of her sense of wonder will draw readers of all ages and all manner of expectations. In that way it surpasses even Arthur Waley's *The Real Tripitaka* (London, 1952). Written with unmatched grace and style, Waley's book makes an important scholarly contribution but leaves the pilgrim and his experiences beyond the reader's touch. Perhaps that is because Waley never traveled to Asia, whereas Wriggins has walked the ground that Xuanzang trod. Wriggins puts him directly into our company, and having thus come to feel and breathe with him, we cannot forget him. It is a memorable accomplishment.

Frederick W. Mote
Professor Emeritus, East Asian Studies
Princeton University

Preface

A Chinese emperor called him "the jewel of the empire," this Buddhist monk who journeyed from China to India on the Silk Road in the seventh century. Xuanzang (Hsuan-tsang), one of the Silk Road's most famous travelers, is as well known in Asia as Marco Polo is in the West. He wanted to go to the holy land of Buddhism in India to obtain the true scriptures instead of having to rely on the sometimes confusing translations then available in China. He also hoped to study with famous religious teachers and to see the sacred places of the Lord Buddha. During his journey, from 629 to 645 C.E., he traveled an astonishing 10,000 miles.

Xuanzang was both a symbol and an instrument of cultural exchange between the two great civilizations in Asia—India and China. He was one of the disseminators of Buddhist faith and Indian philosophy in China, opening new horizons for the Chinese at a time when they were singularly open to influences from the outside world. His *Record of the Western Regions*, which he wrote for the Tang emperor, has been used by scholars in many disciplines. Even now in the twentieth century, it remains a major source on seventh-century Asia before the coming of Islam. It is still a guide for those seeking to learn more about the art and archaeology of Afghanistan, Pakistan, Central Asia, India, and China. When contemporary art historians wish to interpret cave paintings and sculptures, or when modern archaeologists seek to learn more about the sites they are studying, they look to Xuanzang. He provided an introduction to the Silk Road and to a wonderful medieval world in which pilgrims were great adventurers as well as philosophers and ambassadors of goodwill.

As an adventurer, he crossed the Great Unknown, the Taklamakan Desert, which had been called "an abomination of desolation." He traversed the icy glaciers of three of the highest mountain chains in Asia, losing one-third of his men in the first range he climbed. He crisscrossed the subcontinent of India, traversing swinging rope bridges in the upper reaches of the Indus River and facing leopards, robbers, or both in the tropical forests in the south.

From this standpoint Xuanzang seems rather more like some of the Irish monks who set forth in their tiny coracles to spread Christianity in Europe. Xuanzang traveled much farther than they did, but their motivation may have been similar to his. What led them to leave home and face the unknown? What was this restless energy, this questing urge, this passion to seek new spiritual horizons? The Irish monks were bringing a purer form of Christianity to the continent; the Chinese pilgrim was seeking to bring the real truths of Mahayana Buddhism to China.

Unlike the Irish monks, Xuanzang was also an ambassador of goodwill. He consorted with the kings of the Silk Road oases, the Great Khan of the Western Turks and the king of Samarkand in Central Asia; with the kings of the smaller kingdoms in what is now Afghanistan, Pakistan, and northern India. He was a great favorite of King Harsha, the uniter of northern India. Subsequently the Tang emperor twice asked him to be one of his political advisers, and Xuanzang became his spiritual mentor in the last year of the emperor's life.

Xuanzang was also a philosopher, metaphysician, and translator of Buddhist texts. For fifteen years prior to his journey he studied the various schools of Buddhism in China. He was drawn to the sophisticated ideas of the founders of an Idealist school of Buddhism; he toured India for another fourteen years, going on pilgrimages, talking with Indian philosophers, lecturing at monasteries, and debating before large crowds. Finally, he spent the last two decades of his life translating the texts he had brought back with him to China.

What guidance is there in trying to understand this man of so many parts, this adventurer, diplomat, and philosopher? Along with the passion that drove him from a quiet monastic life, Xuanzang is clearly portrayed by his biographer as someone who is extraordinarily dispassionate, possessing an equilibrium that made him indifferent to the flattery of kings, and a calm presence that soothed even the most vicious pirate robber. "As the turbulent waves of a river do not disturb its pure water underneath so was he." This was the Asian Buddhist ideal and perhaps also what Xuanzang was striving for when he set out on his journey.

This same quality of extraordinary equanimity can be seen and understood more easily by viewing some of the Buddhas and Bodhisattvas, or Compassionate Ones, from famous caves in China. In these Buddhas are the paradoxes of Mahayana Buddhism, the supramundane calm and radiating energy, or unearthly detachment and great compassion. By standing and gazing long enough, one begins to understand the mission of Xuanzang and the medieval world in which he lived.

Xuanzang looked down on an early Buddhism, called Hinayana (the Lesser Vehicle, or Theravada Buddhism), which was addressed largely to monks. Their ideal was the *arhat*, or holy man who occupies himself only with his own salvation. Xuanzang was devoted to a later Buddhism (Mahayana, or the Greater Vehicle), which preached universal salvation to laypeople as well as monks. Much of its appeal comes from the role of the Bodhisattvas, the Compassionate Ones, who help all sentient beings attain salvation. They represent wisdom and mercy with their half-closed eyes and mysterious smiles. Xuanzang sought their guidance for his journey.

Part of my fascination with Xuanzang is connected with my love of Buddhist art, especially an image from childhood—a supramundane sandstone Buddhist head with its secret smile—and a look of remoteness such as I had never imagined possible. The combination of detachment and compassion in this Khmer head in the Seattle Art Museum was the image upon which my heart first opened. Perhaps also the lure of "the lands farthest out," symbolized by the Silk Road, accorded with my childhood among the mountains of the Pacific Northwest, one of the wilder parts of the United States.

Many visits to Asia stimulated my interest in Xuanzang. When I talked to curators from the Kabul Museum in the mid-1970s about this pilgrim and his journey, they produced a map showing me exactly where he had passed through Afghanistan on his way to India and also on his way back to China. To me, such a detailed knowledge of the places he visited was unbelievable. Wasn't this pilgrimage only a century after the legendary King Arthur is supposed to have lived in mist-shrouded Wales or northern England? What impressed me even more was that they described Xuanzang in the same way modern detectives talk about a "live witness."

I had already encountered Xuanzang when I was researching the Chinese classic *Monkey*, or *Journey to the West*. His pilgrimage had inspired a cycle of legends in China, which became this sixteenth-century epic novel. But it wasn't until my husband and I were traveling in Burma with Jeannette Mirsky that I seriously considered writing about the journey of this remarkable Buddhist. Jeannette had just completed a biography of the great explorer and archaeologist Aurel Stein; Xuanzang had been his patron saint. One evening with her I ventured to compare King Arthur and the Chinese pilgrim; both had lived about the same time, and both had inspired a vast corpus of literature hundreds of years after they had died. Jeannette exploded, "King Arthur is a myth and Xuanzang was a *real* person." She added significantly that my excitement was palpable whenever I talked about Xuanzang. I knew in that moment that I, too, had a book to write.

Good sources on Xuanzang and his travels are available, for after the pilgrim's return to China, the Tang emperor asked him to make a record of his pilgrimage. Xuanzang did so on the basis of notes he had made describing the social, economic, and political life in the foreign lands he visited. He also included several chapters on the Buddhist holy land in India, its holy sites and monuments, the eight places of pilgrimage for every Buddhist, and the chief miracles of the Lord Buddha.

Several years after Xuanzang completed his *Record of the Western Regions* in 646 C.E., Shaman Huili (Hwui-li) wrote *The Life of Hiuen-Tsiang*. Huili, a younger man and an expert on Buddhist literature, was assigned by the emperor to assist Xuanzang in translating the Sanskrit texts he had brought back from India. I can picture the two of them after their day's work of translating, sitting down over a cup of tea, with Xuanzang telling his fellow monk his ordeals and triumphs on the Silk Road to India.

Their two books complement each other. Huili put Xuanzang and his personal experiences in the foreground of what is a reverential tribute. In Xuanzang's own narrative, which begins on an oasis on the Northern Silk Road, the pilgrim stays in the background and rarely refers directly to himself. His style is unemotional and highly detached. He is, after all, writing a report for the Tang emperor. Both Huili's biography and Xuanzang's record contain solid factual information spiced with fictional elements. By embroidering on adventures that are already heroic, Huili gives them a storybook quality, so that Xuanzang is already on his way to becoming a legend.

As Fritz Mote points out in the Foreword, most people in East Asia know Xuanzang. His image in the popular culture is a powerful, albeit fanciful, one. His role as a Chinese folk religious hero is a vital part of his legacy.

The Xuanzang I present in this biographical account is also an intellectual, a theologian, a translator of great precision, a diplomat, and a keen journalistic observer. I have not stinted in presenting his substantial achievements that will endure, as they have for centuries already. Yet the religious hero, the man every Chinese knows and loves, is in this book too.

I have tried to capture the appeal of Xuanzang as a folk hero by using italics and simple language, as I distilled the best of his two biographers, Huili and Li Yongshi, to make their stories more vivid. These are dramatic incidents showing his visions, how his religious devotion saved him from death by starvation, robbers, and pirates. Sometimes the stories are dreams and omens foretelling his fate or accounts of great courage and triumph.

Unfamiliar names of people and places, difficult Buddhist nomenclature, and arcane language in their accounts are daunting. If only Xuanzang's name had been simple like Marco Polo's. As it is, his name was written in a bewildering variety of ways even before China adopted its modern pinyin system of spelling in 1958. In the earlier Wade-Giles system, he was known as Hsuan-tsang, Hhuen Kwan, Hiouen Tsiang, Hiouen Thsang, Hiuen Tsiang, Hsuan Chwang, Hsuan Tsiang, and Hwen Thsang. Additional ways of spelling his name are Yuan Chang, Yuan Chuang, Yuen Chwang, and Yuan Chwang. Place-names undergo

Preface

many transformations. The great Tang capital was known as Ch'ang-an in Wade-Giles spelling and Chang'an in pinyin spelling. It then became known as Sian in Wade-Giles; now it is Xi'an in pinyin. The countless names on the Silk Roads are even worse, for art historians have used Turkic, Uighur, and other names for some of the sites. For example, some old Turkic names on the Silk Road are still in use, such as Bezeklik or Dandan Oiluq. Because readers, in following Xuanzang's journey, may want to examine modern maps with pinyin spelling or twentieth-century Indian names, I have used both modern and the best-known earlier usages.

Added to the spelling difficulty is a generous sprinkling of the nearly indecipherable titles of Buddhist Sanskrit texts and obscure Buddhist terminology used by Buddhist writers. To take a sample from Huili at random: "In a mango wood east of Ghosilarama were the old foundations of the house in which Asanga P'usa composed the Hsien-yang-sheng-chiao-lun." Maybe this combination of spelling and terminology is one of the reasons that Xuanzang is not better known in the West.

Rene Grousset's *In the Footsteps of the Buddha,* with its emphasis on art as illuminating the culture of a brilliant era in Buddhist history—the seventh century—whetted my interest in Xuanzang. But the real inspiration for me was Xuanzang himself, the individual behind the extraordinary achievements. By retracing his path, I sought to rediscover Xuanzang as a person of deep religious feeling with a powerful mind, a man of adventure with a strong personality and a gift for friendship.

The peculiar qualities of the man sometimes seem to be overwhelmed by the legends that grew up about him, even in his lifetime. Yet there were moments when he showed human frailties, such as when he, surrounded by Indian monks who dismissed China as inferior, staunchly defended his homeland. He was very Confucian in his reactions to some of the excesses of Hinduism, so that he was driven to comment, "the naked man who covered his body with ashes is like a cat who has slept in the chimney corner." After almost twenty years of seeking the truths of Buddhist philosophy, he arranged to study with the pundit Jayasena, asking him for explanations of passages *that still caused him doubt.* What tenacious truth seeking! Finally his anguish welled up at Bodh Gaya, where the Buddha had attained enlightenment. He wondered in what cycle of life he had been at the time when the Buddha perfected himself in wisdom; he reflected on the depth and weight of his own imperfection and wept. When his great teacher at Nalanda died, he said that he felt "his heart was deeply stabbed and he could not recover from such a wound."

When he defended his country, when he had doubts, when he wept at Bodh Gaya, when he mourned the death of the head of Nalanda, those were the moments when he broke the mold of the ideal Buddhist. Those were the times when I no longer followed in his shadow on the pilgrim road. Instead he had become fully human and I felt that he was by my side.

Sally Hovey Wriggins

Acknowledgments

Two women and two men have been my mentors, Jeannette Mirsky, Edith Wallace, Frederick W. Mote, and Victor Mair. Vidya Dehejia, Angela Howard, Victor Mair, Frederick W. Mote, Madge Cooper, Katherine Sherman, Matthew Kapstein, and Morris Rossabi have all read my manuscript at least once and provided useful advice. Irene Bloom, Nancy Dupree, and Aileen Ward have read appropriate chapters. My energetic husband has read it countless times over the years.

I have been fortunate in working with Susan McEachern at Westview Press. She is an ideal editor, who has a sharp intelligence enhanced by an open, generous, and knowing spirit. Her colleagues Marian Safran and Shena Redmond help to maintain her high standards.

Before publication Ellen E.M. Roberts worked closely with me, challenging me to rethink many parts of my manuscript. She also provided detailed advice on all aspects of producing the manuscript as well as constant moral support during its long gestation period.

Phil Schwartzberg developed a series of expert maps that add so much to making Xuanzang's journey come alive. Kathy Swatek translated *Xuanzang Xiyouji* (Xuanzang's journey to the west), by Zhu Qi, from Chinese into English for me.

Many have lent general advice or very specific help in America: Janet Baldwin, Doak Barnett, Kanta Batia, Patricia Berger, Ed Bernbaum, Paddy Booz, Jane Brown, Gloria Burkhardt, Lee Caldron, Katherine Caldwell, Debbie Chodoff, Roy Craven, S. Czuma, Louis Dupree, Ainslie Embree, Anne Goodrich, Carrington Goodrich, Uta Gouras, Barbara Harrison, Amy Heinrich, Sheila Hixon, Paul Ignatieff, Ernst Kitzinger, Lucy Lo, David S. Magier, Patrick Maveety, Florence Kate Millar, Freda Murck, P. Pal, Theodore M. Riccardi Jr., Glynn Robinson, Joseph Schwartzberg, Erma Shelton, Susan Sinberg, Judith Smith, Alexander Soper, Walter Spink, Robert Thurman, Audrey Topping, S. Heng-Ting Tsay, Trish Young, Masallo Watanabe, and Zhu Ming.

One other person deserves special mention, the one who rescued me whenever the computer (or I) misbehaved, Zhu Fang.

My agent, Carolyn Gilbert, whose zest was so attractive, "kept the faith."

In the course of many trips to Europe and Asia I have been helped by friends, diplomats, scholars, and museum officials in many countries:

In China, Ambassador Arthur and Betty Lou Hummel, Karl Olson, Huang Shengzhang, in Beijing; Stan Brooks, consul general, and Nancy Elizabeth Boulton, in Shanghai; Abbot Changming Master and Head Monk Xinqi, master of Xiangjiao Temple (Temple of Flourishing Teaching), in Xi'an. In Russia, D. Lesnichenko, Nathalie Dayanakova, and Maria Menshikova, from the Hermitage Museum, Leningrad. In India, D. Devahuti, Maya Sen, who accompanied me to the Buddhist holy land, Himani Lal Khanna, and Rolf and Ronnie Lynton; Chaya Hassner, National Museum, New Delhi; H. S. Bora, director, Photographic Sections, Archaeological Survey of India; Pradeep Mehendiratta, director, American Institute of Indian Studies; D. Misra, photographer, Mathura Museum; Puah Thakurel, assistant curator, Mathura Museum; M. A. Dhaky, director, American Institute of Indian Studies, Benares; V. R. Nambiar, associate director, American Institute of Indian Studies; Gerhardt Roth, director, Nalanda Maha Vihare. At Nalanda, H. Prasad, librarian, N. K. Prasad, registrar, C. K. Prasad and S. B. Singh, expert guides, as well as H. K. Prasad, Patna Museum. In Pakistan, Humera Alam, Lahore Museum; Barry Walkley, USIS cultural affairs officer, and Aallam Almakky, USIS photographer, Lahore; Al Thibout, consul general, Lahore; Dan O'Dell Rawalpindi, Gulzar Mohammed Khan, director, Taxila Museum; Fidaullah Sehrai, director, Peshawar Museum; Mike Malinowski, consul general, Peshawar. In Afghanistan, Ambassador Theodore and Patricia Eliot, Mrs. H. T. Motamedi, Kabul Museum. In Great Britain, W. Zwalf, British Museum, Ernest Gombrich, Oriental Institute, Glen Dudbridge, China Institute, Oxford. In France, Robert and Monique Jera-Bezart, College de France, Francine Tissot, Musée Guimet, and Dominique Darbois. In Belgium, Claude de Marteau. In Sweden, Bo Sommerstrom, curator for Asia, Ethnological Museum Stockholm.

S.H.W.

Notes on Spelling and Pronunciation

One reason so little Central Asian scholarship has been made available to the general public in the United States is the tremendous task of presenting Chinese, Indian, and Central Asian names in a clear and simple way. It has proved impossible to adopt a uniform system of orthography for this book because there are too many differences in sources and scholarly traditions as well as discrepancies between ancient and modern names. I have tried to encourage readability by confining complicated elements to the glossary.

Chinese Orthography

For Chinese words I have used the pinyin system throughout the book. This system, adopted by the Chinese government in 1958, superseded the Wade-Giles method of romanizing Chinese names. If the spellings differ significantly, I have listed the Wade-Giles spelling in parentheses at the first use of the name in the text. I have also listed the Wade-Giles spelling in parentheses in the Glossary. When unfamiliar names have been spelled in the Wade-Giles system in extracts from works published in English, I have added the pinyin spelling in brackets.

Pronunciation of Chinese names presents perhaps the largest hurdle. However, according to Madge Huntington, pinyin words are pronounced more or less according to the rules of English phonetics. There are five significant exceptions:

C: *C* followed by vowel(s) is pronounced "ts" as in i*ts*; thus Cao Cao becomes "Tsao Tsao."

OU: *OU* is pronounced like the "oe" in hoe. Zhou, as in Zhou dynasty, becomes "joe."

Z: *Z* is pronounced like the "j" in déjà vu or *J*acques.

Q: *Q* is pronounced "ch" as *ch*in. Thus Qin and Qing (dynasties) become "*ch*in and *ch*ing."

X: *X* is spoken like a lisped "s"—also described as an aspirated "s" or "hs." Xi'an becomes "*H*si-ahn"; Xuanzang becomes "*H*su-wan Tsahng."

Local Names

In the case of places, I have usually taken the best-known name: Kashgar instead of Kashi; Khotan instead of Hotan, Hetan, He-tien, Yutian, or Kustana. Some of the alternative names are included in the Glossary.

Indian/Sanskrit

In keeping with modern practice, I have eliminated diacritical marks in Indian and Sanskrit words. Names of important Buddhist texts appear in English in the book; Sanskrit equivalents appear in the Glossary. When pronouncing words, one must sound each letter. Vowels are pronounced as in Italian; consonants as in English. The sound of every letter is invariable:

C: *C* is pronounced "ch" as in "*ch*urch."
H: When *h* appears after *p, t, d, g, b,* or *k*, it begins a new syllable. For example, *ph* as in "u*ph*ill," not as in "*ph*iloso*ph*y."
V: *V* is pronounced like *w*.
A: *A* is pronounced like the second *a* in "Americ*a*."
E: *E* is pronounced like the French *é*, as in "*été*."
I: *I* is pronounced "ee" like the *i* in "l*i*ter."

ONE

THE PILGRIM & THE EMPEROR

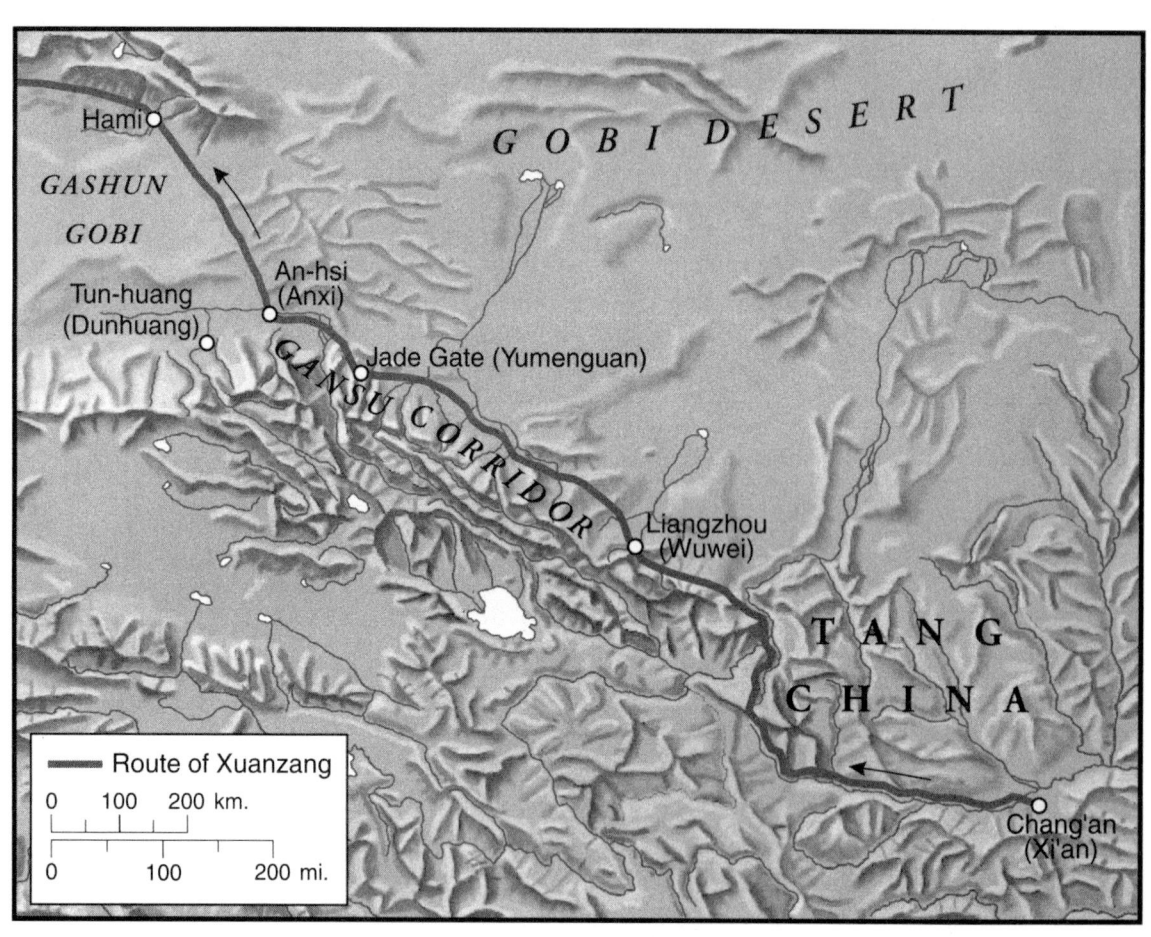

MAP I.I
Itinerary of Xuanzang on the Silk Road in China (from Chang'an to Hami) (Philip Schwartzberg, Meridian Mapping)

IN 629 C.E. A YOUNG MONK named Xuanzang left China with a warrant on his head; he departed in secret by night. He made his way safely past five watchtowers in the desert and the Jade Gate, the last outpost of the Tang Empire. The fears of this solitary pilgrim were not over, for he was traveling against the wishes of the Emperor Taizong (T'ai-tsung, 626–649 C.E.) (Fig. 1.1).

This young ruler of the Tang dynasty had little sympathy for Buddhism at the time and did not want Xuanzang or any other of his subjects in the dangerous western regions. His power was far from secure and he was still grappling with the hostility and even treachery of several of the peoples of Central Asia. Disobeying the emperor would carry a heavy price, but Xuanzang was determined to go on a pilgrimage to the holy land of Buddhism in India.[1]

In April 645, after his 10,000-mile quest for truth to India, the pilgrim returned and approached the Tang capital Chang'an, modern Xi'an. The news of his arrival soon spread; the streets were filled to overflowing, so much so that Xuanzang could not make his way through the crowds. People had heard about his pilgrimage to far-off and strange lands and wanted to see him. He was obliged to spend the night by a canal on the outskirts of the city. The magistrates, fearing that a large number of people would be crushed in the crowd, ordered everyone to stand quietly and burn incense. The emperor was away at the time, but an audience was arranged. A huge procession of monks carried the relics, images, and books that Xuanzang had brought back with him from India. The return of a hero.

In the sixteen years between Xuanzang's lonely departure and his triumphant reentry in 645, both the pilgrim and the emperor had succeeded in the eyes of the world. The twenty-seven-year-old fugitive had become China's best-known Buddhist and one of the most remarkable travelers of all time.[2] The thirty-year-old emperor, who was of Turkish-Chinese descent and therefore an expert horseman, had become one of China's greatest emperors, presiding over the expanding Tang Empire (Fig. 1.2)

Xuanzang accomplished his religious mission and returned safely with a large collection of Buddhist scriptures. He had seen "traces not seen before, heard sacred words not heard before, witnessed spiritual prodigies exceeding those of nature." He had consulted with the rulers of the oases of the Northern and Southern Silk Roads; the Great Khan of the Western Turks; King Harsha, uniter of northern India; and many potentates in between. He would remember a close friendship with the

FIGURE I.I
Portrait of the Emperor Taizong, who at first forbade the young monk Xuanzang to go to India and after the trip asked him to write an account of his journey, which is one of the principal sources for this book (The Metropolitan Museum of Art. Gift of Mrs. Edward S. Harkness, 1947 [48.81 lj])

head of India's most illustrious monastery all his life. He had crossed the most dangerous rivers and three of the highest mountain ranges in Asia (Fig. 1.3).

Not only had the new Tang emperor consolidated his power in China; he had conquered Central Asia. First he defeated the Eastern Turks in Mongolia in 630 C.E. Then he turned his attention to the Western Turks. By a curious stroke of fate, the Great Khan of the Western Turks was murdered shortly after Xuanzang's visit; six months later his mighty empire collapsed. The Tang emperor then began to reestablish protectorates over the oases of the Northern and Southern Silk Roads, where the pilgrim had also been. As a result of these conquests, China exercised direct control as far as the Pamirs. On occa-

The Pilgrim & the Emperor

FIGURE 1.2
Relief from the tomb of the Emperor Taizong (ruled 626–649 C.E.), showing a general removing an arrow from a wounded horse (University of Pennsylvania Museum [Neg. #23298])

sion, the emperor extended his power through diplomacy, such as when he arranged a marriage alliance with a Tibetan royal family. He had already sent two Chinese envoys to King Harsha in India in 643 C.E. after Xuanzang's visit. Religious missions such as Xuanzang's would extend the reach of China even beyond the Pamirs.

What a difference in background and temperament of these two men! Brought up with Confucian values, Xuanzang was a bookish boy who read Confucian classics and became a scholarly Buddhist intellectual. But he broadened his intellectual skills, and far from staying in a monastic cell, he overcame robbers and pirates and became a mountaineer and survivor in the desert. The emperor, whose early education was horsemanship and archery, was a rough soldier and heroic warrior

FIGURE 1.3
Copy of a traditional fourteenth-century portrait of Xuanzang with a modern-looking frame pack filled with the Buddhist scriptures he brought with him from India. Portrait from a rubbing taken from a stele at Xuanzang's burial place, at the Temple of Flourishing Teaching, outside Xi'an. (Courtesy Abe Dulberg, photographer)

The Pilgrim & the Emperor

who had come to the throne after assassinating his elder brother. Yet the emperor in the early years of his reign came to be regarded as a moderate, frugal, and wise Confucian ruler who sought the advice of his ministers and was concerned for the welfare of his people.[3] As a final irony, it was Xuanzang's secular knowledge of foreign affairs gained from years of arduous travel that interested the Tang ruler, although toward the end of his life, the ailing emperor changed his views on Buddhism, sought out Xuanzang for solace, and accepted him wholeheartedly as his spiritual mentor.[4] At the first meeting of the emperor and the pilgrim in 645, both men were at the height of their careers. The experiences of the Chinese pilgrim and the political interest of the emperor coincided in a remarkable way. With the expansion of his new empire, the emperor needed firsthand information about the successes and failures of his imperial policies. Xuanzang was the ideal informant. The emperor questioned the forty-three-year-old monk in detail about the rulers, climate, products, and customs of the countries he had been through. Impressed by Xuanzang's knowledge of foreign lands, Taizong asked him to be a minister to advise the emperor on the new Asian relationships and problems of his kingdom. Xuanzang declined. Then the emperor requested that he set down a detailed account, country by country, of the western kingdoms that he had visited. What interested Xuanzang the most—information on the monks, their schools of philosophy, and especially the monuments and stories of the Buddha—were matters of indifference to his patron.

No matter. Writing an account of the western regions was a new kind of request for Xuanzang who was used to those who sought his advice on religion or philosophy. A man of many parts, adventurer, intellectual, theologian, priest, and ambassador, he had given spiritual advice and inspiration to many political leaders and potentates in Central Asia. A "Prince among Pilgrims," this Buddhist monk moved easily in both religious and secular worlds. His powerful personality had impressed both the Emperor Taizong and the great Indian King Harsha. A man of unusual flexibility, open to the new and strange wherever he found it, Xuanzang was an ideal observer of foreign cultures.

Studying in Monasteries

Who was this Chinese pilgrim, and how did he happen to go on his long journey? According to his biographer, Xuanzang was born near Luoyang in the province of Henan in 602. He was the youngest of four sons, an heir to a long line of literati and mandarins. His grandfather had been an official in the Qi (Ch'i) dynasty (479–501 C.E.) and held the post of eminent national scholar. His father had been well versed in Confucianism and was also distinguished for his superior abilities and elegance of manner. However, this Confucian gentleman preferred to busy himself in the study of his books and pleaded ill health rather than accept offers of government service at the time of the decaying Sui dynasty (581–618 C.E.).

Xuanzang was brought up in a Confucian household. At the age of eight he amazed his father with his filial piety, a strong virtue in Confucianism. He even began to study the Confucian classic books about this time. But the intellectual vitality of Confucianism was waning,[5] and Xuanzang's older brother became a Buddhist monk. He took an interest in his younger brother and saw to it that he began to study Buddhist scriptures at his monastery in Luoyang at a young age.

Xuanzang was the kind of serious boy who was old before he was young. When he was only twelve years old, an unexpected royal mandate announced that fourteen monks were to be trained and supported by the state at his brother's monastery in Luoyang, the eastern capital of the Sui dynasty. Several hundred candidates applied at the Pure Land Monastery for this important ordination. The young adolescent Xuanzang loitered at the monastery gate until the imperial envoy, who was about to supervise the ceremony, engaged him in conversation. "What is your name? Your age?" And when Xuanzang revealed how very much he wanted to be a monk, the official asked him why. "My only thought in taking this step," he replied, "is to spread abroad the light of the Religion of Tathagata (Buddha)."[6]

Such an unexpected and formal reply impressed the official, who recognized the boy's remarkable qualities from his eagerness, confidence, and modesty. The official selected him as one of the novices to be ordained despite his youth, for, as he explained to his fellow officials, "To repeat one's instructions is easy, but true self-possession and nerve are not so common."[7]

For the next five years Xuanzang lived with his brother at the Pure Land Monastery. He plunged into the study of Buddhist scriptures, both the austere doctrine of early Buddhism and the mystical doctrine of the Greater Vehicle, or Mahayana. Xuanzang was irresistibly drawn to this later Buddhism, whose two key words were "Emptiness," signifying the object of wisdom, and "Bodhisattvas," or Enlightened Beings, who postponed their own salvation for the sake of others (Fig. 1.4).[8]

His philosophical studies were interrupted in 618 C.E. when the Sui dynasty collapsed. Because of the anarchy that followed its downfall and the civil war between the Tangs and their rivals, many parts of the empire fell into chaos.[9] Xuanzang and his brother fled first to Chang'an in the northwest, which the Tang rulers had proclaimed their capital.

FIGURE 1.4
Wall painting and sculpture in one of the earliest Dunhuang Caves in China. Center figure is a Bodhisattva, or Maitreya (these are beings who postpone their own salvation so that they may help others). (The Lo Archive)

They found the city swarming with soldiers, so the two brothers, along with a large community of monks who were gathering from various parts of the empire, made their way to Chengdu, in Sichuan. Xuanzang and his brother spent two or three years there studying the different schools of Buddhism.

Xuanzang's biographer compared the two young men: "His elder brother . . . was elegant in his manners and sturdy physically just like his father. . . . His eloquence and comprehensiveness in discussion and capacity to edify people were equal to those of his younger brother." He continued, "But in the manner of loftiness of mind, without being affected by worldly attachments; in profound researches in metaphysical aspects of the cosmos; in ambition to clarify the universe . . . and in the sense of self respect even in the presence of the Emperor," Xuanzang surpassed him.[10]

In 622, when he was twenty, Xuanzang was fully ordained as a monk. Shortly afterwards he left his brother behind in Chengdu and returned to the capital.

Preparing Himself in Chang'an

Chang'an had much to offer Xuanzang. It was the greatest city in China—perhaps in the entire medieval world. Tang historical sources are so detailed that we know, for example, that it occupied an area of more than 30 square miles.[11] Rome at its height occupied 5.2 square miles. Chang'an, a city of a million people in the seventh century, became the center of the great culture of the Tang dynasties. In 742 C.E. its population had swelled to two million inhabitants, of whom five thousand were foreigners.[12]

With its rich cultural life, prosperity, and the variety of nationalities that came to live there, Chang'an was a radiating center of Asian civilization. New stimuli from northern India and the kingdoms of Central Asia enriched Chinese Buddhism and made it the most lively and influential system of thought in its day. From Iran and Central Asia came other new religions, including Islam, Zoroastrianism, Manichaeanism, and Nestorian Christianity. Together with these intellectual and spiritual influences came many new developments in the arts, ranging from music and the dance to metal working and fine cuisine, as well as important technical and scientific influences in mathematics and linguistics. A galaxy of poets and artists were also part of this glittering capital. The latest in Buddhist doctrine and in pictorial models, the newest in entertainment and fashion, could be found in Chang'an.

A time of preparation. Xuanzang continued his Buddhist studies in Chang'an and sought out those foreigners who could give him instruction in the languages spoken beyond China's borders. He probably went to the Western Market, the area of the city connected with the Silk Road, to learn some Tokharian, which was spoken in many places in Central Asia, such as Turfan. His gift in languages would serve him well in the future. He also began to study Sanskrit in 626 C.E. so that he would be able to communicate with foreign monks whose native language was unfamiliar to him. Like Latin in the Christian monasteries of medieval Europe, Sanskrit was the language of Buddhist scriptures and monasteries in all of northern Asia.

Indian scriptures had been translated into Chinese since the first centuries of the common era. Missionaries from India and Kashgaria (modern Xinjiang), Parthians from Iran, and Sogdians (from the area of Central Asian republics of the former Soviet Union) had founded monasteries in Luoyang and Chang'an, where individual monks and teams of monks were busily translating the vast Buddhist literature coming out of India. There were also many Chinese monks who had gone to the west. At least fifty-four clerics before Xuanzang, the first one in 260, had traveled westward, though not all of them reached the land of their faith. Among those who did, the pious Faxian (Fa-hsien) and Zhiyan (Chih-yen) stirred his imagination.[13]

By this time Xuanzang had spent fifteen years in Luoyang, Chengdu, and Chang'an, studying languages and mastering the teachings of the various schools of Buddhism. In so doing he formed serious doubts about some of the Chinese translations. They were conflicting, garbled, or simply inadequate. He came to feel also that each abbot uncritically followed the teachings of his particular school. Like the Indian fable of the blind men, each touching a different part of the elephant and taking it for the whole, these men were blind to the strange discordances and contradictions among them. Some of their theories were either vaguely or manifestly in contradiction with the holy scriptures. Which precepts were authentic? Was it true that all men or only part of humanity could attain Buddhahood? He was bewildered and unable to decide which theories should be accepted. Thus he made up his mind to go to India to clear up his doubts and to bring back the complete Sanskrit text of what came to be called *Treatise on the Stages of Yoga Practice*, by Asanga.

Xuanzang was drawn to the sophisticated writings of Asanga and his brother Vasubandhu, who were the founders of the Yogacara school of Buddhism, only part of whose huge compendium of philosophy had reached China.[14] This school of thought professed a metaphysical idealism in which the outside world did not exist but was a projection of one's own consciousness.

> *As stars, a fault of vision, as a lamp,*
> *A mock show, dew drops, or a bubble,*
> *A dream, a lightning flash, or cloud,*
> *So should one view "the world of birth and*
> *death," or Samsara.*[15]

This verse from the *Diamond Sutra* tells us that the material world is an illusion. It is similar to Bishop Berkeley's idealism, according to which "all the choir of heaven and furniture of the earth,—in a word all those bodies which compose the mighty frame of the world—have not any subsistence without a mind."[16] The Yogacarins, however, based this concept not merely on a number of logical arguments that proved the impossibility of an external object, but also on the living experience of insight meditation.

It seems more a philosophy for the theoretically oriented than for one who was willing to meet with storms in the Taklamakan Desert, avalanches in the Tian Shan Mountains, or murderous pirates on the Ganges River. Although Xuanzang was attracted to this school, he enjoyed and was skillful in the art of dialectics. Part of him liked mastering the subtleties of numerous doctrines, a capability that would serve him well as he talked with the eminent doctors of philosophy in India and Central Asia.

With a firm sense of truths only dimly perceived, he knew that he must plumb to the source.[17] Having decided to go, Xuanzang, along with several other monks, sent a petition to Emperor Taizong to be allowed to leave China. Xuanzang's petition was not answered, but an imperial decree made it clear that laymen and possibly monks, unless they had official business, had better stay home. For such a passionate young man as Xuanzang, that was hardly a deterrent.

> *629 C.E. the month is uncertain. Dangers and untold difficulties lie ahead of him. He retires into the seclusion of a sacred tower in Chang'an in order to pray for guidance. He has a dream. In it he sees Mount Sumeru, a sacred mountain at the center of the universe, made of gold, silver, beryl, and crystal, surrounded by a Great Sea. Lotus flowers of stone support him as he crosses the waters, but so slippery and steep is the way up this Asian Mount Olympus that each time he tries to climb its sides he slides to the bottom. Of a sudden, a mighty whirlwind raises him to the summit; the world stretches out as far as the eye can see. The pilgrim beholds an unending horizon, a symbol of the countless lands he hopes to visit. In an ecstasy of joy he awakes; he has been shown a vision of what he must do. He now knows that it is meant for him to go. He will be severely tested, but he is ready to depart.[18]*

Beginning His Journey

Xuanzang was twenty-seven years old. A little less than six feet tall, he was an exceptionally handsome young man, with broad eyebrows, bright eyes, a clear complexion, and a noble forehead. He liked to wear ample garments and a broad belt, which gave him the appearance of a scholar. He spoke elegantly and had a clear, sonorous voice. He carried himself gracefully and looked straight ahead as good Buddhist monks do, without a glance to either side.[19]

It happened that owing to untimely frosts the harvests had failed, and a decree was issued ordering both monks and laymen to disperse to parts of China that were less affected. Xuanzang took advantage of the decree. He traveled with several companions from Chang'an to the high valleys and gorges of Gansu, one of the westernmost Chinese provinces. The long Gansu corridor cuts between the Land of Grasses and the wild plateau of Quinghai, until it reaches the sands of the Taklamakan Desert. Liangzhou, or modern Wuwei, was the last town of importance in Gansu province, as well as the start of the caravan routes leading over the desert to both Mongolia and the Tarim Basin in the Taklamakan Desert.

The pilgrim stayed in Liangzhou a month preparing himself for his journey. While there, he preached to monks as well as to traders and merchants at a large religious gathering. The governor, who had heard that the monk was about to go to the west, called him to his presence and urged him to obey the emperor's edict and return to the Tang capital. After this interview, Xuanzang knew he had to be careful. So, sheltered and guided by two young disciples of Liangzhou's most revered monk, he hid by day and traveled by night. His companions guided him to Guachou, not far from the oasis at Anxi, the last halting place with local supplies before the wide desert. At this frontier outpost he halted for another month, "so sad and silent," his biographer observed. His new friends had left him, his horse had died, and spies from Liangzhou had informed the district governor of his intentions. Happily the official was a man of piety who tore up the edict in Xuanzang's presence, but he urged him to depart in all haste.

Xuanzang bought a new horse. He was praying in a Buddhist hall when a Central Asian named Bandha made himself known and asked if he might take the five vows to become a dedicated layman. Xuanzang told him of his need for help in starting for the west. Bandha readily offered to conduct him past the Jade Gate and the five watchtowers in the desert.

The next day Xuanzang waited and waited for his guide. At last Bandha appeared, followed by another very aged fellow riding a skinny roan horse. The "grandfather" appeared to be there for the purpose of giving advice on dealing with the demons and perils of the desert crossing, for he claimed to have made the crossing more than thirty times. Xuanzang suddenly recalled that a fortune-teller in Chang'an had said: "I see you leaving China on a skinny roan horse. You are riding on a lacquered saddle with an iron stud in front of the saddle hump."[20] As the old man's horse and saddle fit the prediction exactly, Xuanzang agreed to exchange horses. So the aged man made a very good bargain in selling his decrepit horse, and the zealous monk set forth.

> The hour is early, possibly before dawn. The pilgrim, his guide, and their horses make their way as far as the Hu Lu River. Both men are weary after their first day's journey and finally spread out their mats within sight of the Jade Gate, one of the last outposts of the empire. Xuanzang's body slowly relaxes, and sleep steels over him as it does to all tired travelers. But suddenly he awakens. He can see his pious companion, Bandha, stealing toward him with a drawn sword! When Bandha is less than 10 feet away, he appears to hesitate; then he retraces his steps.

Xuanzang begins to recite scriptures and prays to the Compassionate Bodhisattva Guanyin (Kuan-Yin) to protect him from assassins. Bandha goes back to his sleeping place, and the monk sleeps lightly until dawn. Not long afterward Bandha departs.[21]

Being Lost in the Desert

Xuanzang was now alone. He set out with his pathetic-looking horse into a broad depression of sand and gravel, with many steep and stony gullies to be crossed. Often he saw the bones of men and beasts, each one with a story of thirst, exhaustion, and collapse. The sun shone down cruelly. Rising heat waves reflected from the shimmering earth as he slowly made his way. Then a chain of black hills rose up ahead of him, for the desert can change from tan and gray dunes to small mountains looking as if they were made of coal. Near one of these mountains he thought he saw hundreds of armed barbarians clad in felt and fur on the horizon. His devoted biographer described the desert scene: "And now the appearance of camels and horses, and the glittering of standards and lances met his view; then suddenly fresh forms and figures changing into a thousand shapes appeared, sometimes at an immense distance and then close at hand, and then they dissolved into nothing."[22]

Were the shifting forms of men and horses in the midst of the heat waves of the desert sands actually bands of robbers? They could well be armies of Turkish nomads from beyond the Tian Shan Mountains to the north in Turkistan. They might be mirages. Or were they, rather, the demon shapes and strange goblins of other worlds, the configurations of Mara, the wicked, that so many travelers had warned him against?

Ahead of the pilgrim was the first of five signal towers in the desert.

Fearing lest the lookouts should see him, he concealed himself in a hollow of sand until night; then going on west of the tower, he saw water; and going down, he drank and washed his hands. Then as he was filling his water-vessel with water an arrow whistled past him and just grazed his knee, and in a moment another arrow. Knowing then that he was discovered, he cried with a loud voice: "I am a priest come from the capital, do not shoot me."[23]

He was brought before the captain, a Buddhist, who urged him not to cross the nearly three hundred miles of desert to the Hami oasis, but to spend time with the eminent teachers at Dunhuang, the famous Buddhist center at the convergence of what we now call the Northern and Southern Silk Roads.

The Pilgrim & the Emperor

Xuanzang complained that he was shocked that instead of urging him to go forward, the captain was exhorting him to turn back and give up. The Dunhuang Caves housed both a large "art gallery" of paintings and sculpture and a substantial library of Buddhist scriptures and secular writings, but it wasn't India. (See Color Plate 1.)

Xuanzang negotiated the remaining watchtowers safely by leaving the usual route to Hami, following a parallel track to the northwest, and plunging into the heart of the Gashun Gobi (Mo-ho-yen), or what the Chinese call the River of Sand. By that term they mean a desert where the ground is not hard, gravelly, rock-embedded earth, but composed of shifting dunes, more like waves in the ocean. The Gashun Gobi was a place where there were no birds, nor animals, nor water, nor pasturage. When he felt himself to be in danger, he would invoke the name of Guanyin Bodhisattva with utmost devotion and also recite a special magic saying found in the *Heart Sutra*. He had learned it many years before from a sick man whom he took to his monastery and supplied with food and clothes. Out of gratitude the sick man taught him this sutra (Fig. 1.5).[24]

Gusts of hot desert sands obliterated his track, and he was obliged to make long detours. After a while, he knew he was lost. He should have come to the Spring of Wild Horses and he hadn't found it. To add to his panic, in a terrible moment, his water bag fell out of his hands! In an instant his whole supply of water drained out into the sands and was gone. Because of one moment of inattention his pilgrimage would have to come to an end.

> *Time seems to stop. In utter despair he begins to retrace his steps back toward China and the fourth watchtower. Then he remembers his oath that he would rather die with his face toward the west than return and live in the east. Again he sets off. For four days and five nights the pilgrim and his horse struggle westward. Not a drop of water anywhere. His mouth, lips, and throat are parched by the burning heat. The evening of the fifth day the horse and rider fall down exhausted.*
>
> *Xuanzang collapses on the sand. He prays to the Compassionate One, Guanyin. Dew falls on the pilgrim and his horse. He is able to slide into a deep slumber. He dreams of a tall spirit who calls out to him, "Why do you sleep instead of going forward with zeal?"*
>
> *Once more he sets forth with his skinny roan horse. He has gone nearly 4 miles when suddenly the horse starts off in a different direction. He lets himself be guided by the creature's instincts. Soon Xuanzang catches sight of a green oasis. In it is a shining pool as bright as a mirror. The pilgrim drinks long and deep. He refills his water bag with the water of life. He and his horse rest for a day before going on. Xuanzang reaches his destination, the oasis of Hami, on the other side of the Taklamakan Desert.*[25]

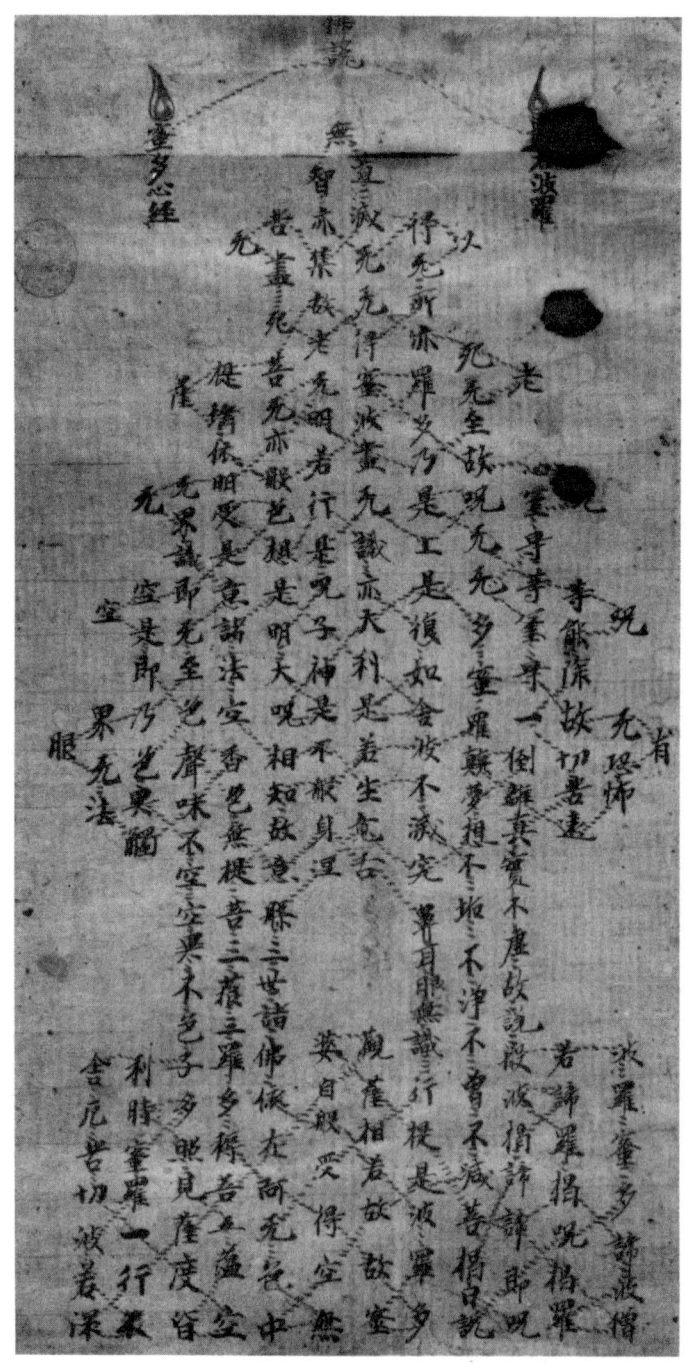

FIGURE 1.5
Scroll on which the Heart of the Perfection of Wisdom Sutra, *in Xuanzang's translation, is written in the form of a stupa, or pagoda. From Dunhuang Caves, China. (By permission of The British Library)*

Who knows what role the skinny roan horse played? Horses and camels in the desert cannot only scent water and grazing spots from considerable distances but seemingly can remember such places from previous journeys. For his pious biographer, Huili, the famous desert crossing from Anxi to Hami was surely the sign of a miracle. The pilgrim was his hero. It was the first of many miracles that he described, especially in the first part of his book. For a modern explorer and archaeologist such as Aurel Stein, it was necessary to retrace the pilgrim's route to find out whether his desert crossing was within the realm of feasibility. After all, Xuanzang's topographical records showed that he fully possessed that "instinct of the compass" that some people have. Stein concluded that the dangers and the quasi-miraculous escape that marked the beginning of Xuanzang's travels were neither exaggerated nor fictionalized.[26]

Both his memorable desert crossing and his vision at the beginning of his 10,000-mile journey in search of truth embody the universal elements of a hero's quest.[27] The Buddhist monk was not simply traveling over thousands of miles of dangerous deserts and mountains as if he were a Chinese Marco Polo; he was on a pilgrimage of the soul. His was both an inward and an outward journey; therefore, it carried an aura of special value.

Since he was a brilliant monk with keen scholarly interests, he began his journey of the soul for intellectual and theological reasons—to seek the truest doctrine. His vision of Mount Sumeru was a spacious vision, a call from his innermost being that would sustain him in his many ordeals ahead. When he passed beyond the Jade Gate, the furthermost outpost of the Tang Empire, he reached a point from which it was difficult to turn back. Going through such a gate is usually a decisive step, taking one from mere investigation to commitment. For the Chinese, especially, one side of the Jade Gate represented their civilized world, with all that it stood for, in culture, tradition, and a knowable world; the other side represented a place of desolation, the land of the unknown. Having passed this threshold as well as having nearly lost his life at the hand of his assassin-guide, he faced his ordeals alone. He circumvented five watchtowers in the desert and then survived a succession of trials, often in a dismal landscape of desert mirages and dust storms, only to lose his way. Xuanzang experienced a "dark night of the soul," a time of crisis when he lost his water bag and collapsed in the desert. His guide was one of the Compassionate Ones of his Buddhist faith, the Bodhisattva Guanyin, and with the help of this guide he emerged victorious.

Because of this heroic quality, which is so marked in the first part of his journey, Xuanzang has all the vividness of a character in an epic. "His kindred, in the world of our imagination," as Arthur Waley phrased it, are "not the great travelers, not Marco Polo, or Vambery, nor the great theologians such as Saint Augustine or Saint Thomas, but rather Aeneas, King Arthur, Cuchulain. He is the hero of a sort of spiritual epic, as they of their knightly sagas."[28]

Thanks to Huili, his biographer, and probably many other monks, Xuanzang became a legend in China even before he died. Whether his desert crossing was a miracle or even a feasible exploit, it was a near-disaster; his trip almost ended before it had begun. As so often happens in legend or in real life, however, it was quickly followed by an event that was to change his fortunes dramatically—his meeting with the king of Turfan.

TWO

THE OASES OF THE NORTHERN SILK ROAD

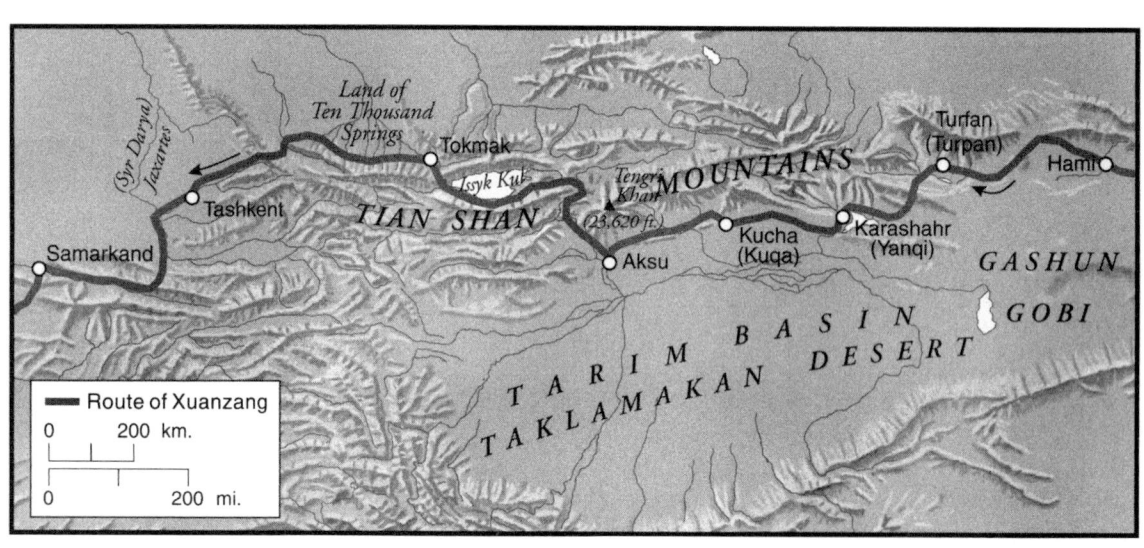

MAP 2.1
Itinerary of Xuanzang on the Northern Silk Road (from Hami to Samarkand) (Philip Schwartzberg, Meridian Mapping)

BEFORE XUANZANG MET UP with the strong-willed king of Turfan, he stopped at the oasis of Hami, the beginning of the string of oases at the foot of the Tian Shan Mountains. When he lifted his eyes to the snow-capped peaks of this range, he was looking at the source of life of the desert oases below. From the icy summits of these mountains rivers flow, passing beside fir-clad slopes, down brown, barren valleys below, rushing ever downward to desert dunes and further west to the Taklamakan Desert, until they disappear eventually in the sand.[1]

Wells begin at the base of the mountains, tapping their subterranean water; these wells and channels, called *karez*, are sometimes 40 miles long. They are necessary because of the intense heat and scant rainfall. From the air they look like earth mounds, because their keepers are constantly digging and piling up the earth so the water flows smoothly. They were first developed in Persia and existed many centuries before Xuanzang passed through on his way to India.

With fertile land and the increasingly prosperous trade of ancient China with the West, and the West with China along the Northern Silk Road, these oases flourished greatly. It was those kingdoms that the young Xuanzang would visit in 629–630 C.E.; that is where he would replenish his caravan of horses and camels, visit with kings, and preach the Buddhist doctrine to merchants and warriors as well as to his fellow monks on his way to India. He would be the most famous pilgrim to travel on this road, one of the longest and oldest trade routes known to mankind—the Silk Road.

Staying at the Hami Oasis

When he was in Hami, he stayed in a monastery where three Chinese monks lived; they were overjoyed to see him. The oldest embraced Xuanzang with tears, saying, "Could I ever have hoped to see a man from my own village?" The Master of the Law showed an unexpected warmth and shed tears of sympathy with him. It was from monasteries such as this one that the teachings of Buddhism radiated from India as far as China, a country that was enlightened by the new religion in much the same way as northern Europe had received the teachings of Christianity from the monasteries of Ireland.

This oasis kingdom of Hami, famous for its melons, had long been inhabited by a Chinese military colony that had accepted suzerainty of the Turks during the troubled times of the Sui and early Tang dynasties. Several months after the monk's visit, the kingdom of Hami reverted back to China. Like many another oasis, it was caught between nomadic hordes from the north and west and the sedentary civilization of China to the south and east.

The impetuous king of Turfan, having heard of Xuanzang's approach, ordered an escort to meet him. A powerful monarch of Chinese descent, the king had sent rare gifts to the Tang emperor and also presented himself in person at the Chinese court. Some time later, he associated himself with the Turkish nomads and cut off the caravans between China and the western kingdoms. It is said that he died of fright as he awaited the arrival of the Chinese armies. In 640 C.E. Turfan was annexed to China.[2]

Opposing the King of Turfan

Since the king of Turfan was also a devout Buddhist, Xuanzang could hardly refuse to see him. The pilgrim had another itinerary in mind, but he changed his route in order to go to Turfan. After a six-day march through the desert, a distance of about 200 miles, he reached the borders of Turfan at sunset. The moment the king was informed of Xuanzang's arrival, he left his palace and proceeded by torchlight to meet him. When the two of them arrived at the king's elegant pavilion, the king personally conducted the monk to a seat. The queen and all her serving women came to pay their respects, and food was served. Then the king, according to Huili, persisted in talking with him all night.

> *630 c.e. The hour grows late. Having stayed for ten days, the Master desires to take his leave and continue his journey. But the king wants him to stay and be a spiritual preceptor for his kingdom.*
>
> *Xuanzang says: "It needs no repeated explanation to understand your deep kindness. But as I am going to the west to seek the Law of the Buddha, it is improper for me to stop halfway before I have found it."*
>
> *The King is adamant.*
>
> *Xuanzang is firm.*
>
> *The king becomes sullen and shouts at the pilgrim, flapping the sleeves of his royal robe, "I have other ways to deal with you." He threatens to detain him by force or else send him back to his country.*
>
> *It is Xuanzang's first confrontation with royal authority and power. There will be other times when he will have to resist a monarch's wish, even that of the emperor himself. He stands firm. Still the king does not let him go, increasing his offerings. Xuanzang decides that he must refuse*

The Oases of the Northern Silk Road

to eat and drink. The king serves him with his own hands. For three days Xuanzang fasts, hoping to change the king's mind. On the fourth day the Master's breath is very feeble. The king is ashamed and gives in.[3]

In the end, Xuanzang promised to preach to his subjects in Turfan for a month (Map 2.2). He also agreed to stop in Turfan for three years on his return journey to China. This was not to happen, for the king's death released the pilgrim from the promise, and Xuanzang returned to China fifteen years later on the Southern Silk Road.

During his stay of a month here in this area, Xuanzang stopped at the ancient city of Gaochang, which lies 29 miles southeast of Turfan. This impressive city of 1.5 square miles was divided into three parts: an outer city, an inner city, and a royal palace, more or less like the pattern of the Tang capital, Chang'an. Today, after more than a thousand years, part of the ancient city wall stands over 30 feet high; the gates, the stupa shrine, the Buddha hall, and the bases of various temples are still recognizable. In such an excessively dry climate, with only

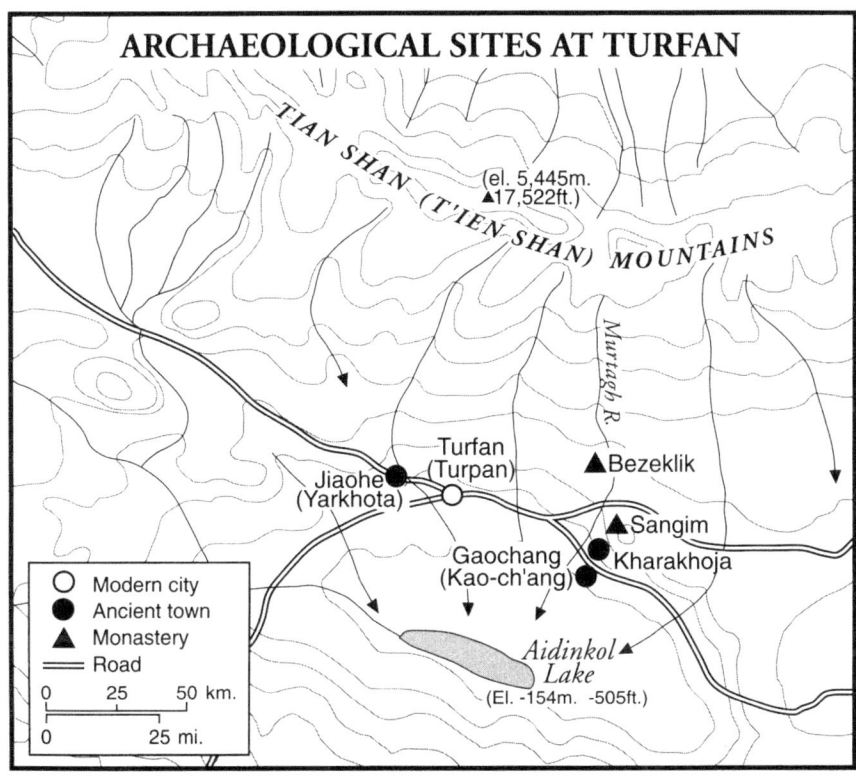

MAP 2.2
Archaeological sites at Turfan oasis, with indication of rivers that flow from the Tian Shan Mountains feeding Aidinkol Lake (Philip Schwartzberg, Meridian Mapping)

one-half inch of rainfall a year, some of the buildings are timelessly preserved, so we may easily imagine a prosperous kingdom even now.

Although the king prepared a special pavilion for Xuanzang to talk to an audience of three hundred, he may also have preached in front of the large Buddha hall, a square structure constructed of sun-dried bricks, with hollowed-out niches 3 to 4 feet high on the exterior of the building. Some of these carved-out spaces still have painted halos in them, recalling the Buddha figures or Compassionate Ones they once contained.

Most probably he also visited Jiaohe, 6 miles west of Turfan town, a natural fortress that stands on a high bluff between two rivers. A stroll across a dusty plain would take him to an unusual stupa with a tall central round pillar surrounded by four towers. Ten years after Xuanzang visited the Turfan oasis, Jiaohe became the main base for administering the western regions of the Chinese empire.

It is likely that Xuanzang climbed in the foothills of the Tian Shan Mountains, passing by the famous Flaming Mountain, so called because of its reddish hue. These red foothills, strangely rent with gouged-out gullies, are the setting and inform the action of the chapter in the famous Ming novel *Journey to the West*, an epic inspired by the monk's own pilgrimage to India. It is but a short walk for such a vigorous, young monk among barren, desolate hills to the monks' cells of the Sangim ravine, where he may have paused on his way to the truly spectacular caves at Bezeklik. (See Color Plate 2.)

Almost hidden until one is right upon them, these cells stand in the Murtok gorge on a steep bank of conglomerate rock. Above the temple cells, partly cut out of the cliff, is a smooth tableland, as if the river, hundreds of years before the monks built their monastery, had been at a higher level and over the centuries had cut its way through to form a wild, narrow gorge. The caves face an equally steep, serrated cliff on the other side of the gushing river. Like the Greeks, the Buddhist monks had a genius for place: Their monasteries usually stand in dramatic settings.

The sounds of the swift-flowing river at night must have been soothing, but who knows about the wailing howls of wolves baying in the gorge at the full moon? Albert von Le Coq, an early-twentieth-century German explorer, heard them in this desolate gorge twelve centuries after Xuanzang passed through and told us that the wolves, though sounding dangerous, were mostly harmless.

After Xuanzang's month-long sojourn in this oasis, the king equipped him in truly grand style for his pilgrimage.

> He had various articles of clothing made suitable for such a climate, such as face-coverings, gloves, leather boots and so on. Moreover he gave him a

hundred gold ounces, and three myriads of silver pieces, with five hundred rolls of satin and taffeta, enough for the outward and home journey of the Master during twenty years. He gave him also thirty horses and twenty-four servants.[4]

The gold, silver, satin, and taffeta would be for the kings and khans whom he would visit on his journey. Most important of all, the king gave him twenty-four royal letters to be presented to the twenty-four different kingdoms. The Turfan king requested these rulers to conduct Xuanzang through their territories and to provide relays of horses. And finally, the king commissioned one of his officers to conduct Xuanzang to the Great Khan of the Western Turks.

In his letter to the Great Khan, the king of Turfan asked him to be kind to Xuanzang, as he had been "to the slave who writes these respectful lines." The relation of the two monarchs was clear. The king of Turfan was a vassal of the Khan and had a right to claim protection for his new friend—a medieval code that seemed to apply in Asia as it had in Europe.[5]

Xuanzang was overcome by his generosity.

> For all these favours, I feel ashamed of myself and do not know how to express my gratitude. Even the overflow of the Chiao River is not comparable with the amount of your kindness, and your favour is weightier than the mountains of the Pamir Range. Now I have no more worry to travel across the suspending bridge over the perilous Icy River, and it is now time to visit the Land of the Heavenly Ladder and the Bodhi tree. If I may achieve my objective, to whom shall I owe my achievement? To nothing but the king's favour.[6]

Xuanzang was more right than he knew, for the empire of the Western Turks at the time extended from the Altai Mountains in the former Soviet Russia to what is now Afghanistan and Pakistan. This protection extended even further, for the monarch who ruled from Kunduz in present-day Afghanistan was both the Khan's son and the king of Turfan's son-in-law. The monk who had left China secretly with a warrant on his head would now have official standing; all the petty kings of the desert oases, all the rulers of the Western Turks, were at his service.

From Turfan, the pilgrim and his now large caravan traveled 200 miles toward the southwest to Karashahr (Yanqi), climbing a range of mountains celebrated for its silver mines. On the other side of the Qoltag Mountains his party was confronted by robber bands; Xuanzang's entourage was able to bribe the bandits to withdraw, but the caravan ahead of them had been killed to a man. After these dangers, Xuanzang reached the remarkable, prosperous kingdom of Karashahr. At one time the number of grottoes that were transformed into Buddhist sanctuaries in the area was so great that the word *Mingoi*, meaning

"1,000 caves," was used to describe the region and came to be used elsewhere. According to Xuanzang's account, there were ten monasteries containing nearly two thousand Hinayana Buddhist monks.

Although the pilgrim was given a very warm reception, he spent only one night before setting out for Kucha. Xuanzang depicted the king as being brave and conceited but without practical ability. This description was confirmed by the action of the Emperor Taizong in 643 C.E. When the king of Karashahr secretly renounced his duty and allegiance to China, just as the king of Turfan had done, the emperor sent an army to invade his kingdom and made the king a prisoner.[7]

Visiting the Monasteries at Kucha (Kuqa)

From Karashahr, Xuanzang followed the historical route running along the foot of the Tian Shan Mountains. Like the king of Turfan before him, the Kucha monarch went out to meet the young pilgrim, accompanied by the chief officers of the court and the monks of the district. The king of Kucha was a devout Buddhist and at the time anxious to win the favor of the Chinese, so it was natural that he should give Xuanzang a warm welcome.

Unlike the king of Turfan, the king of Kucha was not of Chinese descent, nor was his appearance Chinese (Fig. 2.1). He had red hair and blue eyes. He seems also to have been without the fiery temper of the Turfan king. The elegant royal pair who greeted the Chinese pilgrim were representative of an Indo-European people in race and appearance. Xuanzang described the king as a man of weak intellect who was controlled by his ministers. Shortly after the pilgrim's visit in 630 C.E., the king sent the Tang emperor a tribute of horses and received in return an imperial warrant of investiture. Later the same ruler showed his lack of political wisdom in renouncing Chinese suzerainty in favor of an alliance with the Turks. In 648 C.E. the Chinese invaded his country and took him prisoner.

Kucha was perhaps the most important kingdom in Central Asia. Xuanzang was impressed with its wealth and the brilliance of its civilization as well as its great size.

> This country was above 1,000 *li* from east to west and 600 *li* from north to south; its capital being 17–18 *li* in circuit.... This country yielded millet, wheat, rice, grapes, pomegranates, and plenty of pears, plums, peaches and apricots. It produced also gold, copper, iron, lead, and tin: its climate was temperate and the people had honest ways; their writing was taken from that of India, but has been much altered; they had great skill with wind and stringed musical instruments.[8]

The Oases of the Northern Silk Road

FIGURE 2.1
Portraits of the king and queen of Kucha originally on grotto frescoes from the first half of the seventh century C.E. Thought to approximate the appearance of the royal pair who greeted Xuanzang in 630 C.E. (l'Imprimerie Nationale, 1977)

A Kuchan orchestra had in fact been introduced at the Chinese court and during the whole of the Tang period took part in imperial fetes. We even know the names of the pieces it played, such as "The Jade Woman Hands the Cup Around," "Meeting on the Seventh Evening," and "The Game of Hide the Buckle."[9]

A beautiful fresco from the caves at Kizil of a musician and an Indian goddess exerts such charm and fascination that we might even come to believe the legend that the enchanting melodies of the Tokharian music were taken from the sounds of a waterfall. Although this fresco is in a museum in Germany, at Kizil there are still many other frescoes that reveal flying *apsaras*—like our angels—playing musical instruments and gods and musicians playing flutes, oboes, and four-stringed lutes. (See Color Plate 3.)

Along with its cultural richness, Kucha seems to have been a very important center of Buddhism along the Northern Silk Road. Xuanzang indicated that on either side of the western gate of the city was a Buddhist statue over 90 feet tall. One month before and one month after the autumnal equinox large crowds would gather there for ten days for religious celebrations and Buddhist sermons. All the monasteries in the region participated in an elaborate "procession of images" with highly adorned statues of the Buddha mounted on floats, decorated with precious substances or covered with silken stuffs. Xuanzang visited twelve monasteries in Kucha, and this kingdom, he said, had no fewer than five thousand monks.

Among the especially famous monasteries, Xuanzang mentioned a few by name, such as the Ascharya Monastery: "Forty *li* north of the depopulated city at the slopes of the hills, and separated by a river, were two monasteries which bore the common name Chao-hu-li [Zhaohuli] distinguished respectively as Eastern and Western. The images of the Buddha in these monasteries were beautiful almost beyond human skill: and the Brethren were punctilious in discipline and devoted enthusiasts."[10]

Numerous stupas, worship halls, and Thousand Buddha caves crowd one another at Subashi old city, a site covering about 2 acres, 12 miles north of Kucha. Subashi old city is spread along the east and west banks of the Kucha River and might well have been the Zhaohuli that so inspired Xuanzang.

Heavy snows in the high passes of the Tian Shan Mountains lying to the north of the oasis that year obliged the pilgrim to remain two additional months at Kucha. Close by was a ring of monasteries that he surely did see. Several of them were far enough away from the thriving cities for the idly curious not to be tempted to come and disturb the monks in their meditations and yet near enough for the devout to visit and bring them offerings.

A climb ascending a steep Yanshui gorge and down in a westerly direction would take him to the 236 caves at Kizil 35 miles away. Local people call the cave complex the High Thousand Buddha Cave. In the wild ravines of the Muzart River, caves connected by interior galleries and staircases had been hollowed out of the soft sandstone of the

The Oases of the Northern Silk Road

mountain. A dramatic photograph taken by the German expedition of Von Le Coq, a view from a monastic cell, shows much the same landscape that spread out before the eyes of Xuanzang 1,300 years ago.

Little has changed in other ways, too. The openings of the ancient chapels still present the same darkness and light as they did then: darkness, for the caves are lighted only by the front entrance of the grotto or by torchlight; and light, for the very brilliance of the blue lapis lazuli, the copper green, and the chalky white of the flesh tones combine to make bright and pleasing patterns.

The Buddhism practiced at Kucha at the time of Xuanzang's visit was Hinayana Buddhism in spite of the fact that Kucha was well known as the birthplace of Kumarajiva (344–415 C.E.), one of the greatest translators of Mahayana Buddhism. This scholar of Kucha was so distinguished that he was called to Chang'an, where he stayed ten years working with a team of translators, rendering some of the most important scriptures into Chinese, most notably the *Lotus of the True Law*.

Instead of the illustrious Kumarajiva, an aged local philosopher in Kucha spent many long hours debating with Xuanzang. But the pilgrim seems to have challenged him on so many points that the older man was glad to see this bright, young Chinese intellectual head for the mountains.

Two days out of Kucha, Xuanzang had another narrow escape when his caravan encountered a band of two thousand Turkish bandits. (Was this a poetic figure or a contingent of roving tribesmen on the loose?) Luckily, the marauders were quarreling about the spoils they had acquired from their previous haul and showed no interest in Xuanzang's party. At length he came to the oasis of Aksu, which was in many ways similar to Kucha.

Crossing the Tian Shan Mountains

From Aksu Xuanzang's party entered the Tian Shan range. They climbed around the giant peak of Tengri Khan, 23,620 feet high, and crossed the chain of the Tian Shan by the Bedal Pass. Its slope was covered with glaciers.

> This mountain is steep and dangerous, and reaches to the clouds (*heaven*). From the creation the perpetual snow which has collected here in piles, has been changed into glaciers which melt neither in winter nor summer; the hard-frozen and cold sheets of water rise mingling with the clouds; looking at them the eye is blinded with the glare, so that it cannot long

gaze at them. The icy peaks fall down sometimes and lie athwart the road, some of them a hundred feet high, and others several tens of feet wide.[11]

The heavy snows that caused them to delay their 40-mile-long crossing of the mountains at Kucha should have been a warning; events would show that they had left too soon. Xuanzang's description of mountains of ice that rose up into the sky and the ice peaks that occasionally fell down give us a clue. It took seven days to cross the Bedal Pass, one of the major passes used by Western Turks to communicate with their dependencies in the Tarim Basin. During that time he lost three or four out of every ten men and a great number of oxen and horses. The loss of one-third of his men and many animals might lead one to think that there was an avalanche, but Xuanzang said that his men either starved or froze to death. His 10,000-mile pilgrimage had scarcely begun. Yet not even in Hindu Kush Mountains in Afghanistan, where his party got lost and was rescued, and not in the Pamirs, where he crossed a 16,000-foot pass, did he experience so great a disaster.

On the northern side of the mountains, the sadly depleted caravan rested at Lake Issyk Kul, or the "warm lake," so called because it never froze. The comparative warmth of the water and the sheltered location made it the winter headquarters of the Great Khan of the Western Turks. The Khan's summer capital was at Tashkent (Che-shih), but he often spent time in the valley of the upper Yulduz River.

As Xuanzang and his party went along the southern side of this great inland sea 114 miles long and 36 miles wide, the pilgrim noted:

> On all sides it is enclosed by mountains, and various streams empty themselves into it and are lost. The colour of the water is a bluish-black, its taste is bitter and salt. The waves of this lake roll along tumultuously as they expend themselves (*on the shores*). Dragons and fish inhabit it together. At certain (*portentous*) occasions scaly monsters rise to the surface, on which travelers passing by put up their prayers for good fortune.[12]

He was a man of the seventh century, believing in spirits in the mountains, demons in the desert, and dragons in the lake.

Meeting the Great Khan

In 630 C.E., Xuanzang met the Great Khan of the Western Turks at Tokmak, today in Kyrgyzstan at the northwest side of the lake. The Great Khan's relations to the Tang emperor were friendly at that time. Three years earlier he had offered to the court of the Emperor Taizong a belt of gold adorned with jewels and five thousand horses. By the early years of the Emperor Taizong's reign, the Western Turks had come to control much of the vast region from the Chinese Empire to Persia in the west, and from Kashmir in the south to the Altai Mountains in the north.

At the time of Xuanzang's visit, the Great Khan was at the height of his powers. After he returned from a hunting trip, the Khan gave Xuanzang a warm welcome. This nomad king, in a manner reminiscent of Jenghiz Khan,

> was covered with a robe of green satin, and his hair was loose, only it was bound round with a silken band some ten feet in length, which was twisted round his head and fell down behind. He was surrounded by about 200 officers, who were all clothed in brocade stuff, with their hair braided. On the right and left he was attended by independent troops all clothed in furs and fine spun hair garments; they carried lances and bows and standards, and were mounted on camels and horses. The eye could not estimate their numbers.[13]

The pilgrim handed over the letter and gifts of the king of Turfan. Their party was treated to a feast in the Khan's yurt, a large pavilion

> adorned with golden flower ornaments (*Ta kwan*) which blind the eye with their glitter. All the officers had spread out in front long mats, in two rows, on which they sat; they were clad in shining garments of embroidered silk. The body-guard of the Khan stood behind them. Regarding these circumstances of state, although he was but the ruler of a wandering horde, yet there was a certain dignified arrangement about his surroundings.[14]

(Xuanzang was a bit patronizing here, as if as a civilized Chinese he was surprised that the nomadic tribes were not quite as uncouth as he had expected.)[15]

Quarters of mutton and boiled veal were piled high in front of the guests. Everyone but Xuanzang drank a lot of wine, and all enjoyed the loud, clashing chords of their music. Special rice cakes, cream, mares' milk, crystallized sugar, honey, and raisins were provided for the pilgrim, whose religious beliefs did not allow him to eat meat. At the end of the sumptuous banquet, the Khan asked him to "improve the occasion" by expounding on the Buddhist doctrine. A difficult assignment in such a setting and before such company! The pilgrim spoke on the need for love of all living creatures and the religious life that led to final deliverance. Apparently the Khan was impressed.

Buddhism was not wholly foreign to the Khan, for a monk from India had tried to convert him to Buddhism some years earlier.[16] At Ak-Beshim, only a short distance southwest of Tokmak, two Buddhist shrines that can be attributed to the seventh or eighth century C.E. have been excavated by Soviet archaeologists.[17]

Having taken a liking to Xuanzang, the Khan sought to dissuade him from going to India. "It is such a hot land where people were like savages without any decorum." Theirs was a gentle exchange with no threats of force, like those of the king of Turfan. Xuanzang replied that notwithstanding all this, he was determined to go and gaze at the sacred traces and earnestly search for the law, that is, scriptures. The Khan then sought out a young Chinese soldier to accompany Xuanzang part of the way. The Khan also gave him letters of introduction to the petty princes of the Gandharan region—part of present-day Afghanistan and Pakistan—who were his vassals. He presented Xuanzang with fifty pieces of silk and a set of clothes of crimson satin. Like the kings of Turfan and Kucha before him, the Khan and his officers, with true Eastern courtesy, accompanied him a few miles to start him on his journey.

Xuanzang set out again for the western regions. He crossed the plain on the north of the Alexandrian Mountains where the nine rivers that feed the Chu and the ten rivers that feed its tributary, the Kuragati, have their source. Even today this area, 80 miles west of Tokmak, is called the "Land of One Thousand Springs" (Bing-yul). The pilgrim observed that the Great Khan of the Western Turks often camped in this delightful region of many pools and verdant trees.

In all his travels through Central Asian Turkdom, especially in areas inhabited by Iranian and Turkic peoples that were later to become centers of carpet weaving, Xuanzang made no mention of the production of either *woven* or *knotted* carpets. For those seeking to understand the origin and development of such carpets, Xuanzang's realistic and detailed description of the Great Khan and the nomadic life in Central Asia is crucial evidence that the nomads at that time were producing only felt rugs.[18]

The next important place he visited was Tashkent (Che-shih), the capital of modern-day Uzbekistan. He probably crossed the famous Syr Darya (Jaxartes) at the present village of Chinaz. Finally Xuanzang had to traverse the eastern spur of the Desert of Red Sands in order to reach Samarkand. He found it to be a sandy waste: "North-west from this we enter on a great sandy desert, where there is neither water nor grass. The road is lost in the waste, which appears boundless, and only by looking in the direction of some great mountain, and following the guidance of the bones which lie scattered about, can we know the way in which we ought to go."[19] One hundred fifty-six miles of solitude.... Once again the desert, the land of bleakness, driving winds, and bleached bones. The pilgrim's goal was the golden oasis of Samarkand, the farthest point west on his journey.

Many Western poets, Milton, Keats, Edward Fitzgerald among them, have been charmed with the cadence of the word *Samarkand*, and in the nineteenth century James Flecker romanticized it still more in his book *The Golden Journey to Samarkand.*

> *We are the pilgrims, master; we shall go*
> *Always a little further; it may be*
> *Beyond that last blue mountain barred with snow . . .*
>
> *Sweet to ride forth at evening from the wells*
> *When shadows pass gigantic on the sand,*
> *And softly through the silence beat the bells*
> *Along the golden road to Samarkand.*
>
> *We travel not for the trafficking alone;*
> *By hotter winds our fiery hearts are fanned*
> *We make the golden journey to Samarkand.*[20]

THREE

THE CROSSROADS OF ASIA

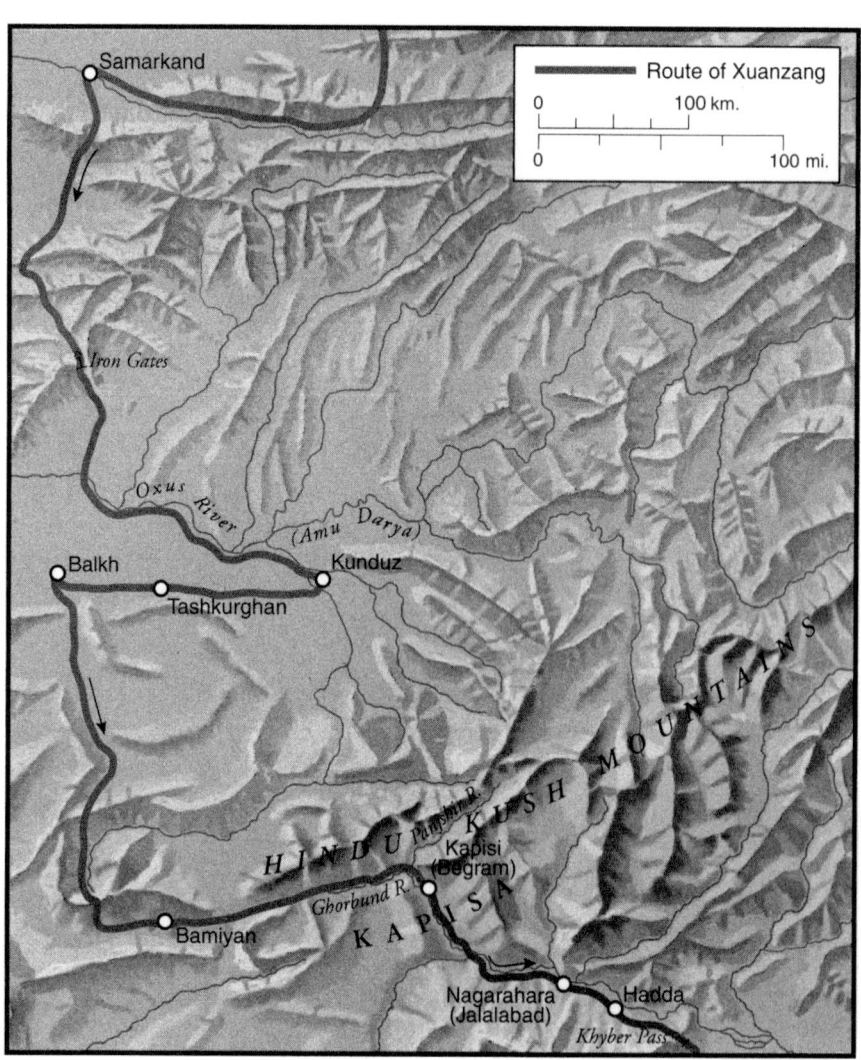

MAP 3.1
Itinerary of Xuanzang in Afghanistan (from Samarkand to Jalalabad) (Philip Schwartzberg, Meridian Mapping)

🕮 THE STREETS OF SAMARKAND.[1] A medley of sounds—trotting horses, camel bells, and wagons creaking along the muddy roads. Smells of incense, cloves, cinnamon, curry spices in round sacks, urine, boiled lamb simmering in huge vats, and always jostling crowds of people. To Xuanzang, who was used to men with small noses, beardless faces, and almond-shaped black eyes, the men filling the roads and the bazaar were clearly foreign traders.[2] In Chang'an and along the oases of the Silk Road, he had already seen some hawk-nosed men whose beards swallowed their faces and whose eyes looked like blue, green, or gray glass.

Now he would go beyond merely foreign faces to discover the characteristic forms of Buddhist culture in the lands south of the Oxus River (Amu Darya), which nowadays divides Tajikistan and Afghanistan. He would learn more about Buddhism's chief form of architecture, called the stupa, and about the great Buddhist Kings Asoka and Kanishka; come to know some of the well-known images of the Buddha, images such as the giant Buddha at Bamiyan or the Dipankara Buddha, called the twenty-fourth predecessor of the Historical Buddha.

In the trading city of Samarkand, "the merchandise of many countries was found and the craftsmanship of artisans appeared superior to that of other countries," Xuanzang observed. Caravans with gems, spices, and cotton coming north from India converged with caravans bearing silks and ironware from China on their way west to Persia and beyond to Rome. Bearded nomads from the steppes farther north brought their fur, cattle, and hides to trade in this important entrepôt of the Silk Road.

Winning Over the King of Samarkand

Although the king of Samarkand was a vassal of the Great Khan of the Western Turks, the local culture was that of Sassanian (226–637 C.E.) Persia. The language of Samarkand, Sogdian, was related to Persian; the religion of the king and the people was akin to Zoroastrianism, the national religion of Sassanid Persia. Two Buddhist monasteries existed there, but they had long stood empty before the arrival of Xuanzang and his caravan. Huili reported that when two of Xuanzang's young disciples went there to worship, they were pursued by the fire-worshipping Zoroastrians with firebrands. When the king heard of the incident, he ordered that the pursuers' hands be cut off. Xuanzang could not bear to see them mutilated and interceded on their behalf, so that their sentence was reduced to one of flogging and expulsion from Samarkand.

Xuanzang described the king of Samarkand as courageous, a man who had a strong army and who was obeyed by the neighboring states. The king's relations with Xuanzang seemed to change during his visit. At first the king was pointedly unfriendly, and then after hearing Xuanzang preach on the second day, the king was so impressed that he allowed Xuanzang to convene an assembly where he ordained a number of monks. This may be an exaggerated account of Xuanzang's influence, or it may show a desire on the king's part to impress the pilgrim so that he himself might turn his kingdom toward China and break away from the Turkish protectorate. Indeed, in 631 C.E. the king sent an embassy to China asking to be received as a vassal state. The Emperor Taizong declined to accede to this request; instead the two countries established diplomatic and commercial relations.

The pilgrim's face turned south now. He passed through Shahr-i-Sabz (Kesh), where one day Tamerlane was to build a great palace. Then once more he entered the mountains, this time a spur of the Pamir massif. After two or three days going through very rugged terrain, bearing always toward the southwest, he entered the famous pass called the Iron Gates. Located 8 miles west of modern Derbent, it marked the boundary of the empire of the Western Turks. This well-known defile was shut in on both sides by high vertical rock walls. "The road is narrow, which adds to the difficulty and danger. On both sides there is a rocky wall of an iron color. Here there are set up double wooden doors, strengthened with iron and furnished with many bells," Xuanzang told us.[3]

He then traveled due south again to the Oxus River, which rises in the Pamirs and, after traversing more than 1,400 miles, ends in the Aral Sea. Staying on the northern side of the river, he stopped at Termez. There he found Buddhism flourishing once again. He noted that there were more than a thousand brethren.[4]

Xuanzang's observations are of special interest in view of the abundance of Buddhist monuments found by Soviet archaeologists in the vicinity of Termez or more broadly the Surkhan Darya Valley.[5] Further east on one of the tributaries of the Oxus in Tajikistan is Adzhina-tepe, the most important Buddhist monastery yet discovered in Central Asia. Along with a very large collection of Buddhist relics is a Buddha lying in the final pose of *parinirvana,* which marks the farthest point reached by Buddhism from India toward the west.[6]

Poisoning at Kunduz

During his long journey Xuanzang was able to take advantage of the many kinship ties of the khans and kings along the Silk Road. So it was that he made a special detour after crossing the Oxus River to stop at Kunduz (in present-day Afghanistan). He carried a letter to the reigning Prince Tardu in Kunduz from his first patron, the king of Turfan. It must have been a warm letter, for the Turfan king was writing to his brother-in-law. Prince Tardu was also the eldest son of the Great Khan of the Western Turks, whom the prince had just been visiting at the latter's hunting quarters near Tokmak.

But Xuanzang came at an unfortunate time. The wife of Prince Tardu had died and the king was in mourning. Something like a Greek tragedy was to follow. Suddenly Prince Tardu married the younger daughter of the king of Turfan. This dastardly new queen started an intrigue with a royal prince, son of the first marriage. While Xuanzang was still their guest, she poisoned Prince Tardu and made her lover the new ruler of Kunduz. Seemingly undismayed by this murder, Xuanzang stayed on for the protracted funeral and marriage ceremonies.

These delays gave him a chance to come to know a monk named Dharmasimha, who had already been to India. Xuanzang's biographer related that his hero tried to find out about the number of scriptures and treatises Dharmasimha knew. "I can explain any of them you like," the monk at Kunduz was supposed to have said. Xuanzang confined himself to asking about the treatises he thought the monk would know and found that he couldn't explain them easily. Dharmasimha's disciples were filled with dismay, but to his credit, he "ceased not to praise the Master, acknowledging that he was by no means his equal."

Visiting Stupas in Balkh

Before he was murdered, Prince Tardu, who was a pious man, had recommended that Xuanzang make a detour to visit Balkh because of its many religious monuments. Accompanied by some monks who had come from Balkh to participate in the funeral services of the prince of Kunduz as well as the investiture of the new rulers, they went 100 miles, through Tashkurghan, westward to Balkh. They saw how large the well-fortified city of Balkh was—20 *li* in circuit.[7]

Xuanzang noticed the barren character of the city and its neighborhood, yet he wrote, "In truth it was a most excellent land." The plains and valleys were extremely fertile. There were one hundred monasteries and three thousand monks belonging to the Hinayana, or Lesser Vehicle. Above all, the countryside was rich in relics in spite of the invasions of a series of foreign invaders.

Balkh was already a city of prodigious antiquity when Alexander the Great used it as his base, 329–327 B.C.E. In the early centuries of the common era Buddhism flourished in what is now Afghanistan, especially during the Kushan Empire (first to third centuries C.E.).[8] After that empire's fall, there were a number of petty kingdoms, and the kings in times of prosperity embellished their capitals with temples, monasteries, and stupas. Both the cave monasteries at Bamiyan and the thousands of stupas at Hadda were built during the period from the third to the fifth centuries. Then came the invasion of the White Huns (455–470? C.E.), who conquered Gandhara (eastern Afghanistan and parts of Pakistan) on their way to India. Xuanzang may have exaggerated their destruction; a combination of floods, a general decline in economic prosperity, and perhaps most decisive of all, a general revival of Hinduism had occurred by the seventh century when Xuanzang passed through the area.[9]

Two rich merchants, Trapusa and Bhallika, according to Xuanzang, brought Buddhism to Balkh. Northwest of the city were two Buddhist shrines, or stupas, associated with those nomad traders. "At this time two householders meeting him in his majestic glory gave him of their travelling provisions parched grain and honey. Bhagavat [the Buddha] expounded to them what brings happiness to men and devas [gods], and these two householders were the first to hear the Five Commandments and Ten Virtues. When they had received the religious teaching they requested something to worship."[10] The Buddha gave them his hair and nail parings. The two men, being about to return to their native country, begged to have a rule and pattern for their worship services. Thereupon the Buddha took his three garments, folded them into four, piled them on the ground, beginning with the largest and ending with the smallest. Next he took his begging bowl and inverted it on his garments. Finally he put his beggar's staff on top and said, "This is how to make a stupa."

This legend carries an important message about the early days of Buddhism and the special grace accorded to merchants. Caravanners were an important means of spreading the new faith; the two traders in the legend had traveled well over 1,000 miles from Balkh to India's holy land. The truth of this story is borne out in history, for both Kushan traders and Sogdian caravans from Bukhara and Samarkand were emissaries for the message of Buddhism to the desert oases and to China. The Sogdian language became the lingua franca of the eastern end of the Silk Road, and both Sogdians and Parthians from Central Asia were among the earliest translators of Buddhist texts into Chinese.[11]

The Crossroads of Asia

This new religion was also no longer identified with the highest caste, or Brahmins, as Hinduism was; it was open to all. The merchants who went back to Balkh and built a stupa also set an example of turning their material wealth into Buddhist works of art. Finally, the story gives a convenient way to represent how a stupa looks with its square bottom, round dome, and tall mast (Fig. 3.1). Over the centuries the stupa form became more complex: More platforms supported the dome, the dome changed, the square railings at its top were enlarged and elaborated, the mast grew taller, and the symbolic parasols on it increased in number.

The Indian ruler, King Asoka (third century B.C.E.), third emperor of the Mauryan dynasty, is said to have initiated the stupa cult. Like the conversion of the Roman Emperor Constantine, six hundred years later, Asoka's conversion to Buddhism was of great historic importance. According to legend, eight stupas had been used to enshrine the last possessions and remains of the Buddha, whence Asoka further divided the relics and erected 84,000 stupas throughout the major cities of his realm. He believed the bones of the human body consisted of 84,000 atoms and desired to build 84,000 stupas over each atom of the Buddha's skeleton.[12] There is evidence that a major redistribution of relics did take place under Asoka's direction. Ever since then, "a monument of this type has been an indispensable element of every monastery or temple in Asia, either in the ancient form of an Indian stupa or its variants, or in the eastern Asian form of a pagoda."[13]

Buried inside these stupas, which Xuanzang would encounter everywhere on his journey, were the relics of the Buddha. The Chinese pilgrims noted that the most valuable relics were usually kept in small receptacles made of crystal or gold; these in turn were enclosed in stone boxes or earthenware containers, which were of decreasing value.

Sometimes a relic was broadly interpreted to include a sacred text or a small statue representing the Buddha. Stupas were also built in praise of disciples or revered holy men or to commemorate important events in the Buddha's life or his previous lives. Part of stupa worship was an ancient Indian rite in which the pilgrim circumambulated the stupa, following the path of the sun.

Originally stupas were burial mounds or sepulchers. Their form and meanings kept evolving. The symbolism is varied, but it has come to be thought of as a cosmic diagram in which the dome represents heaven sheltering the interior as a world mound. The tall mast symbolizes the World Axis. The stupa also stands for nirvana, the ultimate goal and highest consummation for all Buddhists.

The New Monastery, where Xuanzang stayed for a month, had been one of the most splendid monasteries of the Buddhist world.

FIGURE 3.1
A small reliquary dated first century C.E. in the shape of a stupa, the principal form of Buddhist architecture (Copyright British Museum)

> This was the only Buddhist establishment north of the Hindu Kush in which there was a constant succession of Masters who were commentators on the canon. The image of the Buddha in this monastery ... was studded with noted precious substances, and its halls were adorned with costly rarities, hence it was plundered for gain by the chiefs of the various states. In the monastery was an image of Vaisravana deva [god] which had bona fide miracles and in mysterious ways protected the establishment.[14]

There he found Prajnakara, a genial and learned man, with whom he was able to converse profitably and read certain Hinayana texts that interested him. For the first time since he had left China, Xuanzang found a Buddhist teacher whom he respected even though the teacher was a follower of Hinayana Buddhism. They enjoyed each other so much that when it came time to leave, Prajnakara accompanied him south through the Hindu Kush Mountains to Bamiyan.

Like the soldiers of Alexander the Great, they had a very difficult time of it. The snowdrifts were 20 to 30 feet deep, the worst he had encountered. Although Xuanzang didn't lose as many men and animals as he had crossing the Tian Shan Mountains, he seems to have been in the midst of a perpetual blizzard. But let Xuanzang tell it himself: "These mountains are lofty and their defiles deep, with peaks and precipices fraught with peril. Wind and snow alternate incessantly and at midsummer it is still cold. Piled up snow fills the valleys and the mountain tracks are hard to follow. There are gods of the mountains and impish sprites which in their anger send forth monstrous apparitions, and the mountains are infested by troops of robbers who make murder their occupation."[15]

Seeing the Famous Buddhas at Bamiyan

Xuanzang's caravan prevailed against the blizzards, mountain gods, and robbers and finally approached Bamiyan, an oasis town in the center of a long valley separating the chain of the Hindu Kush from that of the Koh-i-baba range. Xuanzang noted that the country produced spring wheat and had flowers and fruit. It was suitable for cattle and afforded good pasture for sheep and horses. He commented that the people of Bamiyan wore fur garments and coarse wool to protect themselves from the cold. Although their "manners were hard and uncultivated," he admired "their simple, sincere religious faith."

The first sight of the valley of the Great Buddha must have made the weary travelers gasp—immense cliffs of a soft pastel color, and behind them indigo peaks dusted with snow, rising to a height of 20,000 feet. They saw the reddish cliffs in the cold, clear air; as they came closer, they could make out two gigantic statues of the Buddha standing in niches carved in the mountains. Closer still, they saw that two colossal figures were colored and glistening with ornaments; the smaller wore blue, the larger one red, and their faces and hands were gilded. (See Color Plate 4.)

When Xuanzang's caravan first arrived in Bamiyan, the king met the pilgrim and escorted him to his palace. Later Xuanzang's fellow monks took him on a tour of their valley. Xuanzang reported that there were some tens of Buddhist monasteries and several thousand monks who were adherents of a rare Hinayana school whose chief tenet was that the Buddhas were above earthly laws, an idea that is perhaps an approach to the conception of the transcendent Buddha of the Mahayana pantheon.[16]

Together they visited the chief monastery at Bamiyan, with its world-famous Buddhas that Xuanzang described. Modern art historians have often quoted his words.

> On the declivity of a hill to the north-east of the capital was a standing image of Buddha made of stone, 140 or 150 feet high, of a brilliant golden color and resplendent with ornamentation of precious substances. To the east of it was a Buddhist monastery built by a former king of the country. East of this was a standing image of Sakyamuni Buddha above 100 feet high, made of *t'u-shih* [bronze], the pieces of which had been cast separately and then welded together into one figure.[17]

These two Buddhas, which face south, an orientation ensuring the full benefit of the sun's warmth, are actually 175 feet and 125 feet tall respectively. They are still standing, although they are badly mutilated. The monk's quarters were in between these two statues (Fig. 3.2).

Xuanzang called the larger figure a "Buddha image" and the smaller one a "Sakyamuni," or Historical Buddha. As a Master of the Law, as he was often called, Xuanzang would have been particular about such differences in theory, even though he was inclined in practice to keep his intellectual sophistication in one place and his devotion and commitment in another. The size of the Buddha statues served as a model later on for other gigantic statues of a divinized Buddha in China and Japan.[18]

Xuanzang described a curious custom that he would encounter again with the great King Harsha in India. The king used to summon an assembly every five years at which he gave away all his possessions, even his queen; afterwards his officials redeemed all his possessions from the monks.

From Bamiyan Xuanzang and his caravan went east, climbing the pass of Shibar, which at an elevation of 9,000 feet gives access to the

The Crossroads of Asia

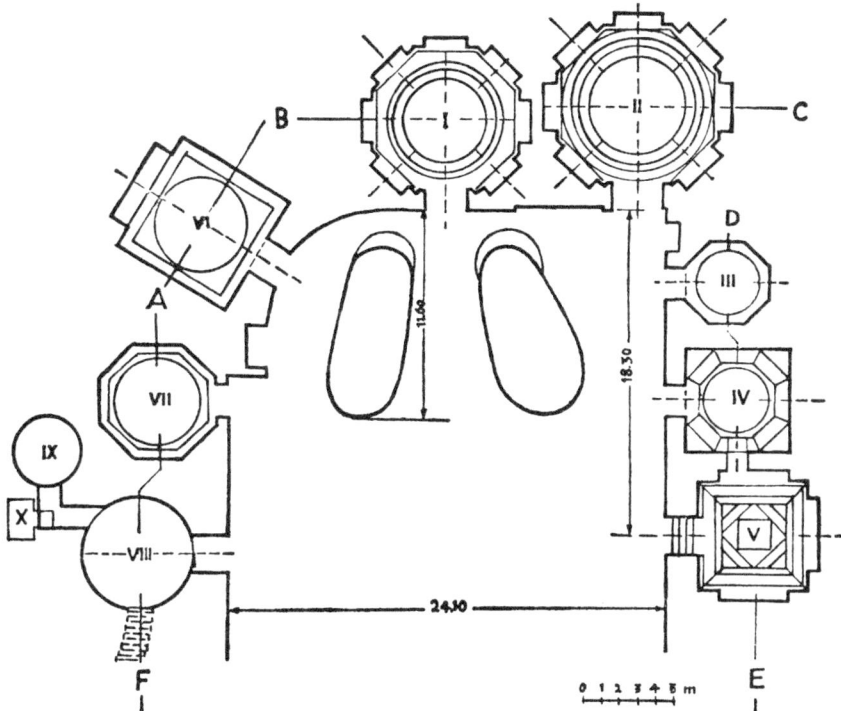

FIGURE 3.2
Ground plan of rock-hewn chapels at Bamiyan, Afghanistan, which form a semicircle around the 175-foot-high figure of the Buddha (Weltbild Verlag GmbH)

upper valley of the Ghorband River. He was overtaken by a snowstorm in the Black Mountains (modern-day Paghman Mountains) and lost his way. Happily, some hunters helped him to follow the winding valley of the Ghorband as far as the meeting of that stream with the Panjshir River. At that point the mountains opened up, and at last the beautiful plain of Kapisa revealed itself.

Finding Hidden Treasures in Kapisa

With its magnificent frame of mountains on three sides, the plain of Kapisa lies in one of the most scenic and historical valleys in all of what is now Afghanistan. Its capital, Kapisi, is an ancient city located on the archaeological site of the village of Begram. Although it is 40 miles north of Kabul, the elevation of the plain is somewhat lower. Now wheat, maize, and sesame fields flourish in this rich alluvial region, along with walnut and mulberry trees.[19] In Xuanzang's time it yielded "cereals of all sorts and every kind of fruit tree, timber and saffron." What a remarkable continuity after so many centuries!

As befitting this important political, commercial, and artistic center, there were one hundred monasteries with more than six thousand monks, chiefly Mahayanist, in Kapisa. "Their *stupas* and *sangharamas* [monasteries] are of an imposing height, and are built on high level spots, from which they can be seen on every side, shining in their grandeur."[20] There were also ten Hindu temples in the kingdom.

The Chinese pilgrim described the people as being of a rude and violent disposition, a little like the inhabitants of Bamiyan. The king, who also went out to meet the pilgrim, was of the merchant class. Xuanzang noted that he was an intelligent, courageous man and a benevolent ruler, whose power extended over ten of the neighboring lands.

Alexander the Great crossed the Kapisa plain in the spring of 329 B.C.E. At Kapisi, the political capital and commercial center of the Kushan Empire, French archaeological missions led by Joseph Hackin discovered the magnificent Begram treasure in 1939. The far-flung nature of Kushan trade with the outside world is revealed in that treasure: exquisitely carved ivories from India, fine Chinese lacquerware from the Han dynasty, an infinite variety of Roman bronzes, and most astonishing of all, a glass vase representing one of the seven wonders of the ancient world—the famous lighthouse at Alexandria. All are in the Kabul Museum (Fig. 3.3). This treasure points to Afghanistan as the true crossroads of the Silk Road, for the area stands halfway between Rome and Chang'an on the east-west roads. On the north-south axis, caravans from Samarkand (from which Xuanzang had come himself so recently) and from India also must have jostled each other in this famous area.

Although Kanishka was a tolerant promoter of religion, he is also known as one of the great supporters of Buddhist art from the first to the third centuries C.E. Like the Tuoba Wei in China who built the large Buddhist caves at Yungang and Longmen, the Kushans had originally been a nomad people from the north who had no artistic traditions of their own. They imported precious objects, such as the Begram treasures, and they borrowed the arts of the contemporary Roman Empire, which came to them over the trade routes, not from Rome itself, but from the eastern outposts of the empire. The union of this Western art with Eastern religion is one of the foundations of Gandharan art and the source of its unique form. Xuanzang had seen an example of this union at Bamiyan, where the drapery of the huge Buddha was modeled after the Roman toga, and the Buddha head was adapted from a classical prototype, such as the Apollo Belvedere.[21]

On a ridge rising to the east of the mound where the Begram treasure was found is the Koh-i-Pahlawan, or Hill of Heroes, a Buddhist

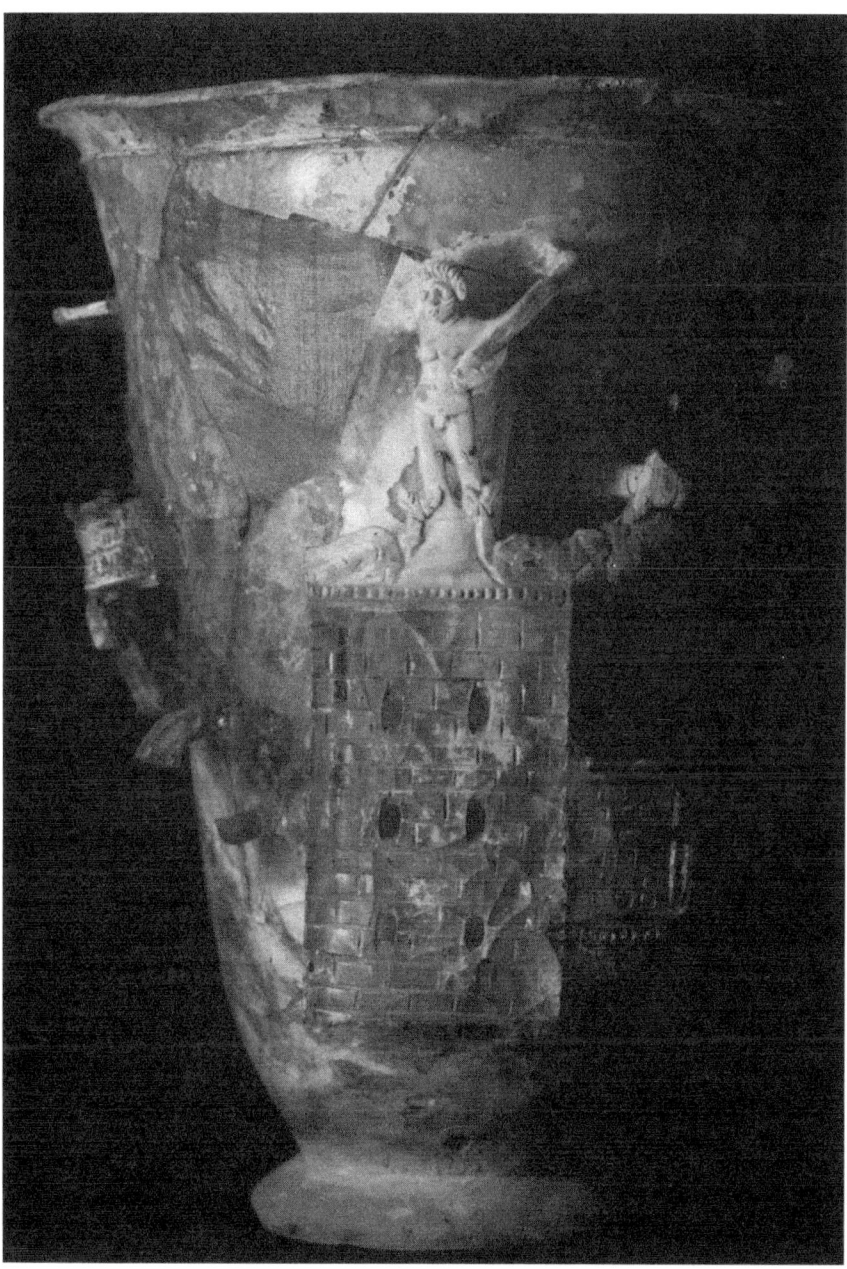

FIGURE 3.3
Carved glass vase from Begram, Afghanistan, showing the Lighthouse of Alexandria, one of the seven wonders of the ancient world (Photo: DAFA)

religious center that flourished from about the third century C.E. on. One monastery, Shotorak, was built especially to house a Chinese hostage, a prince, taken by King Kanishka.[22] Xuanzang was Shotorak's first Chinese visitor since then!

Xuanzang could see for himself on the walls paintings of the Chinese prince. After the hostage prince returned home, he sent religious offerings back to the Monastery of Hostages. Out of gratitude the monks held religious services in his honor at the beginning and end of each Rain Retreat season. This had been done for generations. The Chinese hostage was so generous and wealthy that he also left behind a buried treasure with instructions that it be dug up when the monastery fell into disrepair.

> *The rainy season in the spring of 630 C.E. Who should dig up the treasure? Why, Xuanzang of course. The outer walls of the stupa collapse. The Chinese monk arrives at a crucial moment, a clear sign that it is a propitious time to exhume this treasure. The monks tell him the following story.*
> *"An evil king who is covetous and cruel intends to seize the treasure. He orders his men to dig under the feet of the deity [Vaisravana], but the earth quakes and the figure of a parrot on top of the deity flaps its wings and screams in alarm when it sees the men digging. The king and his soldiers fall down unconscious, and finally they go away in fear." Xuanzang prays to the guardian deity of the monastery for his blessing. Xuanzang supervises the work crew. The monks dig down 7 or 8 feet. To their great delight, they find a large copper vessel containing lustrous pearls and "several hundred pounds of gold."*[23]

While he was at the Monastery of Hostages he most likely stopped to look at one of the several carvings of the Dipankara Buddha. Maybe he learned the story as he gazed at the Buddha carved in gray schist, with its moving portrayal of religious devotion (Fig. 3.4). Some said that a young man went out to meet Dipankara, the last of the Buddhas of the Past, and that the youth first threw five lotus flowers in the direction of Dipankara, which stayed miraculously in the air. He then prostrated himself, put down a deerskin, and offered his long hair as a carpet for the Dipankara Buddha's feet. When he beheld the majesty of this Buddha of the Past, who lived thousands of years ago, he knew that he wanted to seek supreme knowledge of the truth. Dipankara, recognizing the intensity of his desire, which one can feel even in this sculptural fragment, prophesied that he would become the Historical Buddha, Sakyamuni.

Not long after the treasure excavation, the king of Kapisa, who was also a Mahayana Buddhist, asked Xuanzang to take part in a five-day religious assembly. This was a kind of debate similar to the scholastic tournaments held in Europe in the Middle Ages. Xuanzang presided

FIGURE 3.4
A fragment of the Dipankara Buddha, called the twenty-fourth predecessor of the Historical Buddha, Sakyamuni, from Shotorak Monastery, near Kapisa, Afghanistan, where Xuanzang stayed in 630 C.E. This was the Monastery of Hostages, built for a Chinese hostage taken by King Kanishka. (Photo: RMN)

over the debate and, according to his biographer, revealed that he had mastered all the doctrines of the different schools, whereas his opponents understood only their own.

Xuanzang met Jains and Hindu ascetics for the first time on this part of his journey. One was a Saivite who covered his body with ashes and wore a chaplet of skulls on his head. This was a foretaste of what he would meet in the powerful Indian subcontinent to the south, where Hinduism had grown for four thousand years. This religion had no single founder but was composed of innumerable sects. The Hindus were united by the acceptance of caste and devotion to an ancient religious text known as the *Vedas*.[24]

Xuanzang would describe the Hindu people as "given to music. Naturally they are untrustworthy and thievish; their disposition is exacting one over the other, and they never give another the preference over themselves . . . they are little, but they are active and impetuous. Their garments are made of white linen for the most part and what they wear is well appointed."[25]

We recognize in his description the "restless Hindus," as contrasted with his description of the mountain-dwelling Afghans of the Hindu Kush, with their harsh, uncultivated ways, wearing fur garments and coarse wool. A modern view marks British India as beginning on the eastern side of the Khyber Pass, but Xuanzang considered that he had entered India when he came to Jalalabad, his next important resting place.

Xuanzang had already been traveling for about a year, from September 629 to the early fall of 630 C.E. By almost any criterion, it had been an extraordinary year. His physical vigor and toughness were tested by extremes of temperature, sheer distances, and variety of terrain. He crossed both the Taklamakan Desert and the Desert of Red Sands and traversed both the Tian Shan Mountains and the Hindu Kush range. For such a man, only twenty-seven years old, the variety of his experiences and his organizing and personal skills were astonishing: He conversed with kings from cultures very different from his own; he dealt with caravan and pack men of varying nationalities provided by each king; he coped with robbers; and he related and preached to monks and royalty alike. The spiritual challenges were no less demanding: He prayed for guidance before he departed, he prayed in the desert, and he fasted for his beliefs. And now, now, he was approaching the land of many and profound religions—India.

FOUR

THE LAND OF INDIA

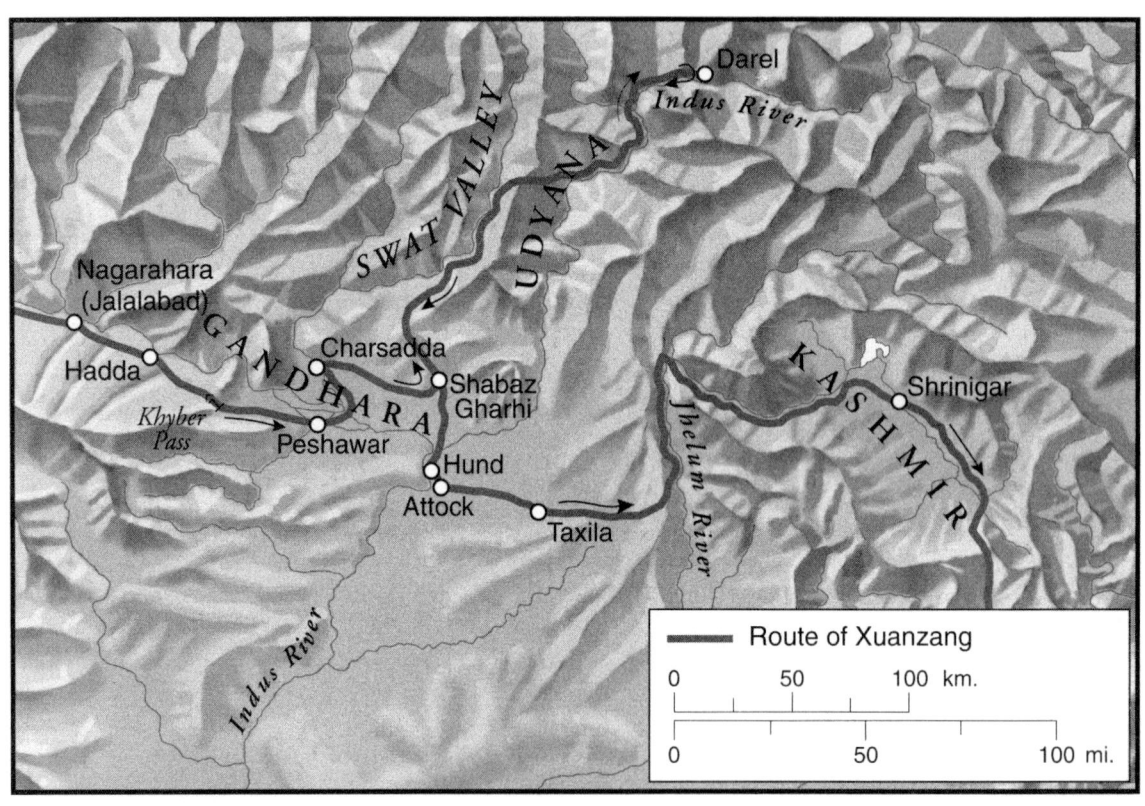

MAP 4.1
*Itinerary of Xuanzang in Gandharan Pakistan (from Jalalabad to Kashmir)
(Philip Schwartzberg, Meridian Mapping)*

✎ WHEN XUANZANG FINALLY reached the neighborhood of Langham, near Jalalabad, he felt, as Alexander the Great had, nine centuries earlier, that he had entered a new world. Alexander offered sacrifices to Athena to inaugurate his new enterprise, and after the division of his army, he began his new campaign. At that point also Xuanzang paused in the detailed narrative of his journey to take an overview of Indian civilization. Evidently, Xuanzang, like Alexander, must have been aware of having reached the gate of a kind of promised land.[1]

Xuanzang began by naming the country, Indu, but did not indicate what kingdoms and states he was including. He overestimated the country's size, although it would be important to know what he is designating as India. The whole territory

> was above 90,000 *li* in circuit, with the Snowy Mountains [the Hindu Kush] on the north and the sea on its three other sides. It was politically divided into above seventy kingdoms; the heat of the summer was very great and the land to a large extent marshy. The northern region was hilly with a brackish soil; the east was a rich fertile plain; the southern division had a luxuriant vegetation; and the west had a soil coarse and gravelly.[2]

His overview was virtually an ethnographic survey, for in it he included measures of time and space and comments on the general characteristics of the people and on both the written and spoken languages. The Indian polysyllabic language, with its alphabetic script so different from the ideograms of Chinese, seemed to appeal to him. He provided information on the condition of cities and villages, public buildings, convents, and private houses. He noted that Buddhist monasteries had "a most remarkable architecture. They have a tower at each of the four corners of the quadrangle and three high halls in a tier. The rafters and roof beams are covered with strange figures, and the doors, windows and walls are covered with strange colors."[3]

He attached great importance to the clothing of different classes. "The inward clothing and outward attire of the people have no tailoring," he said, his Chinese way of describing the saris of Indian women and the dhotis of Indian men. He mentioned the extreme cleanliness of the people, which many have noted.

These material details were followed by a description of the morals, the education of children, and the literature of India. Although he regarded Brahmins as heretics, he did justice to their intelligence, love of learning, and intellectual labors. He was less sparing in his discussion of Buddhists, mentioning the eighteen sects in which they were divided and their often acrimonious discussions. He was amazed that for people whose spiritual attainments were high, the distinctions conferred on them were extraordinary; Buddhist paragons of virtue rode richly caparisoned elephants, just as he himself would do at Nalanda and, later, on King Harsha's elephant. Finally, he outlined the differences in the major hereditary castes—the Brahmins, the highest caste; the Kshatriyas, or the race of kings (and warriors); the Vaisyas, or the class of traders; and the fourth class, the Sudras, or agriculturalists. He also mentioned the particularly Indian phenomenon of the holy men, or wanderers, who did not care for the material things of life.

As if this were not enough, he discussed the law, the army, administration of justice, royal families, and the nine kinds of salutation in India, which had special significance because of caste differences and funeral practices. He devoted the last three chapters to general, but somewhat disconnected, considerations of public administration, agriculture, and mineral resources. It is in many ways a tour de force. Everything is noted and well organized.[4] Then he continued an account of his travels. The next important place he visited was Jalalabad, ancient Nagarahara.

Praying in the Shadow Cave at Jalalabad

Jalalabad was the setting of one of the famous legends of the Sakyamuni Buddha. In a former existence, the Buddha had met Dipankara and received the prediction of his own Buddhahood. King Asoka had a stupa 300 feet tall built to mark the place where the Buddha-to-be had met his distant predecessor, Dipankara. Xuanzang paid his devotions by circumambulating this giant stupa.

But the greatest marvel of all was a cave that the Lord Buddha himself was supposed to have visited, where the Buddha had left his shadow after his combat with the dragon Gopala. This grotto was near the present village of Charar Bagh.[5] Xuanzang had to see it.

> *630 C.E. A few weeks after Kapisa, the Shadow Cave. The approach is said to be hazardous. An old man agrees to be Xuanzang's guide. Hardly do they come near the cave when five robbers appear with drawn swords. The pilgrim explains the purpose of his journey. He knows, he says in answer to their questions, that he might find robbers. "Since I am going to worship the Buddha, I should not be afraid even if I met wild animals on the way, let alone men like yourselves!" The robbers are so surprised by this display of fearlessness that they sheathe their swords and ask if they may join him.*

> *Xuanzang goes inside the gloomy, dark grotto. At first he sees nothing at all. He weeps with regret over his shortcomings and prostrates himself one hundred times; he recites sutras, chants, and prayers with ardor and true selflessness. At last he sees a spot of light on the wall. After two hundred more prostrations, he vows not to leave until he has seen the shadow. Finally the whole cave becomes full of light, and he sees the Buddha's shadow gleaming on the wall. The Buddha's body and his robe are of a yellowish red color. The distinguishing marks of his person are exceedingly glorious. Below, the lotus throne on which he sits is slightly obscured.*[6]

How could Xuanzang commemorate his vision? He had a replica carved of the Buddha of the Shadow Cave. The image, made of sandalwood, was only 15 inches tall, so it could fit in his saddlebags. Perhaps he wanted to take this sacred image as a portable "icon" to venerate on his long journey to the holy land. Having been vouchsafed such a vision, he didn't need to know that this Shadow Cave Buddha was regarded as a unique manifestation of the Buddha's form. Accurate likenesses exist "in only three replicas which the Buddha was said to have granted in his lifetime—the sandalwood image made for King Udayana, the golden image made for King Prasenajit, and the shadow.[7] This was the first in Xuanzang's collection of seven famous images of the Buddha.

With such famous places of pilgrimage as the Dipankara Stupa and the Shadow Cave, it is no wonder that the area of Jalalabad and nearby Hadda have yielded rich archaeological treasures. In the 1840s, Charles Masson, a pioneer in Indian archaeology, discovered a small round container of pure gold repoussé, inlaid with rubies, which had been a container for Buddhist relics (Fig. 4.1). It was enclosed in turn in a stone box in the ruin of a stupa at Bimaran, near Jalalabad. Now in the British Museum, this beautiful reliquary depicts a standing Buddha flanked by two attendants, Brahma and Indra, Indian gods who were incorporated into the Buddhist pantheon. It is one of the early representations of the Lord Buddha.[8]

Ordinary commercialism existed at Jalalabad even in the seventh century. Xuanzang mentioned that the priests were few. He complained about how much he had to spend to venerate the numberless relics of the region—fifty gold coins, one thousand smaller silver coins, four silk banners, two lengths of brocade, and two cassocks were asked of him as he visited various holy sites. Xuanzang depicted the local inhabitants as being full of respect for the Buddha. But there was something puzzling about this rich area of pilgrimage. "The Sangharamas (*monasteries*) are many, but yet the priests are few, the stupas are desolate and ruined."[9]

FIGURE 4.1
The Bimaran reliquary, a work of Gandharan art that shows Western influence and Indian iconography. The standing Buddha is flanked by Brahma and Indra. (Copyright British Museum)

Pursuing King Kanishka Around Peshawar

Sheer cliffs of shale and limestone on both sides of a rugged narrow defile mark Khyber Pass, which leads from Jalalabad to Peshawar. Protruding dun-colored rocks make it an ideal place for robbers to lie in wait for weary merchants and pilgrims. Xuanzang and his caravan had met robbers before on the other side of Turfan near the Qoltag Mountains, and two days out of Kucha he had had a narrow escape. Xuanzang's caravan would be ambushed in a forest later on. Worse still, he would be tied to a stake by a band of robbers on the banks of the Ganges River.

The Land of India

This time Xuanzang and his party emerged unscathed in the valley of Peshawar (Pakistan). At the time of Xuanzang's arrival, Peshawar was no longer an independent state, for it had been annexed to Kapisa. No king or principal officers of the realm would come to welcome him. The valley of Peshawar had once been a place of great importance, with Purushapura (Peshawar), the capital of Gandhara.[10] Then came the White Huns (450–470 C.E.), leaving their trail of destruction and plunder. Buddhism was in a marked state of decline. Xuanzang's lavish welcome in Kashmir by the king and 1,000 monks several months later—in May 631 C.E.—would be all the more heartwarming in contrast to his experience in the valley of Peshawar.

Xuanzang estimated that only one thousand families lived in a corner of the ancient city. The country was still rich in cereals and sugarcane, watered by rivers flowing from the mountains. As the pilgrim looked about, he saw a familiar sight—the dilapidated dwellings of monks where once there had been perhaps one thousand monasteries. Many of the stupas were also in ruins. There were one hundred Hindu temples and "the various sects lived pell-mell."

From roughly the first to the fifth century the prestige of the valley of Peshawar, like that of Jalalabad and Hadda, had rested upon the building of monasteries and stupas and their connection with a number of episodes in the Buddha's legendary life and previous existences. All through the valley, as well as in Swat, in the mountains, Xuanzang heard the many legends that missionaries and monks had invented or brought from the Indian lowlands. He recorded them all.

One of these legends, that of King Kanishka, is a tangled skein of legends and fact. Xuanzang noted that

> about eight or nine li to the southeast of the capital was a large and very ancient Pipphal [Pipal] Tree above 100 feet high with wide-spreading foliage affording a dense shade. When Sakya Julai [the Buddha] was sitting under this tree with his face to the south he said to Ananda, "Four hundred years after my decease a sovereign will reign, by name Kanishka, who a little south of this will raise a tope [stupa] in which he will collect many of my flesh and bone relics."[11]

This was part of the Kanishka legend. Xuanzang went on to relate that when King Kanishka was out hunting in the forest, a white hare approached him. The hare led "the heathen king" to a herder boy who was making a small stupa out of clay or dung. Kanishka was impressed by the little boy, who proceeded to tell him of the Buddha's prophecy. This so moved the king that he was converted to Buddhism on the spot and set about building a stupa "round the site of the small boy's clay mound."

A multistoried tower stupa was actually built and for a long time was regarded as one of the wonders of the world. A small stucco model from Jaulian monastery at Taxila may reflect the appearance of this great shrine, with its impressive mast of parasols, an architectural feature that played a vital part in the evolution of the Indian stupa into the Far Eastern pagoda.[12]

Although Xuanzang found the Kanishka stupa in ruins, he was able to gather information about it from many sources. He established that it was 400 feet high, with a superstructure of gilt-copper disks, the base being in five stages and 150 feet in height.[13] Xuanzang's description played a role in D. B. Spooner's locating the giant Kanishka stupa and his finding the relic box of this great Kushan monarch in 1908 (Fig. 4.2).[14] On the reliquary is a portrait of this Indian monarch exactly as he appears on what is known as the *BODDO* coin, which on its reverse side also contains one of the early portrayals of the Buddha in human form (Fig. 4.3). The design of this coin testifies to King Kanishka's involvement with Buddhism.

After Xuanzang left the ruins of the Kanishka stupa, he visited the old house nearby where Vasubandhu had composed the *Treasury of Buddhist Philosophy*. Although that was an early work closer to the Realist school, Vasubandhu became one of the originators of idealism, and Xuanzang had already spent many years in China studying him. Vasubandhu, as one who was devoted to seeking to "solve that which was beyond language," had been an inspiration to Xuanzang. He noted that a tablet had been set in the old house in commemoration of this great Buddhist philosopher.

Seeking the Four Great Stupas and the Visvantara Site

Xuanzang sought to the north and east of Peshawar the famous stupas that commemorated the Jataka tales of the Buddha's good deeds in his past lives. Many of the stories characteristic of early Buddhism were adapted from the popular culture to point up certain moral truths. They told of unbelievable sacrifice and often depicted absolute pity for all creatures. Near Charsadda was the stupa commemorating the vivid story of the Buddha's giving his eyes for charity. In the hills separating Peshawar and Buner was a stupa connected with the story of the Buddha's giving his flesh so that a dove could live. From Manikyala, a stupa in Swat, came yet another legend reflecting the Buddha's close connection with animals, for with Buddhist concepts of reincarnation, life may assume a variety of forms. This time the legend described how

The Land of India

FIGURE 4.2
Reliquary of King Kanishka, one of the great patrons of Buddhism. Lid has Buddha seated on a lotus pedestal, being worshipped by Brahma and Indra. (Copyright British Museum)

the Buddha offered his life so that a tiger could feed her cubs (Fig. 4.4). The fourth great stupa, which was in the neighborhood of Taxila, related to the gift of the Buddha's head. Although Xuanzang was happy to pinpoint these tales of the former Buddhas and attach them to specific sites, he would see the same stories repeated over and over again engraved in stone or painted on monastery walls in greater India and in China as far away as the Dunhuang Caves.[15]

Xuanzang located the site of the most famous legend of boundless sacrifice at Shahbaz Garhi—the Prince Visvantara Jataka. There was once a generous prince, he told us, who owned a miraculous elephant

FIGURE 4.3
Gold coin with a standing Buddha, clearly identified by the legend BODDO in Greek letters, and King Kanishka on the other side (Copyright British Museum)

that had the magic power of making rain. When a neighboring kingdom had a severe drought, the prince gave the elephant away. He and his family were banished.

> To the northeast of Po-lu-sha city about 20 li or so we come to Mount Dantaloka. Above a ridge of that mountain is a stupa built by Asoka raja; it was here the Prince Sudana (Visvantara) dwelt in solitude. It was here the prince gave his son and daughter to a Brahmin, who, on his part, beat them until the blood flowed out on the ground. At the present time the shrubs and trees are all of a deep red colour. Between the crags (of the mountain) there is a stone chamber where the prince and his wife practiced meditation.[16]

In time the prince was persuaded to give away even his wife. Eventually the children were recognized by the prince's father and purchased by him. In a happy ending his wife was also returned by the gods, who finally took pity on the prince as well.

Across the valley from the ruins of the stupa are Asoka inscriptions

The Land of India

FIGURE 4.4
Part of a frieze from the Dunhuang Caves in China, portraying the Tiger Jataka, a tale in which the Buddha sacrificed his life so that a tiger might feed her cubs (The Lo Archive)

on a large rock, tangible evidence for the most particular historian. These edicts were also inscribed on stone pillars erected in important cities. They made known Asoka's understanding of the nature of the insights and principles of the Buddhist religion as well as their application by the state, the religious community, and the individual. These Asoka inscriptions, believed to be the oldest written records of Buddhism, were on the chief roads throughout India. This particular location, midway on the ancient route from Charsadda to Taxila, was a logical place for the Rock Edicts, especially as it was also the site where Prince Visvantara achieved knowledge of "perfect charity."[17]

Xuanzang also mentioned the story of the Monk of the Single Horn. A stupa is believed to mark the spot where this monk lived. As it happened, the holy monk was led astray by a courtesan, and then disguised as a nun, she rode on his shoulders to the city. It is similar to early versions of the story of Phyllis and Aristotle.

To see how closely Gandharan art and Buddhist worship are intertwined, one can look at the reconstructed Sikri stupa from the same area that is now in the Lahore Museum in Pakistan (Fig. 4.5). Most of

FIGURE 4.5
A reconstructed Sikri stupa (about 20 feet high), with sixteen scenes from the life of the Buddha. Lahore Museum, Pakistan (Copyright Lahore Museum)

The Land of India 63

these friezes are at eye level—Jataka tales, the miracles and stories of the life of the Buddha, such as one depicting the grass cutter offering his grass for the Buddha to sit on prior to his enlightenment. We can easily imagine Xuanzang going slowly around such a stupa, just as he did at the Dipankara stupa, stopping before each scene of the Buddha's life to contemplate its meaning, much as Christians pray before each station of the cross at Easter time.

It didn't seem to matter that the Historical Buddha had never been to Gandhara. So famous were the stories that many Chinese pilgrims were content to visit these great stupas in this second holy land without going to the true holy land of India itself. William Blake captured some of this feeling in relation to England.

> *And did those feet in ancient time*
> *Walk upon England's mountain green*
> *And was the holy Lamb of God*
> *On England's pleasant pastures seen?*[18]

Collecting Healing Sutras and Trekking in the Swat Valley

Xuanzang left the main road from Peshawar to India to go north and east to Udyana in the Swat Valley, fine mountainous country where he found the destruction was even greater than at Gandhara—1,400 monasteries that had once housed 18,000 monks. He found the region in a derelict state with only a remnant of monks. They were Mahayana Buddhists "who occupied themselves with silent meditation; they were clever at reciting their books without penetrating the deep meaning; they lived strictly according to their rules and were specially expert in magical exorcisms. Of the Deva-Temples, there were above ten and various sectarians lived pell-mell."[19]

It doesn't appear as if Xuanzang was necessarily condemning these practices, for the Chinese monk brought back the *Sutra of the Eleven-Faced Avalokitesvara* and other sutras containing spells for charming holy water, incense, firewood, medicinal herbs, and so on.[20] Actually Xuanzang was among the first to introduce esoteric texts to China. He seems to have been far more open to a wide range of Buddhist belief and practice than might be expected.

Xuanzang continued north and east to the Upper Swat and Buner Valleys. Alfred Fouchet, who retraced his steps for thousands of miles in these valleys and mountains south of the Oxus River, grew accustomed to "his tastes and habits of travel, his craving for edification, his foible for monkish stories, his complete disdain of ruins, his obvious preference for beaten tracks and stages of reasonable length." Thanks to "the precision and honesty of his journal," Fouchet was able to follow him through Gandhara, availing himself of "the information which he has recorded and the legends which he has collected in order to determine the principal trade routes and identify the most celebrated Buddhist monuments of the country."[21]

But the Upper Swat and Buner Valleys were only open to diplomats and those on special missions; Alfred Fouchet could not go there, so his description fits very well until the pilgrim's next explorations. Xuanzang went to the source of the Swat River, where the dragon Apalala is supposed to have lived; the pilgrim crossed a mountain range and followed the mighty Indus River, where there were no roads, no beaten tracks, only hazardous paths through gloomy gorges. On his trek he crossed "bridges of rope or iron chain; ... bridges spanning precipices by means of pegs for steps." Modern travelers have described similar paths that are tacked to a cliff by branches and sticks pressed into cracks in the rock wall and covered by brush and rocks piled on top: These trekkers have looked down *through* the path and seen the river hundreds of feet below.

Chinese travelers—just as Xuanzang in the seventh and the pious old Faxian in the fourth century did—made their way along the steep escarpments of the Indus River, crawling along precipices where one false step meant a slip into eternity or, for a pilgrim like Xuanzang who believed in reincarnation, another round of existence.[22]

Their destination?[23] In the upper reaches of the Indus River northeast of the capital of Swat was "a great Monastery by the side of which is a carved wooden image of ... Maitreya Bodhisattva of a brilliant golden hue and of miraculous powers; it is above 100 feet high; it was the work of the arhat Madhyantika who by his supernatural power thrice bore the artist to Tushita Heaven to study Maitreya's beautiful characteristics; the spread of Buddhism eastwards dates from the existence of this image."[24] This was the famous statue at Darel that may have served as a model for the colossal Buddhas of Yungang in faraway China.[25]

In times of distress Xuanzang had often prayed to the Maitreya, the Buddha of the Future. So he didn't need to know, though he might have been interested, that it was in the land of Gandhara as well as in the area around Mathura farther south in India that the first Bodhisattvas and the first human representations of the Buddha had been created.

What is so remarkable is that Buddha images, whether in Sri Lanka, Japan, or Indonesia, have all sprung from these first images. Before the second or third century, the Buddha had been represented for the most part by abstract symbols, such as an empty throne, a stupa, a tree standing for the place where he received his enlightenment, or a wheel signifying the Wheel of Buddhist Law, just as in early Christianity Christ was represented by a fish or a plain cross.[26] Interestingly enough, at the same time that these first human images of the Buddha were created, the first quasi-historical accounts of the Buddha's life were being written.[27] It was almost as if people were asking: "What is this Buddha? What sort of a person is he?"[28]

Similarly, in the early stages of Christianity, Christians wrestled with the problem of the true appearance of Jesus Christ. A relic in St. Peter's Basilica in Rome is said to be the Veronica Veil, from the legend that a woman named Veronica gave Christ a cloth that he put to his face to contain his perspiration as he carried the cross. The imprint from his perspiration, a true picture of his face, helped to satisfy the human desire to envisage the sacred. If a deity walked on earth, people want to know what he looked like—Christians as well as Buddhists.

Xuanzang would have known many of these Gandharan images of Buddhas and Bodhisattvas from worshipping at stupas or monasteries where the type and form of these figures had already been established. Had he not seen that the Buddha's hair was arranged in waves, with a mound of wisdom on top of his head? In order for the Buddha to be distinguished from other holy men, he has wavy hair and his head is not shaved, as befits ordinary monks. The eyes on these early Buddhas are open, though some of them seem to look at an indefinite space in front of them, and there is a little circle or beauty spot between the brows. The earlobes are distended, for he was once a prince who wore heavy earrings. Sometimes he has a mustache. A heavy monk's robe hangs in deep folds to just above his feet, or in a cross-legged Buddha, his feet may be covered completely. The hands are shown in the gestures of reassurance, meditation, preaching, or touching the earth with the right hand, calling the earth to witness. Thirty-two superior and eighty inferior superhuman features were borrowed from the ancient Indian concept of the World King. There is an unusual early dated example of a Gandhara Buddha in a private collection in Belgium (Fig. 4.6). It remained for later generations to suggest that irresistible combination of detachment and pent-up dynamic force that would give the Gupta Buddhas their deep religious quality.

Exploring Monuments at Taxila

How long the pilgrim spent in Swat isn't clear. Xuanzang returned on "this route of hanging chains" to the lowlands, to a place where the

FIGURE 4.6
An early representation (dated 182 C.E.) of Buddha flanked by a Bodhisattva and Avalokitesvara, with Brahma and Indra in the background. Figures like the seated Buddha in this relief were sources for images elsewhere in Asia. (Copyright Claude de Marteau. Courtesy Claude de Marteau Collection.)

The Land of India

Indus River is more than one-half mile wide and the current flows swiftly. He picked up the ancient caravan route to cross the river at Hund. The crossing could still be dangerous: "Its stream is extremely clear and rapid. Poisonous dragons and evil sprites dwell beneath this river in great numbers. Those who cross this river carrying with them rare gems of India, or celebrated flowers . . . or Sariras [the Buddha's relic bones], the boat (*in which they embark*) is suddenly overwhelmed by the waves."[29]

A modern account describes the Indus at Attock 12 miles south-southwest of Hund: In winter the swift torrent makes a rushing, swishing noise like a big bird swooping close, but in summer "the glacier sluice-gates open in the high mountains, the river washes fifty feet further up the cliffs and roars through like a galloping horse."[30]

Dragons, big birds, galloping horses? The Indus River, then as now, seemed alive! On his way home to China in 645 C.E., Xuanzang's boat, on which there were many valuable manuscripts, did capsize when a sudden storm sprang up. He lost many of them.

After his crossing of the Indus River, the pilgrim made his way to Taxila, which Alexander the Great had conquered in 326 B.C.E., and which Asoka had made a center of his provinces in the northwest. The valley, 10 miles square, is enclosed on three sides by mountains. Perhaps as he made his way to the city, the roads were filled with horse-drawn carts, occasional camels, and donkeys bearing farmers kicking their flanks. Perhaps Xuanzang stopped first in the bazaar in the town of Sirsukh to talk with the caravan traders about the price of food, where people had come from, where they were going, and who was running things, the local legends of the place. Or maybe he looked up to see a few monks quietly descending the rock-scarred foothills of the town to beg for food, or turned in the direction of the Jaulian monastery to admire its golden domes and spires. That remains the best preserved monastery in Taxila, with its many Buddhas still in place, a rewarding place to visit even now.

Did he pick up the story of the local dragon in the bazaar or the monastery? What were his sources? How did he know how large the kingdom was? How did he come to know what there was to know about Taxila, so that he could write:

> This was above 2,000 *li* in circuit, the capital being above ten *li* in circuit. The chiefs were in a state of open feud, the royal family being extinguished; the country had formerly been subject to Kapisa but now it was a dependency of Kashmir; it had a fertile soil and bore good crops, with flowing streams and luxuriant vegetation; the climate was genial; and the people, who were plucky, were adherents of Buddhism. Although the Monasteries were numerous, many of them were desolate, and the Brethren, who were very few, were all Mahayanists.[31]

Xuanzang stayed in Sirsukh, the last of the ancient cities of Taxila. According to the Baedeker for South Asia valid from the British period until 1915, the distances and directions mentioned by Xuanzang around Sirsukh could be used to guide the modern traveler. There are few examples in history of an ancient source so reliable that it was still useful after almost 1,300 years.[32]

Xuanzang described several famous Buddhist monuments in the neighborhood of the city. One of these was the tank (artificial lake) of Elapattra, the Dragon King; another, across the Taxila Valley, was the stupa of "the sacrificial head," said to have been built by Asoka. This is the present-day Bhallar stupa, which stands like a mighty drum perched high on a hill.

A third monument, the Kunala stupa, presumably had been built by Asoka, too, to commemorate the spot where his son's eyes were put out. The story of Kunala was told by Xuanzang: Kunala's stepmother fell in love with him, and when he rejected her advances, she induced Asoka to send him to Taxila; this wicked lady forged a letter in her husband's name and sealed it with his teeth while he slept. The letter contained an order that Prince Kunala's eyes be put out. The king's ministers shrank from executing the order until the prince himself insisted on obedience to his father. After he was blinded, he wandered forth with his wife and begged his way to the far-off capital of his father. When he sang and played the lute at his father's palace, his father recognized his voice and the string of his lute. The king then had the cruel and vindictive queen put to death. The prince's eyesight was restored at Bodh Gaya through the help of a Buddhist holy man, according to one of the many versions of the Kunala story.

This drama, reminiscent of the Greek tragedy of Hippolytus and Phaedra, is said to have taken place on a rock-scarred foothill above the south end of the village of Sirkap. Steps of rock lead to the rectangular base of the Kunala stupa, dating from the third or fourth century C.E. Buried in the northwest corner are the remains of a tiny first-century stupa, which, in Sir John Marshall's day, stood about 10 feet in height. Not far away are the remains of the spacious Gaia Monastery. Xuanzang wrote that blind people used to go to this stupa to pray for the restoration of their eyesight, and many had their prayers answered. Though the Kunala stupa has crumbled, the tradition lingers; the best medical facility for eye patients, the Mission Hospital, is in Taxila today.[33]

Before Xuanzang reached Kashmir, he found yet another Asoka stupa and more than ten tanks, or artificial lakes, large and small. He was enchanted by what he called "a scene of sunshine."

> The banks of these tanks were of carved stone representing various forms and strange kinds of creatures. The struggling water (that is, the rivers

which supplied the tanks) was a clear brawling current; dragons, fish and other watery tribes moved about in its cavernous depths; lotuses of the four colours covered the surface of the clear ponds; all kinds of fruit trees grew thick making one splendour of various hues and, the brightness of the wood mixing with that of the tanks, the place was truly a pleasure-ground.[34]

Among his many sensibilities, Xuanzang here showed, like many Chinese, a nice appreciation of nature.

Studying the Law in Kashmir

Ahead of him was Kashmir, roughly 200 miles to the northeast in the mountains. After climbing precipitous passes and traversing more chain bridges, Xuanzang seems to have gone through the Barula Gorge, made by the Jhelum River flowing with "extraordinary fury on account as the natives affirm, of its angry feeling at being obliged to quit the peaceful plains of Kashmir."[35]

Xuanzang was met at the inside edge of the pass by a maternal uncle of the king, who had been sent to escort the pilgrim to Srinagar. He spent the night at Hushkara Monastery, where the night before his arrival, the monks had been told in a dream that a strange monk from China had come to their land to study the sacred books and adore the holy sites. When the party approached the capital, the king provided Xuanzang with an elephant upon which to make his entrance to the city. The king himself came to meet him, along with his ministers, and 1,000 Buddhist monks bearing colorful standards and parasols. The heavy fragrance of incense filled the air, and the road was strewn with flowers for his arrival. The king provided hospitality at his palace and invited Xuanzang to read and expound scriptures, giving him twenty clerks to copy out manuscripts.

Xuanzang included a short general description of Kashmir in his usual manner. The country was surrounded by high, steep mountains over which there were narrow difficult passes. The district had good agriculture and produced abundant fruit and flowers; it also yielded horses of the dragon stock, saffron, and medicinal plants. Fields of bluish purple saffron flowers with red stamens still grow in Kashmir today. The people were volatile but timid, good-looking but deceitful. "Being protected by a dragon," the pilgrim added, "they crow over their neighbors."[36]

From remote times Kashmir was distinguished for its learning. Xuanzang mentioned four Asoka stupas housing Buddhist relics, but he seemed much less interested in visiting sacred places than previously and was clearly challenged by the intellectual atmosphere of Kashmir. He reported that there were five thousand Buddhist monks and one hundred monasteries. Best of all, he found a venerable Mahayanist sage.

In the morning the sage lectured on that great treatise, the *Treasury of Buddhist Philosophy*, by Vasubandhu, in the afternoon on another text, which confuted that treatise. The evening was devoted to secular studies, such as grammar and logic. Here was the kind of intellectual and spiritual challenge Xuanzang had been waiting for.

The Kashmir sage spoke to Xuanzang in words that were quoted by Xuanzang's biographer:

> This priest of China possesses wonderful (*vast and immeasurable*) strength of wisdom. In all this congregation there is none to surpass him. By his wisdom and his virtue he is competent to join in succession to the fame of his brother Vasubandhu. What a subject for regret, indeed! that belonging to a distant land he cannot at once form a part in the bequeathed fragrance of the saints and sages![37]

Xuanzang was equally enthusiastic about the aged sage. Such a meeting of minds gives us a clue as to why Xuanzang spent two years in Kashmir—from May 631 to 633 C.E. Along with the Idealist doctrine to which he subscribed, there was also in Kashmir a thriving Realist school of Buddhism. Xuanzang was glad to study these two important and contrasting schools and to collect treatises from both to take home to China.

Not far from the Kashmir district of Jalandar, King Kanishka, with a collaboration of two celebrated patriarchs, is said to have summoned a council of 500 Buddhist scholars. Xuanzang filled us in on how this might have come about.

> In his leisure hours he [Kanishka] studied the Buddhist scriptures, having a monk every day in the palace to give him instruction. But as the Brethren taught him different and contradictory interpretations, owing to conflicting tenets of sectarians, the king fell into a state of hopeless uncertainty. Then the Venerable Parsva explained to His Majesty that in the long lapse of time since Buddha left the world disciples of schools and masters with various theories had arisen, all holding personal views and all in conflict. On hearing this the king was greatly moved, and expressed to Parsva his desire to restore Buddhism to eminence, and to have the Tripitaka explained according to the tenets of the various schools.[38]

Xuanzang could appreciate the nature of Kanishka's desires from his own anguish in trying to sort out conflicting interpretations of Buddhist texts in China.

He reported the story that King Kanishka had the finished treatises written out on copper plates and enclosed in a strongbox, which he de-

The Land of India

posited in a stupa made for that purpose. They have not been found, and almost all information on this Fourth Buddhist Council comes from Xuanzang.[39]

Tradition has it that the Buddhist canon, the equivalent of the Scriptures for Christians, was written down in Sanskrit under Kanishka's auspices. Buddhists call this the Three Baskets, or *Tripitaka*—the Sayings of the Buddha, or *Sutras*; the Rules of Discipline, or *Vinaya*; and the Systematic Philosophy, or *Abhidharma*.

Xuanzang was also fascinated by Indian logic and studied systematic treatises dealing with logic, which were almost unknown in China. India produced many systems of logic and many forms of syllogistic reasoning. The Old Logic of Vasubandhu and Asanga laid down detailed rules for conducting a debate. The New Logic, founded by Dignaga in the late fifth century C.E., simplified the set form in which an argument was to be stated. It also enumerated and defined valid and invalid inferences, means of proof, and so on—the famous Thirty-Three Fallacies. A few Indian texts had been translated into Chinese, but the New Logic was Xuanzang's special gift to China.[40]

Xuanzang had already participated in a religious debate before the king of Kapisa, and he would do so most successfully in India before the powerful King Harsha. The rules of logic, common laws of thought, were necessary for these grand scholastic tournaments between men of differing faiths—Hindus, Buddhists, Jains, who would put their case before powerful rulers who might become their patrons. This idea is partly connected with the fact that for centuries so many of the rulers of northern India had been foreigners who had to make up their minds which sect it would be politically advantageous to support. Many Hindu and Buddhist biographies of great teachers mention such disputations in the presence of reigning monarchs.[41]

The vale of Kashmir, with its snow-covered peaks and misty lakes, was not only a beautiful place to stay, but Xuanzang's two years there would prepare him for future studies with Buddhist philosophers and religious debates. He had already showed his wide-ranging intellectual interests in esoteric Buddhist texts and practices and the New Logic. It was also a foretaste of what he would find in seventh-century India: an increasing emphasis in Buddhism on intellectualism and metaphysical inquiry.

COLOR PLATE 1
Exterior of the Dunhuang Caves, which were at the juncture of the Northern and Southern Silk Roads in China. Xuanzang stopped there on his return journey from India. (Courtesy Paddy Booz, photographer)

COLOR PLATE 2
General view of Bezeklik Monastery, which, like many Buddhist monasteries, overlooks a river. The caves are filled with beautiful wall paintings, which are now largely destroyed. (Copyright Sally Hovey Wriggins, photographer)

COLOR PLATE 3
Wall painting of an Indian goddess and a celestial musician, from cave at Kizil. (Museum of Indian Art, Berlin. Museum für Indische Kunst, Staatliche Museen Preussischer Kulturbesitz, Berlin)

COLOR PLATE 4
The valley of Bamiyan, set between the peaks of the Hindu Kush and the Koh-i-baba ranges. One of the two colossal Buddhas described by Xuanzang is visible in this long-distance view. (Courtesy Lee Coldren, photographer)

COLOR PLATE 5
At Sanskaya, so the legend goes, the Buddha descended from heaven after preaching to his mother. Xuanzang visited the site of this miracle, which is one of the eight traditional places of pilgrimage for all Buddhists, even now. (By permission of The British Library)

COLOR PLATE 6
General views of Sarnath, where the Buddha preached his first sermon, the Doctrine of the Middle Way. It is one of the four most sacred places of Buddhist pilgrimage. (Courtesy of Sheila Hixon, photographer)

COLOR PLATE 7
View from Stupa 3 at Nalanda Monastery: The outline of one of the monastic courtyards can be seen, with the flat, verdant, countryside of Bihar in the background. (Copyright Sally Hovey Wriggins, photographer)

COLOR PLATE 8
Chinese painting on silk scroll from Dunhuang, called *Return of Xuanzang with the Buddhist Scriptures*. (Courtesy Fujita Museum)

FIVE

PHILOSOPHERS & PIRATES IN NORTHERN INDIA

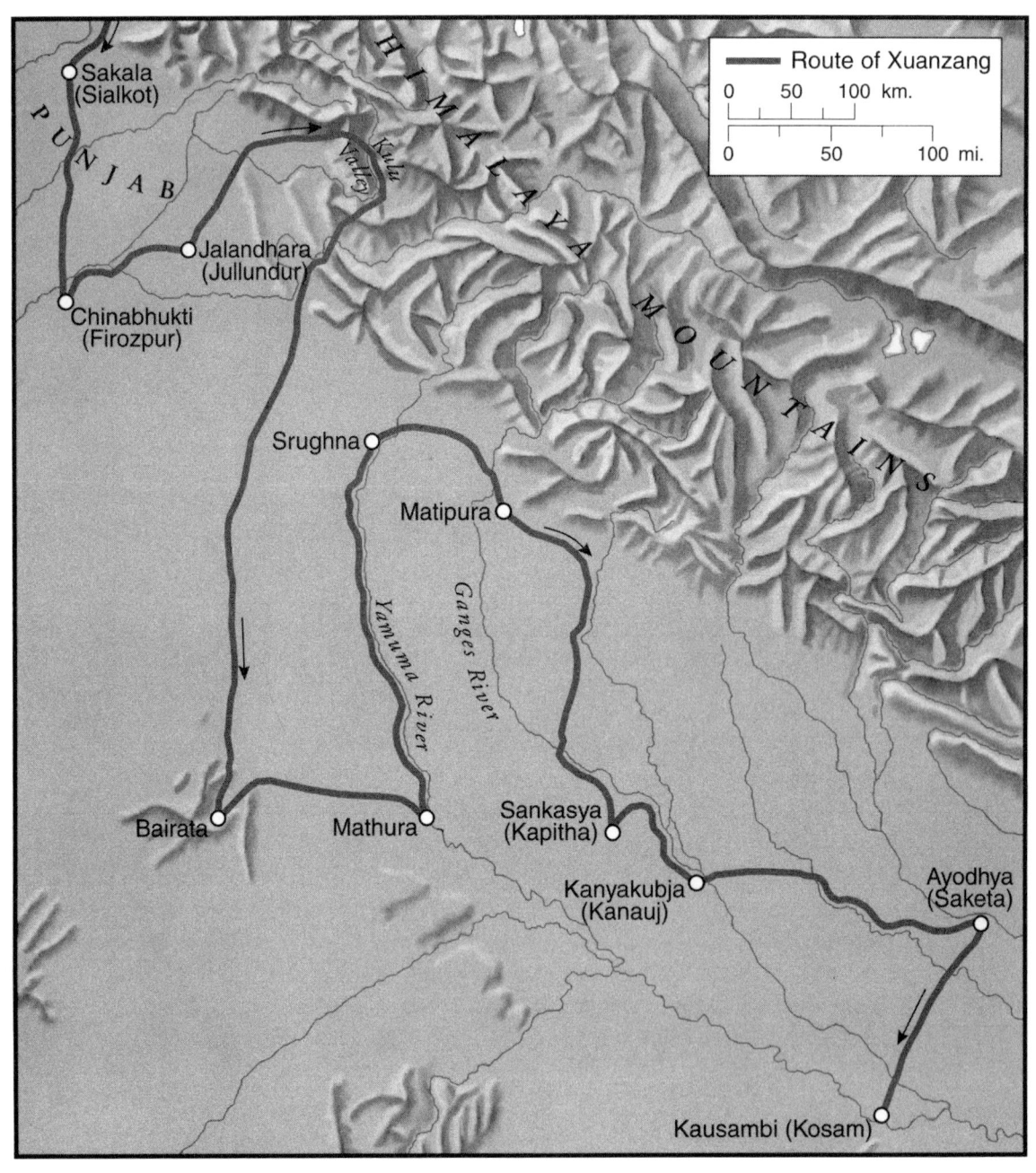

MAP 5.1
Itinerary of Xuanzang through northern India (from Kashmir to Kausambi) (Philip Schwartzberg, Meridian Mapping)

NEAR-CALAMITIES AND unexpected dangers lay ahead of Xuanzang in northern India—hazardous paths up mountain ravines to reach the pointed conifers of the Kulu Valley and forests infested with elephants and wild beasts on his way to Kausambi. At one moment the pilgrim would be exerting every ounce of strength to escape from a band of robbers, and the next moment he would linger with a group of monks to discuss the implications of the Buddhist doctrine of Not-Self. What was reborn if the existence of Self, or soul, was denied?

Fleeing from Robbers in the Punjab

633 C.E. No warning. It had been a spring day like any other. Xuanzang and his entourage descend from the vale of Kashmir to find their way down to the great Gangetic plain of north India. The setting is a forest near Sakala, present-day Sialkot; fifty robbers are lying in wait for just such a caravan. They ambush the pilgrim and his party, strip them of their clothes, steal their goods, and chase them into a dried-up marsh. The former lake, enclosed by a wall of matted vines and thorns, makes an ideal pen for slaughter. The brigands are already beginning to tie up some caravan members when a young monk helps Xuanzang escape. The two of them get away and seek help from a village a mile away. The rescuers from the village free those who had been tied up. Everyone is shaken by the loss of their possessions and their narrow escape from death. Xuanzang alone seems untouched by what had happened.
"Life is the most precious thing in existence," declares Xuanzang.[1]

This high degree of detachment seems unattainable or alien to most modern people, and yet Xuanzang, as his trip continued, showed this same equanimity, this extraordinary imperturbability. Even when he was captured by pirates who hoped to burn him on their altar as a sacrifice to the god Durga, he seemed above it all. As Huili put it so well, "As the turbulent waves of a river do not disturb its pure water beneath, so was he."[2]

At Chinabhukti, said to correspond to modern Firozpur, just to the south of the Sutlej River, Xuanzang was pleased to study with Vinitaprabha, a north Indian prince, for more than a year (633–634 C.E.). Xuanzang was able to continue his study of logic, for the prince, who was also a monk, was an authority on one of the two surviving texts of the New Logic.[3] He had also written commentaries on Yogacara

Buddhism, including one on the *Thirty Verses*. That treatise was by Vasubandhu, whose house Xuanzang had visited in Gandhara a short time before, and who was one of the founders, along with Asanga, of the school of Yogacara idealism. An immense body of literature has grown up around these thirty verses, which summed up the doctrine of the Idealists, the philosophy that was closest to Xuanzang's own personal sympathies.

Part of the background of this elusive philosophy, which applies to Buddhism generally, has to do with the doctrine of Not-Self. In the *Questions of Milinda*, a wise monk asks a Greek Bactrian (whose views would be more materialistic and literal) to explain what a chariot is.

> "Is the pole the chariot?"
> "No, reverend Sir!"
> "Is then the axle the chariot?"
> "No, reverend Sir!"
> "Is it then the wheels, or the framework, or the flagstaff or the yoke, or the reins, or the goad-stick?"
> "No, reverend Sir!"
> "Then is it the combination of pole, axle, wheels, framework, flagstaff, reins and goad which is the 'chariot'?"
> "No, reverend Sir!"[4]

Therefore, "chariot" is a designation, or a mere name, that has no ultimate reality. Not only is the human personality much less solid than once thought; it may indeed be a simple stream of phenomena. Another Buddhist image is that of the flame of a candle. Is the flame of the candle at the beginning of the night the same as the flame in the middle of the night and the flame in the morning?[5]

In 634 C.E. Xuanzang spent the Rain Retreat at Jalandhara (Jullundur), the last large town in the eastern Punjab. Afterwards he left the hot plains of northern India, crossing mountains and ravines by hazardous paths, to climb up to the beautiful fir-clad Kulu Valley. There he found twenty Buddhist monasteries and more than a thousand monks, mostly Hinayanists. He observed that the country produced medicinal roots of value; that gold, silver, and copper were found there; that the people were much afflicted with goiter and tumors, which is still true today in Kulu and perhaps even more in the neighboring valleys. North of Kulu was the Rothund Pass, at 14,000 feet, and beyond were exotic lands, such as Lahul and Leh in Ladakh. But the holy land of India drew him inexorably; he changed direction again to head for the torrid plains of the Punjab and the very heartland of India, the valleys of the Yamuna (Jumna) and Ganges Rivers. These valleys, reminiscent of Mesopotamia and the rich lands between the Tigris and Euphrates

Rivers, were very productive. He journeyed 2,000 li due south and then east to Mathura, on the Yamuna River.

Reaching Mathura, the Heartland of India

Mathura was a thriving cultural center and had also been the southern capital of King Kanishka. At Mathura Xuanzang commented: "The soil was very fertile and agriculture was the chief business." He found two kinds of mangoes. "The country produced also a fine striped cotton cloth and gold; its climate was hot; the manners and customs of the people were good; the people believe in the working of karma and paid respect to moral and intellectual eminence."[6] Culturally Mathura was a Hindu center, even though Xuanzang said that there were two thousand monks of both Buddhist branches along with the Hindus.

The land was very flat. Buddhist monasteries there could not be on a cliff, ridge, or mountain by a river, overlooking the city, as they usually were. Most of them seem to have been in a large semicircle on the west side of the Yamuna River. The old town, according to this interpretation, was probably located 10 miles from the present city. Among the finds in the Mathura museum are huge symbolic begging bowls, which may have stood in front of those monasteries, containers that replaced individual begging bowls of the monks and that were perhaps not so much for food as for collecting alms for the monks.[7]

Xuanzang had been following the career of King Kanishka in what is now Afghanistan and Pakistan. When the pilgrim stayed at the Monastery of Hostages, he learned of the king's kindness in caring for his Chinese forerunners. In what is present-day Pakistan he first heard the story of King Kanishka's conversion to Buddhism and saw the ruins of the stupa built by the king, said to have been the tallest Buddhist structure in Asia. An impressive statue of King Kanishka himself, with an inscription incised in the king's mantle identifying him as "The Great King, King of Kings, His Majesty Kanishka," is in the Mathura museum (Fig. 5.1).

The statue, built on a larger-than-life scale, is now headless. The king's powerful hands rest on his sword and mace. If one looks at coins with portraits of Kanishka that are similar to this statue, one can with half-closed eyes easily add a massive bearded head, crowned by a tall cap. The king, with his long-skirted coat and heavy padded boots with spurs, would have been most uncomfortable in the steaming heat of Mathura. His ceremonial dress was imported from the steppes, the original home of this nomadic Kushan dynasty. A seated statue of the king's father shows the same authority and primitive strength.

FIGURE 5.1
Headless statue of King Kanishka, in ceremonial dress, with inscription visible on his long-skirted coat. (Courtesy Government Museum, Mathura)

The sculptors of Mathura also created the earliest entirely Indian representation of the Buddha (Fig. 5.2). Whether this figure is earlier than or contemporary with the Gandharan image is a matter of endless discussion among art historians. In the first centuries of the common era, these early Buddhas were depicted somewhat as archetypal Indian sages seated with crossed legs in yogic meditation. Xuanzang might have seen them in the twenty Buddhist monasteries he mentioned as being in Mathura.[8]

In Mathura, in spite of foreign invaders—Greek, Scythian, Parthian, and Kushan—Indian classical art, the art of the Guptas (c. 320–480 C.E.), was born. Earlier Kushan Buddhas, with their eyes wide open, *look out* at the world, but during the Gupta years, the Buddhas with half-open eyes begin to *look inward* at the heart, suggesting inward vision and serenity. The Buddhas carved in Mathura in the fourth and fifth centuries were the first to express a higher transcendental wisdom and compassion, which will reach its height at Sarnath.

Mathura is a place of sacred remembrance for Hindus and Jains as well as Buddhists. Hindus regard it as the fatherland of their god Krishna, whose worship, during the era of Xuanzang's travels, was gradually replacing that of Buddhism. An earlier Chinese pilgrim, Faxian, visited Mathura during the reign of Chandragupta II (375–413 C.E.), at a time when both Brahmanism and Buddhism were lavishly patronized by the Gupta court. In this golden age of Indian culture, there was a flowering of art, literature, science, and religion. Alas, few Buddhist structures remain standing today that are sufficiently intact to provide a ground plan, so complete was the destruction by Islamic invaders. Archaeologists as recently as 1976 were still uncovering large Buddha statues from mounds in the area.

As Xuanzang drew closer and closer to the cradle of Buddhism near Benares, he stopped again for a winter and the early part of the following spring (634–635 C.E.) at Srughna, on the upper reaches of the Yamuna River. There he paused to acquaint himself with the thinking of yet another Hinayana Buddhist sect. Traditionally, Buddhist monks pursue serious studies during the rainy season, but Xuanzang seized every opportunity to learn.

The Rain Retreat varies from country to country; in India it is usually around the middle of June, although it may be a month later when the countryside becomes flooded and torrents of rain oppress the earth. A very ancient practice, it is still the rule observed by monks in all Asian countries to take up residence around this time. Initially monks were peripatetic and participated in settled community life only during the three months of the Rain Retreat, when wandering was difficult. Gradually monasteries developed for year-round use on land given to them by pious laymen or Buddhists.[9]

FIGURE 5.2
Seated Buddha from Katra Mound, Mathura (second century C.E.). This prototype—a cross-legged figure in yogic meditation posture—is an excellent example of an entirely Indian representation of the Buddha. (Courtesy Government Museum, Mathura)

Seeing the Sacred Ganges River

A journey to the southeast of the Yamuna River brought Xuanzang and his party to Matipura, where he stayed the second half of the spring and summer of 635 C.E. on the Ganges River. The most sacred river in India, the Ganges rises in the foothills of the Himalayas and flows 1,500 miles east to the Bay of Bengal. Xuanzang observed that it was about 3 or 4 li wide in its upper reaches, whereupon it flowed to the sea, where it was roughly 10 li in width. The "waters of the river vary in color and great waves rise in it: there are many marvelous creatures in it but they do not injure any one; its waters have a pleasant sweet taste and a fine sand comes down with the current."[10]

Xuanzang reported that it was called the "Water of Felicity"; but he dismissed as superstition the belief that the sins of those who bathed in it were erased or that those who drowned themselves in it were reborn in heaven with happiness. His usual tolerance didn't extend that far.[11]

Upon learning that the Ganges was the cradle of Indian civilization, he might have remembered the Yellow River of his own country, often called the womb of Chinese civilization. And when he thought of his own country, as the Chinese saying has it, "his heart touched on 10,000 things."

Thirteen hundred years later, Jawajarlal Nehru, the first prime minister of independent India, asked that after his death a handful of his ashes be thrown in the river at the sacred confluence of the Yamuna and Ganges Rivers at Allahabad, to be carried to the great ocean that washes India's shores. In his will, dated June 21, 1954, Nehru said that the Ganges especially was "the river of India, beloved of her people, round which are intertwined her racial memories, her hopes and fears, her songs of triumph, her victories and her defeats."[12]

For Nehru the river was changing, ever flowing, yet ever the same. It reminded him of the Himalayas, the snow-covered peaks and deep valleys and the rich plains below, where he had lived and worked. He saw the river as smiling and dancing in the morning and dark and "full of mystery as the evening shadows fall." And he contrasted the Ganges in winter and when the river was in full spate during the monsoon: "broad-bosomed, almost as the sea with something of the sea's power to destroy." For Nehru, the Ganges was "the symbol and memory of the past of India, running into the present and flowing on to the future."[13]

Paying Reverence at the Heavenly Staircase

When Xuanzang thanked the King of Turfan in a gracious letter for his many gifts in 629–630 C.E., he said that it was time for him to go to "the Land of the Heavenly Ladder and the Bodhi tree," where the Buddha received enlightenment. As the pilgrim journeyed beside the Ganges River, always bearing toward the southeast, he felt a deep yearning to visit Sankasya (Kapitha), which even now is one of the eight traditional places of pilgrimage for all Buddhists. Four great pilgrimage sites were so proclaimed—where the Buddha was born, at Lumbini; where he received enlightenment, at Bodh Gaya; where he preached his first sermon, at Sarnath; and where he died, at Kusinagara.[14] Gradually four other sites came to assume importance. These were where he performed the Great Miracle, at Sravasti; where the Buddha tamed the wild elephant, at Rajagriha; where the monkey gave the Buddha a gift of honey, at Vaisali; and where the Buddha descended from heaven, at Sankasya, the Land of the Heavenly Ladder.

"To visit the scenes of the eight great events is to experience in a direct way the life of the Buddha as both a demonstration of his perfection and the perfection of all Buddhas."[15] So says the Mahayanist doctrine. Xuanzang believed in these miracles; he simply saw no reason why the spiritual should be powerless in the material world.

At Sankasya, so the legend repeated by Xuanzang goes, the Buddha descended from heaven after preaching to his mother. (See Color Plate 5.) "Then Indra by his divine power, set up the triple stairs of precious substances, the middle one of gold, the left one of crystal, and the right one of silver. The Buddha descended on the middle stair, Brahma holding a white whisk came down with him on the right stair, and Indra holding up a jeweled sunshade descended on the left stair, while devas in the air scattered flowers and praised the Buddha."[16]

The legend may be interpreted to mean that the Buddha is superior to the Hindu gods because Indra and Brahma are his attendants. The legend also speaks to the human need that is expressed in Christianity in the hymn "Descend to Us, We Pray." Perhaps it is also analogous to the Ascension of Christ; both miracles describe the movement from an earthly to a heavenly realm.

Xuanzang wanted to obtain a model of the Buddha descending from heaven to the temple at Sankasya. He found a large silver one, more than 4 feet tall. This was the second in his collection of seven famous images of the Buddha, a collection that he would take all the way back to China with him.

By Xuanzang's time later kings had reconstructed the precious stairs in stone and brick ornamented with various gems, to a height of 70 feet. Over the stairs a temple was built; it had in it a stone image of the Buddha and figures of Brahma and Indra. Little remains at the present time except for the ruins of the Stupa of the Triple Stairs and an impressive Asoka pillar with a crouching elephant on top.[17]

Visiting King Harsha's Kingdom

From this famous pilgrimage site of Sankasya, Xuanzang went south to the region of Kanyakubja (Kanauj), where the capital of King Harsha was located. It was on the Ganges River, about 50 miles south of present-day Cawnpore. The great King Harsha (607–647 C.E.), uniter of northern India, was away at the time. Xuanzang found evidence of his energy and imagination on every side. His capital had lofty walls, solid trenches, and was strongly defended. Yet there was a sensitivity to beauty too. Attractive gardens, artificial lakes of clear waters, as well as impressive towers and pavilions, were everywhere. The people were largely traders. The rarest wares from other lands were to be found in Kanyakubja and families of great wealth lived there. They had a refined appearance and dressed in glossy silks; many were given to learning and the arts. Only Chang'an or Luoyang in China could compare to it.

Xuanzang found one hundred Buddhist monasteries of both Buddhist sects, housing ten thousand monks (the largest number he had encountered in his travels in a long time), as well as two hundred deva temples. Everything he saw and heard showed that King Harsha was a patron of Buddhism; he had grown as fond of the grand processions of religion and of religious debates as he had been formerly of the magnificent array of battle and the glories of military victory.[18]

Xuanzang learned of the murder of the king's brother and the details of his coming to power.

> The people having lost their ruler, the country became desolate. Then the great minister Po-ni (Bhandi) whose power and reputation were high and of much weight, addressing the assembled ministers, said: "The destiny of the nation is to be fixed to-day. The old king's son is dead; the brother of the prince, however, is humane and affectionate, and his disposition, heaven-conferred, is dutiful and obedient. Because he is strongly attached to his family, the people will trust in him."[19]

Harsha was reluctant to become king in spite of his public support and fasted and prayed to a Bodhisattva statue on the banks of the Ganges River before he accepted the throne.

> As soon as Siladitya [Harsha] became ruler he got together a great army, and set out to avenge his brother's murder and to reduce the neighboring countries to subjection. Proceeding eastwards he invaded the states which had refused allegiance, and waged incessant warfare until in six years he had *fought* the Five Indias. . . . Then having enlarged his territory he increased his army, bringing the elephant corps up to 60,000 and the cavalry to 100,000, and reigned in peace for thirty years without raising a weapon.[20]

Xuanzang also learned that the usual practice was to make this huge elephant corps drunk before they engaged in battle.

King Harsha, having been ruler of a small state in the upper Ganges Valley, had forged an empire by 612 C.E. and was regarded as "the lord of the entire north" of India. The kings of Assam and Gujarat also accepted his sovereignty, and his army advanced as far as the snowy mountains of Tokharistan, in modern-day Afghanistan.

Xuanzang reported that during years of peace the king devoted one-third of his time to affairs of state and two-thirds to religious work, the latter including feeding five hundred Brahmins and one thousand Buddhist monks every day and establishing travelers' rests throughout his dominions. Those were regarded as acts of spiritual merit. He was given credit for being one of the major benefactors of Nalanda Monastery. Like Asoka and Kanishka before him, he took an active part in the life of Buddhist institutions. He assembled the monks of all India, discussing points of doctrine with them as well as strengthening their faith. Like Asoka, he constructed thousands of stupas and monasteries and attempted to forbid the slaughter of animals. Every five years he held a great almsgiving to which he invited the poor of every faith and the clergy of every religion; it was similar to the ceremony Xuanzang had encountered at Bamiyan, only much grander.

The monks were enthusiastic about this generous benefactor. So too, presumably, were men of letters, whom he encouraged and rewarded as well. All signs, all evidence, pointed to a humane, intellectually curious man of versatile interests, whom Xuanzang would call the Sun of Virtue.[21]

Gradually, during the three months he stayed in Kanyakubya in 636 C.E., Xuanzang was able to build up a portrait of this patron and great king, whom he would not meet until he had traveled the length and breadth of India for thirteen years. King Harsha apparently sent a diplomatic envoy to China in 641 C.E.: "Motives both of political and of prestige . . . as well as intellectual curiosity, may have guided Harsha in opening up diplomatic relations with China."[22] When the king and the pilgrim finally did meet in 642 C.E., the king was very impressed by Xuanzang and staged a grand debate to honor the pilgrim, which was one of the major triumphs of his journey.

Xuanzang spent his first visit, while the king was absent, reading the commentaries on the standard works of the Hinayana Realist school. It seems strange that Xuanzang, who regarded Hinayana Buddhism as incomplete and elementary, spent so much time studying their texts. Perhaps he realized that in order to make his mark in India, he had to be skillful against all opponents. "Complete understanding of an opponent's arguments," Arthur Waley suggested, "was one of the twenty-seven 'points' by which speeches were judged."[23] It might also have been that Hinayana sources were easier to come by.

Pursuing Philosophy and Escaping from Pirates in Ayodhya

Xuanzang was eager to go to Ayodhya, ancient Saketa, for that was the home of Mahayana idealism, the fountainhead of Yogacara Buddhism. Just south of the capital he found the ancient monastery in a mango grove where the brothers Asanga and Vasubandhu had composed their sutras and expounded Yogacara idealism in the fifth century. When the two brothers came from the land of Gandhara to Ayodhya, Vasubandhu still remained faithful to many Hinayanist ideas. His conversion to the pure idealism of the Mahayana came about at the monastery of the mango trees next to the river, "where the Ganges is full of mystery as the evening shadows fall," in Nehru's words.

Asanga arranged a meeting place with his brother at the mango tree monastery.

> At nightfall he led him onto a terrace which overlooked the river, and then withdrew. It was a cloudless autumn night, and the moon was shining on the water. A voice rose, an unknown voice reading a Mahayanist treatise. Doubtless it was speaking of the freeing of the spirit for its flight on the wings of idealism. According to this fluid and luminous theory, the world of forms was destined to vanish away, as at this moment the appearance of earth and water were floating in the lunar haze of the Gogra [Ganges]. Above vain material things, beyond all that was concrete, a dream was filling the Indian night; objects were no more than this—the dream of a dream. The ideality of the universe was taking the place of the material cosmos, and under this new aspect all was becoming intelligible, accessible and possible.[24]

Vasubandhu understood at last the beauty of the Idealist philosophy of his brother Asanga. According to that philosophy, the ideality of the universe takes the place of the material world. For example, "In a picture painted according to the rules, there is neither hollow nor raised part, and yet one sees them; thus in our imagination there is never duality and yet one sees it."[25]

In this Mind Only philosophy, it would seem that external reality becomes a dream, a mirage, a cloud. Vasubandhu said, "No doubt things are unreal (*nirathanas*)—with regard to that reality (*atman*) that exists in nature proper, but they are not without existence in the indescribable manner of being which is of the domain of the Buddhas."[26]

The word *yogacara* actually means "the practice of yoga." And so we move from Idealist philosophy into the world of mysticism.

Perhaps that is why the Bodhisattva Maitreya, or Buddha of the Future, and the Yogacara Idealists have a special affinity for each other. Followers of the cult of Maitreya, our pilgrim among them, believed that the meritorious would go to the Tushita Heaven to await rebirth in a joyous new age. Xuanzang himself related the legend of how Asanga went at night to the Tushita Heaven, where the Maitreya dictated to him the Sanskrit text now known as the *Treatise on the Stages of Yoga Practice*. Scholars surmise that in fact Asanga received the words from a historical person, presumably his teacher, who happened to bear the name of Maitreya.[27] Xuanzang's own translation of the treatise was made about 647 C.E.

Xuanzang was closer to his paradise than he realized; a dramatic incident took place that very nearly put an end to his journey.

> 636 c.e. Any week. Time is unimportant to the unsuspecting pilgrim. The banks of the Ganges River. The pilgrim is going with eighty people in a boat down the river. Ten boats filled with pirates attack and force them ashore. Then they notice how handsome Xuanzang is and decide that he is the perfect specimen for their annual sacrifice of human flesh and blood to their god Durga. But Xuanzang appeals to their chief: "If this poor and defiled body is suitable for sacrifice, then I dare not grudge this offering. As my intention in coming such a distance is to pay reverence to the image of the Buddha and to inquire as to the character of the Sacred Books and Buddhist doctrine, if you kill this body of mine, I fear it will bring you misfortune."
>
> The pirate captain pays no heed and orders his men to tie up the pilgrim. Xuanzang makes one last request, that he be given time to compose his thoughts. Then the pilgrim, with undivided mind, thinks on the Bodhisattva Maitreya and earnestly prays to be born in the Tushita Heaven that he may hear the most holy words of Buddhism and attain perfect understanding. Exalted by joy, he is oblivious of the altar on which he is about to be sacrificed.
>
> Suddenly a black typhoon arises. The pirates are terrified by this miracle. "Who is this man?" they ask.
>
> When they are told that Xuanzang is a famous monk from China, the pirates ask his forgiveness. Xuanzang pardons them, inviting them to change their ways. Then and there the pirates take vows to become lay members of the Buddhist community.[28]

After this high drama, the pilgrim and his party, their gear having been returned by the pirates, made their way to the confluence of the sacred Yamuna and the sacred Ganges River at modern Allahabad (Prayaga).

Finding the Sandalwood Image at Kausambi

Before Xuanzang reached the true holy land of Buddhism, his last important stop was at Kausambi. He had to pass through forests filled with wild elephants to visit that ancient Gupta capital. There by the Yamuna River he was shown a large Buddhist temple, more than 60 feet high, in which there was a sandalwood image of the Buddha with a stone canopy suspended over it.

"This image made miraculous manifestations, and no power could move it from its place: so paintings made of it were worshipped, and *all true likenesses of the Buddha have been taken from this image,*" Xuanzang observed.[29] It was said to have been made for King Udayana during the three-month period that the Buddha was in heaven preaching to his mother.

According to tradition, the king, thinking of the Buddha with affection, requested that one of the Buddha's disciples, by means of his spiritual power, transport an artist to heaven to observe the excellent marks on the Buddha's body and carve a sandalwood statue. The artist did so, and when the Lord of the World descended to earth, the statue *rose* and saluted the Buddha. Whereupon the Buddha graciously said, "The work expected of you is to toil in the conquest of heretics and to lead in the way of religion in future ages," that is, the task of spreading his teaching among future generations.

A touching representation of a king presenting just such an image to the Buddha is housed in the Peshawar Museum (Fig. 5.3). Xuanzang saw to it that a model of the Udayana sandalwood image 2 feet 9 inches tall, with a shining pedestal, was carefully packed in his baggage. Sandalwood, the yellowish heartwood of an Indo-Malayan tree (*Santalum album*), is much used in oriental carving; the wood itself is fragrant, with an unmistakable aroma of spices from Asia. This was the third in his collection of seven Buddha images to take back to China.

Xuanzang had already collected two replicas of the Buddha. His first sandalwood image was modeled after the Buddha of the Shadow Cave in Jalalabad in present-day Afghanistan; it would forever call to mind his own rapture at seeing the Buddha there. At Sankasya, in northern India, he had obtained a second statue, a large silver one of the Buddha descending the staircase from heaven. And now he had the most famous of all images, the Udayana image, whose iconographic type still exists in Japan. These and other portable images were one of the means

FIGURE 5.3
King Udayana presenting to the Buddha the sandalwood Udayana image, carved by an artist sent to heaven while the Buddha was there (Copyright British Museum)

by which the styles of Indian art were introduced into the Far East.[30] It wasn't that Xuanzang was the first to bring them, for the Udayana First Image was well known in the Six Dynasties period (489–581 C.E.) in China. However, the classical Gupta images were very beautiful, and Xuanzang's reputation gave them added importance.

Apparently the greatest asset for a Buddha image was an origin in India, "the homeland of faith and magic, and a link of some sort, the closer the better, with the person of the historic *Sakyamuni* [Buddha]."[31] Often those that were supposed to work the greatest miracles had been found under mysterious circumstances.

Xuanzang's images were not of that sort, but he seems to have had a special feeling for them. After his return to China he had two hundred images executed in the dry lacquer technique. Many years later when he knew that he would die and his disciples asked him to translate yet another Buddhist text, he refused. "Let us go instead to the Orchid and Mushroom valley so that I may say goodby to my Buddhas."[32] He set out with his fellow monks and it was with tears in their eyes that they watched him perform his devotions. This quality of piety would be apparent as he continued his travels in the holy land of Buddhism.

SIX

THE BUDDHIST HOLY LAND

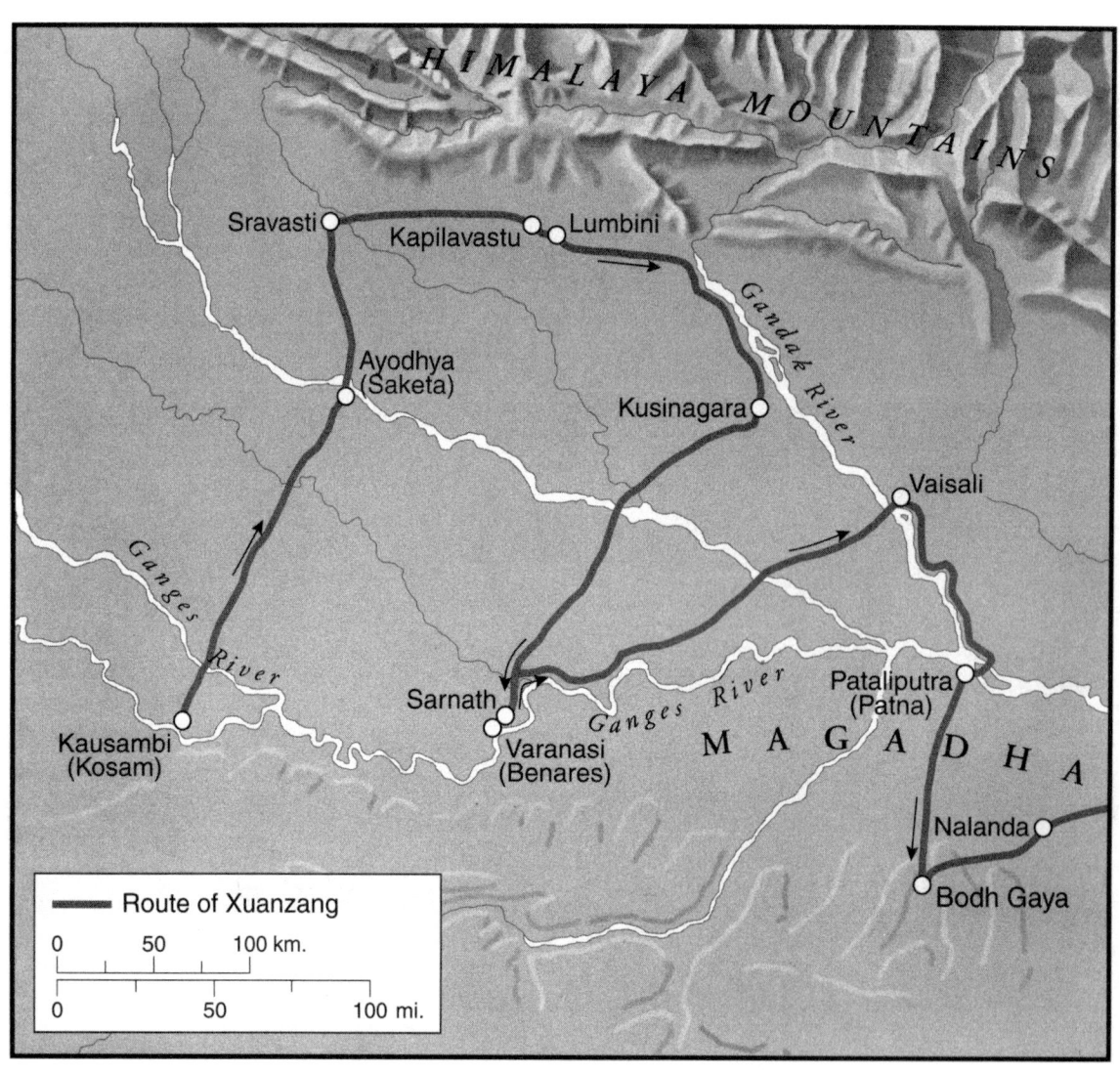

MAP 6.1
Itinerary of Xuanzang in the Buddhist holy land (from Kausambi to Bodh Gaya) (Philip Schwartzberg, Meridian Mapping)

WHEN HE WAS A YOUNG MAN, Xuanzang had once been so absorbed in reading the *Sutra of the Glorious Decease* that he forgot to sleep. "There are four places," the Buddha is supposed to have said in this sutra, "which the believing man should visit with feelings of reverence and awe"—where the Buddha was born, the place at which he received enlightenment, the place at which he preached the first sermon, and the place at which he died.[1]

The sites associated with the main events of the Buddha's life—Lumbini with his birth, Bodh Gaya with his enlightenment, Sarnath with his first sermon, and Kusinagara with his death—gradually became places of pilgrimage.[2] Xuanzang had been to the site of the descent from heaven, one of the lesser sites, at Sankasya. Now he would go to each of the four most sacred places as well as the three other lesser sites, where the Buddha performed miracles. He would write about the sacred traces of the Buddha in loving detail.

When Xuanzang visited the sacred sites he went usually as a careful observer of Buddhist history, legends, practices, and the location and existence of Asoka pillars and other monuments. But this time he would go as a pilgrim, expressing his own religious feelings. At Lumbini he would celebrate the Buddha's birth as a joyous pilgrim; at Sarnath he would have a replica made of the famous Teaching Buddha; at Kusinagara he would remember a Chinese tree at the Sal grove where the Buddha died; at Bodh Gaya he would weep with profound emotion under the tree of the Buddha's enlightenment.

When Xuanzang went farther down the Ganges-Yamuna Valley where the Buddha had lived for so long, he had been on his pilgrimage for almost eight years; now at last he was approaching the true holy land of the Buddha.[3] There he would forget about pirates and metaphysics, the abstruse arguments that had so occupied him in the past few years.

To walk where the Buddha had walked and performed his many miracles; to go to the very places where he had been born, where he had lived and worked and died, and the greatest shrine of all, at Bodh Gaya, where he had received enlightenment under the Bodhi tree: These sacred places would be the pilgrim's goal. He would be pursuing a different kind of understanding, the kind that begins with God's word to Moses: "Take off your shoes. You are on holy ground."

He knew the stories of the Buddha's life from his fifteen years of study in Chinese monasteries; he learned more details from reading Faxian's account of his western journey. He was reminded of each incident in the Buddha's life by the reliefs portraying the cycle of Buddhist legends on monastery stupas, pillars, and walls in every land he visited. And as he went from one pilgrimage place to another, he was responding to the compass of the heart.

As usual, his accounts begin with geographical facts about the kingdom he was passing through and data on the number of worshippers and what sect they belonged to. But such mundane matters paled in the face of the great mystical drama of the Buddha's life. Spiritual realities, as so often happens in India, tended to overwhelm the particularity of historical details. And so we have what is called the Buddha Legend, wonderfully conceived, whether we accept it literally as religious truth, as Xuanzang did, or understand it as myth or symbolic truth.

Beholding the Site of the Great Miracle at Sravasti

After Kausambi, Xuanzang changed direction. He was eager to go north to the place where the Buddha had been born, in Lumbini. His first stop on the way was Sravasti, in the present Sahet Mahet District. While the Buddha was alive, it had been the capital of King Prasenajit. Xuanzang viewed the ruins of the king's palace and the foundations of a preaching hall that the king had erected for the Buddha. Among the many monasteries he saw in ruins, Xuanzang mentioned only one by name, the Jetavana Monastery. On this site he found a brick shrine that contained an image of the Buddha commissioned by King Prasenajit. It was a 5-foot-high copy of the image made for King Udayana of Kausambi.

At the Jetavana Monastery the Buddha had established a monastic community and also given his consent for women to form their own community of nuns. Xuanzang related how a wealthy layman named Sudatta acquired a site in a beautiful park not far from Sravasti for the new Buddhist community. The only piece of available land was owned by Prince Jetavana.

> When the Elder [Sudatta] asked the prince to sell his park the prince said jokingly—"Yes, for as many gold coins as will cover it." This answer delighted Sudatta, and he at once proceeded to cover the ground with gold coins from his treasury. When all the ground except a small piece was covered the prince asked Sudatta to desist, saying—"The Buddha truly is an excellent field, it is meet I sow good seed": so on the uncovered ground he erected a temple.[4]

Xuanzang reported that near Jetavana park King Prasenajit held a magic contest between the Buddha and six leaders of various sects. The Buddha overwhelmed them all. This is his only reference to the famous miracles at Sravasti, which are so often depicted in Buddhist art. One of these portrayals is of the Buddha with flames issuing from his shoulders and streams of water coming from his feet, symbolizing his victory over fire and water. An even more popular miracle is that of the Buddha multiplying himself thousands of times.[5]

The miracle of multiplying his personage that is supposed to have taken place at Sravasti, one of the required pilgrimage sites, is similar to the Buddha's descent from heaven at Sankasya, the first of the eight places of pilgrimage visited by Xuanzang. Both have a kind of psychological or inner truth to them: the understanding that the godhead is infinite and is everywhere at once.

Guided by the footsteps of the Historical Buddha, Xuanzang explored the places where so many of his teachings had taken place. Xuanzang visited the site of the Angulimala stupa, named after the wicked man who had gone around killing people and cutting off a finger from each of his victims in order to make "a finger-garland necklace" for himself. When he was about to kill his own mother, the Buddha took her place and not only convinced the murderer to repent but inspired him to become a devout monk. Near the grounds of the Jetavana Monastery Xuanzang also saw the stupa that marked the spot where the Buddha had cured a sick monk and restored the eyesight of the criminals arrested by King Prasenajit who had been punished by having their eyes put out.

Although both Xuanzang and his predecessor Faxian were bent on learning about Buddhist philosophy and monastic rules, they were often chiefly observant of the stories and miracles of Buddhist lore. Both described at length the seemingly bottomless chasms that were supposed to show where the Buddha had vanquished his enemies and consigned them to these fathomless depths of hell. There had been several of these unfortunate people—the woman who sought to slander the Buddha, saying that he was the father of her child, and his cousin Devadatta, the Judas Iscariot of Buddhism, who had put poison under the Buddha's nails while in the act of paying respect in order to kill him.

The Buddha stayed at Sravasti for the Rain Retreats during twenty-five years. Unfortunately little stands now but a few low walls, stupas, and mounds of earth. The area has only been partially excavated, although it was there that many of the teachings of the Buddha were offered for the first time.[6]

Seeking the Sacred Traces at Kapilavastu and Lumbini

As Xuanzang approached Kapilavastu and Lumbini, the long-familiar tales and legends of the Buddha's life and death were probably uppermost in his mind and heart. In order to reach Kapilavastu, Xuanzang had to travel northeast to what is known as the Terai, a semitropical area in southern Nepal in the foothills of the Himalayas. He found the countryside very fertile and the monasteries deserted.

With reverence and awe, he sought the sacred traces of the Buddha. Within the walls of Kapilavastu, the kingdom where the Buddha had been born and had grown up, Xuanzang located a number of hallowed sites.[7] Among them were the ruins of the palace of the Buddha's father, King Suddhodana, and a dilapidated foundation that was supposed to have been the sleeping palace of his mother, Queen Maya.

Inside the shrine he saw a representation of the white elephant descending from heaven. The conception of the Buddha had been miraculous, like that of the Christ. During the night of the full moon in August, Queen Maya had dreamed that she saw a small white elephant entering her right side. When she related the dream to her husband, he and his ministers knew at once that she would give birth to an extraordinary human being, for a white elephant was part of the patrimony of a universal king (Fig. 6.1).

To the northeast of the palace of "spiritual conception," Xuanzang found the stupa that marked the place where the astrologer Asiti cast the horoscope of the royal prince. On the day of the Buddha's birth, King Suddhodana summoned all his soothsayers, for he wanted to know what were the lucky and what were the unlucky signs. The answer came that if his son remained in secular life, he would be a universal king, and if he left home, he would be a Buddha. It was a prophecy the king would heed well, though he would prove powerless to affect the outcome.

Before Xuanzang reached the place of the Buddha's actual birth in Lumbini Garden, he stopped on the hallowed ground of the stupa that marked the foreshadowing of the enlightenment of the Future Buddha, which is told in many Buddhist books.

> This is the spot where the prince sat in the shade of a tree to watch the ploughing festival. Here he engaged in profound meditation and reached the condition of "absence of desire." The king seeing the prince in the shade of the tree and engrossed in quiet contemplation, and observing that whilst the sun's rays shed their bright light around him, yet the shadow of the tree did not move, his heart, recognizing the spiritual character of the prince was deeply reverent.[8]

Perhaps by this supernatural demonstration the king knew that he could not contain his son within the palace walls. The young Buddha-to-be, like the young Jesus in the temple, would have a life that would be different from that of other men.

At the southeast gate of Kapilavastu, Xuanzang found a shrine that must have been especially poignant to him. It was the place where the

The Buddhist Holy Land

FIGURE 6.1
The dream of Maya. The conception of the Buddha took place when Maya, his mother, saw in a dream an elephant enter her right side. (Copyright British Museum)

young prince, having left the luxurious life of the royal palace, had seen for the first time an old man, a sick man, a dead man, and a monk. This fateful encounter had led directly to what is known as the Great Departure from his father's kingdom.

Always Xuanzang traveled toward Lumbini, the most sacred place in the region, 9 or 10 miles east of Kapilavastu.[9] How his steps must have quickened when he saw the beautiful bathing tank there and about twenty-four paces from it, the old Asoka tree where the Buddha had been born. Nearby he saw a broken pillar and then came closer to see the figure of a horse on top. The pillar had been placed there by King Asoka, and there was an inscription on it stating that King Asoka had worshipped in the twenty-first year of his reign on the very spot where the Buddha had been born. This pillar had been completely engulfed by the jungle until it was discovered in 1895 by an archaeologist, A. Fuhrer, thus verifying the exact location of the park of Lumbini.

According to tradition, Queen Maya went to this pleasure ground in May 563 B.C.E. The birth took place as she stood erect in an attitude popularized by sculpture, under an Asoka tree, grasping a branch in her right hand. The newborn baby came out of her right side and was immediately caught by the gods who had gathered for the event. And the gods said, "The queen may rejoice indeed at having given birth to such a fortunate child." The heavenly kings proclaimed, "If the gods rejoiced at the event, how much more should men!"

Xuanzang continued:

> When Bodhisattva was born, he walked without assistance in the direction of the four quarters, seven paces in each direction, and said, "I am the only lord in heaven and earth; from this time forth my births are finished." Where his feet had trod there sprang up great lotus flowers. Moreover, two dragons sprang forth, and, fixed in the air, poured down the one a cold and the other a warm water stream from his mouth to wash the prince.[10]

Xuanzang mentioned that near the Asoka pillar there was a small stream flowing to the southeast that the people called the oil river. He explained that it was originally a tank of pure oil created by the gods for the use of Buddha's mother after the birth of her son, and he added that they changed the tank back to a stream of water that still retained its oily character.[11]

Paying Reverence at Kusinagara, Where the Buddha Died

After Lumbini the pilgrim road would take Xuanzang in early 637 C.E. to Kusinagara, where the Buddha had died. Kusinagara has been identified with the present site of Kasia, on the left bank of the Gandak River. The journey was not an easy one then, nor is it now. Xuanzang had to pass through a sizable forest filled with wild oxen, elephants, and savage bandits. When he finally arrived safely, he came to several deserted towns and villages and the ruins of a city wall. One of the Buddha's favorite disciples, Ananda, wondered why the Buddha had to die in "this wattle and daub town, a town in the middle of the jungle, a branch township."[12]

Xuanzang described the scene of the "Great Decease," or *Parinirvana*, at a Sal grove. The Sal "tree resembles the Ho tree. It is like the Chinese oak with greenish white bark and very glossy leaves," at once personalizing the place for himself and a Chinese audience. This is one of the very few times that Xuanzang made a connection between what he saw in India and what he had known in China. There were four trees of extraordinary height, and it was at the feet of these four that the Buddha passed away.[13]

According to tradition, Xuanzang reported, the Buddha attained nirvana at the age of eighty. Just before his death in 483 B.C.E., he converted a Brahmin named Subhadra. In bidding his monks farewell, the Buddha said that the laws he had taught them and the discipline he had established should be their Master. His last words are presumed to have been: "All that is composed is perishable. Work diligently for your salvation."

Xuanzang saw a great temple built of brick standing nearby. Inside was a figure of the Buddha's nirvana, with his head turned toward the north. His appearance, Xuanzang said, was "as if he were asleep." By the side of the temple stood a stupa built by Asoka, 200 feet high, which recorded the circumstances of the nirvana, "but he does not state the year or month." Xuanzang was once again the careful chronicler with each of these telling details.[14]

Here and there Xuanzang's eyes picked out more stupas marking the places where Chandra the blacksmith had given the Buddha his last meal, and where he had converted Subhadra. Xuanzang's heartfelt response to many of these sites is shown by what he wrote of a simple well from which the Buddha drew water for drinking: "A mysterious sense of awe surrounds the precincts of the place; many miracles are manifested also. Sometimes heavenly music is heard, at other times divine odors are perceived."[15]

He paid homage at the place where the Buddha's body, surrounded by flowers and clouds of incense, was wrapped in a shroud before it was put in a coffin. He also stopped beside each of the three towers that commemorated the three times the Buddha appeared from his coffin; first, when he put his arm out and asked Ananda if he had prepared the way; second, when he sat up and preached the law for his mother's sake; and third, when he showed his feet to the great Kasyapa, one of the Buddha's favorite disciples.

Tradition has it that after seven days both mortals and immortals carried his bier to the river. They filled it with scented oils and piled wood around it, but it would not burn until the arrival of Kasyapa. After Kasyapa had completed his devotions, the wood caught fire of its own accord. And finally, after the cremation, eight kings came with their armies and begged for their share of the relics. As a crowning touch, Xuanzang repeated the familiar legend: "Then Indra claimed a share for the gods, and the Dragon-kings also claimed a share. So the brahmin divided the relics into three lots, one for the gods, one for the Dragon-kings, and the third was sub-divided into eight shares for the kings. The gods, dragons and kings were all deeply affected."[16]

Paying Reverence at the Deer Park, in Sarnath

Traveling southwest through densely wooded country, Xuanzang headed for the holy city of Varanasi, modern Benares, on the Ganges River. This City of Light epitomized the essence of Hinduism in all its luxuriant variety of phenomena. The pilgrim described it as being 3 miles long and 1 mile wide: "The city-wards were close together, and the inhabitants were very numerous and had boundless wealth, their houses being full of rare valuables. . . . Of Deva [Hindu] temples there were about 100, and there more than 10,000 professed adherents of the sects, the majority being devotees of Siva."[17]

He was ever alert, even as to secular details that might interest a modern audience. Although he was a devout Buddhist, he admired a 100-foot-high statue of Siva, noting that it radiated an awe-inspiring majesty.

Xuanzang went on to portray the radical ascetics who went without clothing or who smeared their bodies with ashes. A walk around Benares today still reveals a stream of wild-eyed ascetics, beggars, merchants, naked children, goats, sacred cows, and rickshaws, as well as thousands of pilgrims carrying their dead for burning on the banks of the holy Ganges.

But his destination was the Deer Park at Sarnath, 5 miles northeast of Benares. A greater contrast cannot be imagined between Benares and Sarnath; from the teeming, roiling, noisy city of pilgrims, animals, and ascetics, he crossed to the quietude of a peaceful green park with Buddhist monasteries and the awesome simplicity of stupas. This was the Deer Park where the Buddha had preached his first sermon. (See Color Plate 6.)

The Doctrine of the Middle Way, which the Buddha first enunciated at Sarnath, could have been in Xuanzang's mind and heart while he stayed at the Deer Park Monastery, where there were 1,500 monks residing. His biographer described the monastery as connected at its four corners by long galleries with lofty turrets like those Xuanzang would see at Nalanda, where "the upper rooms are above the clouds." Huili was clearly impressed with the height of the buildings.

Xuanzang found that what is now called the Main Shrine had a large metal image of the Buddha preaching his first sermon, which the Buddhists refer to as Turning the Wheel of the Law. We know the name of the Main Shrine was the Original Hall of Fragrance. The Main Shrine, although largely in ruins, has the massive walls characteristic of ancient architecture (Fig. 6.2). Some historians believe that the Main Shrine was the pyramidal temple that Xuanzang described. He said that it was "about two hundred feet high and surmounted by a golden *amra*, or mango, fruit."[18]

The Buddhist Holy Land

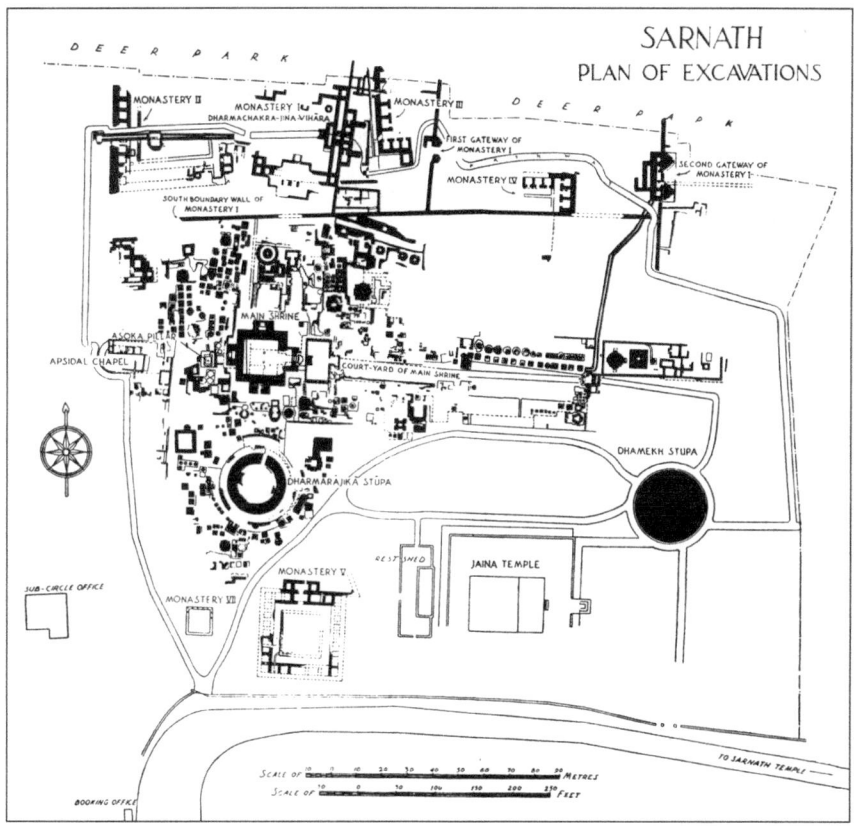

FIGURE 6.2
Site map of Sarnath: plan of excavations showing the location of the Dhamekh stupa, the main shrine, the Asoka column, the Dharmarajika stupa, and the monasteries (Courtesy Archaeological Survey of India)

Just west of the Main Shrine was an Asoka column that Xuanzang saw rising out of the ground. It seemed to him "as bright as jade. It is glistening and sparkles like light," Xuanzang wrote. The lion capital still shines agelessly in the Sarnath Museum; it is so highly regarded that it adorns not only the modern Indian flag but also the coins of India. The shaft of the pillar is still in its original place in the ground (Fig. 6.3).

Xuanzang mentioned that the ill-fated Dharmarajika stupa, built by King Asoka, was about 100 feet high. Its ruins now barely rise above the earth. The world-famous image of the Buddha in the attitude of preaching was discovered near the stupa ruins in 1904. Xuanzang saw the latter in its natural setting near the Dharmarajika stupa; today we

FIGURE 6.3
Lion capital of the pillar erected by King Asoka, the first great patron of Buddhism, at Sarnath c. third century B.C.E. The capital is in the Sarnath Museum. The shaft remains in the ground. (Courtesy American Institute of Indian Studies. Photographed by permission of Archaeological Survey of India.)

The Buddhist Holy Land

can see it only in the Sarnath Museum.[19] With its strength and beauty and power, the statue of the Buddha Preaching the First Sermon (Fig. 6.4) is one of the masterpieces of sculpture in the world. The Buddha is seated in a yoga posture, and his hands are "Turning the Wheel of the Law." His eyes are lowered; the gaze of the Buddha is inward. On the large halo behind the Buddha are two celestial beings worshipping him. The proportions of the figure are perfectly balanced; the head is at the top and the horizontal legs are the base of an equilateral triangle, giving the whole a quality of perfect spiritual poise and equilibrium. Both the countenance and form contribute to the effect of spiritual calm and extraordinary energy.[20] No wonder Xuanzang arranged to have a sandalwood replica of this image to take back with him to China—the fourth of the seven famous images that would be carried in a grand procession in the capital shortly after his return.

The greatness of the sculpture commemorating the first sermon is matched by the freshness and originality of what the Buddha is presumed to have said. According to legend, the Buddha was speaking to the five ascetics with whom he himself had practiced austerities during his six years of forest wandering after he had left the palace. They had been determined to scorn him, but instead they found themselves down on their knees. His personal appearance overwhelmed them: "His whole person breathed serenity and spread a divine radiance. His body was like fine gold," Xuanzang wrote.

What had the Buddha preached?

"Two extremes there are, O monks, which he who strives after Enlightenment must avoid, which two? A life addicted to pleasure, which is vulgar and worthless, and a life given to self-mortification which is painful and equally profitless." He who has gained knowledge of the *Middle Path* has found the way that leads to rest, to knowledge, to enlightenment and nirvana.[21]

The Buddha then spoke to them about the Noble Eightfold Path of (1) right views, (2) right intention, (3) right speech, (4) right action, (5) right livelihood; and the ways of virtue, which he described as being (6) right effort, (7) right mindfulness, and finally (8) right meditative concentration, which leads to wisdom.

The Four Noble Truths, he said, were suffering, the source of suffering, the destruction of suffering, and the way that leads to the destruction of suffering. Beginning with his own experience of his first view of a dead man, a sick man, and an aged man, he defined suffering as old age, sickness, death; separation from objects one desires and joining in with what one does not desire; and even birth itself as suffering. And the Buddha defined the source of suffering as desire; the way of its destruction was the Eightfold Path of the Middle Way.

FIGURE 6.4
Considered the most beautiful of all Buddha statues, known as the Buddha Turning the Wheel of the Law or Preaching the First Sermon (Courtesy of American Institute of Indian Studies. Photographed by permission of Archaeological Survey of India.)

The Buddha's teaching is generally said to have taken place in the third watch of the night—from 2 until 6 A.M.—and to have been accompanied by many miraculous signs as well as the visitation of Indra and Brahma, the four great heavenly kings, and many other beings. The event is known in Buddhist texts as Turning the Wheel of the Law.

Visiting Holy Places at Vaisali

With his heart full of these great memories of the Buddha's life and teachings, Xuanzang journeyed east to the land of Magadha, in southern Bihar, which has more holy places connected with Buddhism than any other region in India.[22] He would visit Vaisali, Pataliputra (Patna), and last, Bodh Gaya, which would be the climax of his searching for the sacred traces of the Buddha.

Several months earlier, Xuanzang had seen two of the lesser sites of the eight places of pilgrimage, Sankasya and Sravasti. Now he was on his way to the Stupa of the Monkey's Gift at Vaisali, another of the four lesser places of pilgrimage. It was there that monkeys, taking the alms bowl of the Buddha, had climbed a tree and gathered some honey for him. Near an Asoka stupa and column was a tank, or lake, where Xuanzang said there was a figure of a monkey.[23]

Vaisali had an additional interest for him; it was there that Vimalakirti, a lay follower of the Buddha, had lived. Vimalakirti had a special attraction for the Chinese. Perhaps that was because he had been the symbol of the lay householder and yet had been capable of defeating Manjusri, the Bodhisattva of Wisdom, in debate. The Vimalakirti legend inspired many paintings and pieces of sculpture in the Longmen, Yungang, and Dunhuang Caves. In the Tang dynasty, the legend was the subject of popular stories and ballads. Xuanzang himself had made a translation of the *Vimalakirti-sutra*, which was well known in China.

Xuanzang, the metaphysician and theologian, was also interested in the stupa where seven hundred sages had made the second compilation of the *Dharma*, the law, and the *Vinaya*, the Rules of Discipline for monks. The Second Buddhist Council, held at Vaisali (367 B.C.E. or 383 B.C.E.), had assembled representatives of various districts and centers of Buddhism in India. A new codification of rules seems to have been especially important. In describing the council, Xuanzang said:

> Then Sambhoga, with his right shoulder bared and on his knees in the great Congregation, addressing the assembled Brethren prays to them to be orderly, sedate and attentive. He proceeds—"Although years have passed since our spiritual sovereign in his wise discretion passed away, his

oral instructions still survive—Irreverent bhikkhus [priests] of Vesali city have gone astray in Vinaya [rules] in ten matters violating the teaching of the Buddha—Reverend Brethren, ye understand what accords with and what is opposed to this teaching. As ye have been instructed by the Bhadanta Ajanta show gratitude for Buddha's kindness, and make a second promulgation of his ordinances."[24]

At this council Hinayana Buddhism was divided into several sects; it also marked the beginnings of the Mahayana school. Vaisali was famous for all Buddhists as the place where the Buddha had made the announcement of his coming nirvana.

With so many associations, it was natural that Xuanzang would want to bring back an image from Vaisali. The one he chose was made of sandalwood and was sculpted after a model of a similar one representing the Buddha as he went around Vaisali in his work of conversion. This was the fifth of the seven famous images that he would take back to China.

On his way south to Bodh Gaya in the kingdom of Magadha, Xuanzang stopped at Pataliputra, roughly 50 miles away, which had been the seat of King Asoka's empire and also the site of the so-called Third Buddhist Council.[25] Little remained of the magnificence seen by Faxian in the fourth century; when Faxian was there, he couldn't believe that it had been made by mere mortal hands.

Worshipping at the Bo Tree, in Bodh Gaya

Always thinking of Bodh Gaya, Xuanzang wended his way along with the other monks and pilgrims to the Bo tree—the place of the Buddha's ultimate triumph. His fellow pilgrims were also searching for the Bo tree, with its sheltering branches. The long-awaited moment had finally come. Xuanzang, the observer, described the sacred precincts with his usual precision (Fig. 6.5). It is a description largely applicable even to the present-day remains. From him we learn that

> a journey of 14–15 *li* south-west from the Pragbodhi Hill brought one to the Bodhi Tree. The enclosing walls ... are built of brick, high and strong; the inclosure is long from east to west, and narrow from north to south, and it is above 500 paces in circuit.... The principal gate opens east toward the Nairanjana River, the south gate is connected with a large flower-tank, the west limit is a natural defense, and the north gate communicates with the grounds inside the walls of a large monastery.[26]

What a sense of awe Xuanzang must have felt as he walked with his fellow pilgrims in the garden of the Bo tree! What a feeling of exhilara-

The Buddhist Holy Land

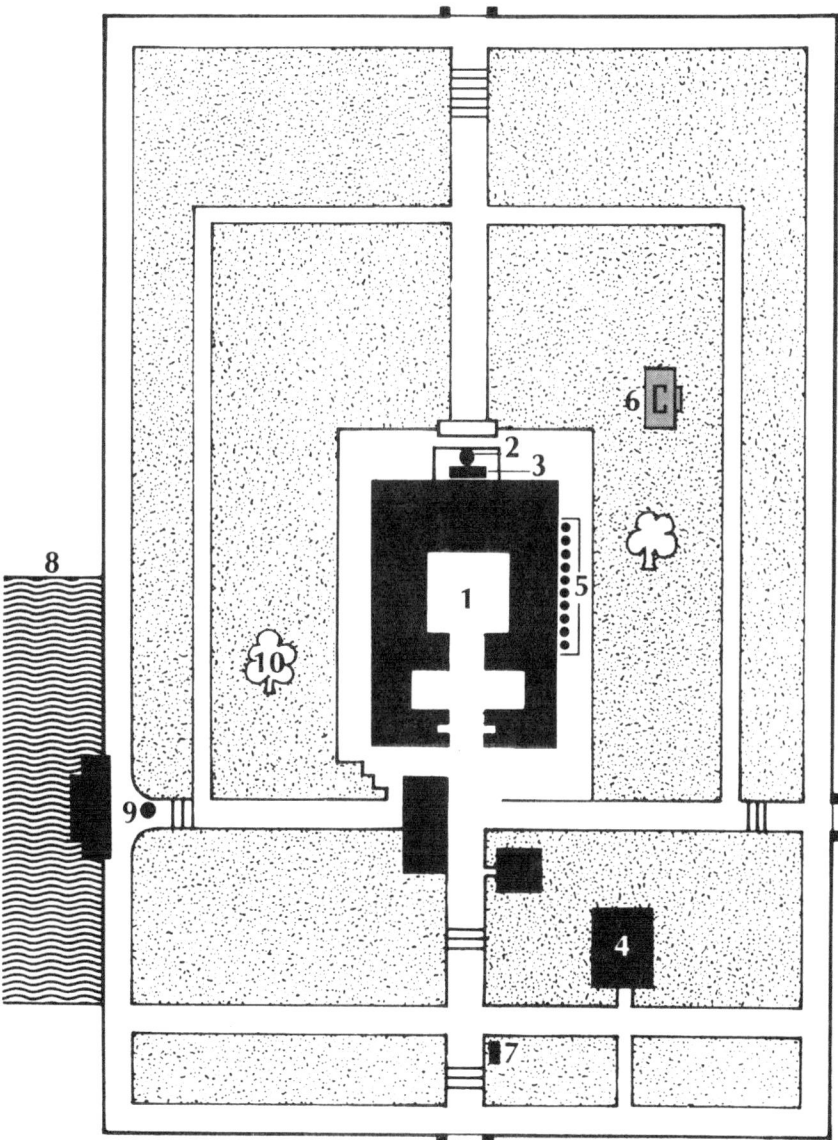

FIGURE 6.5
Site plan of Mahabodhi temple at Bodh Gaya, where the Buddha achieved enlightenment: (1) temple, (2) Bodhi tree, (3) Diamond Throne, (4) Unblinking Shrine, (5) Jeweled Walk, (6) Rainbow Shrine, (7) Goatherd's tree, (8) Muchalinda lake, (9) Asoka column, (10) Rajata tree. (Copyright Alistair Shearer. Reprinted by permission of Alfred A. Knopf, Inc.)

tion as they exchanged glances with the knowledge of common purpose, their eyes meeting, their hearts knowing that this was where the Buddha achieved enlightenment. Like mountain climbers who have finally reached a summit at 18,000 feet, so these pilgrims must have felt a sensation of infinite peace and happiness.

Xuanzang wandered from one holy place to another with his fellow pilgrims at Bodh Gaya, each shrine recalling to him the path by which the Buddha had come to meditate under the Bo tree. Perhaps he stopped first at the Stupa of the Five Ascetics, the ones who believed that the way to truth was to starve the body. Or maybe he lingered at the temple with the image of the Buddha in an emaciated condition, a subject popular with the artists of Gandhara. For six years the Buddha had tried this path but found it taught him nothing. That was one extreme. The other extreme had been the life of pleasure he knew well from his palace years. And thus he had sought the Middle Way.

Walking among the rare trees and fine grasses, Xuanzang reached the place where the Buddha, having obtained an old shroud, stopped to wash his clothes. The god Indra had created a tank for him as well as a large rock. It was sometimes alluded to as "Hit by the Hand Pond," recalling the way the women slapped their clothes on rocks to get the dirt out.

Continuing to visit the shrines for seven days, Xuanzang noted the strange plants and flowers everywhere. He went down to the Nairanjana River, where the Buddha had bathed to rid himself of impurities. He paused at a shrine marking the home of the two cowherd maidens who had presented the Buddha with rich boiled milk before his enlightenment.[27] Nearby was the stupa marking the place where the Buddha had received four bowls from the gods. In order to avoid jealousy, he accepted them all, put them together, and compressed them into one, which is why the Buddha's bowl has a fourfold rim.

Xuanzang might have searched his memory at yet another shrine, for it was dedicated to Buddha's first disciples, two nomadic traders from Balkh who had fed the Buddha his first food after his enlightenment. The legend said that the gods of the place told the traveling merchants that the Buddha's mind had been fixed in contemplation for forty-nine days, and that by offering him whatever they had, they would reap great and excellent benefits. Accordingly they gave him some parched-grain flour and honey from their traveling stores. Years before, Xuanzang visited the Balkh stupa north of the Hindu Kush mountains, which was dedicated to those intrepid traders.

Every time he went near the Bodhi tree, he saw people meditating by the Mahabodhi temple, lighting little oil lamps or offering incense and flowers. Many, like himself, were from faraway countries, thankful to have reached their destination at last. Not far from the Bo tree, with its ever-fluttering green leaves, Xuanzang stopped by an Asoka stupa. One hundred feet tall, it commemorated the spot where the Buddha, when he was on his way to the sacred tree, had obtained grass for a seat from Indra disguised as a grass cutter.

Xuanzang described the famous Bodh Gaya temple.

The Buddhist Holy Land

> To the East of the *bodhi* tree there is a *vihara* [temple] between sixty and a hundred and seventy feet high, with a base of about fifty feet. It is carved with several niches, each of which contains a gilded statue of the Buddha. On all four sides the walls are covered with beautiful sculptures, festoons of pearls and figures of sages. On its summit there is a gilt copper *amalaka* fruit. The architraves and pillars, the doors and windows are all ornamented with gold and silver casings, amongst which pearls and precious stones are inserted. To the right and left of the outer door are two large niches containing statues of Avalokiteshvara and the *buddha* Maitreya. Both statues are of solid silver and are about ten feet high.[28]

For nearly three centuries after the visit of Xuanzang no repairs or improvements to the temple appear to have been carried out. Major alterations were made after the eleventh century, but what we see now is more or less the same building he has just depicted (Fig. 6.6).[29]

Xuanzang observed that the sacred tales of the Buddha legend were so numerous he could not recount them all; neither could he bear to leave out three of the most important stories—legends of the Temptation of Mara, the wicked one. Like Christ, who was faced with three temptations, the Buddha was tempted by Mara, representing the forces of evil. Xuanzang described how Mara marshaled all his forces in battle array, with spears, bows, and arrows, to terrify the Buddha. He created thunder and lightning and filled the air with sands and stones and darkness. At that moment the Buddha went into the *samadi* (meditation) of great compassion. All the warlike weapons were changed into lotus flowers, and Mara's army fled in panic.

A second stupa, commemorating yet another Mara story, related to the time Mara challenged the Buddha's authority, whereupon the Buddha called the earth to witness and stretched his right hand to the ground. Immediately the earth goddess emerged to testify to the Buddha's multitude of past lives of accumulated achievement. Xuanzang also described the third temptation. Mara tempted the Buddha with the magic of his daughters, but the Buddha was able to change their fascinating bodies, so that "they went away tired and decrepit in each other's arms."

The Chinese monk, along with a host of pilgrims, walked with reverence and joy in the Buddhist rite of circumambulation of the Mahabodhi temple and the Bodhi tree. Perhaps even then there were some Tibetans in their wine-colored robes, prostrating themselves before the miraculous Diamond Throne.[30] Xuanzang told us that "the throne reached from the surface of the earth to the Golden Wheel," the center of the Buddhist world: "It was the seat on which the thousand Buddhas of this *kalpa* attained Emancipation." It had remained "undisturbed by cosmic convulsions and is the sacred point from which all else in Buddhist faith emanates."[31]

FIGURE 6.6
Mahabodhi temple at Bodh Gaya, the holiest place of all for Buddhist pilgrims, with the Bodhi tree, where the Buddha achieved enlightenment (American Institute of Indian Studies. Photographed by permission of Archaeological Survey of India.)

The Buddhist Holy Land

To the north of the Bodhi tree, Xuanzang continued, was the place where the Buddha himself walked up and down in ecstatic contemplation. After the Buddha remained motionless under the tree for seven days, he walked up and down, east and west, for seven days. The Buddha's famous walk is now the Jeweled Walk.

> *The moment he had been waiting for. Finally Xuanzang kneels down before the sacred tree. He thinks of the time the Buddha reached Perfect Wisdom. Perhaps he even remembers how the Buddha, in the first watch of the night, meditated on all worlds, the rising and falling of things, the ascending and descending rhythm of existence; how in the second watch, from 10 to 2 A.M., the Buddha reviewed his own life, and in the third watch, from 2 until 6 A.M., he meditated on human suffering and arrived at the Four Noble Truths and the Eightfold Path of Salvation. What an awakening! "His mind was liberated, ignorance vanished, knowledge was acquired, darkness melted away, light sprang out."*
>
> *With the most sincere devotion, Xuanzang casts himself face down on the ground. Filled with grief, he sighs and says: "At the time when the Buddha perfected himself in wisdom, I know not in what condition I was in the troublous whirl of birth and death." To him it is inescapably clear his evil deeds mean that he is condemned to live in this lesser age, when Buddhism is in decline, instead of the golden age of the Buddha's life on earth. His eyes overflow with tears.*[32]

In one of the most touching passages in his book, Xuanzang's biographer described this scene. Thousands of monks were present for the summer retreat. All of them were moved by the words and emotions of their grieving Chinese visitor. In his innermost heart, Xuanzang knew the perfection of the Buddha and his own unworthiness. This fearless traveler and powerful metaphysician was down on his knees weeping; his outpouring of emotion, far from being a sign of weakness, revealed a new depth of feeling.

SEVEN

NALANDA MONASTERY & ENVIRONS

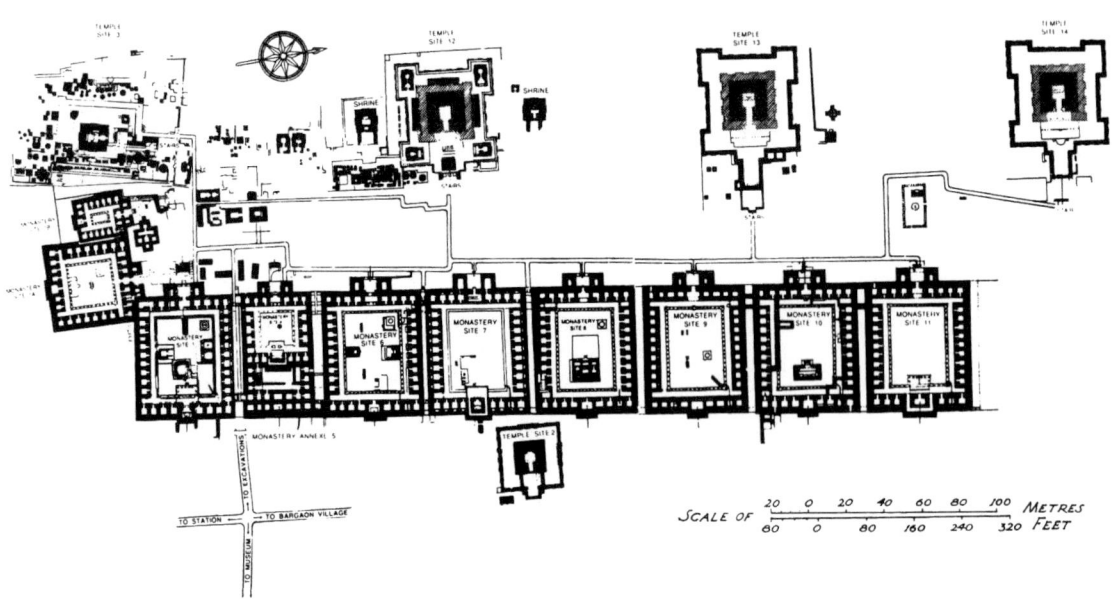

FIGURE 7.1
Survey plan of the excavated remains at Nalanda, showing both monasteries and temples. The monasteries are arranged next to each other like colleges on a university campus. (Courtesy Archaeological Survey of India)

Xuanzang's anguish at living in an age inferior to that of the time of the Buddha was short-lived. Not long afterward, four monks from Nalanda, 60 miles from Bodh Gaya, came to take him back to their monastery (Fig. 7.1). Monks from Korea, Tokhara, China, Mongolia, Tibet all came to study there (Fig. 7.2).[1] What Cluny and Clairvaux were to medieval Europe, Nalanda was to medieval Asia—a cloister for Buddhists from all over the world. It was also the most distinguished of all the monasteries and universities in India.[2]

Meeting the Venerable One

637 C.E. After a night quivering with stars. The monks come to escort Xuanzang to their cloister. They are joined by one hundred other monks and one thousand lay persons who surround him, recounting his praise. With banners, with parasols, with flowers and incense, they make their entrance in Nalanda, where the entire community of ten thousand people awaits Xuanzang. He is welcomed by the presiding monk, who orders the great gong to be sounded and declares, "While the Master of the Law is present, everything is at his disposal." Twenty reverend seniors of the monastery coach him in the proper ways to approach the head of Nalanda, who is so venerable and so saintly that no one dares address him except by the title "Treasury of the Righteous Law." His name is Silabhadra. Xuanzang does homage to him in a scene recalling a Chinese imperial court. He crawls on his hands and knees, kisses the foot of Silabhadra, and touches his head to the ground.

The Venerable Silabhadra orders a seat to be provided for Xuanzang and the other monks. After he is seated, he turns to Xuanzang and asks him, "Where do you come from?"

Xuanzang explains that he has come from the country of China to learn from him the principles of the Treatise on the Stages of Yoga Practice.[3]

When the Venerable Silabhadra heard what Xuanzang had said, he shed tears and begged his nephew to tell about Silabhadra's severe illness and how three years ago it had grown to such an extent that he became tired of his body and wished to end his life.

Xuanzang listens as the nephew explains. One night the Venerable Silabhadra had a dream in which he was visited by three Bodhisattvas who

FIGURE 7.2
Fragment of a hand holding a leaf from a palm-leaf book, found at Nalanda Monastery, where Xuanzang was in residence for at least two years (Courtesy Archaeological Survey of India)

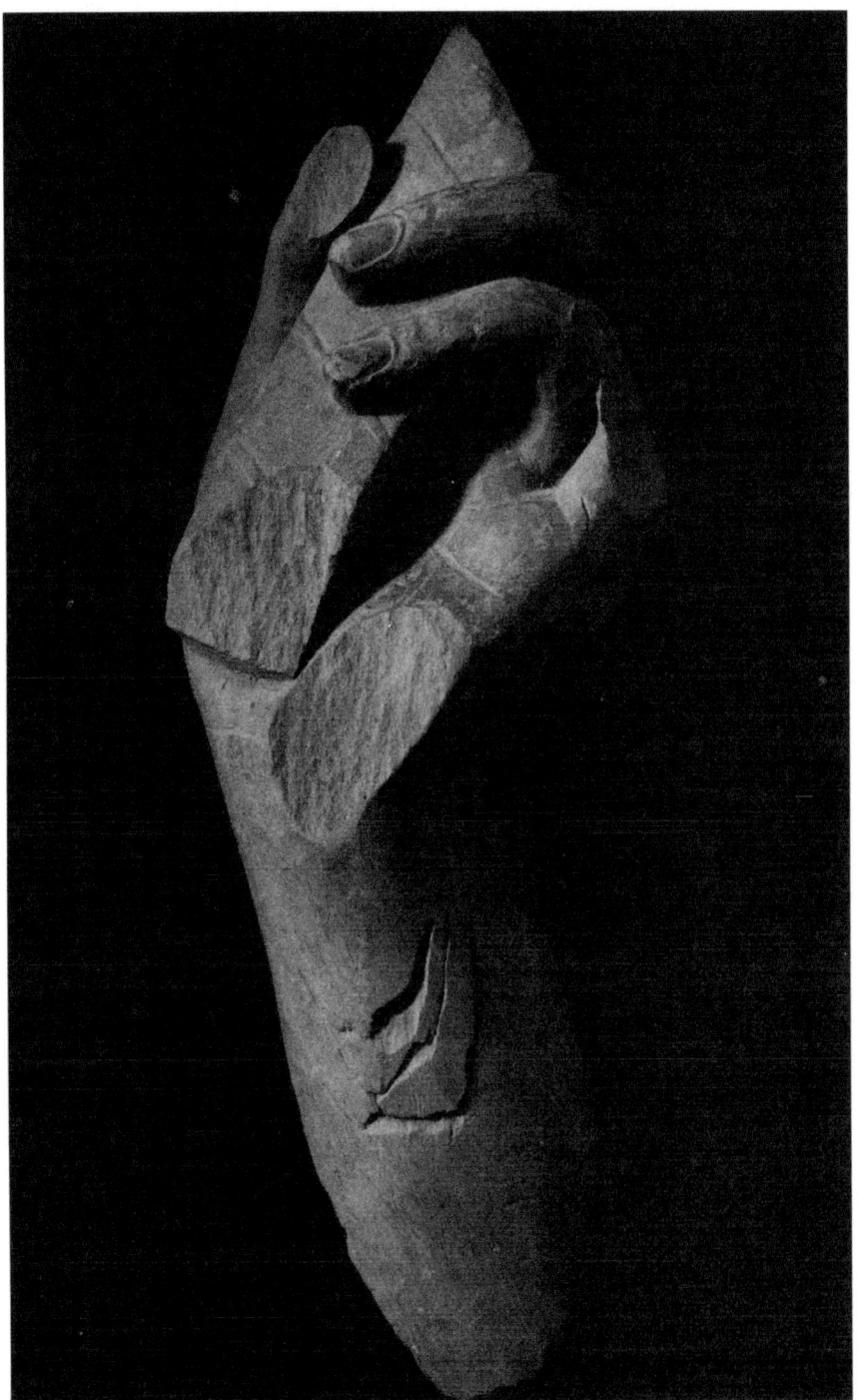

told him that it was taught not to give up the body. They said that in one of his past lives he had been a king and had caused much pain to his people, and that he was suffering his retribution now. He should not think of starving himself to death, but rather he should propagate the Right Law and preach the Treatise on the Stages of Yoga Practice *and other books to the people who had not read them. If he did so, they said, he would recover. Finally they declared that a Chinese monk who wished to learn the great Law would come to study with him. "You may wait to teach him," they said.*

His disciples conclude by saying that he is relieved of his painful illness and is now teaching this scripture.

The Venerable One asks, "How many years have you spent on the way?"

Xuanzang is unable to control his feelings of joy. The fact that the message of the Bodhisattvas in the Venerable Silabhadra's dream that he should preach the very doctrine he had come to India to understand is overwhelming; the Master's task in life is to teach, and his to learn, the very same scriptures. In the awe and excitement of the tremendous moment, Xuanzang forgets everything and replies, "three years."

Both men are enchanted that the prophecy seems to have been confirmed.[4]

While he was traveling around Magadha, Xuanzang reported that he came across the Silabhadra stupa. In the course of telling the story behind its building, he noted:

Silabhadra was a scion of the Braminical royal family of Samatata [in East India]; as a young man he was fond of learning and of exemplary principles. He travelled through India seeking the wise, and in Nalanda he met Dharmapala P'usa who gave him instruction, and in due time ordained him as a bhikshu. Then Silabhadra rose to be eminent for his profound comprehension of the principles and subtleties of Buddhism, and his fame extended to foreign countries.[5]

Xuanzang didn't indicate to us that he remembered the Silabhadra stupa and perhaps it isn't important, for he had finally found the great master, the incomparable metaphysician who would reveal to him new insights about the mystic philosophy of the Yogacara.

After his meeting with Silabhadra, Xuanzang was shown to his quarters at Nalanda. He was the guest of the Venerable One's nephew for seven days, staying on the fourth floor of a convent built by the king of Magadha. Later he moved to another dwelling. From his quarters Xuanzang could look out at the beauty of the extensive grounds.

The whole establishment is surrounded by a brick wall, which encloses the entire convent from without. One gate opens into the great college, from which are separated eight other halls standing in the middle (*of the Sangharama*) [monasteries]. The richly adorned towers, and the fairy-like turrets, like pointed hill-tops are congregated together. The observatories seem to be lost in the vapours (*of the morning*), and the upper rooms tower above the clouds.

From the windows one may see how the winds and the clouds (*produce new forms*), and above the soaring eaves the conjunctions of the sun and moon (*may be observed*).

And then we may add how the deep, translucent ponds, bear on their surface the blue lotus, intermingled with the Kie-ni (*Kanaka*) flower, of deep red color, and at intervals the Amra groves spread over all, their shade.

All the outside courts, in which are the priests' chambers, are of four stages. The stages have dragon-projections and coloured eaves, the pearl-red pillars carved and ornamented, the richly adorned balustrades, and the roofs covered with tiles that reflect the light in a thousand shades, these things add to the beauty of the scene.

The Sangharamas of India are counted by myriads, but this is the most remarkable for grandeur and height.[6]

Down below him were monks in their orange robes going to and fro among the eight lecture halls, numerous stupas, five temples, and many monastery complexes for students and priests, spacious libraries, the observatory building, ten ponds, and garden courts on campus. Maybe even he watched the building of a new brass temple, which had been commissioned by King Harsha, that was occurring while he was there.[7] (See Color Plate 7.)

Did Xuanzang often visit the great temple, which must have dominated Nalanda then as it does today? Now called Stupa 3, it was enlarged and beautifully embellished in the seventh century; the foundations of the original structure must have been laid two centuries earlier. Xuanzang mentioned a large temple, 300 feet high, which "recalls the form" of the Mahabodhi temple at Bodh Gaya (Fig. 7.3).[8]

When Xuanzang visited Nalanda, the monastery may have been in existence for seven centuries. Successive Indian kings had contributed to its welfare. The monastery was richly endowed by—among others—the king of Magadha, who provided that the revenues of one hundred villages should be given for the upkeep of Nalanda. Day by day two hundred householders of these villages contributed several hundred pounds of rice, butter, and milk. Clothes, food, beds, and medicines were also provided.

Every day Xuanzang received 120 betel leaves for chewing, 20 areca (a variety of betel palm) nuts, the same number of cardamoms, an ounce of camphor, and about one and one-half pounds of Mahasali rice. He recalled that this rice, grown only in Magadha, had grains as large as black beans and was scented and of an exquisite flavor and shining

Nalanda Monastery & Environs

FIGURE 7.3
Stupa 3, remains of the great stupa at Nalanda Monastery, which has some resemblance to the temple at Bodh Gaya (Courtesy Archaeological Survey of India)

color. His daily rations also included ghee (clarified butter) and other staples.

Water clocks were used to keep track of the time. The entire day was divided into periods of study and worship. A gong sounded every morning to remind priests of the bathing hour. "Sometimes a hundred, sometimes several thousand" priests left their rooms together and proceeded to take a bath in one of Nalanda's ten ponds. And so we may picture Xuanzang going out with his fellow pilgrims in the cool, early morning hours. This bath was followed by the devotions before the holy images of Buddhas, Bodhisattvas, Tara, Hariti, the Mother Goddess, either in the cells of individual monks or in large courtyards.

Monks offered incense and flowers and lighted lamps in adoration, or in the case of Hariti, they proffered food as well. Neither Xuanzang nor Yijing, who stayed at Nalanda from 675 to 695 C.E., spoke of any Tantric images, but perhaps those came later.

After public lectures there was a large meal, which was probably brought directly to the monks' cells, for there seem to have been no community kitchens or common dining rooms. Four strokes of a drum, the blowing of a conch shell, followed by two more strokes, announced the noon hour.[9]

Study and discussion seem to have continued until twilight, when there was an evening service. At Nalanda, owing to the large size of the monastery, instead of the monks walking three times around a central stupa performing their devotions, a precentor was sent to chant and offer hymns around the three hundred apartments. He was preceded by lay servants and children carrying incense, lamps, and flowers. "At every hall he chanted the service, every time three to five *slokas* [stanzas] in a loud tone, so the sound was heard all around."[10] There seems to have been an evening service in which a reader intoned selected texts. The night was also divided into watches; the first and third were occupied by meditation and chanting. During the middle hours, the monks could take rest.[11]

Even if there were only one-third as many monks at Nalanda as the figure of ten thousand given by Huili, the sound of thousands of monks chanting by the light of a full moon in the Indian night must have been overpowering; their male voices would have risen and fallen like the ascending and descending tones of a Gregorian chant.[12] The last verses of the popular *Heart of Wisdom Sutra* are "Gone, gone, gone beyond, gone altogether beyond. O, what an Awakening! All hail!" Xuanzang had chanted to himself the same sutra in the desert. Over and over their deep voices would have repeated this sutra. At last there would have been the long, brooding cry of the conch shells. Silence. And the monks would return noiselessly to their cells to meditate or to sleep.

Riding an Elephant to Rajagriha (Rajgir)

Most monks had two lay servants to attend to their needs. As a special guest coming from so far, Xuanzang was also given two servants and the use of a palanquin or an elephant for his excursions outside the university. Of the thousands of host and guest monks only ten persons were given such privileges. Riding elephants was not usually the prerogative of ordinary citizens but was confined to religious processions and royal usage.[13] Xuanzang would ride on an elephant again in a glorious religious procession for King Harsha's grand debate. In addition, King Harsha, in an unusual gesture, would give the pilgrim his best elephant for his journey back to China.

Riding high on a howdah on his elephant, Xuanzang visited the holy places of Rajagriha (modern Rajgir), where the Buddha had spent many long periods of his life. It was the central point of the kingdom of Magadha, where King Bimbisara (c. 544–493 B.C.E.) had fixed his capital at the time of the Buddha. Xuanzang's description explains why: "High mountains surround it on each side, and form as it were its external walls. On the west it is approached through a narrow pass, on the north there is a passage through the mountains. The town is extended from east to west and narrow from north to south (Fig. 7.4).[14]

One can imagine Xuanzang on his high perch on the elephant's back jotting down notes about this fine natural fortress. Xuanzang repeated a colorful legend attached to Rajagriha that fits in with this dramatic countryside. It is the story of the Buddha taming the wild elephant Nalagiri, which marks the last of the eight miracles, and the last of the traditional places of pilgrimage.

The drama took place as the Buddha went about the city of Rajagriha with some of his disciples to gather food. A mad elephant was drugged by palace guards at the instigation of the wicked Devadatta. This Judas had tried several times to murder the Buddha and failed, but this time he felt that he would surely succeed. The crazed elephant galloped through the city, creating panic everywhere; it had just thrown its guard to the ground, killing him instantly, when it saw the radiance of the Master. Immediately, the elephant sought forgiveness and knelt before the Buddha (Fig. 7.5).

Climbing Vulture Peak

Xuanzang must have been eager to climb to Vulture Peak, where the Lord Buddha is supposed to have preached some of his most famous sermons; among them was the *Lotus Sutra,* which enjoyed such popularity in China. To the northeast of Rajagriha, on a small spur of what is now called Chhatha Hill, is this most picturesque of the five mountains surrounding the old city. Xuanzang noted that the mountainside had clear springs, trees covered with thick foliage, and extraordinary rock formations. This is still true. Scrub bushes, fewer trees perhaps, but orange-and-black-striated rocks dot the foothills, and gray rocks streaked with white, all of them with peculiar, almost anguished shapes, are at the summit. Some see them in the shape of vultures, and others describe the peak as a resting place for vultures.

FIGURE 7.4
Site plan of old and new Rajagriha. Xuanzang traveled from Nalanda to the old town on his elephant. (Courtesy Archaeological Survey of India)

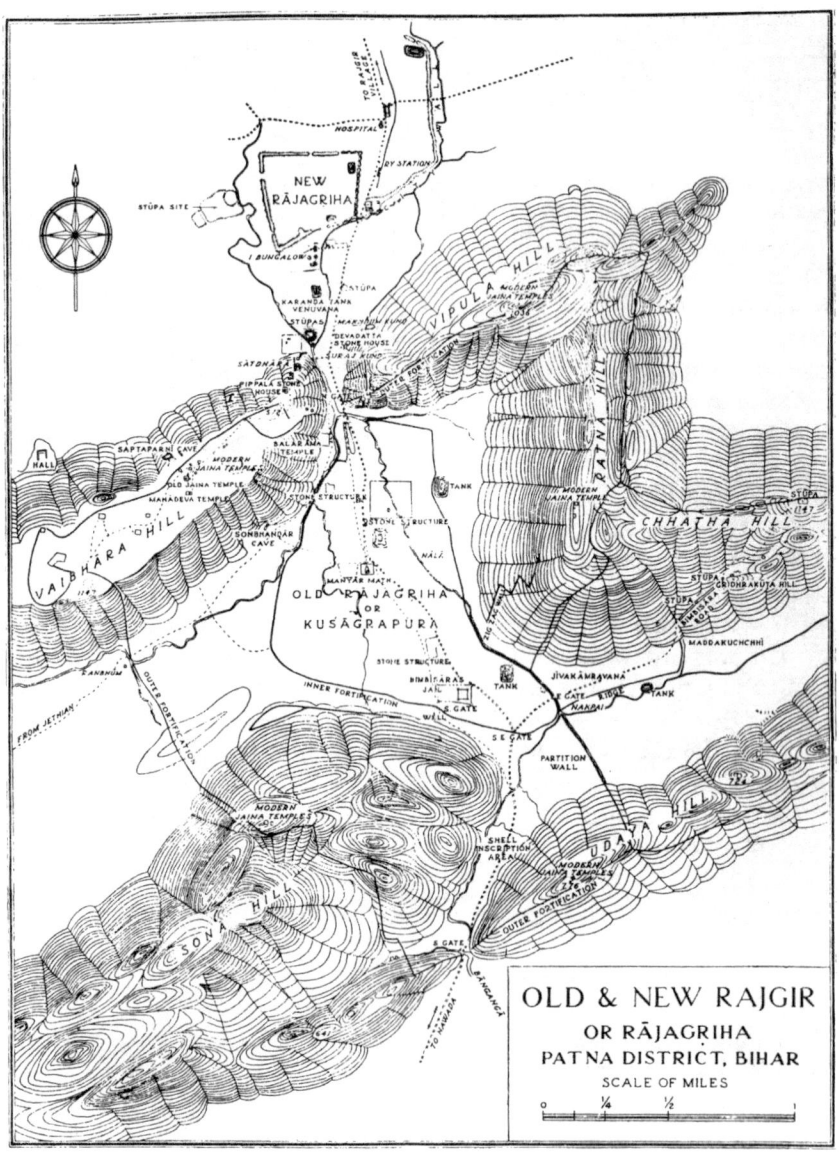

At the foot of the hill is the beginning of King Bimbisara's road. "Bimbisara raja [king], for the purpose of hearing the law, raised a number of men to accompany him from the foot of the mountain to its summit. They levelled the valleys and spanned the precipices, and with the stones made a staircase about ten paces wide and 5 or 6 *li* long."[15]

FIGURE 7.5
Taming of the elephant Nalagiri at Rajagriha, one of the eight famous miracles of the Lord Buddha. The Buddha is depicted as much larger than the elephant. (American Institute of Indian Studies. Photographed by permission of Archaeological Survey of India.)

In the middle of the road, Xuanzang observed, were two small stupas, one called "Dismounting the Chariot" because the king, when he got there, went forward on foot. The other was called "Sending Back the Crowd" because the king, separating from the common folk, would not allow them to proceed with him.[16]

Climbing on this Bimbisara Road of rough undressed stones, pausing where the king stopped, and exploring the mountain caves along the way, one reaches the flat terrace at the top of Vulture Peak. A sense of timelessness pervades the air. Xuanzang surely would have made his prayers and offerings of flowers and incense at the top, remembering that the pious Faxian had done so and had spent the night in meditation on this very peak two centuries earlier. As a symbol of remembrance, he obtained a golden model of Buddha preaching the *Lotus*

Sutra on Vulture Peak. This was the sixth of the famous images that he would take back to China as part of his continuing search for genuine artifacts that would be useful when he returned. The seventh and final image was also made of gold; it came from the Dragon Cave not far from Bodh Gaya.

Descending from the mountain by elephant, Xuanzang probably went through the north gate of the old city to visit the famous hot springs where the Buddha's disciple Ananda had bathed. Nearby was the Venuvana, or the Bamboo Grove of Kalanda, presumed to be the first piece of land ceded to the early Buddhists. Later this beautiful garden, given to them by King Bimbisara, became one of the favorite places of the Lord Buddha, where he stayed after his enlightenment.

About 6 *li* southwest of the Bamboo Grove, Xuanzang visited another forest of bamboo and a large cave. His interest was theological. That is where a few months after the Buddha's final nirvana, Kasyapa, a senior monk, presided over a meeting to establish the Buddhist canon called the *Tripitaka*, or the *Three Baskets*. The canon was in effect created by Kasyapa's questioning of five hundred monks regarding what the Buddha had said. Xuanzang wrote that Kasyapa told Ananda, "The Tathagata [Buddha] used to praise you among monks, saying that you were the most learned disciple and could understand all the Dharmas. Now you may take the chair to recite the Sutra-pitaka, i.e., all the scriptures, for the assembly."[17]

After Kasyapa said this, Ananda rose to his feet, paid homage in the direction of the far-off place where the Buddha entered nirvana, and then he took a chair and recited the scriptures. The monks listened carefully and orally corrected what he said. That is why when each sutra begins, "Thus I have said," it is Ananda speaking. Thus the first compilation of the Buddha's sermons was established but not written down.

At this same First Buddhist Council, Upali expounded the *Vinaya*, the Rules of Discipline. The third basket, or *Abhidharma*, consisting of scholastic elaboration of the doctrine, was done by Kasyapa himself. A second meeting was held, according to Xuanzang's biographer, which included lay folk as well as *arhat*s.

Attending Lectures at Nalanda

After touring the nearby holy sites, Xuanzang returned to Nalanda and was finally able to hear his master, the Venerable Silabhadra, lecture on the basic Yogacara scriptures, only a portion of which had been transmitted to China. At long last Xuanzang had found an incompara-

Nalanda Monastery & Environs

ble teacher in the very school of Buddhism that had inspired him to leave China in the first place. From him Xuanzang could learn *the pure tradition* handed down from master to pupil, beginning with Asanga (fourth century C.E.) and Vasubandhu (fourth–fifth century C.E.), who had both come to Nalanda, one from Peshawar and the other from Ayodhya. Next in the chain after these two luminaries of the Yogacara school was Dignaga (late fifth–sixth century C.E.), founder of the New Logic, who was succeeded by Dharmapala (sixth–seventh century C.E.), the head of Nalanda Monastery before the period of Xuanzang's arrival. Finally there was Silabhadra, the Venerable One, who was the pupil of Dharmapala and succeeded him, and who had greeted Xuanzang with such joy and accepted him as his pupil.

Over a period of fifteen months the Venerable One—some said he was 104 years old—expounded on the *Treatise on the Stages of Yoga Practice* no less than three times. Xuanzang listened carefully to each exposition. He praised his teacher for making clear the most abstruse points. In a famous letter Xuanzang said of the Venerable One:

> He was thoroughly conversant with the teaching of all sects ... whether they were deficient or perfect; and even with the writings of heterodoxy. ... They not only permeated his mind, but also liquified in his heart. His literary style was circuitous while thoroughly expressing his ideas. His reasoning was allusive while clearly putting across his message. All this led to a mass following of his teachings, both the religious and the secular hail him as a spiritual leader of India.[18]

Xuanzang also attended courses in grammar, logic, and Sanskrit. His biographer interrupted the narrative to include a three-page summary of Sanskrit grammar.[19] Huili seemed impressed with Xuanzang's linguistic skills and might have thought that he could best show Xuanzang's expertise by demonstrating to the Chinese reader the complexity of Sanskrit grammar.[20] Xuanzang himself recognized that Indians were expert scholars of their own language and wanted to show that Sanskrit was structured entirely differently from Chinese.[21] He noted, "One who is skilled in the language may write his compositions without any ambiguity and may express himself in a most elegant manner."[22]

The longer he stayed, the more impressed he became with the whole atmosphere of Nalanda.

> The priests, to the number of several thousands, are men of highest ability and talent. Their distinction is very great at the present time, and there are many hundreds whose fame has rapidly spread through distant regions. Their conduct is pure and unblamable.... The rules of this convent are severe, and all the priests are bound to observe them.

> The day is not sufficient for asking and answering profound questions. From morning till night they engage in discussion; the old and the young mutually help one another. Those who cannot discuss questions out of the *Tripitaka* [canon] are little esteemed, and are obliged to hide themselves for shame. Learned men from distant cities, on this account, who desire to acquire quickly a renown in discussion, come here in multitudes to settle their doubts, and then the streams (*of their wisdom*) spread far and wide.[23]

Several thousand monks lived at the monastery-university, and it appears that secular researchers and non-Buddhist scholars pursued studies there. One hundred pulpits were used and set up daily for the delivery of discourses, which the students attended without fail. The monks studied Mahayana Buddhism and the eighteen schools of Hinayana Buddhism, Indian subjects such as the Vedas, logic, grammar, philosophy, medicine, mathematics, Sanskrit, astronomy, as well as literature and the works of magic. Such a broad curriculum was based on the notion that logic, grammar, and literature should be studied in order to vanquish one's adversaries; the science of medicine to administer health to others; and that of metaphysics to acquire knowledge of oneself.[24]

Xuanzang naturally was put into the top level. It was reserved for those who had mastered fifty books, a very select group consisting of only nine monks when Xuanzang arrived. The Venerable One, Silabhadra, had read and fathomed all the sutras and *sastra*s without exception, and the high rank he occupied was due to his eminent virtue, his learning, and his age.

Lecturing and Writing at Nalanda

At the end of 642 C.E., after an extended tour of the whole continent of India that took several years, Xuanzang returned to Nalanda for another period of study. The Venerable One asked him to give some lectures on Idealist texts. Xuanzang did so and also wrote a 3,000-stanza work called the *Treatise on the Harmony of Teaching*. The Venerable Silabhadra thought highly of it, and it was widely read.

The Venerable One, recognizing Xuanzang's abilities, chose him as one of four monks to debate with Hinayanists at Orissa. The other three were not at all certain of success. But Xuanzang told them, "I have learned the whole Tripitaka of the various sects of Hinayana Buddhism while I was in my own country and when I was staying in Kasmira and thus I thoroughly understand their teachings." He added in a self-deprecating tone worthy of any Chinese, "I am not deeply learned with but little wisdom, I shall be able to deal with them, and therefore you need not worry about it. If I am defeated in debate, it will be the failure of a Chinese monk and will have nothing to do with you."[25]

Xuanzang's final meeting with Silabhadra before he left for China shows that the Venerable One appreciated Xuanzang's mission. After the priests of Nalanda had urged him to stay because China was but a frontier land, an evil country, they took him to see Silabhadra so that Xuanzang could set forth his intentions. Xuanzang expressed his affection for India and his gratitude that Silabhadra had explained the *Treatise on the Stages of Yoga Practice*, and he explained that he had visited sacred vestiges and heard the profound exposition of different schools. Nevertheless, he desired to return in order to translate and explain to others what he had heard. In this way he could repay the kindness of his teacher, and that is why he did not want to linger any longer.

The Venerable One joyfully replied: "This is indeed the wish of a Bodhisattva, and it is also what I expect of you. Let him make the necessary arrangements, and you people need not try to detain him any more."[26]

Xuanzang heard that the Venerable One, on his deathbed, had inquired about Xuanzang. He wrote: "I felt my heart deeply stabbed and could not recover from such a wound. Oh, it was as if a boat had capsized in *duhkha-sagara* [ocean of misery] or a celestial being lost the light of his eyes. How unexpectedly soon had come the pain of bereavement!"

Xuanzang's letter to the Venerable One's most prominent pupil continued:

> The great *Dharm-akara* [Dharma-keeper] Master had cultivated virtue in the past, and accumulated merits for a long time to come. This was why he was endowed with a harmonious and noble nature and uniquely outstanding talent. He inherited the virtue of the Buddha, the Aryadeva, and extended the brilliance of Nagarjuna. He rekindled the torch of wisdom and re-hoisted the flag of *dharma*. He extinguished the volcano of heterodoxy, and stopped the river of untruth from flooding. He led the exhausted travelers to the spiritual treasury, and opened up new vistas for those who had lost their bearings. He was at the same time a vast ocean and a lofty mountain, and a pillar of the edifice of *dharma-paryaya* [Gate of Buddhism].
>
> When I was seeking truth (in India), I had the honour of association with His Reverend and of benefiting by his teachings. Much as I was mediocre and unintelligent, I became amenable in his noble company.

When I bade him farewell to return to my country, he offered me deep and sincere advice which is still ringing in my ears. I had wished that he would live long to provide a noble example of emulation. Never had I imagined that he would one day depart from us eternally—how unbearable!

Your Reverend had for long received his noble teaching and risen in status in the *asrama* [hermitage]. It must have been difficult for you to suppress your longing for the departed guru. What can we do? Such are the laws of the universe, what can we do? I wish you could overcome your sad-feelings.[27]

A close tie had developed between Xuanzang and Silabhadra when he was at Nalanda. When Xuanzang wrote to the Venerable One's most prominent pupil about how difficult it must have been "to suppress his longing for the departed guru," or that he wished the pupil "could overcome his sad feelings," it was as if Xuanzang was talking in part to himself.

EIGHT

PHILOSOPHERS, ROCK-CUT CAVES & A FORTUNE-TELLER

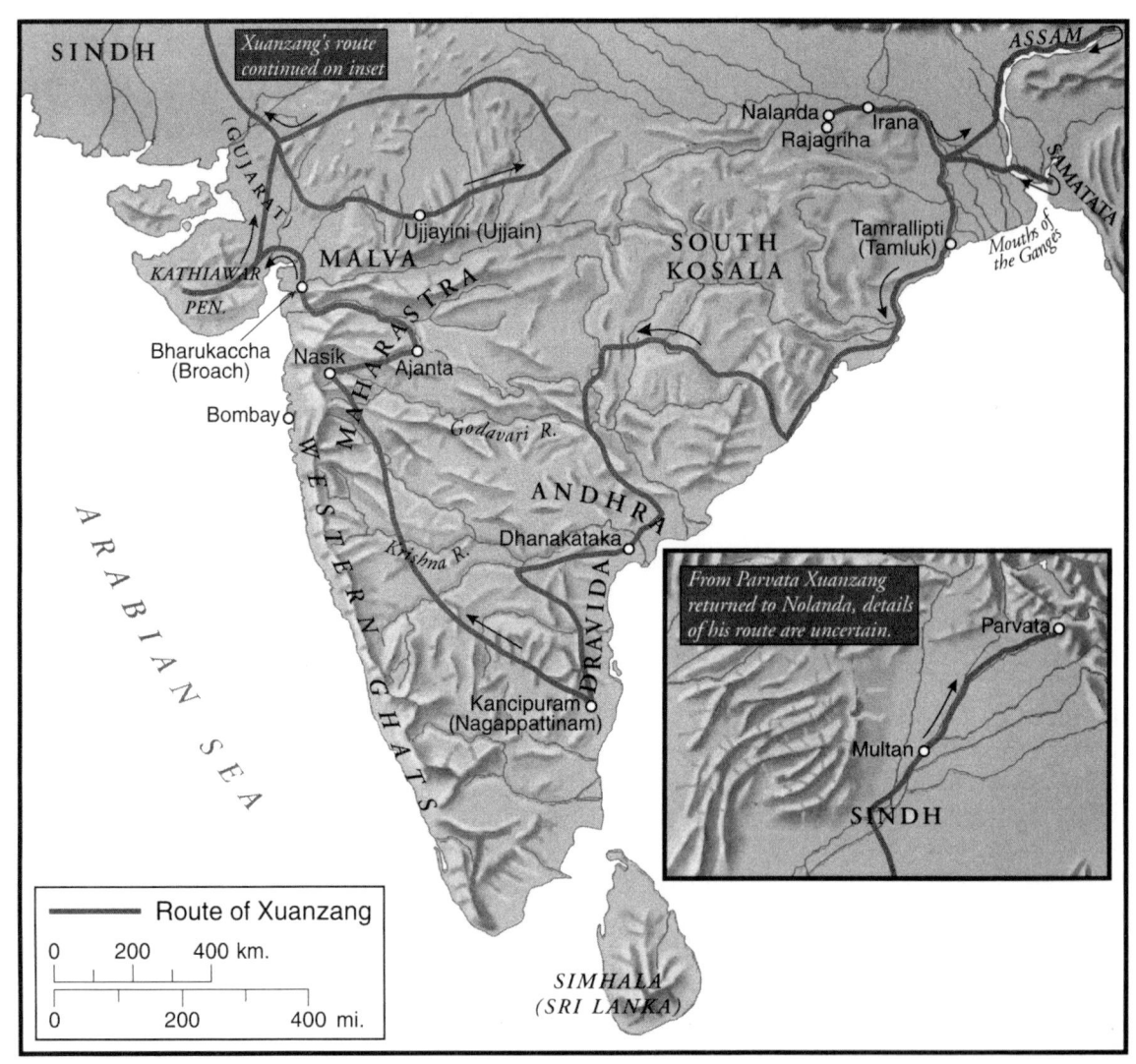

MAP 8.1
Itinerary of Xuanzang around the Indian continent (from Nalanda to Parvata) (Philip Schwartzberg, Meridian Mapping)

638 C.E. The best time of day in India—dawn. The place is Kapota Monastery, east of Nalanda. Xuanzang worships at a famous sandalwood statue of the Bodhisattva, called Avalokitesvara, on his way to Bengal. It is a precious statue surrounded on all sides by a wooden balustrade. People go there seeking an omen, which depends on their garlanding the image with flowers. If the flowers rest on the image, pilgrims believe, their innermost wishes will be answered. Xuanzang kneels and makes three prayers.

His first is that if the flowers rest on the hand of the Sandalwood Buddha, he may safely return to his own country after he has completed his studies. His second prayer is that if the flowers hang on the arms of the Sandalwood Buddha, he may be reborn in the Tushita Heaven to serve the Maitreya Buddha. His third is that if the flowers rest on the neck of the Buddha, he will know that he has the Buddha nature and may become a Buddha of the Future. The garlands stay on all the places he prays for, and the Bodhisattva is covered with flowers.[1]

IT DOES SEEM EXTRAORDINARY that Xuanzang was really in doubt about his Buddha nature. Yet he did come to believe, along with the Venerable Silabhadra, that not everyone had the Buddha nature, that not everyone could attain salvation. This belief very much lessened the attraction of the Buddhist school he tried to found when he returned to China.[2]

Xuanzang's intellectual curiosity was insatiable. At a time when it seemed as if he had achieved most of his goals, he was determined to go on, to see what was there, to try to understand, to explore the rest of the vast subcontinent of India. For four years, from 638 to 642 C.E., Xuanzang would be touring both coasts of India, and much of the interior, a trek of 3,000 miles and more. Was it that having opened the door to Buddhist philosophy and metaphysics, he found that there was always more to know, always yet another school to master? Another attraction must have been to visit the birthplace of some of the other great Buddhist philosophers—Nagarjuna, the skeptic; Dharmapala, the teacher of Silabhadra; and Dignaga, the logician, just as in the north he had been to the places connected with the Idealist philosophers Asanga and Vasubandhu, who had meant so much to him.

Probably by this time on his journey he felt an ever-greater urge to collect new scholarly treatises, discourses on Ultimate Reality, works on logic and grammar, and healing sutras from other Buddhist centers. These could be packed in the 527 boxes he would take back with him to China. Xuanzang was not only seeking the truth for himself but he was also collecting 224 sutras and 192 treatises from Mahayanist works, as well as the sayings, rules of discipline, and treatises from six Hinayanist schools—to form a "library of truths." His Chinese compatriots at home need never be confused by varying translations; they could read the texts for themselves from original sources.

Xuanzang had become the Master of the Law of Buddhism, but he was also an explorer who relished adventure. He knew the lure of the next country, the mists on the far horizon, the attraction of wild and awesome places in India or even of countries beyond its border—Simhala (Sri Lanka) and Persia (Iran). Always he was hungry for experience as well as knowledge.

His energy in the most torrid parts of India was remarkable. Even in the area around the mouths of the Ganges River he said that the climate "was soft and agreeable because of the sea." Not many would concur with him—unless the climate of the seventh century was drastically different than it is now.

Or it may be that he was inspired by the Buddhist ideal as it was expressed in one of the Wisdom Sutras: "If thou goest eastward . . . abandon all thy thoughts about growing tired, about sleep, eating and drinking, day and night, cold and heat; do not trouble thyself at all about such affairs; have no thought whatever about them."[3]

Traveling Around the East Coast

Xuanzang's written account of the kingdoms he visited in the rest of India is much less detailed than his account of northern India and much vaguer about the duration of his stays in each place.[4] However, we do know that he spent time in the kingdom of Irana, to the east of Nalanda, in western Bengal. He reported that there were ten monasteries and four thousand priests in the area. He immersed himself once again in studying Hinayana scriptures, books that were the farthest removed from his own Idealist beliefs.[5]

From there Xuanzang followed the Ganges River until he reached modern-day Bangladesh, which was then an area of dense forests inhabited by wild elephants, rhinoceroses, wolves, and black leopards.[6] Keeping a path in a northerly direction, the pilgrim reached Assam.

The country was low and moist; the crops were regular; the Jack fruit and Cocoa were in great esteem though plentiful; there were continuous streams and tanks to the towns; the climate was genial. . . . The reigning king . . . was a brahman by caste. . . . His Majesty was a lover of learning and his subjects followed his example; men of ability came from far lands to study here; though the king was not a Buddhist he treated accomplished sramanas [scholars?] with respect.[7]

Later on Xuanzang would visit Assam on the invitation of the king, even though the king was a Hindu.

In Assam Xuanzang learned that the borders of Sichuan in China were only two months' journey distant. However, the mountains and rivers were filled with poisonous snakes and pestilential vapors. When he was farther south along the coast, at Samatata (near present-day Dacca), he heard of six kingdoms lying to the east; among them were what are now Burma, Thailand, Cambodia, and Vietnam.

Perhaps he felt a surge of homesickness before he turned back toward India, recrossing all "the mouths of the Ganges River," as they are called on modern maps, to reach the famous seaport from whence both Faxian and Yijing had made their sea journeys back to China! There at Tamrallipti (Tamluk), 41 miles southwest of Calcutta, he heard that in the middle of the ocean was a country called Simhala (Sri Lanka), which was distinguished for its scholars of early Buddhism. A south Indian whom he met explained that this holy island was thousands of miles away. He should not go by sea because of the dangers of storms and bad weather; it would be far better to go south through Orissa, see the sacred traces along the east coast, and talk with scholars, traveling until he reached the southernmost tip of India. From there he might take a boat across the Palk Strait and reach Simhala in a few days.

This he proceeded to do. On his way south he happened upon a stupa that was built to honor the man who had defeated a boasting philosopher from south India. "This bullying braggart had come to the city and strutted about with his stomach protected by copper sheathing to prevent him from bursting with excessive learning, and bearing on his head a light to enlighten the ignorant and stupid."[8]

Xuanzang stopped at an Orissa seaport. On hot tropical nights when the sky was clear and without clouds, he sometimes fancied that he saw "at a great distance the glittering rays of the precious gem placed at the top of the Stupa of the Tooth of Buddha; its appearance [was] like that of a shining star in the midst of space."[9] This imagining of emanations from Simhala (which was at least 1,000 miles away by sea) is in great contrast to his precision in debate, his fine-tuned discrimination in matters of philosophy, and his general accuracy in reporting. It seems rather to be a kind of imaginative leap in which Simhala becomes the beckoning star for his long journey to the south of India (Fig. 8.1).

Exploring a Rock-Cut Cave in South Kosala

The next important Buddhist center Xuanzang visited was South Kosala.

> This country, more than 6,000 *li* in circuit, was surrounded by mountains and was a succession of woods and marshes, its capital being above 40 *li* in circuit. The soil of the country was rich and fertile, the towns and villages were close together; the people were prosperous, tall of stature and black in colour; the king was a kshatriya by birth, a Buddhist in religion, and of noted benevolence. There were above 100 Buddhist monasteries; and about 10,000 Brethren, all Mahayanists.[10]

South Kosala was well known as the home of the famous Nagarjuna, who is thought to have lived around 100–200 C.E. Nagarjuna was a founder of the Madhyamika school of Buddhism, whose principal ideas have survived to the present day in Tibet, China, and Japan. The Madhyamika school was known especially for the systematizing of the *Perfection of Wisdom Sutra*. Madhyama means middle; the Madhyamikas are those who take the middle way between affirming and denying.

FIGURE 8.1
Temple of the Tooth in present-day Sri Lanka. When Xuanzang was on the northeast coast of India, he thought he saw the glittering of the gem topping the Stupa of the Tooth. (Courtesy Howard Wriggins, photographer)

Nagarjuna was among those who developed the Mahayana concept of Emptiness and opposed the rigid categories of existence and nonexistence, seeking a middle way between affirmation and denial. He believed that the way to salvation was the contemplation of unreality or emptiness. The Doctrine of Emptiness, or void, provided a new basis for Buddhist art, for it became possible to render the Buddha without asserting that it was a representation of true reality, but rather a pale reflection of it.[11]

While Xuanzang was in South Kosala, he heard some of the legends that had grown around "this second Buddha," as Nagarjuna was sometimes called.[12] There were several about Nagarjuna as a magician, but one of the legends Xuanzang recorded was how the king was having a monastery quarried for Nagarjuna in the mountains and ran out of funds. The monastery, sometimes called the Pigeon Monastery, was an extraordinary place, with cloisters and lofty halls: "These halls were in five tiers . . . with temples containing gold life-sized image of the Buddha of perfect artistic beauty . . . the chambers were lighted by windows cut in the rock."[13] And even more intriguing: "From the high peak of the mountain, descending streamlets like small cascades, flow through the different stories, winding round the side galleries and then discharging themselves without."[14] But in the building of this monastery the king's treasure became exhausted; Nagarjuna then provided an abundant supply of funds by transmuting the rocks into gold!

This wonderful rock-cut monastery, with golden Buddhas and cascading waterfalls, was also described by Faxian after his visit to India two centuries earlier. Caves were particularly adapted to Indian climate for they are both cool in summer and warm in winter.[15] Several of these monastery caves, such as Ellora and Ajanta, are as grand in size as the Pigeon Monastery; their sculpture and wall paintings are of world renown.

In the 1950s, during the Cultural Revolution in China, a historian retold Xuanzang's journey to the west in the form of a novel.[16] The book has a haunting description of Xuanzang visiting a cave set deep in the side of the mountain. The cave was inhabited by a demon, and men were afraid to enter. Its pavilions had fallen into ruin. Xuanzang found candlesticks that had fallen over, spiderwebs, and pitch-black halls. Behind jeweled curtains were images of the Three Buddhas of the Past, Present, and Future. Xuanzang prostrated himself, feeling saddened and cold. Then he dusted the altar in front of the Buddhas. The farther he went in the mountain, the higher were the halls. Passing through several courtyards, he climbed a tall tower. A fox—or was it a cat?—ran past his feet. One building was for storing sutras, Sanskrit texts written on palm leaves, now covered with dust and mildew. He heard the whirring wings of bats as he came to a tall, seated, jade-covered body of the Buddha. In the flickering light of his torch, it almost seemed as if the Buddha had come to life in a moment of discovery and reward.

Visiting Andhra and the South

From South Kosala, where he had heard that the king was well disposed toward learning and the arts and that there were a hundred monasteries and ten thousand monks, Xuanzang headed back toward the coast through a vast forest to the ancient kingdom of Andhra, between the Godavari and Krishna Rivers.[17] He stated that there were twenty monasteries and five thousand monks. This was the home of Dignaga, the great logician, whose writings Xuanzang knew very well. He had studied them both in Kashmir and more recently in South Kosala. A stone stupa marked the place where Dignaga had composed his classic, the *Treatise on Logic*. Xuanzang related the legend of Dignaga listening to the advice of the Bodhisattva of Wisdom, Manjusri, a story that is meant to show that Dignaga gave up Hinayana Buddhism when he listened to the Bodhisattva.

From South Kosala he went on to the kingdom of Dhanakataka, usually equated with the modern city of Bezwada. Xuanzang wrote that there was a large number of Buddhist monasteries, many of them deserted. About twenty were still in use; there were three thousand monks, mostly adherents of Nagarjuna's philosophy. Xuanzang studied with them during the rainy season in 639 C.E., and in turn, he taught them some of his favorite texts. The most famous site in the kingdom was the great stupa at Amaravati, a third-century C.E. structure, whose exquisite carvings have given it importance in the history of Indian sculpture.[18]

He was eager to reach Dravida, the land of the Tamils, in the south, whose capital was Kancipuram. He stayed there for a considerable period during the Rain Retreat in 640 C.E. on his way to Simhala. Kancipuram was the birthplace of Dharmapala (c. seventh century C.E.), who has been called Xuanzang's spiritual grandfather because he was the teacher of the Venerable Silabhadra. Xuanzang recounted a dramatic story of the young Dharmapala: He was about to be married to the princess of Kancipuram, and on his wedding night when he was in the midst of his prayers, he was suddenly whisked off by a god to a monastery where he might pursue the vocation of a monk.

Xuanzang was greatly influenced by this follower of the Yogacara school, who was the author of a number of celebrated works of Mahayana literature; among them was his commentary on Vasubandhu's *Thirty Verses*. In 649 C.E., when Xuanzang returned to China, he made a synthesis of ten commentaries by Indian philosophers on the *Thirty Verses* based chiefly on Dharmapala's commentary. It became the standard textbook of idealism in China and Japan.[19]

Imagining Simhala (Sri Lanka)

It is not too surprising that Xuanzang, who had dreamed or imagined that he saw glittering rays from the Stupa of the Tooth in Simhala when he was in northern India, devoted an entire chapter to the holy island when he got to the south. He had thought that the monks in Simhala were knowledgeable about the *Treatise on the Stages of Yoga Practice,* but when he talked with a Simhalese monk about it, it turned out that the latter could not give a better explanation than the Venerable Silabhadra had. However, Faxian had written a glowing account of his two years in Simhala, which perhaps whetted his desire to see it. Xuanzang did not fail to repeat its most famous legends, that of the founding of its people and the story of Mahendra, the son of Asoka, who brought Buddhism to the island. Xuanzang described the Temple of the Tooth, referring to it as the Land of Gems because of the many precious stones found there. It continues to be known by that name, for the same reason.

Xuanzang recounted that the monks "were very precise in the observance of rules, perfectly clear in meditation and wisdom, and very grave in their model deportment." Fine words of praise, but the country as a whole was not as blessed as its monks. While Xuanzang was making his way to Kancipuram, Simhala was enduring both civil wars and famine as a result of a palace revolution. Just as he was about to leave on the three-day sail to Simhala, three hundred Simhalese monks who had fled their land came to him and urged him to abandon his plans.

Touring the West Coast

Xuanzang did not have much to say about his journey from Dravida, in the south of India, to the area around what is now called Bombay, in the north on the west coast, a distance of roughly 900 miles. Accompanied by seventy Simhalese monks, he made his way to Nasik, the capital of King Pulakesin II. This area was already known as Maharashtra. The king was a powerful monarch with strong military inclinations who boasted of his arms. The people of the country preferred death to disloyalty, and the king, being of the warrior caste by birth, loved the military arts. Xuanzang's biographer related that whenever "generals went to fight with his enemies and were defeated in battle, they were not inflicted with any punishment, but were simply ordered to wear women's dress in order to humiliate them."[20] Many of them committed suicide. Like King Harsha, King Pulakesin kept several hundred wild elephants to which, as the time of battle approached, he gave much wine to drink; then they routed the enemy. Relying on military strength and discipline as well, he held his enemies' kingdoms in contempt. Xuanzang wrote:

> The king in consequence of his possessing these men and elephants, treats his neighbors with contempt. He is of the Kshattriya caste, and his name is Pulakesi.... His plans and undertakings are wide-spread, and his beneficent actions are felt over a great distance. His subjects obey him with perfect submission. At the present time Siladitya Maharaja [King Harsha] has conquered the nations from east to west, and carried his arms to remote districts, but the people of this country alone have not submitted arms to him.[21]

Xuanzang's description of these warlike characteristics of the people of Maharashtra reflects their reputation even in British imperial times; they were the last to submit to colonial rule.

Although the Calukya dynasty was Hindu, there were one hundred Buddhist monasteries in the kingdom. What is of greatest interest is Xuanzang's description of one of them:

> In the east of this country was a mountain range, ridges one above another in succession, tiers of peaks and sheer summits. Here was a monastery the base of which was in a dark defile, and its lofty halls and deep chambers were quarried in the cliff and rested on the peak, its tiers of halls and storeyed terraces had the cliff on their back and faced the ravine.... Within the establishment... was a large temple above 100 feet high in which was a stone image of the Buddha above seventy feet high; the image was surmounted by a tier of seven canopies unattached and unsupported. ... The walls of this temple had depicted on them the incidents of the Buddha's career as Bodhisattva, including the circumstances of his obtaining bodhi and the omens attending his final passing away, all great and small were here delineated.[22]

Xuanzang captured the monumentality of the monastery. He mentioned that the logician Dignaga "stayed much in this place"—surely a special attraction for him. This monastery has been identified with the magnificent caves of Ajanta and its famous rock temples. Huili did not mention Ajanta, although the distance and direction of the pilgrim's next journey support the claim that he did indeed visit Ajanta and see the splendid wall paintings there. The setting is dramatic, with spectacular cliffs sheering down to an emerald pool, an enchanting waterfall spilling into it at one end. Thirty rock-hewn caves were cut into the scarp of a horseshoe-shaped cliff (Fig. 8.2).

Like the monasteries on the Chinese Silk Road oases, the Indian monks' retreats were usually located near ancient trade routes. Because of salt marshes along the coast, these routes passed from the western seaports near Bombay, through the Western Ghats, which Xuanzang described, to the inland center of Ujjaini (Ujjain) or to Bharukaccha (Broach) on the coast. Xuanzang undoubtedly followed such a trade route when he went from Ajanta in Maharashtra to Broach (Map 8.2).

During the summer of 641 C.E. at Nasik, he might have visited the rock-cut caves of Bhaja to the south (Fig. 8.3), or stood in Ajanta's pillared hall, where religious ceremonies or meetings of the Sangha were held, or worshipped at a sanctuary with a stupa or a solid figure of the Buddha at one end. Or perhaps he stopped before the majesty of a painting known as "the Bodhisattva of the Blue Lotus." If indeed he viewed the perfect peace and tranquillity of this face, he would have been part of an endless stream of pilgrims throughout the centuries who have done so (Fig. 8.4).

Farther north, Xuanzang visited Malva, a cultured and civilized part of India, which he compared with Magadha. He said that there were several hundred monasteries and more than twenty thousand Hinayana Buddhists, by far the largest number he mentioned. "Their language is elegant and clear," he told us. "Their learning is wide and profound." In the fifth century, Malva was the home of Kalidasa, perhaps the greatest of the Sanskrit poets.

Xuanzang was on his way to the Kathiawar Peninsula. There he found more traders than farmers; then as now, the people of the kingdom of Valabhi on the peninsula lived on trade with the Persian Gulf. In one of the west coast seaports he learned about Persia, then on the eve of the fall of the Sassanid Empire. Xuanzang reported:

> They draw the water up to irrigate their fields. The people are rich and affluent. The country produces gold, silver, copper, rock crystal . . . rare pearls, and various precious substances. Their artists know how to weave fine brocaded silks, woollen stuffs, carpets and so on. They have many *shen* horses and camels. . . . There are two or three *sangharamas* [monasteries] with several hundred priests, who principally study the teaching of the Little Vehicle.[23]

He also learned about Hormuz, a city on the Persian Gulf, and an island to the southwest called the Land of the Western Women.[24]

At this point, the pilgrim's travels become more difficult to follow. His own account and that of his biographer diverge.[25] He traveled

FIGURE 8.2
Ajanta Cave #1: Interior shrine door and large Buddha image. The cave (late fifth century C.E.), one of the most famous of the more than thirty rock-cut Hinayana and Mahayana caves at Ajanta, may have been visited by Xuanzang. (Photo by Walter Spink, Archives of Asian Art, University of Michigan, Ann Arbor)

Philosophers, Rock-Cut Caves & a Fortune-Teller 141

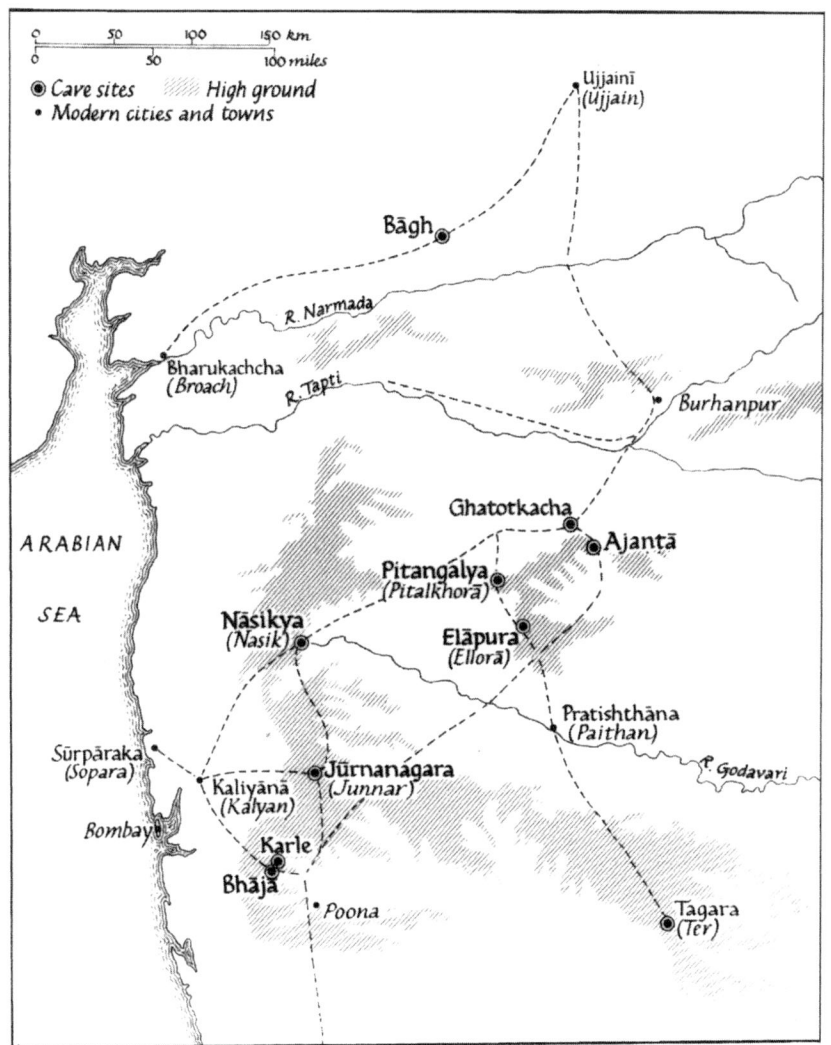

MAP 8.2
Archaeological Survey of India map of trade routes and sites of major rock-cut caves, including Ajanta and Bhaja. Monks often located their retreats near ancient trade routes, which passed from the western seaports to the inland centers. (Courtesy Archaeological Survey of India)

around northern India and through Sindh, in what is now Pakistan. Multan, in the country of Morasampuru, is the only place he mentioned that we can distinguish with certainty. The people there sacrificed to the gods and worshipped the Sun God, Surya. Xuanzang visited

FIGURE 8.3
Exterior view and entrance to the sanctuary of the ancient rock-cut cave at Bhaja, dating from the late second–early first century B.C.E. Such caves, important centers of ritual and places of pilgrimage and learning, had large halls of worship. (Photo by Roy C. Craven)

the famous sun temple at Multan and described it vividly: "There is a temple dedicated to the sun, very magnificent and profusely decorated. The image of the Sun-deva is cast in yellow gold and ornamented with rare gems. Its divine insight is mysteriously manifested and its spiritual power made plain to all."[26]

Xuanzang observed that even the kings and high families of the Five Indias never failed to make offerings of gems and precious stones:

FIGURE 8.4
Painting known as the Bodhisattva of the Blue Lotus, on the wall of Cave #1 at Ajanta. The only Buddhist paintings that survive in India are at Ajanta. (Photo by Walter Spink, Archives of Asian Art, University of Michigan, Ann Arbor)

"Men from all countries come here to offer up their prayers; there are always some thousands doing so." There was also a house of mercy, which provided food, drink, and medicines for the poor and sick.[27]

Perhaps Xuanzang remembered seeing the portrayals of the Sun God at Bodh Gaya and Bamiyan. There were several important temples dedicated to Surya worship in northwest India. "Even in primitive Buddhism, Sakyamuni [the Historical Buddha] had come to be identified with the sun-god, and his nativity likened to the rising of another sun."[28]

The Sun God statue and temple at Multan, as Xuanzang reported, were surrounded by ponds and flowery groves of trees, tastefully arranged tiles, surrounding steps, all of which inspired feelings of admiration. Such an oasis does not accord with the popular Persian rhyme about Multan:

> *With four things rare Multan abounds,*
> *Dust, beggars, heat and burial grounds.*[29]

Staying at Nalanda Monastery Again

Xuanzang remained for two months at Parvata, in the region of the Jamur River, 700 li northwest of Multan, before returning to Nalanda in 642 C.E. for his second visit there. After paying his respects to his teacher, the Venerable Silabhadra at Nalanda, he went a short distance away from the monastery to study for two months with a philosopher who was an authority on grammar and logic. Then he went on to study with the distinguished scholar and eccentric named Jayasena, who had his own school of wisdom. Xuanzang was becoming well versed in the hidden meanings of various schools of Buddhism, though there were many difficulties in the rich, speculative commentaries of each; Buddhist philosophy had become one of the best developed systems of Indian thought.[30]

Xuanzang studied the *Lankavatara Sutra*, a verse compendium of Idealist philosophy, with Jayasena. He stayed several months with him trying to solve some of the ambiguous parts of the *Treatises on the Stages of Yoga Practice*, a work that he knew well; this scripture was the very text that had lured him to India in the first place. He struggled over passages of a work in logic having to do with methods of refutation and argumentation. He kept asking for explanations of passages that *yet caused him doubt.*[31] Did he, like the French philosopher Abelard in the twelfth century, regard healthy skepticism as the key to knowledge and understanding? What was the nature of his doubts?

Philosophers, Rock-Cut Caves & a Fortune-Teller

Even after twenty years of study, he wasn't sure of some of the ideas and interpretations he encountered on his Indian travels.

Yet his fundamental character seems to suggest someone with a well-defined goal, a set of principles. It may be that when the young Xuanzang journeyed forth from China he was inspired by the Buddhist Ideal, as expressed in one of the Wisdom Sutras. After urging that the true pilgrim should not think about food, sleep, fatigue, cold, heat, it advises being completely detached in the human sphere. Finally it goes to the heart of Buddhist doctrine:

> Assert no dualistic notions as to subject and object, inner and outer, etc.; while walking along, do not turn either side, left or right; do not think of the points of the compass, front or behind, above or below; do not be disturbed with thy form (*rupa*), sensation (*vedana*), thought (*samjna*), conformation (*sanskara*) and consciousness (*vijana*). Why? Because he who is disturbed in these walks into birth-and-death, and not into the Buddhist life and will never attain Prajnaparamita [True Wisdom].[32]

While he was at Jayasena's hermitage, Xuanzang had an ominous dream. He saw the cells of Nalanda deserted and filthy, and when he looked more closely, they seemed to be inhabited by water buffalo. Then he beheld the Bodhisattva of Wisdom, Manjusri, who showed him a fierce fire burning through all the villages and towns outside the monastery. Manjusri said to him: "You should return soon, for after ten years, King Harsha will be dead and India will be laid waste. Remember what I have said."

In fact, King Harsha died in 647 C.E., even sooner than had been foretold. India, however, suffered famine and disorder, as the dream predicted. For a period of five or six hundred years there was obscurity, confusion, and disintegration. Apparently the death of King Harsha "loosened the ties which held the empire together."[33]

In 642 C.E. Xuanzang returned once more to Nalanda Monastery. This time he lectured occasionally and devoted himself to writing a treatise called *On the Harmony of Principles*. In it he tried to reconcile the Idealist school, which sprang from the two great Idealists, Asanga and Vasubandhu, and the School of the Middle Way of the skeptic, Nagarjuna. He attempted to show that there was no significant difference between believing that mental happenings alone are real (idealism), and believing that the only reality is the wisdom that consists in denying all reality (Prajna school).

His return coincided with an invitation from King Harsha to send four men from Nalanda to engage in a religious debate with Hinayana believers in Orissa. Although Xuanzang was among those chosen to go, for some reason this debate was put off. Instead Xuanzang found himself engaged in a dispute with a Hindu Brahmin. This man, like Luther, who would nail his famous ninety-five theses on the doors of All Saints' Church at Wittenberg, had hung up forty-four propositions on the monastery gates of Nalanda, declaring that if anyone could refute a single one of the propositions, the supporter would be willing to forfeit his head!

Xuanzang took up the challenge. Before he dealt with the Brahmin, he criticized the adherents of the Samkhya and Vaiseshika systems of Hindu philosophy, two of the most famous rival schools of the day. After addressing the arguments of the adherents of those schools, he reproved them for the variety of Hindu ascetics, saying that the man whose body was smeared all over with ashes looked just like a cat who had slept in a chimney corner; that the man wearing only a chaplet of skulls reminded him of a vampire in a graveyard; and that the man belonging to a sect whose members smeared themselves with dung and ate human excrement "stank like a pig in a cesspool." He asked, "How can you Hindus regard these things as proofs of wisdom? Are they not evidences of madness and folly?"

For all his attraction to Buddhist philosophy in India, a part of Xuanzang stayed true to a belief in moderation, consistent with his Confucian upbringing. And as he began to think about going home to China, this side of Xuanzang became more evident.

In the end, Xuanzang was victorious in argument against everyone, including the Brahmin who had issued the challenge. Instead of asking him to "forfeit his head," Xuanzang first asked him to be his servant. Then he insisted that the two of them engage in many long conversations, and on the basis of these talks, he composed *The Destruction of Heresy*, refuting Hindu and Hinayana arguments. Then Xuanzang released the Brahmin, who, filled with joy, went forth to the king of Assam to tell him of the remarkable qualities of the Master of the Law. The king lost no time in dispatching a messenger bidding Xuanzang to come to his court.

Meeting with a Fortune-Teller

The end of 642 C.E. An ordinary day, a day like any other. One day before the King of Assam's messenger arrived, a naked Jain named Vajra, unexpectedly walked into Xuanzang's cell at Nalanda. Knowing that Jains are famous for their fortune-telling skills, he asked him a series of questions. "Should I return immediately? Should I stay longer in India? Will I get back safely? How much longer am I going to live?" The Jain diviner gave the kind of answers that could be construed in several ways. However, when Xuanzang told him that he had collected so many sacred images and books that he didn't know how he could carry them back to China, the fortune-teller gave him some interesting information.

> "King Harsha and King Kumara of Assam will supply you with transport," he said.
> "But I have never met either of them," objected Xuanzang. "There is no reason for either of them to do me such a kindness."
> "Do not be anxious." The diviner then told him that both kings would despatch escorts for him and that he would successfully return without accident.[34]

Xuanzang made up his mind to return to China. When the monks at Nalanda heard about it, they begged him to remain, saying that India was the place of the Buddha's birth and that the sacred traces of the Buddha were in India. What is more, China was a country of no importance, with a shallow religion. Of course the Buddhas were never born there. The people were narrow-minded and their coarseness was profound. The climate was cold there and the road dangerous. "Why do you think of going back?"

The Indian monks underestimated the deep and underlying loyalties of his nature. "The King of the Law in establishing the principles of his doctrine, designed them for universal diffusion," retorted Xuanzang, the Chinese monk. And then Xuanzang, the Chinese patriot, subject of the Tang Empire and loyal to the Emperor Taizong, launched forth: "Moreover, China is a highly civilized country where the people have a high standard of behaviour, the Emperor is sagacious, and his ministers are loyal, and the father is kind toward his son, while the son is filial toward his father. Kindness and righteousness are esteemed and the aged and wise are respected."[35]

That was pure Confucian doctrine, for Confucianism regards a benevolent social order as the highest good. This order begins with the ruler at the top, with the prince, through officials, scholars, and gentlemen, and goes down to the father of the family, each with authority over those below them, but each also with the responsibility to set a good example. "Right relationships" are carefully defined for each association, father and son, subject and ruler, husband and wife, older brother and younger brother, and so on.[36]

This benevolent order extends to the right relation to the ruler of Heaven, or the gods. Thus the Confucian patriot continued: "Their wisdom is corresponding with that of the gods. They act in accordance with the laws of nature.... They are able to enslave the birds and beasts, inspire the ghosts and spirits and employ the principles of negativity [Yin] and positivity [Yang] for the benefit of all creatures."[37]

A panegyric composed after he returned to China? Perhaps, but certainly one that might have come from Xuanzang's own lips at the very thought of returning to his homeland.

And Xuanzang reminded the monks that no less a sage than their own Vimalakirti had once asked, "Why does the sun travel over the world of men?"

"To disperse the gloom" was the answer. This also was the reason he proposed to return to his native land. To his teacher, the Venerable Silabhadra, he elaborated the reasons for his return.

> This country is the place of Buddha's birth; it is impossible not to regard it with affection; only Hiuen-Tsiang's intention in coming hither was to inquire after the great law for the benefit of his fellow creatures. Since my arrival here, you, sir, have condescended to explain (or, *recite*) the Yogacharya-bhumi-sastra, and to investigate doubtful passages. I have visited and adored the sacred vestiges of our religion, and heard the profound exposition of the different schools. My mind has been overjoyed, and my visit here, has, I protest, been of the utmost profit. I desire now to go back and translate and explain to others what I have heard, so as to cause others also to be equally grateful to you, with myself, in hearing and understanding these things; and for this reason I am unwilling to delay my return and remain here.[38]

Xuanzang began to gather up his books, his statues, his manuscripts, preparatory to his return. Two days later the king of Assam's messenger appeared. With his arrival began the dramatic finale of Xuanzang's stay in India.

NINE

THE JOURNEY HOME TO CHINA

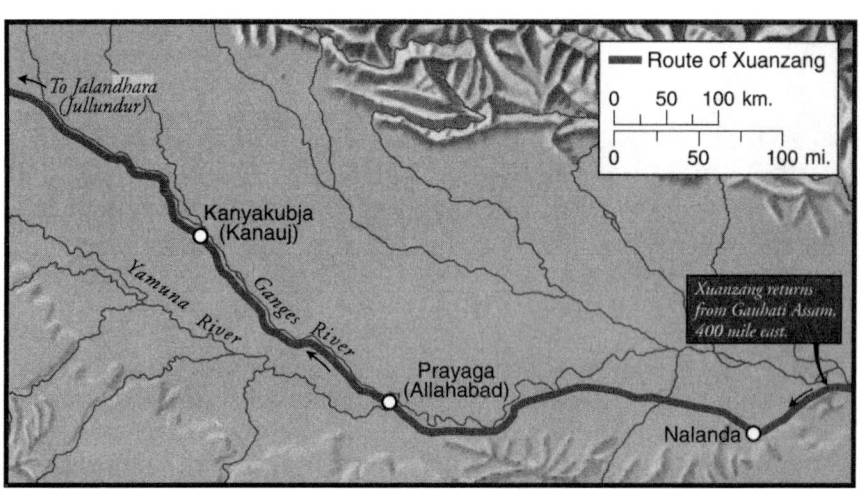

MAP 9.1
Itinerary of Xuanzang from India to western China (Nalanda to Jalandhara) (Philip Schwartzberg, Meridian Mapping)

THE SCENE OF XUANZANG'S greatest triumph in debate took place at the capital of King Harsha, on the Ganges River, in the twelfth month, 642 C.E. The pilgrim was at the height of his powers; he had consorted with kings, with the Great Khan, and with eminent Buddhist leaders. He had spent twelve or thirteen years crisscrossing the Indian continent, becoming one of the greatest metaphysicians of medieval Buddhism.

Meeting King Harsha

At age forty he would have the heady experience of being sought out and even quarreled over by both the king of Assam and King Harsha, who was the last of the great Buddhist rulers before the triumph of Hinduism and the invasion of Islam.

Just as the fortune-teller had foretold, a messenger from the king of Assam arrived with an invitation to visit his capital, Gauhati, 400 miles east of Nalanda. Xuanzang, having already promised King Harsha that he would visit his court at some future date, was uncertain about what to do. In the end he spent two months with the king of Assam, who not only received him with honors but became, even although he was Hindu, a lay member of the Buddhist community. For the king's benefit, Xuanzang composed the third of the treatises that he wrote in India, a work on the *Three Persons of the Buddha:* the Phantom Buddha, who seemed to lead an earthly existence; the Social Buddha, who communicated with the Bodhisattvas; and the Transcendental Buddha.[1]

King Harsha, having returned in the interim from a military expedition in Orissa, heard that the Chinese pilgrim was with the king of Assam. He demanded that Xuanzang return at once. After a rather foolish display of bravado, the vassal king of Assam complied. He equipped a grand river flotilla and made his way with his Chinese guest to the capital of King Harsha on the Ganges River.

In a dramatic middle-of-the-night rendezvous (presumably the king could not wait until morning), several hundred men played golden drums by the light of flaming torches. As the king marched, he was always accompanied by drummers who "beat one stroke of the drum for every step taken"; no other king was permitted to march with drums keeping time to his gait. King Harsha came to Xuanzang's pavilion, bowed at his feet, scattered flowers, and recited long verses praising him.

Such was the respect paid to religious leaders in India. Such also was King Harsha's reaching out to Xuanzang and to Mahayana Buddhism. Like many a ruling monarch, he had a conscious policy of evenhandedness toward the ardently competing religions of his kingdom. He engaged publicly in the sun worship of his father, sacrificed to the Hindu god Siva, and supported Buddhist endeavors. When he began to favor Xuanzang and lose sight of this balancing of many religions, the consequences were serious and nearly cost him his life.

King Harsha placed a high value on talented men in his kingdom, according to Xuanzang, often leading them "to the lion throne," or highest place of honor, and listening to what they had to say. The king himself was both a poet and a dramatist. One of the luminaries of his court had been the illustrious Hindu poet named Bana, who subsequently wrote about him in a famous Sanskrit poem. King Harsha was continually rewarding "the learned, the clever and the pious."[2]

For this patron of learning, Xuanzang had an additional exotic attraction—he was from far away, specifically from China. King Harsha, perhaps from political motives and prestige, as well as from general curiosity, had established diplomatic relations with China a year before Xuanzang's visit. Drawing on this experience, King Harsha said, "You come from China, and I have heard you have a musical composition called the 'Triumph of the Prince of Chin' [Qin] in your country. I do not know who this Prince of Chin is and what meritorious deeds he has done to earn such praises for himself."[3]

Xuanzang replied in an unusual passage. Normally it was only his biographer who recorded his personal reactions. This time he included his own reply to King Harsha in his *Record of the Western Regions* for the emperor. He explained to King Harsha that his emperor had been the Prince of Qin and the people had composed this song and dance to celebrate his victory in 620 C.E. over the last opponents of the Tang dynasty. Then Xuanzang used the opportunity to deliver in high-flown Chinese a eulogy of his emperor.

> At that time the whole country was in a condition of complete tumult without a lord to rule over the people. Human corpses piled high in the wild fields and human blood flowed in the rivers. Evil stars appeared in the sky at night and an ominous atmosphere condensed during the day. The three rivers were suffering under avaricious pigs and the four seas were troubled by poisonous snakes. Being a son of the emperor, the prince led his troops personally and suppressed the rebellious forces, in compliance with the order of Heaven. With his military power he established peace in the whole country and restored tranquillity in the universe, making the sun, the moon and the stars shine brightly again. As people in the whole country felt grateful to him, they composed music in praise of him.[4]

The Journey Home to China

At their next meeting at King Harsha's palace, the king was eager to see *The Destruction of Heresy*, a treatise Xuanzang had composed at Nalanda. After examining this polemic against the opponents of Mahayana Buddhism, both Hinayana and Hindu, the king addressed his court: "I have heard that when the sun rises in its splendour, the light of the glow-worm is eclipsed, and when the sound of heaven's thunder is heard, then the noise of the hammer and chisel is silenced, so with regard to the doctrine which the Master defends, all the others have been destroyed."[5]

King Harsha was so impressed that he proposed a grand tournament at Kanyakubja, to which he invited the disciples of all religious schools. Xuanzang had participated in a five-day religious debate called by the king of Kapisa many years before, but that was on a small scale compared to this one.

Debating in the Grand Tournament

642 C.E. Twelfth month. Kanyakubja. Hour after hour of waiting. Xuanzang watches the kings of eighteen vassal kingdoms, three thousand Buddhist monks, three thousand Hindus and Jains gather. Some of the visitors arrive on elephants, others in chariots, some are carried in palanquins, many are surrounded by parasols and standards, and all the celebrated visitors are accompanied by a retinue of servants. King Harsha and the king of Assam lead the procession. A huge, elaborately caparisoned elephant carries a golden image of the Buddha on its back. King Harsha, dressed as the god Indra and holding a white fly whisk, walks on the right of the image, and the king of Assam, disguised as Brahma and holding a parasol, is on its left.

Monks chant holy verses. Flowers are scattered in the path of the holy procession. In front of and behind the statue one hundred elephants carry musicians beating drums. Xuanzang and the king's chaplains also ride on elephants, followed by vassal kings and distinguished visitors. King Harsha places the golden Buddha image on a jewel-encrusted throne. This celebration of "more than oriental splendor" takes place on a mile-long ride from the king's palace to the place of the Great Debate. As a grand climax King Harsha provides a sumptuous banquet and makes offerings of gold, robes, and other valuables to the Buddha image and gives presents to all the monks. Only then is the Buddhist Master of the Law permitted to speak. Xuanzang explains in a voice that is clear and forceful, and in language elegant and harmonious, his treatise on the superiority of Mahayana Buddhism. He deports himself gravely and is as handsome as a figure in a painting.[6]

The drama intensified. During the five-day meeting, their theological battlefield became a bloody one. Xuanzang's opponents were seething with rage and made threats on his life. When the king heard of their vicious intent, he issued a proclamation that anyone daring to harm the monk would be beheaded, and anyone insulting him would have his tongue cut out. As no one dared to refute Xuanzang's teaching during the eighteen-day period in which challenges were entertained, the king declared him winner of the debate and arranged a triumphal procession to celebrate his victory.

Xuanzang recorded in his account that the Buddha shrine was set on fire. The fire was extinguished, but the irate Brahmins went even further in their fury: They hired a man to kill King Harsha. The brave monarch was able to subdue the assassin and hand him over to his officers. The political wisdom that King Harsha had until then shown in encouraging all major religions had been violated this time, and the consequences were immediate.

Xuanzang, too, was in a difficult position. He was becoming closer and closer to the king, who was attracted to him and to Mahayana Buddhism. Although Xuanzang had experience with many monarchs by this time, he must have reminded himself of the injunction in the Buddhist Wisdom Sutras: "Be done away with flattery; cherish no self-conceit, or arrogance; free thyself from the idea of being, from the desire of making a name, of amassing wealth; free thyself from the five hindrances, from envy."[7]

Many years later Xuanzang acknowledged in a letter to one of his opponents: "As one of us expounded the tenets of the Mahayana school, the other advocated the aims of the Hinayana. In the course of debate, our arguments unavoidably got heated. In order to defend the truth there was scant regard for personal feelings. Thus, there were clashes. But, as soon as the debate was over, we did not take each other amiss."[8]

Xuanzang was longing to begin his journey home, but King Harsha insisted on taking him to Prayaga, modern Allahabad, where the king was about to celebrate his sixth Quinquennial Almsgiving. The king gave away all his possessions with the exception of his war horses, war elephants, and so forth. Rare jewels, precious stuffs, and special foods were offered first to the Buddha, next to the Sun God, then to the Hindu god Siva, on down the line to ten thousand monks, to the Brahmins, the Jains, and last of all, to the poor and orphans. At the end, the king—like Prince Visvantara of the Buddha legend, who donated his possessions and his family to charity—also gave away all his jewels and his outer garments until he was obliged to cover himself with tattered rags.

Then came the turn of his eighteen vassal kings to go from one beneficiary to another and ransom back the king's gifts. Xuanzang had encountered this curious ceremony before at Bamiyan; what was perhaps different this time was that it took place at a site that was especially holy for Hindus, at Prayaga on "the field of charity."

Starting His Journey Back to China

When the almsgiving was over, Xuanzang sought permission to depart. Both kings tried to detain him on one pretext or another. Finally Xuanzang was desperate. In order to emphasize the urgency of his mission, he quoted the scriptures: "whoever hinders men from receiving a knowledge of religion shall, for generation after generation, be born blind."[9]

In April 643 C.E., the kings finally agreed to his departure, and Xuanzang was given a north Indian king's military escort to carry his precious books and images on horseback, and one of King Harsha's best elephants to ride. This elephant was of unusual size, capable of carrying eight men in his howdah as well as the 3,000 gold pieces and 10,000 pieces of silver given to Xuanzang to defray his expenses along the way. The elephant's appetite was also prodigious, for he could consume forty bundles of hay and twenty buns in two days. People could remember no other example of an elephant being given to a monk.

Three days later, as Xuanzang's procession was making its way, the two kings and their horses came galloping up like happy schoolboys to Xuanzang's caravan. They presented him with letters bearing impressive red seals, letters that commanded the rulers of the countries through which the pilgrim would pass to furnish him with escorts in relay. As far as it lay within his powers, King Harsha tendered his help to the western borders of China. Only four years later, this remarkable, versatile monarch was gone; for the next three centuries there would be chaos in northern India.

Losing Scriptures in the Indus River

Having decided not to return by sea, Xuanzang and his party turned to the northwest. They stopped in the rainy season of 643 C.E. at a monastery north of Kanyakubja. Then they crossed northern India by way of Jalandhara and Taxila, returning in the opposite direction by roughly the same route Xuanzang had taken thirteen years before (Map 9.2).

Xuanzang's caravan had been joined at Jalandhara by one hundred priests also carrying scriptures and images, who were glad to have the

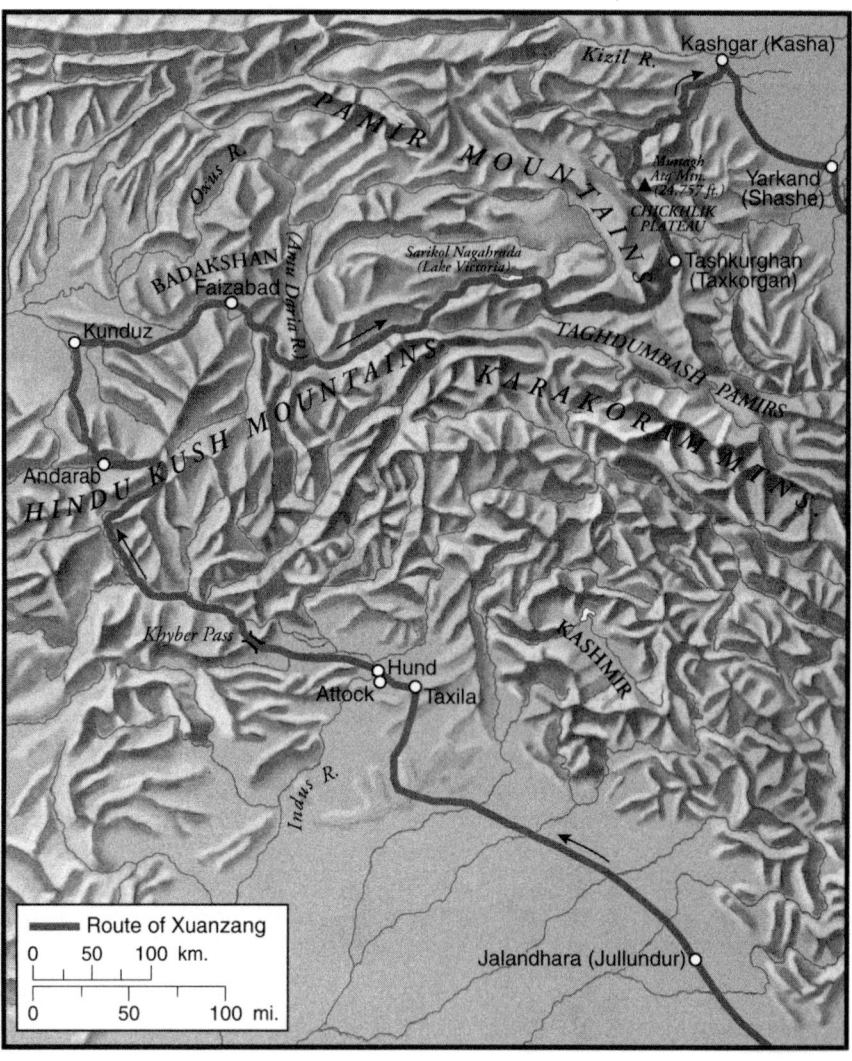

MAP 9.2
Itinerary of Xuanzang from India to western China (Jalandhara to Kashgar) (Philip Schwartzberg, Meridian Mapping)

protection of numbers as they made their way through robber-infested passes. Xuanzang took the precaution of sending a monk ahead of the caravan who was instructed to say if he was stopped: "We have traveled a great distance to see the Law. Our baggage contains only Scriptures, images and holy relics. We pray you to protect us and do not do us violence."[10] By this time their loads of Buddhist manuscripts must

The Journey Home to China

have been substantial, but apparently this declaration worked, for the many bandits they met did them no harm.

> *644 C.E. The beginning of the year. Having traveled roughly 900 miles from Prayaga, Xuanzang is finally at Hund, ready to cross the Indus River. He pauses astride his magnificent elephant before he makes the dangerous crossing. The rest of his retinue are in boats piled high with scriptures, relics, statues, and rare flower seeds that he had gathered from the four corners of India. But then a terrible calamity occurs; a storm springs up while they are in the middle of the mile-wide Indus River, shaking the boats and nearly overturning them. The guardian of the scriptures and flower seeds falls overboard and has to be rescued. Fifty of his precious manuscripts and all his seeds fall in the water.*
>
> *The king of Kapisa is nearby at the time of the catastrophe. When he comes to meet Xuanzang, his very first question is, "Did you not bring with you any Indian flower seeds? That is the sole reason," the king explains, "for the storm that damaged the boat. It has been so from the days of old until now. Whoever attempts to cross the river with the seeds of flowers is subject to similar misfortunes."*[11]

Xuanzang sent to Udyana for fresh copies of these scriptures and waited for nearly two months for their arrival at the king of Kapisa's winter capital, at Hund, north of Attock. The king of Kashmir also came to pay homage and to visit with Xuanzang. Their interest could be explained on political as well as religious grounds; they were seeking the help of the Chinese court to defend them from the perceived menace of possible enemies.

Crossing the Hindu Kush and Pamir Ranges

The king of Kapisa personally escorted Xuanzang as far as the Hindu Kush mountains and then provided him with a guide and the one hundred porters needed to transport provisions, including hay for the elephant. Like Hannibal's crossing of the Alps with his elephants and baggage train, their crossing in July 644 C.E. of Kawak Pass proved to be far more difficult than they had imagined. Most of the porters seem to have given up before they reached the pass, which we know to be 13,200 feet in height. Xuanzang's biographer said that the caravan at this point consisted of only seven priests, twenty followers, one elephant, ten asses, and four horses. But let Xuanzang tell it:

This mountain pass is very high; the precipices are wild and dangerous; the path is tortuous, and the caverns and hollows wind and intertwine together. At one time the traveller enters a deep valley, at another he mounts a high peak which in full summer is blocked with frozen ice. By cutting steps up the ice the traveller passes on, and after three days he comes to the highest point of the pass. [Apparently the weather was also against them for he went on to say:] There the icy wind, intensely cold, blows with fury; the piled snow fills the valleys. Travellers pushing their way through, dare not pause on their route. The very birds that fly in their wheeling flight cannot mount alone at this point but go afoot across the height and then fly downwards. Looking at the mountains round, they seem as little hillocks. This is the highest peak of all.[12]

Struggling on for three days more, they finally descended the pass and came to Andarab, where there were three small monasteries. Here they rested five days before pushing on to Kunduz, on the banks of the Oxus River. Xuanzang had stayed at Kunduz before, at the time of a family intrigue and palace tragedy. Nothing happened this time. Xuanzang and his party rested again, this time for a month, waiting for copies of some of the important scriptures that he had lost in the Indus River. With an escort provided by the ruler of Kunduz, and in the company of some merchants, Xuanzang's entourage departed.

Instead of returning the way he had come to India on the northern caravan road to Samarkand, he would ascend the upper reaches of the Oxus River, going over the Pamirs to Kashgar.[13] This was the route followed later by Marco Polo on his way to China, in 1271 C.E. From Kashgar Xuanzang would be traveling on the Southern Silk Road, which would take him to Yarkand and Khotan, eastward along the southern edge of the Taklamakan Desert to Dunhuang, at the juncture of the Northern and Southern Silk Roads.

In the upper reaches of the Oxus River, the caravan came upon a settlement of White Huns who had been driven to take refuge in this wild terrain. Xuanzang told about their strange customs.[14] About 40 miles farther on, Xuanzang and his caravan halted for a month near Faizabad, in the kingdom of Badakhshan, because the passes of the Pamirs were blocked with heavy snow. The area was famous for its horses, lapis lazuli, and ruby mines. There were three or four Buddhist monasteries and a number of monks in this remote outpost.

Still heading east, Xuanzang and his company walked about 200 miles up this bleak, trackless, and nearly inaccessible Penj Valley. On some of the makeshift bridges along the river, they felt as if they were "a tear on an eyelash," to use a Russian writer's words.[15] They passed by scrabbly collections of mud and stone huts until they came to the Pamir ranges. These upland plains, he explained, were situated among the snowy mountains, and "on this account the climate was cold and the winds blew constantly." Here, at the height of 13,526 feet, they reached the banks of the Great Dragon Lake, which was rediscovered by John Woods in 1838 and renamed Lake Victoria.

The Journey Home to China

With his unerring eye, Xuanzang noted the huge size of the lake, 200 *li* from east to west and 50 *li* from north to south, and the water's dark blue color, fresh taste, and clarity.[16] Xuanzang remarked on the aquatic monsters that lived in its depths, the frogs of an infinite variety, and some birds about 10 feet high, with eggs as large as a water pitcher. He even conjectured that they might have been ostriches. Fantastic as this may seem, the *Encyclopedia Britannica* of 1911 mentions the possibility of there having been ostriches in the lower Oxus.[17]

But for the swelling rivers, which made traveling with heavily laden animals impossible, Xuanzang might have crossed at Wakhjir Pass at 16,880 feet! This is the Great Divide of Central Asia. The Taghdumbash Pamirs are the source of the Oxus River, which drains 1,000 miles to the west, ending up in the Aral Sea, and of the Yarkand River, which sweeps down hundreds of miles to the east into the Taklamakan Desert, in China. He probably went by the Great Pamir Road at another pass.[18] In any event, Marco Polo called this mountain mass, this amphitheater of high peaks, the Roof of the World, for the ranges of the Hindu Kush, crossing modern-day Afghanistan, the Karakorum in northern Pakistan, the Pamirs in Afghanistan and Tajikistan, and the Tian Shan range in China all meet in the Pamir knot (Fig. 9.1).

FIGURE 9.1
View of the Pamirs, which Xuanzang crossed in order to go from Afghanistan to Kashgar. (Neg./Trans. No. 2A. 17278. Morden Clark Expedition. Courtesy Department of Library Services, American Museum of Natural History.)

Stopping at the Kashgar Oasis

Xuanzang rested from his arduous climbing for a month at Tashkurghan, where the Sarikol people lived. He was impressed with the king, whom he described as being upright and honest and as one who greatly honored Buddhism. In the old palace was a monastery associated with the monk Kumarajiva, one of the great translators of Mahayana Buddhism. Xuanzang had been to Kumarajiva's birthplace at Kucha on his way to India.

At Tashkurghan he saw the ruins of a famous fortress called the Maiden's Castle and heard its fantastic legend. A Chinese princess of the Han dynasty had been betrothed to the king of Persia and was being escorted to his capital. At Tashkurghan the way was blocked by robbers, so her escort placed her on an isolated peak protected by rock precipices. "When tranquillity was restored, and the journey was to be continued, the king's envoy in charge of the bride discovered that she was *enceinte*. On making enquiry he found that the sun-deva had visited the lady every day at noon, and that it was by him that she was with child."[19]

The people of Tashkurghan were so impressed that they begged her to remain and to rule over them; the chiefs ruling this region were supposed to have sprung from her miraculously born son. Stein assured the reader that the fort on the west side of the Tashkurghan River was the site visited by Xuanzang.[20]

Robbers also attacked Xuanzang's caravan as they went from Tashkurghan to Kashgar, making their way through a narrow gorge between high overhanging rock walls. A robber band came swooping down this treacherous defile; Xuanzang's merchant companions took fright and bolted up the mountain. The mighty elephant from King Harsha stampeded. The robbers pursued the frightened elephant until he plunged into the river and drowned. Stein surmised that Xuanzang lost his elephant in the Tangitar Gorge below Tar Bashi (Fig. 9.2).

At the time Xuanzang was following the track that went across the desolate Chickiklik high plateau, passing by the western slopes of the massive, white dome of Muztagh-Ata.[21] The second-highest peak in the Pamirs, Muztagh-Ata is 24,388 feet in elevation: "A mountain," said Xuanzang, "the vapors of which soaring up, and coming into contact with the rocks, raised clouds; its sheer cliffs of imposing height seemed on the verge of crashing down. On the summit of this mountain was a magnificent tope [stupa]."[22] He reported that it had been built in memory of an *arhat* who, according to the legend, had lived in a trance since the time of the Lord Buddha.

Xuanzang seems to have reached Kashgar by way of the River Gez, a tributary of the Kizil (Qizil) River. His first impression of the approach

The Journey Home to China

FIGURE 9.2
Tangitar gorge, which Aurel Stein suggested was the narrow defile where Xuanzang's Indian elephant was chased by bandits, fell into the river, and drowned. Source: Aurel Stein, Serendia, vol. 1 (Oxford: Clarendon Press, 1921), Plate 29. (By permission of The British Library)

to China's westernmost oasis was of many sand heaps and little fertile soil. Commenting on the oasis itself, he said that "it yielded good crops and a luxuriance of fruit and flowers." How inviting the orchards, the city walls, the winding lanes, and the mud-brick walls of houses must have been! After the bleak and thinly populated Pamirs, how heart-warming the sight of streams of people coming and going, ponies and donkeys laden with goods, heralding an important trade center. Xuanzang went to the famous bazaar at Kashgar: "One gets from this country felt and cloth of excellent quality as well as fine woolen materials. Moreover, the inhabitants are clever at weaving various kinds of fine, fleecy carpets." Xuanzang also remarked that the people had green eyes, suggesting the Sogdian or East Iranian origin of some of the population.[23]

In Kashgar there were hundreds of Buddhist monasteries, with more than one thousand monks, most of whom were of a Realist Hinayana school. Remains of two Buddhist sites near Kashgar still exist. The first, the Cave of Three Immortals, dating from the second century, is hewn from the cliffs of the Quiakmakh River. It now stands 30 feet high above the riverbed. It has two chambers; traces of wall paintings survive in the left chamber. The second site, the ancient village of Hanoi, had been a thriving Buddhist settlement in Tang times. Xuanzang is believed to have visited the Mauri-tim stupa there (Fig. 9.3). Xuanzang did not comment on the form of government in Kashgar, but we know that in the Tang period it was under Chinese administration and the military governor was a Chinese official (Map 9.3).[24]

Waiting at the Khotan Oasis

Xuanzang's next goal was Khotan, a fortnight's journey on the caravan road. Khotan was the largest oasis on the Southern Silk Road and was at the foot of the bleak, serrated Kunlun Mountains separating China and Tibet. He halted for a few days at the flourishing oasis of Yarkand (Shache) on the way. The king of Khotan, hearing that Xuanzang was in his territory, went forth to escort him into the capital in September 644 C.E. Xuanzang stayed in a Hinayana monastery. This is puzzling, for he told us that there were one hundred monasteries and more than five thousand monks, chiefly Mahayanist.

The remains of the ancient city of Yotkan are believed to be those of Khotan. Xuanzang was clearly impressed.

> This country he describes as being above 4,000 *li* in circuit, more than half of it being sand-dunes; the cultivated land, which was very limited, yielded cereals and fruits of various kinds; the country produced rugs, fine felt, and silk of artistic texture, it also yielded white and black jade. The climate was genial, but there were whirlwinds and flying dust. The people were of gentle disposition, fond of the practical arts; they were in easy circumstances, and had settled occupations. The nation esteemed music and the people were fond of dance and song; a few clothed themselves in woollens and furs, the majority wearing silk and calico.... The system of writing had been taken from that of India.[25]

FIGURE 9.3
Mauri-tim stupa, which Xuanzang is believed to have visited in the ancient city of Hanoi, not far from Kashgar (Copyright Sally Hovey Wriggins, photographer)

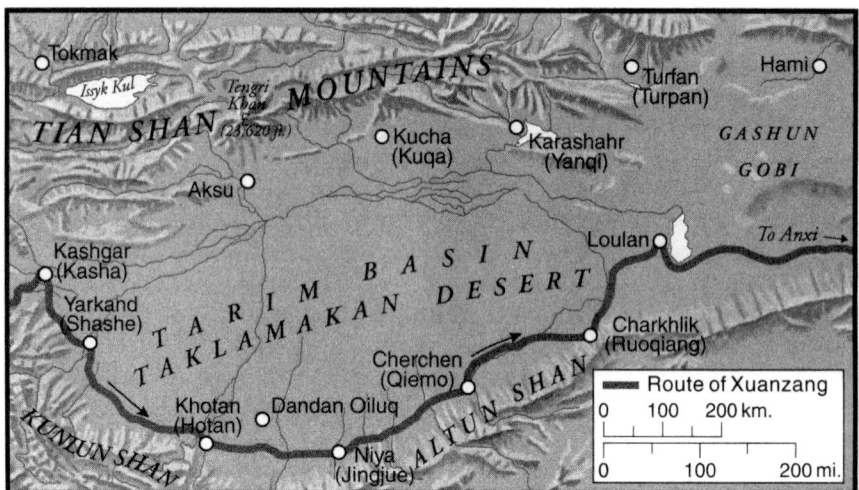

MAP 9.3
*Itinerary of Xuanzang from India to western China (Kashgar to Loulan)
(Philip Schwartzberg, Meridian Mapping)*

Southeast of the capital, Xuanzang visited a monastery that had been built to commemorate the successful introduction of silk culture from China. (At the time Khotan was an independent kingdom.) China had been jealously guarding the secret of making silk, and under imperial decree, disclosure meant death by torture. Thus many centuries passed before any knowledge of the source of this fabulous fabric spread. According to an old legend recorded by Xuanzang, in about 140 B.C.E., silkworm eggs and mulberry seeds were carried to Khotan. The king of Khotan, who married a Chinese princess, had instructed her to procure the means of making silk. She hid the silkworm eggs and mulberry seeds in her headdress. At the customs barrier the guards searched everywhere, but they did not dare to remove the headdress of the princess. Later she founded a convent, where the first silkworms were bred. Xuanzang saw the ancient mulberry trunks that were supposed to be the remains of the first trees planted (Fig. 9.4).[26]

Everywhere Xuanzang went, he found evidence of Indian influence in Khotan. The king himself claimed to be a descendant of Vaisravana, a Buddhist deity of northern India. The Khotanese ascribed their conversion to Mahayana Buddhism to Vairocana, the Indian Buddha of Tantric and Esoteric Buddhism, who had come expressly to Khotan. A monastery was built in his honor. Indian influences were also seen by Xuanzang in the local tradition that the territory of Khotan was colo-

FIGURE 9.4
A votive tablet depicting the Silk Princess's headdress, in which she hid silkworm eggs and mulberry seeds, in order to bring the secrets of silk-making from China to Khotan (Copyright British Museum)

nized by Indian immigrants from Taxila. They claimed to be descendants of the men who blinded Asoka's son Kunala, for which they were banished.[27]

Xuanzang visited the site of a splendid figure of the Buddha with a precious jeweled crown, which came from Kashmir. He saw the famous sandalwood image at Pima, outside of Khotan, which came all the way from Kausambi, in central India. This was the illustrious Udayana statue commissioned by the king of Kausambi while the Buddha was still alive.[28] How did all these statues get to Khotan? Some of them flew, and a charming legend says that a pilgrim carried a statue by day, and the statue carried the pilgrim by night.

Xuanzang spent seven or eight months in Khotan, partly because the king wished him to stay, and partly because he was still waiting for the arrival of replacement copies of some of the scriptures he had lost in the Indus River. This was the third time he waited for the replacement of the lost manuscripts; he stayed a month at Hund waiting, a month at Kunduz waiting, and now many months waiting in Khotan. That sheds light on the high value he attached to bringing a complete library of original sources back to China. He had an additional reason for lingering. Early in his stay in Khotan he found a Turfan trader who was going to the Tang capital, so Xuanzang was able to write and send a long "memorial" to the emperor advising him that the monk would be coming home.

With his lively curiosity undiminished, Xuanzang visited a number of monasteries and sacred sites in the area. Often these were "the sand-buried ruins of Khotan" near the rivers that had once flowed down from the Kunlun Mountains and then dried up; the cities were the buried sites of Dandan Oiluq, Rawak, and Niya (Jingjue), made famous by the archaeological expeditions of Aurel Stein. To the east of Khotan was a once very prosperous region that Xuanzang observed had become a dried-up old city until a Khotanese nobleman sacrificed his life by marrying the "Naga spirit of the river." Once the nobleman married this Naga, the river waters reappeared and the people could irrigate their land again.[29] The legend has been useful in interpreting a fascinating painting Stein found at Dandan Oiluq (Fig. 9.5).

West of the capital were mounds inhabited by rats. Xuanzang recounted the legend about the origin of the worship paid to these rodents. A rat-headed divinity in another painting from Dandan Oiluq had puzzled knowledgeable British Museum curators until Stein recalled Xuanzang's story of how sacred rats and their Rat King, by destroying the horses' harnesses of an invading Hun host, had caused its defeat and thus saved the land.[30] Herodotus told a similar story in which the overwhelming threat of an invasion by the Egyptian army was stopped by mice who gnawed away so much of the enemy's paraphernalia that they were rendered helpless.

In between his explorations in and around Khotan, Xuanzang engaged in a kind of teaching marathon. During one 24-hour period he lectured to the king and his people on his old favorites, the *Treatise on the Stages of Yoga Practice* and the *Treasury of Buddhist Philosophy*, written by Vasubandhu while he was still a Realist of the Hinayana school, and a famous compendium of Mahayana philosophy translated by Paramartha in 563 C.E., all of which Xuanzang had studied years before when he was yet a very young monk in Chengdu. He also lectured on a fourth commentary, which Waley described as being "the one with the unimaginably long name," which the Chinese call *Abidharma*.[31]

Entering the Desert

From Khotan Xuanzang pushed on to Niya in the Taklamakan Desert.

> Going east from this, we enter a great drifting sand desert. These sands extend like a drifting flood for a great distance, piled up or scattered according to the wind. There is no trace left behind by travellers ... and oftentimes the way is lost, and so they wander hither and thither quite bewildered, without any guide or direction. So travellers pick up the bones of animals as beacons. There is neither water nor herbage to be found, and hot winds frequently blow. When these winds rise, then both men and beasts become confused and forgetful, and then they remain perfectly disabled (sick). At times sad and plaintive notes are heard and piteous cries, so that between the sights and sounds of this desert men get

The Journey Home to China

FIGURE 9.5
Painting of a curvaceous woman standing in a tank and a statue of Vaisravana. The woman is thought to be the Nagini, or water spirit. (By permission of The British Library)

confused and know not whither they go. Hence there are so many who perish in the journey. But it is all the work of demons and evil spirits."[32]

Marco Polo expressed similar beliefs, saying that if travelers lag behind their company, "they hear spirits malignant in the air, talking in a way that they seem to be their companions, for they call them sometimes by their names . . . (they) follow those voices and get out of the right way so that they are never reunited to their fellows and found . . . and in this way they know not how to return and being without food and drink, many of them are dead in the past and lost." Sometimes they hear "many instruments of music sounding in the air, and especially drums more than other instruments, and the clashing of weapons."[33]

But the stark realities of brackish water and no fodder for animals or food for human beings were daunting enough. Xuanzang's caravan, with all its precious statues and manuscripts, finally reached the present-day Cherchen (Qiemo). The desert is blasted by sand, which is blown by Force 5 winds on average 145 days of the year, bearing out Xuanzang's and Marco Polo's descriptions of the perils of desert travels.[34] Xuanzang provided us with few details of his journey to Charkhlik (Ruoqiang), the next oasis, or the desolate lands of the vast region comprising the dried-up Lake of Lop Nor, whose salt-encrusted bed was worse to walk on even than glacial ice.

Not far from the Charkhlik oasis is the astonishing archaeological site of Miran, where there are many statues and yet another portrayal of the Visvantara Jataka, the tale of the self-sacrificing prince. Xuanzang probably saw the ruined temples there. At the site Aurel Stein reflected once again on his patron saint, Xuanzang: "In a region where all is dead and waste, spiritual emanations from those who have passed by centuries ago, seem to cling much longer to the conspicuous landmarks than in parts where life is still bustling."[35]

Unfortunately Xuanzang ended the record of his travels with his arrival in the territory of Loulan, a once-powerful kingdom 1,500 li from Khotan. Evidently he considered the remaining portion of his journey home as being within the borders of the Chinese empire and hence outside the scope of his record. Huili, his biographer, included to Dunhuang, but the pilgrim ended with a few graceful sentences, which form a stylish epilogue.

> I have set forth at length national scenery and ascertained territorial divisions. I have explained the qualities of national customs and climatic characteristics. Moral conduct is not constant and tastes vary; where matters cannot be thoroughly verified one may not be dogmatic. Wherever I went I made notes, and in mentioning what I saw and heard I recorded the aspirations for [Chinese] civilization. It is a fact that from here to where the sun sets all have experienced (His Majesty's) beneficence, and where his influence reaches all admire his perfect virtue. The whole world having been united under one sway I have not been a mere individual on a political mission traveling a myriad li along a post road.[36]

Xuanzang considered this the end of his journey. He was in China now.

TEN

BACK IN CHINA

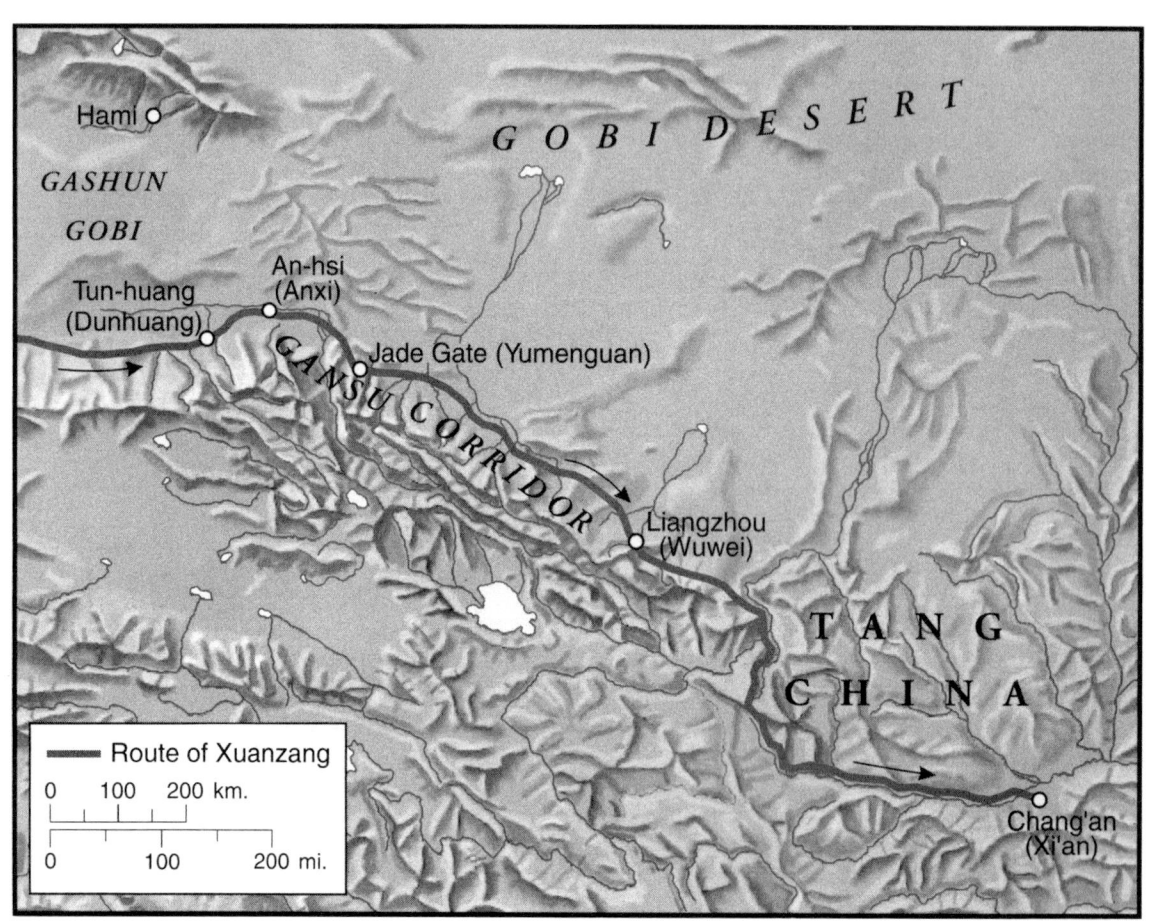

MAP 10.1
Itinerary of Xuanzang from western China back home (Loulan to Chang'an)
(Philip Schwartzberg, Meridian Mapping)

Sixteen years earlier, Xuanzang had left China with a warrant on his head; he had departed in secret by night, against the wishes of the emperor. As he drew closer to the borders of the Tang Empire on his return, he was not sure how he would be received. It might be best for him to advise the emperor that he was returning as a loyal subject. A young Turfanese traveling with a caravan of merchants to China had given him the opportunity of writing ahead to the emperor.

In his letter Xuanzang wrote of his search for Buddhist learning and of the sublime words of the scriptures. He outlined his travels across the vast plains of shifting sands, over precipitous mountains covered with snow, and along by the tumultuous waves of the hot sea.

> Thus I accomplished a journey of more than 50,000 *li*, yet, notwithstanding the thousand differences of customs and manners I have witnessed, the myriads of dangers I have encountered, by the goodness of Heaven I have returned without accident, and now offer my homage with a body unimpaired and a mind satisfied with the accomplishment of my vows. I have beheld the Ghridrakuta Mountain [Vulture Peak], worshipped at the Bodhi tree; I have seen traces not seen before; heard sacred words not heard before; witnessed spiritual prodigies, exceeding all the wonders of Nature; have borne testimony to the high qualities of our august Emperor; and won for him the high esteem and praise of the people.[1]

He concluded by saying that after the great elephant had drowned, he had not succeeded in obtaining enough horses for the library of scriptures that he had brought back, but despite this difficulty he hoped to go forward at once to visit His Majesty.

Seven or eight months elapsed. Finally a messenger returned with a reassuring reply from the emperor.

> I am highly delighted to hear that the teacher is returning home after seeking the Way in the foreign lands. You may come to see me as quickly as possible, and you may, as well bring the foreign monks who understand the Sanskrit language and the meanings of the scriptures to come with you. I have already ordered the authorities of Kustana [Khotan] and the other regions to escort you, and so you will not be in want of carriers and horses. I have also instructed the officials of Tunhuang [Dunhuang] to receive you at the Desert, as well as those of Shanshan [Charkhlik] to receive you at Chemo [Cherchen].[2]

Resting at the Dunhuang Oasis

Shortly after he received the emperor's letter, Xuanzang departed from Khotan. The king had provided him richly with guides and equipment and help was furnished at every oasis along the way, but desert travel is always arduous and uncertain. Like many an exhausted traveler before him, Xuanzang rested at the Dunhuang oasis. He is likely to have paused before some of the fine paintings and sculpture of the impressive shrine, library, and gallery of Buddhist art at the Cave of a Thousand Buddhas. He probably saw many of the cave interiors and read some of the inscriptions of merchants who contributed funds out of gratitude for successful journeys or in the hopes that their caravans would arrive safely at their destinations. Dunhuang was the gateway to one of the oldest long-distance trade routes in history, the Silk Road, dating from the first centuries of the common era and perhaps earlier. Camel and horse caravans from India and the Turfan Basin in Central Asia in one direction, and from the Tang capital Chang'an on the other, all stopped there.

Xuanzang's record stopped at Loulan, before he reached Dunhuang, which was part of the Tang Empire. His biographer said only that Xuanzang wrote a second letter to the emperor at Dunhuang. However, a painting in Cave #103 at Dunhuang shows Xuanzang's caravan before the elephant given to him by King Harsha was drowned on the way down the Pamirs from Kashmir (Fig. 10.1); it also portrays the pilgrim giving thanks for a safe journey.[3] Several Dunhuang paintings on silk depict the prototype of the pilgrim traveler. A wonderfully suggestive example can be seen in the Musée Guimet in Paris (Fig. 10.2).

By a curious twist of fate, more than twelve centuries after he rested at Dunhuang, Xuanzang played a crucial role in a strange drama that unfolded there. Aurel Stein had heard that a vast hoard of manuscripts was sealed in one of its caves. On his second expedition (1906–1908), Stein met the ignorant and somewhat eccentric Daoist Abbot Wang, self-appointed guardian of the caves, which by the early nineteenth century had fallen into ruin. The abbot had commissioned a local artist to illustrate familiar scenes from the legendary travels of Xuanzang on a Dunhuang temple loggia. When Stein saw these portrayals, he told Abbot Wang how he had followed in the pilgrim's footsteps for 10,000 li from India to Dunhuang.

The moody abbot opened the hitherto sealed-up cave for Stein; it had been closed since the eleventh century because of marauding armies. Stacks of manuscripts were piled up to the ceiling and silk temple banners were wrapped in stout sheets of canvas. The size of this treasure trove—30,000 manuscripts and 20,000 other artifacts, including paintings on silk and paper, banners, and embroideries—was beyond belief.

Back in China

FIGURE 10.1
Wall painting at Dunhuang Cave #103 showing Xuanzang returning from India with the great white elephant given to him by King Harsha (The Lo Archive)

Many were in Chinese: Sinologist Paul Pelliot examined those when he visited the shrine in 1908, a year after Stein (Fig. 10.3).

This opening of Cave #17 alerted the world to the long-forgotten caves of Dunhuang. Not unlike Angkor Wat, which had been swallowed up by the Cambodian jungle, Dunhuang with its mile-long galleries of medieval art had been lost or ignored until Stein was allowed to enter. Later a copy of what is one of the world's earliest documented printed books, the *Diamond Sutra*, dated 868 C.E., was found inside.

FIGURE 10.2
Silk temple banner showing an itinerant monk, the prototype of the pilgrim traveler. (Musée Guimet, Paris; photo: RMN)

FIGURE 10.3
Photograph of Paul Pelliot, a French Sinologist, in Cave #17 at Dunhuang, examining by candlelight one of the thousands of manuscripts found there. Early twentieth century. (Archives Pelliott, Musée Guimet)

Triumphant Return to Chang'an

From Dunhuang Xuanzang wrote again to the Emperor Taizong and then hurried to meet him in person. Because the emperor was conducting a military expedition in the northeast, he ordered one of his lord-lieutenants to arrange for Xuanzang's reception in Chang'an. The news of the pilgrim's return soon spread, and the streets were filled to overflowing; Xuanzang was obliged to spend the night by a canal at the western outskirts of the city.

> *Seventh day of the first month in 645 C.E. Morning comes slowly. A body of high officials clears the way to bring Xuanzang to the capital. They arrange for a huge group of monks to parade his books, relics, gold, silver, and sandalwood images through Chang'an. The procession the next day begins at the Street of the Red Bird and ends at the main gate of the Monastery of Great Happiness. All the monasteries send monks and nuns in their ceremonial robes for the occasion. The people vie with one another in preparing their best banners, tapestries, umbrellas, precious tables, and carriages. When they reach the Street of the Red Bird, they march forward with the sound of pearls and jade hanging from their belts tinkling in the air, amidst golden flowers scattered on the road. Scholars and local officials line the ceremonial path.*
>
> *The authorities, fearing that people may tread on one another, order them to stay still, burn incense, and scatter flowers where they are standing. Then the whole congregation witnesses a colored cloud in the sky that seems to float over the scriptures and the gold, silver, and sandalwood images as if it is welcoming the holy objects. It is indeed "the most splendid event since the death of the Buddha."*[4]

Xuanzang was proud to donate 150 pellets of the Buddha's flesh and a box of his bone relics at the Monastery of Great Happiness. That was not all. He brought seven statues of the Buddha, among them statues as tall as 4 feet, which had been transported all the way from India. What a flood of memories must have passed through his mind as he deposited these precious likenesses!

First, there was a sandalwood image, 3 feet 5 inches tall, of the Buddha preaching his first sermon, at Sarnath, on a glittering pedestal; then another sweet-smelling sandalwood statue, 2 feet 9 inches tall, after the image commissioned by King Udayana when he was desirous of seeing the Buddha. Each statue called up the setting, the experiences, of the famous places of pilgrimage that Xuanzang had visited. The third image, which was the largest statue in his baggage train from India, was a shining silver Buddha, fully 4 feet high, in imitation of the Buddha descending from heaven at Sankasya. The fourth replica, 3 feet 5 inches high, may have been made of gold. It was the Buddha preach-

Back in China

ing the *Lotus Sutra* at Vulture Peak. Xuanzang could well remember his feelings when he had gone, like the pious Faxian before him, to pay reverence to this holy mountain. Xuanzang knew that this statue would be well received, for the *Lotus Sutra* was popular in China. To these he added a fifth image, an aromatic sandalwood statue about 15 inches high, carved in imitation of the Buddha's shadow left in the cave at Nagarahara. This was where Xuanzang himself had been vouchsafed a vision of the Buddha. It was one of the first statues he had collected on his journey. Somehow he had located a golden image 3 feet 3 inches tall from the Dragon Cave at Pragbodhi Mountain, near Magadha. This sixth replica resembled the Sarnath image of the Buddha Turning the Wheel of the Law. Finally, he deposited yet another sandalwood image of the Buddha, this one with the Buddha making his daily rounds at Vaisali, where he preached so many sermons.[5]

We know what three of these images looked like. One was the Udayana image, copies of which are believed to have been made century after century. The Udayana images were typically standing images garbed in long robes with folds arranged in a very symmetrical fashion and with the hands assuming gestures of reassurance and charity. Two of the images were copies of an image of the Buddha preaching. Pratapaditya Pal wrote that some of the images Xuanzang brought back with him must have looked very much like Fig. 10.4, the bronze of a standing Buddha from the J. D. Rockefeller collection.[6]

Xuanzang also collected 657 books with strange Indian writing either on birch bark or the trimmed leaves of palm trees strung together in layers, bound in 520 cases. These were classified as 224 Mahayanist sutras and treatises; writings from a number of Hinayanist sects that were for the most part quite unknown, and no less than 36 general works of logic and 13 works on grammar.[7] A charming silk scroll painting from Dunhuang shows twenty horses bearing these scriptures trotting into a temple with elegantly dressed priests and officials looking on. (See Color Plate 8.) Once safely home, Xuanzang's greatest wish was to translate as many of these scriptures as possible.

Being Interviewed by the Emperor

Xuanzang had two interviews with the emperor in the Palace of the Phoenix at Luoyang, the second imperial capital. Their second meeting was well documented.

> Having sat down the emperor asked: "Why did you go (to India) without telling me?"

FIGURE 10.4
Bronze image of a Sakyamuni Buddha standing with his right hand raised in the "fear not" gesture. (The Asia Society, New York, Mr. and Mrs. John D. Rockefeller 3rd Collection; photo by Lynton Gardiner)

The Master replied with apology. "When I was preparing for my journey, I had sent petitions to Your Majesty several times, but as my project was unworthy, I did not enjoy the favour of being granted with an official permission. Because of my utmost sincerity for seeking the Law, I went away privately for which offence I beg the pardon of Your Majesty."

The emperor said: "Since you are a monk, you are different from lay people in this matter. I am delighted that you went to seek for the Law at the risk of your life for the benefit of all the people. There is no need to ask my pardon."[8]

When the emperor showed astonishment that he had been able to make such a journey, Xuanzang replied in the language of diplomacy that it was the universal prestige of the new dynasty that had made it possible.

I have heard that it is not far to reach the Heavenly Lake for those who could ride on a speedy wind, and it is not difficult to cross a stormy river, if one sailed in a dragon-boat. Since Your Majesty ascended the throne to rule over the country, your virtue and benevolence prevailed in all the areas, with the wind of morality blowing to the hot countries in the south and your political influence reaching as far as beyond the Pamirs.[9]

Here Xuanzang was acknowledging the notable foreign policy successes of the emperor. He was no longer the young idealist who defied the king of Turfan; he spoke with the poise of a man who had been honored by King Harsha and who, on his journey, had consorted with the Great Khan of the Western Turks as well as with many kings and princes.

The emperor found Xuanzang full of clear information on the climate, products, rulers, customs, and history of the peoples of Central Asia and India. The emperor suggested that he write a book. "These Buddhist kingdoms," said the emperor at last, "are so far off that up until now our history books have given us very imperfect accounts of the sacred sites and the religious teachings. As you have recently seen it all for yourself, you ought to write a book containing this new information."[10] This was an unusual comment from an emperor who is usually portrayed as being anti-Buddhist because of the powerful influence of one of his Confucian advisers.

That same emperor, realizing that Xuanzang was a man of great talent who could be useful, exhorted him to become his adviser on Asian relations. Xuanzang explained that he had become a monk at an early age and had been totally absorbed in Buddhist studies: "If your Majesty orders me to return to secular life, it would be like dragging a boat from the water to the land." The emperor had been busy giving instructions to his general about launching a campaign in the northeast. He had intended to give Xuanzang a few minutes' audience, but the conversation was of such interest that the emperor's brother-in-law had to remind him that Xuanzang was staying in the official hostel and would be locked out if he didn't leave soon.

According to Huili, the emperor protested: "I have not yet said all I wish to say in our hasty conversation. I wish you to go with me to the East on my political inspection, so that I may talk with you beside my work of commanding the troops. What do you think of it?"[11]

Xuanzang tried to decline, excusing himself on grounds of fatigue. The emperor reminded him that he had been able to travel all alone in foreign countries and that this trip was but "a short distance for him."

Xuanzang protested that he would add nothing to the campaign and furthermore that monastic rules stated that a monk was forbidden to watch a military campaign: "Since this is the teaching of the Buddha, I must report it to Your Majesty. It will be good fortune for me if your Majesty will have compassion on me." The emperor took him at his word and dropped the subject.[12]

Writing the Record of the Western Regions

Xuanzang lost no time in beginning his book, *Record of the Western Regions*, which took a year to write and was completed in 646 C.E. He had brought back with him a mass of papers consisting partly of accounts of his own experiences and impersonal records of various kingdoms in India and elsewhere. Xuanzang noted that each province had its own official for preserving a record of events in writing: "Official annals and state papers, good and bad, are recorded and instances of public calamity and good fortune are set forth in detail."[13] These materials from "the above seventy kingdoms" in India must have been useful to him as he collected information for his book.[14]

It is doubtful that anyone had drawn on them in such a comprehensive way or used so many sources. No one had made fresh observations after traveling the length and breadth of India before: Xuanzang has become a major source for historians studying the India of the seventh century—before the coming of Islam.

The writing of history has been one of China's great strengths. Chinese annals dating back to the first century C.E. exist. Indeed, the greatest literary achievement of the Han dynasty (206 B.C.E. to 220 C.E.) was historical writing.[15] The Chinese have traditionally viewed human affairs in a temporal framework and have excelled at compiling detailed, fact-laden, objective histories. (In contrast to the Chinese concept of time, which is linear, the Indian concept of time is often described as cyclical.[16]) Xuanzang exhibited the Chinese pattern of historical awareness and scholarship even in his travel chronicle.

Although he was heir to this tradition, Xuanzang carried with him certain predilections reflecting his background. With his keen interest in government and administration, his early reading in Confucian classics, and his enthusiasm for Buddhism, he showed a bias in those areas.[17] However, Xuanzang was not blindly partial to Buddhist rulers or oblivious to the qualities of non-Buddhist kings.[18] It could have been just this impartiality that impressed the Emperor Taizong.

Modern historian Ainslie Embree wondered if Xuanzang found India so pleasant because it was a Buddhist country and he was trying to convince both himself and the people of China how advantageous it would be if they, too, were Buddhists. What aroused Embree's suspicions about his reliability was that when Xuanzang was traveling around northeast India, he found the climate so warm and agreeable.[19]

Other historians such as Percival Spear and Vincent Smith were grateful for the vivid records of the pious Faxian and Xuanzang. Spear expressed his gratitude that they put "flesh and blood" on the bare bones of dates, dynastic names, and official inscriptions, which are the historian's stock-in-trade for this early period.[20]

The Death of the Emperor and the Big Wild Goose Pagoda

Xuanzang continued to work diligently on his translations with an expert board of translators provided by the emperor. Among them was Huili, his biographer. Whenever possible Xuanzang used his prestige to strengthen the position of Buddhism in Tang China.[21] The emperor asked him a second time to be one of his advisers. Xuanzang again declined. This seemed to be a turning point, for the emperor suddenly expressed interest in Xuanzang's translation of his favorite, the *Treatise on the Stages of Yoga Practice*. After examining this treasure, the emperor expressed his regret that his preoccupation with political and military affairs had deprived him of a chance to study Buddhism in detail. He went further: He proclaimed Buddhism as superior to Confucianism, Daoism, and other philosophies. The emperor ordered nine copies for distribution to the nine divisions of his empire and agreed to grant an imperial preface commemorating Xuanzang's new translations.

In the last year of the emperor's life, at a time when his health was failing, he sought out Xuanzang as his spiritual guide. He often summoned him to the palace, where they spent many hours discussing Buddhism. The emperor, realizing that he might die soon, often asked Xuanzang about the Buddhist doctrine of retribution of good and evil deeds and the earthly manifestations of Buddhist sages in India. A month before his death, he was so moved that he lamented, "It is a pity that I met you so late, and I could not propagate Buddhism to a greater extent."[22] On the twenty-fifth day of the fifth month, the emperor complained of a slight headache and made Xuanzang spend the night in the palace with him. The next day he died.

The Emperor Taizong was succeeded by his ninth son, known as the Emperor Gaozong. The new emperor, like his father, held Xuanzang in high esteem, providing abundant support for his translation work. He sponsored two important monasteries in Chang'an, although unlike his father, he showed no real interest in Buddhist doctrine.

Xuanzang boldly suggested that the Emperor Gaozong build a pagoda on the site of the first monastery to house the Buddhist scriptures and images that he had brought back from India. He pointed out that in a stone structure they would be less exposed to the risk of loss by fire; Chinese temples were usually built of wood. Xuanzang had been thinking of a tall, multistoried stone building like the ones he had seen in India. Xuanzang designed the pagoda to "show the magnificence of a great country and to be a monument for the Sakyamuni Buddha." However, before construction was begun, the imperial secretary to the emperor was asked to inform the Master: "As the pagoda you intend to construct is so tall, it will perhaps be difficult to build with stone. It should be constructed of brick" (Fig. 10.5). It was much smaller than Xuanzang had in mind and was built in Indian style with five stories. Xuanzang himself helped to carry bricks for the construction of the Big Wild Goose Pagoda, as it came to be called. It took two years to complete.

The Big Wild Goose Pagoda still stands in what was the Tang city of Chang'an, present-day Xi'an. Chang'an was the greatest city of the world in the seventh century. It had nourished both the Tang emperor and the Chinese pilgrim "who had seen traces of the Buddha not seen before and heard sacred words not heard before." In the dream of Mount Sumeru that Xuanzang had before he departed on his pilgrimage, the young monk saw an unending horizon, a symbol of the countless lands he hoped to visit. With this vision he overcame his fear of the unknown and traveled vast distances on the Silk Road.

In this splendid period of medieval Buddhism he forged new bonds between the two major civilizations of Asia. Xuanzang served as a fine diplomat throughout his sixteen-year-long journey. He showed himself to be fully conscious of places, situations, and relationships wherever he was. With few exceptions, he had an attitude of openness and

FIGURE 10.5
The Big Wild Goose Pagoda, which was erected in the seventh century to house the scriptures Xuanzang had brought back with him and which has been restored many times (Courtesy Dr. Glen Dudbridge, photographer)

receptivity. All this was accomplished without a loss of his own warmth and integrity. The Tang Emperor Gaozong called him "the jewel of the empire" and rightly so.

On Xuanzang's journey, his heart was guided by the Compassionate Bodhisattvas and the Wisdom Sutras, his head was in the clouds of Indian philosophy, but his feet were steady even on the iciest glacier. His sandals were full of glory as he returned to ancient Chang'an. His homecoming was triumphant, befitting the Prince of Pilgrims.

Afterword: The Legacy of Xuanzang

What do these people have in common: a historian writing about medieval India, an archaeologist interpreting an ancient painting in the British Museum, a visitor in Kyoto looking at a well-known Buddha image in Japan, a Chinese reading *Monkey* or *Journey to the West* or an American watching a dramatization of it on TV, and a Buddhist priest chanting a popular translation of the *Heart Sutra*? All are looking to Xuanzang, whether they know it or not, and are coming into contact with his legacy to the world. Xuanzang has made a contribution to the fields of Indian history, archaeology, art history, Chinese literature, and the translation of Buddhist scriptures.

Xuanzang himself would probably be surprised by the range of his influence. What seemed most important when he returned to China after his pilgrimage, even as he walked through the streets of Chang'an as the hero of the hour, was undoubtedly very different. He would have been pleased that the seven images he brought had survived the years of their long journey intact, and that he had managed to bring 657 books, a library of Buddhist texts. But the other parts of his legacy? Archaeologists, and art historians, and general historians interested in his work? Becoming one of the characters in an epic Chinese novel? Being a popular religious folk figure? All would have been quite beyond his understanding.

Even though it wasn't quite so grand as the building he had in mind, he would have been pleased that the Big Wild Goose Pagoda in Xi'an still stands as a famous landmark. He had asked the Emperor Gaozong to build it to house the Buddhist scriptures he brought back with him from India.

Archaeological Legacy

Xuanzang's record has inspired generations of archaeologists and art historians. Sir Alexander Cunningham, the first director of the Archaeological Survey of India (1861), used Xuanzang as his guide in reconstructing Indian archaeology. Cunningham followed in the pilgrim's footsteps, traversing the length and breadth of the land; thus he was able to locate its principal cities and Buddhist monuments. Cunningham's chief guides for his *Ancient Geography of India* (which covers what he called the Buddhist Period up to the eighth century) were the campaigns of Alexander the Great and the travels of the Chinese pilgrim. He wrote: "But the fortunate discovery of the travels of several Chinese pilgrims in the fifth, sixth and seventh centuries of the Christian era, has thrown such a flood of light upon this hitherto dark period, that we are now able to see our way clearly to the general arrangement of most of the scattered fragments of the Ancient Geography of India."[1]

Cunningham, in his analysis of ancient settlements, quoted Xuanzang's memoirs extensively for the location and measurements of monuments, cities, and territories. He summarized Xuanzang's route through India to show "the great extent and completeness of his Indian travels," which, as far as Cunningham was aware, had "never been surpassed."

Alfred Foucher, a nineteenth-century French scholar, was able to discover the famous Kanishka tower stupa after reading Xuanzang's precise descriptions of the area. As he followed in Xuanzang's footsteps in present-day Pakistan and Afghanistan, Foucher could determine "the principal trade routes and identify the monuments" as well as the setting of famous Jataka tales and stupas, thereby illuminating his studies of Gandharan art. We can picture Foucher in his travels in India tracking the Buddha legend, walking around Vaisali, one of the eight major sites of pilgrimage, and saying: "Of course we should be carrying with us our Hsuan-Tsang [Xuanzang]. . . . Sure enough, raising our eyes from our book we find facing us the tall, monolithic column crowned with a lion, seen thirteen centuries ago by the Chinese traveller."[2]

Aurel Stein, explorer and archaeologist extraordinaire, followed Xuanzang in India, Pakistan, and Central Asia. He made many archaeological reconnaissances to verify Xuanzang's records, reconciling record and site, and thus giving them life and meaning for future scholars. Because Xuanzang was so richly informative and so useful in understanding Indian geography, Stein described him as his Buddhist Pausanius (an ancient Greek traveler and geographer). James Fraser, he said, had written in his introduction to the translation of Pausanius that "without him the ruins of Greece would be a labyrinth without a clue, a riddle without an answer."

Stein, during his first expedition to Chinese Turkestan, promoted Xuanzang to the status of patron saint. As Jeannette Mirsky put it, "At a crucial moment, his [Xuanzang's] name would, like the magic lamp of Sinbad the Sailor, reveal a treasure to Stein." Thus Stein was able to find a cache of thousands of manuscripts dating from 406 to 995 C.E.,

Afterword: The Legacy of Xuanzang

which Mirsky said was a discovery of more general importance than that of the Dead Sea Scrolls.[3]

Among Art Historians

Art historians look to Xuanzang for descriptions of monuments that have since been destroyed and for ideas of the appearance of damaged works. Or even more broadly, according to Seckel: "It is the report of Chinese pilgrims which constitute the richest source of knowledge about life in these oases, and also about Bamiyan, the sacred places of India, and even southern Asia."[4]

It is tempting to say that Xuanzang is best known among art historians for his portrait in words of the giant statues at Bamiyan. Yet the descriptions by both Faxian and Xuanzang of the tower stupa of King Kanishka are perhaps equally important: "It is only in the accounts of the Chinese visitors . . . that we can get any idea of the sumptuous splendour of Buddhist architecture of the days of Kanishka and his successors," according to Rowland.[5] The descriptions of Nalanda, the most illustrious monastery in Asia, which Xuanzang saw at its height, and the account of the temple and grounds where the Buddha attained enlightenment are often cited. Xuanzang's picture of the highly polished Asoka pillar at Sarnath and the setting of many of the eight places of pilgrimage are also referred to with profit.

Xuanzang knew all the varieties of Buddhism. His commentary included not only valuable descriptions of famous sculptures, monuments, or sites, but usually which sect of Buddhism was dominant in each area or each monastery. This helped to combat some of the oversimplifications about Buddhist art, such as the labeling of plain work as Hinayana and more complex art as Mahayana.[6]

In Xuanzang's record, we find useful clues about Buddhist beliefs and practices that help interpret the iconography and subject matter of Buddhist art. The Buddhist pantheon developed in complex ways into many Buddhas—the Historical Buddha, the Sakyamuni of the Hinayana Buddhists, the Transcendental and Cosmic Buddhas of Mahayana Buddhism, as well as Buddhas of the Past, the Four Directions, Bodhisattvas with many names, and so on. Furthermore, the way in which devotees hold onto one or another set of beliefs is an involved subject with many uncertainties. There are usually two ways to tell Hinayana and Mahayana Buddhas apart—by general context or by special attributes. For example, Xuanzang called one of the giant Buddhas at Bamiyan, which have been badly mutilated, Sakyamuni, the Historical Buddha, and the other a "Buddha image," or Transcendental Buddha, because he knew the context, the special kind of Buddhism, that flourished there.

Since Buddha legends—Xuanzang's account is full of them—are so often the subject matter of Buddhist art, his narrative not only places these tales geographically but also provides insight as to their meaning. In Greater India especially it has been important to give these legends a place of origin. Buddhist art was often a storytelling medium, using the rich materials of the lives of the former Buddhas as well as that of the Historical Buddha for its monastery friezes. The Buddhist monks seemed to know that art gives life to legends and legends give life to art, and the people learn their faith from both.

Xuanzang also provided us with a quasi census of monks and monasteries in India and Central Asia, even though, by modern standards, the numbers are approximate and often exaggerated or misleading.[7] There would seem to have been between 4,000 and 6,000 monasteries in India and another 1,000 on the Northern and Southern Silk Roads in China and Central Asia.[8] What is perhaps more valuable is his information that the reach of Buddhism extended to such out-of-the-way and unexpected places as Badakhshan, in Afghanistan.

Like the pious Faxian before him, Xuanzang has helped modern art historians to reconstruct the history of several of the best-known and most holy images of Buddhism, such as the first sandalwood Buddha, commissioned by King Udayana. The Udayana image that Xuanzang saw at Kausambi was the most popular of all these images. At Dunhuang it was depicted on the *Banner of Famous Indian Images* (a painting now in the Museum for Central Asian Antiquities in New Delhi). All manner of legends grew up about this famous Buddha image prototype. Xuanzang brought a replica back to China, where more copies were made. In 985 C.E. the Japanese monk Chonen had another copy made, which he took back to Japan with him. It is one of the most famous Buddha images in Japan and still stands in the temple of Seiryoji near Kyoto, where it continues to serve as a model for a large number of other replicas (Fig. A.1).[9] And so the past, present, and future Buddha images survive, not just in Buddhist doctrine, but also in art in a chain of authentic images, the prime concern being that something of the omnipresent and beneficial essence of the Buddha be contained in it.

The Gupta images that Xuanzang collected and brought back with him had an impact on Tang art, giving it a new plasticity:

> Hsuan-tsang [Xuanzang] brought seven Gupta images back to China from his travels in India. The 7th and 8th centuries were the critical period for the new influences from India on Chinese workmanship, and the Chinese sculptures seem to have surrendered momentarily to them. Even at this distance one can sense the tremor of delight with which the Chinese in the luxury of the 7th century saw the Gupta images. . . .

FIGURE A.1
Udayana image of the Buddha in bronze from the Seiryoji Temple in Japan (Courtesy Seiryoji Temple)

Xuanzang contributed to this delight. "After the impassive planes of early Yunkang [Yungang] torsos and the heavy concealing drapery of later Northern Wei figures, diaphanous draperies reveal soft lines and warm flesh of living, physically desirable beings."[10]

Even more mysterious than the transfer of artistic influences from India to China was the way in which Xuanzang's journey, and indeed his character, began to be changed in the public imagination from a real journey to a fantastic and legendary one in which the true hero was no longer a pilgrim but a trickster monkey.

Literary Heritage

How did a popular religious folk hero come to acquire his bizarre animal guardians, especially Monkey? The shared motifs of some of Monkey's characteristics with the monkey hero of an Indian epic known as the *Ramayana* have caused some to try to establish a connection between the two, and the evidence is impressive.[11] We do know that Xuanzang's biographers enriched and enlarged the facts and history of his life with stories and miracles. Something about Xuanzang and his exotic travels stirred the Chinese imagination. His seventh-century exploits became folktales, part of a living oral tradition told first in Chinese monasteries. "Do you know how the Chinese monk subdued the demon in the cave? How did he get away from the pirates?" Later they were repeated in Chinese inns. In nearly a millennium of development, the story of Xuanzang and his acquisition of scriptures was told, retold, and written down in short poetic tales, stories, plays, and partial narratives. Finally there was a fully developed narrative using both prose and verse. In 1592, probably after the author died, the earliest extant full edition came out. This epic Ming novel, *Journey to the West*, was said to be written by Wu Cheng'en.

It is one of the three great Chinese novels of the last several centuries. Sometimes it is compared to *Don Quixote* or *Pilgrim's Progress*, more often to the former, with its playful tone, inexhaustible fun and humor, and layers of philosophical and religious meaning, than to the latter. Buddhist, Daoist, and Confucian themes are all present in the very long novel.[12] The English translation of *Journey to the West* is divided into three parts: (1) an early history of Monkey; (2) a pseudo-historical account of Xuanzang's family and life in which there is an astonishing parallel to the biblical story of Moses (the baby Xuanzang is put into a basket to float down a river, where he is eventually picked up by monks); (3) the principal story, which consists of eighty-one calamities suffered by the pilgrim and his guardians.

Afterword: The Legacy of Xuanzang

In the sixteenth-century classic, Xuanzang has been renamed Tripitaka, meaning the "Three Baskets" of Buddhist wisdom. Not only does he slip into the background, but he becomes a timid and peevish monk. He has been upstaged by the mischief-making Monkey, a slovenly, greedy pig, and a somewhat nondescript monk named Sha, sometimes translated as "Sandy." Tripitaka's animal attendants are, however, delinquent immortals gifted with supernatural powers. They have all been naughty, and their task is to redeem themselves by taking care of Tripitaka on his way to the west.

During World War II, Arthur Waley translated and published about a third of *Journey to the West*, calling it *Monkey*; it was popular with the general reading public. A brilliant scholar, Anthony Yu, made the first complete translation into English of the one hundred chapters over a period of six years, from 1977 to 1983. His four-volume edition—about 2,000 pages—was meant for scholars. Two well-known contemporary authors, Mark Salzman and Maxine Hong Kingston, have used Monkey as a chief protagonist in modern novels.[13]

The stories of Monkey are so popular in China that they have become part of the repertoire of shadow plays, puppet companies, and Chinese opera for years, not to mention a TV series, comic books that every Chinese child knows, paper cutouts, and masks. In China there are even murals with a Monkey theme on the walls of the Summer Palace in Beijing as well as folk temple sculpture in such places as Kunming. Chairman Mao wrote several poems about Monkey. His wife, Jiang Qing, ruthless in her persecution of Chinese artists and literati, was nicknamed the White Bone Demon after one of the chapters of this famous classic. Korean and Japanese children also know the Monkey story.

It is not surprising that the earliest legendary depiction of Xuanzang sprang from this literary tradition. The rendering of Xuanzang is from a recently discovered wall painting 100 miles from Dunhuang at Yulin. The scene by a river figures prominently in early versions of *Journey to the West*, and dates from between 1038 and 1227 (Fig. A.2).[14]

Translation Legacy

There were four preeminent translators of Buddhist works into Chinese between the second and the thirteenth century C.E.: Kumarajiva, Paramartha, Xuanzang, and Amoghavajra.[15] In his influence on later Buddhist thought, Xuanzang is second only to Kumarajiva; he translated more Buddhist scriptures than anyone else. In the course of twenty years he and his specially recruited team of scholars produced over seventy-three works, totaling more than one thousand scrolls.

FIGURE A.2
Wall painting of a pilgrim with a monkey and a horse bearing scriptures, the earliest legendary depiction of Xuanzang, recently discovered at Yulin, 100 miles from Dunhuang. Source: Weng Wen 7-12 (July–Oct. 1980), p. 8.

These were sanctioned by the emperor and later supported financially by other members of the royal family.

The most famous of these texts is perhaps the *Heart Sutra*, whose words "Form is Emptiness, Emptiness is no other than Form" are still recited by Zen Buddhists all over the world.[16] Perhaps his most popular and influential translation, the *Thirty Verses*, became a bible to the followers of the Idealist school, which survives in Japan as the Hosso, a small sect.[17] Many Chinese and Japanese soldiers carried the *Thirty Verses* on their persons; during World War II a copy of Xuanzang's translation was found on the body of a Japanese soldier killed in the

Afterword: The Legacy of Xuanzang

war in China. Today that copy is in Fritz Mote's library. But the Idealist text that was the magnet for Xuanzang's journey was his *Treatise on the Stages of Yoga Practice.* The emperor honored him by writing a foreword, and copies were distributed throughout the empire. It is still used as a text for persons entering the Buddhist clergy.

Xuanzang was the founder of an Idealist school known as Faxiang (Fa-hsiang), a branch of the Buddhist tree that stopped growing and survived his death by only seventy years.[18] Possibly it was too abstruse, too intellectual, and not practical enough to suit the Chinese. Also Xuanzang eventually came to believe in a sectarian view that certain types of persons could never hope to attain enlightenment, a belief he shared with Silabhadra, the head of Nalanda Monastery. It is indeed ironic that the later years of Xuanzang, who had been the greatest traveler in his day, were marked by a narrowing of focus. It is also ironic that he may have contributed to the beginning of "sectarianism": The very reason he left China was to search for a broader vision.[19]

Nevertheless, as often happens, what he thought was his most valuable contribution was not that which lasted. A branch of esoteric Buddhism, the Cult of the Healing Buddha, appears to have gained special popularity in China and the Far East after his excellent translation of the *Master of Lapis Lazuli Radiance Tathagata.*[20] This sutra, relating to a healing spell or healing mantra, is of a totally different order than perhaps his most important contribution, bringing the New Logic of Buddhism to China. Waley noted that "systematic treatises dealing with logic were almost unknown" and that "they caused a considerable stir even in the lay intellectual world."[21] The New Logic, founded by Dignaga, simplified the set forms in which an argument was to be stated and enumerated the kinds of argument that ought and ought not to be accepted—the famous Thirty-Three Fallacies.[22]

Toward the end of his life Xuanzang was finally persuaded to attempt the translation of the vast compendium known as the *Perfection of Wisdom* (Fig. A.3). It comprises sixteen long scriptures supposed to have been preached by the Buddha over an extended period. Xuanzang's disciples wanted him to cut the many repetitions in the work, which in his version ultimately filled 600 volumes. The *Perfection of Wisdom* is said to be eighty-four times the length of the Bible. Xuanzang's last illness followed shortly. He died in 664 C.E., on February 5. It was much more than a particular school that translators like Xuanzang revealed to China. Their contribution was a whole treasury of concepts of being, philosophies of the mind, and the methods, or the ground, of knowledge.[23]

Like a dead star that keeps releasing energy for thousands of years, Xuanzang is a resource for historians, archaeologists, and art historians. He was the inspiration for one of China's major epics and a

FIGURE A.3
Frontispiece of the Perfection of Wisdom, *one of the many Buddhist texts translated by Xuanzang. Depicts the pilgrim meeting the Buddha to receive the* Tripitaka *(Buddhist canon). (By permission of The British Library)*

well-known translator of Buddhist scriptures. He continues to shine as a pilgrim-diplomat, one of the greatest travelers of all time.[24] Xuanzang was also a fully realized human being who excelled in intellectual achievements, physical strength, and prowess, the human skills of a diplomat, and the spiritual devotion of a true pilgrim.

Glossary

Terms

Abhidharma: Philosophical commentaries composed between the third century B.C.E. and the third century C.E. They are part of the Buddhist canon (*Tripitaka*).

Arhat: One who strives after his own salvation, in Theravada Buddhism.

Atman: Individual self or soul.

Avalokitesvara: Bodhisattva of Compassion; Bodhisattva of Enlightenment. After about the sixth century C.E., he became the most popular Bodhisattva of Buddhism; later depicted as a female in East Asian Mahayana Buddhism; see Guanyin.

Bhallika: One of Buddha's first disciples from Balkh; he fed the Buddha after his enlightenment.

Bodhisattva: Enlightened Being who renounces entry into nirvana until all other beings are saved.

Bodhi Tree, Bo Tree: Fig tree under which the Buddha attained enlightenment.

Brahma: Creator, chief of the Hindu trinity with Vishnu and Siva.

Brahmin: Member of the highest of the four Hindu castes of India.

Buddha Legend: The stories and miracles associated with the life of the Buddha.

Caste: Hereditary social-class system in Hinduism that restricts both the occupations of its members and their associations with members of other castes.

Confucianism: Moral and religious system in China. Its origins go back to *The Sayings of Confucius* and to ancient commentaries such as *The Book of Mencius*. Before the third century B.C.E., it was entirely a system of ethical precepts for the management of society.

Daoism (Taoism): Major religious philosophy in China. The Dao (Tao, The Way) is hard to define, since basic Daoist axioms include silence and even inaction. Of far greater importance than the world of immediate human concerns is the greater cosmic world of nature.

Deva: Divine beings or gods who inhabit Buddhist heavens.

Dharma: Universal norms that govern human existence; variously translated as "the law," "the truth," et cetera. In Buddhism, it is the law of the universe discovered and preached by the Buddha. Can also mean a potential object of consciousness.

Diamond Sutra: Discourse that is part of the *Prajnaparamita-sutra*. It shows that all phenomenal appearances are not ultimate reality but illusions or projections of one's own mind.

Dipankara Buddha: The first of the twenty-four Buddhas preceding the Historical Buddha, Sakyamuni.

Emptiness Doctrine: *Sunyata*, emptiness, nothingness, void. The mental state that is to be achieved as the final result of Buddhist practices; neither existence nor nonexistence, a state of complete neutrality that is considered to be the ultimate reality seen as a dynamic, not a passive, state.

Faxiang (Fa-hsiang): A school founded by Xuanzang and his disciple, Kuiji (K'uei-chi) (632–682 C.E.). Also called the Wei-shih, Consciousness Only school.

Guanyin (Kuan-yin; Japanese, Kannon): Goddess of Mercy. East Asian name for Avalokitesvara. Originally represented as a male, later popularized as a female deity.

Harmika: Base of a parasol shaft on a stupa. Sometimes a balcony or railing surmounting dome.

Heart Sutra, Heart of Wisdom Sutra, Heart of Perfection of Wisdom Sutra (*Prajnaparamitahridaya-sutra*): Important Mahayana sutra, especially emphasized in Zen. "Form is Emptiness, and Emptiness is no other than Form." It concluded with the mantra: "Gone, gone, gone beyond, gone altogether beyond. O, what an Awakening! All hail!"

Hinayana (Lesser Vehicle): Southern Buddhism, an early form of Buddhism emphasizing the ideal of the *arhat*, rather than worship of Bodhisattvas. Practiced in Sri Lanka, Southeast Asia.

Hinduism: Dominant religion of India, emphasizing dharma, its ritual and social observances, and other mystical and ascetic practices.

Indra: In Hinduism the deity that controls thunder, lightning, wind, and rain. Adopted as one of the protective deities of Buddhism.

Jainism: Religion founded in sixth century B.C.E. in India. Emphasis on austerity, penance, and the practice of nakedness.

Jataka: Stories about the Buddha's previous incarnations.

Journey to the West (*Xiyouji* or *Hsi-yu chi*): A sixteenth-century epic novel by Wu Cheng'en that drew its inspiration from Xuanzang's seventh-century journey.

Kalpa: An aeon, an infinitely long period of time.

Karma: The idea of retribution in the life cycle, whereby acts in a previous existence lead to inevitable results in the shape of good or bad incarnations in later lives.

Kuan-yin: See Guanyin.

Lankavatara-sutra (*Sutra of the Descent into Lanka*): A verse compendium of Idealist philosophy.

Lapis Lazuli–sutra (*Master of Lapis Lazuli Radiance Tathagata*): Discourse relating to the Cult of the Healing Buddha and the *Bhaishajya-guru-sutra*, which flourished in China, Japan, and Tibet.

Li: A Chinese unit of distance; one li is equal to about one-third of a mile.

Logic: See New Logic.

Lotus Sutra (*Saddharmapundarika–sutra; Sutra of the Lotus of the Good Dharma*): Discourse delivered by the Buddha toward the end of his ministry on Vulture Peak.

Madhyamika: Centrist school of Mahayana Buddhism, which affirmed the middle way between affirming and denying. Founded by Nagarjuna and Aryadeva.

Mahaparinibbana-sutta (*Sutra of the Great Decease; Sutra of the Glorious Decease*): Early Pali account of Buddha's last days, his final sermon, death, and funeral. This Hinayana sutra also lists four places of pilgrimage for Buddhists. Composed about 480 B.C.E.

Mahaparinirvana-sutra: Discourses concerning the *Great Parinirvana* sutra. A collection of Mahayana sutras. They deal mostly with "the Buddha nature" and other Mahayana concepts.

Mahayana (Greater Vehicle): Northern branch of Buddhism. Its ideal is the Bodhisattva, the Compassionate One, who helps others attain salvation.

Maitreya: Both a Bodhisattva who is said to reside in the Tushita Heaven, where he awaits birth as the next Historical Buddha, and a Future Buddha who will preside over an earthly paradise.

Manichaeanism: A hybrid religion founded in Persia about the third century B.C.E.; derived partly from both Zoroastrian dualism and Christian soteriology.

Manjusri: Bodhisattva of Wisdom. Often depicted riding a lion.

Mara: The evil one, or tempter.

Maya: Refers to the illusory nature of the phenomenal world. Also creation of illusion or artifice. The power of the gods to assume different shapes.

Mount Sumeru: World Mountain at center of the universe, dwelling place of the gods.

Naga; Nagini (Naga, male; Nagini, female): A serpent, especially a serpent divinity.

Nestorian Christianity: A fifth-century heresy, maintaining that Jesus Christ was two distinct persons. Nestorius held that the father of Jesus was God and that Mary bore him as a human being.

New Logic (*Hetuvya sastra*): A system founded by Dignaga in the late fifth century C.E. Employed to win points in religious debates.

Nirvana: Ultimate goal of Buddhist endeavor, the extinction of craving and separate selfhood, a life that has gone beyond death.

Pali: Ancient language derived from Sanskrit. Used as the liturgical and scholarly language of Hinayana Buddhism.

Parinirvana: Sometimes called the "Great Decease." Complete nirvana. Final passing away of Sakyamuni Buddha.

Perfection of Wisdom Sutra: See *Prajnaparamita-sutra*.

Prajnaparamita-sutra (*Perfection of Wisdom Sutra*): Discourses gathered together dealing with wisdom (*prajna*). Best known in the West are the *Diamond Sutra* and the *Heart Sutra*.

Questions of Milinda: The most important noncanonical work of the Hinayana; a dialogue between the monk Nagasena and King Milinda (Menander) the first-century B.C.E. Greek conqueror of northern India. Milinda is said to have converted to Buddhism.

Quinquennial Almsgiving: Gathering in which a ruler gives away all his possessions, which his officials ransom back afterwards.

Rain Retreat: A variable period of monsoon when Buddhist monks take up residence in monasteries.

Record of the Western Regions Full name: Account of the western lands of the Great Tang Dynasty (*Da Tang Xiyouji [Ta T'ang Hsi-yu chi]*): Xuanzang's account of his journey (646 C.E.).

Reincarnation: Rebirth of the soul in a new form of life.
Samadi: A concentration of mind, the deepest form of Buddhist meditation.
Samsara: Continual bondage of life, death, and rebirth experienced by the unenlightened, from which only nirvana offers release.
Sangha: The Buddhist community; usually limited to the priesthood.
Sanskrit: The ancient and sacred language of India; oldest known member of the Indo-European family.
Sastra (Shastra): Commentaries, as distinct from original Buddhist teachings.
Siva: Major Hindu deity, part of Hindu trinity; embodies principle of creation and destruction.
Stupa: Monument originally shaped like a stylized tumulus commemorating the death of the Buddha or an Enlightened Being, often containing relics.
Sutra; Sutta (Sutra, Sanskrit; Sutta, Pali): A short text "threaded together," considered to be the teachings of the Historical Buddha.
Sutra of the Eleven-Faced Avalokitesvara: Discourses containing spells for charming holy water, incense, firewood, medicinal herbs, and so on.
Tantric Buddhism: Later branch of Buddhism associated with emphasis on female sexual symbolism and secret esoteric traditions and practices.
Taoism: See Daoism.
Tathagata: One of the ten titles of Buddha that he himself used when speaking of himself or other Buddhas.
Thirty Verses: Vasubandhu's *Treatise in Thirty Verses on Consciousness Only*, or *Vijnaptimatrata-trimsika*. Summary of essentials of Yogacara Buddhism.
Transcendental Buddhism: Belief that Cosmic Buddhas have supernatural powers beyond our experience but not beyond our knowledge.
Trapusa: One of Buddha's first disciples from Balkh, who fed him after his enlightenment.
Treasury of Buddhist Philosophy (Abhidharma Storehouse Treatise, *Adhidharma kosa–sastra, Abhidharmakosha*): Composed by Vasubandhu; reflects transition from Hinayana to Mahayana Buddhism.
Treatise on the Stages of Yoga Practice: *Yogacarabhumi-sastra, Yogacharabhumi-shastra*. Composed by Asanga and Vasubandhu. Basic text of the Yogacara school. Presents seventeen stages on the path to enlightenment.
Tripitaka: "Three Baskets." Pali canon with three parts: *Sutra-pitaka* (Sayings of the Buddha), *Vinaya-pitaka* (Rules of Discipline), and the *Abhidharma-pitaka* (Systematic Philosophy).
Tushita Heaven: The third-lowest heaven, in which Bodhisattvas await their last rebirth. This heaven is presided over by Bodhisattva Maitreya.
Udayana Image: Authentic Buddha image commissioned by King Udayana of Kausambi; he ordered an artist to go to heaven to carve a likeness of the Buddha. A copy exists in Japan today. ("Udayana" is often confused with Uddiyana or Udyana, the area in Pakistan.)
Vairocana Buddha: "Illuminator," one of the Five Transcendental Buddhas. His symbols are the wheel of teaching and the sun.
Vaisravana Buddha: Guardian deity of northern India, associated with wealth.
Vimalakirti-sutra; Vimalakirtinirdesha-sutra: Discourse named for its principal character, a rich adherent of the Buddha who lives a worldly life and yet treads the path of the Bodhisattva.

Glossary

Vinaya: Rules of Discipline.

Visvantara Jataka: In a famous Jataka tale a prince named Visvantara makes the supreme self-sacrifice: He gives up his elephant, his wife, and his children.

Yoga: Practices by which the individual attempts "to yoke" himself with the Universal. The chief yogas are: *hatha yoga* (mastery of the body); *bhakti yoga* (emphasizing devotion); *jnana* (intellectual yoga); *karma* (work yoga).

Yogacara: Buddhist school founded by Asanga and Vasubandhu. It maintains that everything is experienced as mind only, as processes of knowledge. The external world is purely mind. There is no subject who experiences. Process explained with the help of "storehouse consciousness." Also teaches that there are three bodies of the Buddha.

Zen (Chinese: Ch'an): A stream of Chinese and East Asian Buddhism that rejects the scriptural tradition and preaches a sudden experience of enlightenment as the culmination of meditation.

Zoroastrianism: Ancient Persian religion teaching that the worship of God, Ahura Mazda, requires men's good deeds to help in his cosmic struggle against the evil spirit. Founded in sixth century B.C.E. by the prophet Zoroaster.

People and Dynasties

Alexander the Great: King of Macedon, conqueror of much of Asia and one of the greatest leaders of all time (lived 356–323 B.C.E.).

Amoghavajra: Indian monk and translator known for his espousal of Esoteric Buddhism in China at Chang'an (705–774 C.E.).

Ananda: The Buddha's disciple. His exposition of the Buddha's discourses became the basis for the codification of Buddhist scriptures.

Asanga: One of the founders of the Yogacara Buddhist school. Elder brother of Vasubandhu (c. fourth century C.E.).

Asoka: King of Mauryan dynasty who ruled all but the southern tip of India (third century B.C.E.). His edicts inscribed on stone pillars and rocks were famous. Many Buddhist legends record his conversion and support of Buddhism.

Bimbisara: King of Magadha who was the Buddha's patron. His capital was Rajagriha (lived c. 544–493 B.C.E.).

Buddha, Gautama: Founder of Buddhism, i.e., Sakyamuni (563–483 B.C.E.).

Calukya Dynasty: Rajput warriors who organized the Mahratta people. Ruled over the northwest Deccan. Pulakesin II was their most famous ruler (sixth century C.E.).

Chandragupta I: Emperor and founder of the Mauryan Empire who ruled over much of north India from about 322 to about 298 B.C.E.

Ch'i: See Qi.

Chih-yen: See Zhiyan.

Chonen: Japanese monk and pilgrim who brought a copy of the Udayana image to Japan (tenth century).

Dharmapala: Spiritual grandfather of Xuanzang; follower of Yogacara school, authoritative commentator on Vasubandhu (c. sixth–seventh century C.E.).

Dignaga: Principal teacher (late fifth century–sixth century) of Yogacara Buddhist school, a founder of the New Logic.

Fa-hsien: See Faxian.

Faxian (Fa-hsien): Famous Chinese monk who traveled to India (399–414 C.E.) to seek the true scriptures.

Gaozong (Kao-tsung): Successor (649–683 C.E.) to Tang dynasty Emperor Taizong; completed his father's work in foreign expansion in early years of his reign. At the end was a weak ruler swayed by harem intrigues.

Genghis Khan: See Jenghiz Khan.

Great Khan of the Western Turks (T'ung Shih-hu): A seventh-century Central Asian emperor who defeated the Epthalite Huns and expanded the Turkic empire into Persia and China.

Gupta: Empire in India during period of flowering of Sanskrit literature, classical sculpture, and monument building, which began at the end of third century C.E. It reached its zenith during the reign of Kumaragupta (415–455 C.E.).

Han: Dynasty that consolidated China into a unified empire; during its reign many Chinese political and social patterns were set (206 B.C.E.–220 C.E.).

Harsha: Last monarch of classical India; built an empire that extended from the Himalayas to the Vindha range and from Bengal to Gujarat. Patron of Xuanzang (lived 607–647 C.E.).

Hsuan-tsang: See Xuanzang. Other spellings of his name beginning with "H" are Hhuen Kwang, Hioen Tsiang, Hiouen Thsang, Hiuen Tsang, Hsuan Chwang, Huan Tsang, Hsuan Tsiang, Huan Chwang, and Hwen Thsang.

Huili (Hui li or Hwui-li): Monk and friend of Xuanzang; wrote Xuanzang's biography in 648–649 C.E.

I-ching: See Yijing.

Jayasena: Famous philosopher of Mahayana Buddhism who lived near Nalanda. Xuanzang studied with him (seventh century C.E.).

Jenghiz Khan (Genghis Khan): Mongol conqueror who ruled most of China, Turkestan, Transoxiana, and Afghanistan. He raided Persia and ruled one of the largest land empires the world has ever known (1167?–1227 C.E.).

Jetavana: Prince who aided in establishing the Jetavana Monastery in Sravasti in India, one of the Buddha's favorite sojourning places (sixth century B.C.E.).

Kanishka I: Kushan ruler of northern India, most of present-day Afghanistan, Tajikistan, and parts of Central Asia. Estimates of the beginning of his reign range from 78 B.C.E. to 225 C.E. Ruled for more than twenty years, was a patron of Buddhism, the arts, and scholarship.

Kao-tsung: See Gaozong.

Kasyapa: One of Buddha's chief disciples, along with Ananda.

Kumarajiva: Monk from Kucha who was taken to Chang'an by imperial order to be head of the State Translation Bureau (lived 344–415 C.E.).

Kushan: Famous dynasty whose invasion of India began during the first century C.E. Empire established in Afghanistan and northern India; its influence extended into Central Asia. Kanishka I was its most famous king (reigned for more than two decades c. 100 C.E.).

Glossary

Marco Polo: Venetian traveler to China then ruled by the Mongol Yuan dynasty; he became a favorite of Khublai Khan. During the Renaissance, his report was a popular source of information on the East (1254?-1324?).

Mauryan: A dynasty (320-180 B.C.E.) that gave a considerable degree of unity to the Indian subcontinent. Its most illustrious rulers were Chandragupta and Asoka.

Maya: Queen, the mother of the Historical Buddha.

Nagarjuna: One of the most important philosophers of Buddhism and founder of the Madhyamika school (c. 100-200 C.E.).

Nehru Jawajarlal: Independent India's first prime minister (1889-1964).

Paramartha: Famous translator (500-569 C.E.); brought the Yogacara school to China in 545.

Parthians: Ancient Iranian people whose empire was at its height in the first century B.C.E. It extended from the Euphrates across Afghanistan to the Indus River and from the Oxus to the Indian Ocean. Conquered by the Sassanians in 226 B.C.E.

Prasenajit: Ruler of Kosola in India who was a contemporary and patron of the Buddha (reign: sixth century B.C.E.).

Pulakesin II: Warrior king of Mahratta people. Calukyan king who was so strong that King Harsha could not defeat him (reign: 608-642 C.E.).

Qi (Ch'i): One of the five dynasties (479-501 C.E.) in southern China when China was divided before the unification under the Sui dynasty.

Sakyamuni: The Historical Buddha, the sage of the Sakya clan.

Santideva: Poet who wrote of the mystic doctrine of Mahayana Buddhism; he lived (c. seventh century C.E.) during the reign of the son of King Harsha.

Sassanian: Last dynasty (224- or 228-651 C.E.) of native rulers to reign in Persia before the Arab conquest.

Scythians: Nomadic conquerors and expert horsemen in regions to the north and northeast of the Black Sea. Noted for their gold ornaments and implements (eighth to fourth centuries B.C.E.).

Silabhadra: Buddhist scholar, teacher, head of Nalanda Monastery; he was Xuanzang's spiritual mentor (seventh century C.E.).

Sogdian: People of ancient Persian empire between the Jaxartes (Syr Darya) and Oxus (Amu Darya) Rivers. Sogdian people were known as caravaners on the Silk Road.

Suddhodana: King. Father of the Historical Buddha, Sakyamuni (sixth century B.C.E.).

Sui: Dynasty (581-618 C.E.) that reunited China for the first time after the collapse of the Han dynasty. The Sui supported Buddhism and built great art works.

Taizong (T'ai-tsung): Tang dynasty emperor (626-649 C.E.) and patron of Xuanzang; one of China's greatest emperors, integrated China and expanded the Tang empire into Central Asia.

Tang (T'ang): Dynasty (618-907 C.E.) that brought to China its great golden age of culture. The empire expanded, and the capital Chang'an became the greatest city in the world.

Tardu: Prince in Kunduz in Afghanistan (seventh century C.E.).

Tokharian: A people of considerable culture and presumably Indo-European origin dwelling in Central Asia in the first millennium of the common era until they were overrun by the Uigurs. Term also refers to their language.

Tuoba Wei (T'o-pa Wei): Turkish tribe that settled in Shanxi province, united north China, and founded the Northern Wei dynasty (386–535 C.E.). The Buddhist caves of Yungang were built (452–512 C.E.) during this period.

Turkic: Relating to a subfamily of Altaic languages, including Turkish, and its speakers.

Uighur (Uigur): Turkic-speaking people who live in northwest China and Xinjiang.

Vasubandhu: One of the founders of the Yogacara Idealist Buddhist school (fourth or fifth century C.E.).

White Huns (Epthalite Huns): Proto-Mongol nomadic people who dominated the steppes; invaded north India, Persia, and parts of China and remained until they were displaced by the Turks in the middle of the sixth century.

Wu Cheng'en (Wu Ch'eng-en): Author of *Journey to the West*, which features Xuanzang as a Buddhist monk who travels to the west in search of Buddhist scriptures (c. 1506–1582 C.E.).

Xuanzang (Hsuan-tsang): Chinese pilgrim and translator who went to India in search of Buddhist scriptures (lived 596– or 602–664 C.E.).

Yijing (I-ching): Chinese Buddhist scholar and translator (634–713 C.E.) who was the first to go to India by sea. He wrote about sixty other Buddhist pilgrims who went to India in the Tang period.

Yuan: Mongolian dynasty that ruled China at time Marco Polo came to China (1271–1368).

Yuan Chang, Yuan Chuang, Yuen Chwang, Yuan Chwang. See Xuanzang.

Zhiyan (Chih-yen): A Chinese traveler who, like Faxian, inspired Xuanzang to undertake his journey.

Gazetteer

Afghanistan: Country in western Asia, east of Iran. Capital is Kabul.

Ajanta: Buddhist caves in Maharashtra, north-northeast of Arungabad, in India.

Aksu: Oasis 162 miles west of Kucha oasis in Xinjiang.

Allahabad (Prayaga): City in north India, in south Uttar Pradesh, on the Ganges River, west of Benares.

Amu Darya (Oxus): River more than 1,400 miles in length in central and western Asia, flowing from Pamir plateau into the Aral Sea.

Andarab: Settlement on the north side of the Hindu Kush.

Andhra: State in eastern India, north of Madras, bordering on Bay of Bengal. Corresponds to modern state of Hyderabad.

Anxi (An-hsi): Oasis in Gansu province, straddles juncture of Silk Roads; was once of considerable importance.

Assam: State in northeast India at edge of Himalayas.

Attock: Site used for modern crossing of Indus 12 miles from Hund.

Glossary

Ayodhya (Faizabad or Saketa): City in northern India in Uttar Pradesh. Legendary capital of Rama.
Bactria: Ancient country in Southwest Asia between Hindu Kush and Oxus River.
Badakhshan: Settlement in mountainous area in Penj Valley, in eastern Afghanistan, surrounded by the Pamirs. Near modern Faizabad.
Balkh (Fo-ho): Ancient walled city in northern Afghanistan at juncture of caravan routes linking China, Iran, India, and Central Asia.
Bamiyan: Buddhist site in Hindu Kush Mountains in Afghanistan.
Bangladesh: Country in South Asia bordering on India and Bay of Bengal.
Begram (Hilo): Archaeological site 40 miles north of Kabul, Afghanistan.
Benares: See Varanasi.
Bezeklik: Buddhist cave site 35 miles east of Turfan.
Bihar: State in northeastern India bordering on Nepal; goal of Buddhist pilgrimages.
Bodh Gaya: Site of Buddha's enlightenment, 5 miles from Gaya, in Bihar in northeastern India.
Burma (Myanmar): Country in Southeast Asia on Bay of Bengal.
Cambodia (Kampuchea): Country in Southeast Asia bordering on Gulf of Siam.
Central Asia: Area composed of Afghanistan, Uzbekistan, Kazakhstan, Kyrgyzstan, Turkmenistan, and Tajikistan, i.e., the region west of the Pamir Mountains and east of the Caspian Sea.
Chang'an (Ch'ang-an): See Xi'an (Sian).
Charkhlik (Ruoqiang): Oasis near Loulan, in Xinjiang, China.
Charsadda (Pushkalavati): City 12 miles northeast of Peshawar.
Chengdu (Ch'eng-tu): Capital of Sichuan (Szechuan), province in southwestern China.
Cherchen (Qiemo): Oasis city in China on Southern Silk Road in Xinjiang.
Chinabhukti: City near modern Forozpur, south of Sutlej River in Himalchal Pradesh in northern India.
Dandan Oiluq (Dandan Uiluq): Archaeological site in China between the Khotan and Keriyan Rivers in Xinjiang.
Darel: Site of famous statue on the upper Indus River in Pakistan.
Dhanakataka: Kingdom southeast of Andhra, on the lower Krishna River.
Dravida: Ancient kingdom in southern India. Capital was Kancipuram.
Dunhuang (Tun-huang): Oasis town on western edge of Gansu province; for millennia it served as a major entrepôt of the Silk Road.
Faizabad: The name of two different cities, one in northern Afghanistan, and the other in India. The Indian city is usually known as Ayodhya. See Ayodhya.
Gandhara: The boundaries of Gandhara are variously defined according to the period and subject of reference. Usually Gandhara refers to eastern Afghanistan and Pakistan. Also, area where school of art flourished in Afghanistan, northwestern India, and Pakistan.
Ganges: River 1,550 miles in length. Flows from Himalayas southeast and east to unite with the Brahmaputra and empty into Bay of Bengal.
Gansu (Kansu): Province in north-central China. Contains so-called Hexi corridor.

Gaochang (Kao-ch'ang, Kocho): Ancient Buddhist center, 29 miles southeast of Turfan.

Gashun Gobi (Mo-ho-yen): Desert in China between Anxi and Hami, east of Taklamakan and west of Gobi Deserts.

Gobi: Desert located in Inner Asia in Mongolia and China; covers an area about 500,000 square miles.

Hadda (Hi-lo): Famous archaeological site near Jalalabad in Afghanistan.

Hami (I-Wu in Tang period; Kumul in Marco Polo's time): Oasis in China in eastern Xinjiang northeast of Taklamakan Desert.

Himalayas: Mountains in South Asia on border between India and Tibet, and in Kashmir, Nepal, and Bhutan.

Hindu Kush: Mountain range crossing the center of Afghanistan.

Hotan: See Khotan.

Hund: Former crossing on the Indus River. Both Alexander the Great and Xuanzang crossed there. Downstream 12 miles is Attock, modern crossing place.

India: Subcontinent of South Asia, south of Himalayas between the Bay of Bengal and the Arabian Sea.

Indus: A river 1,800 miles long, in South Asia, flowing from Tibet northwest, and southwest through Pakistan into Arabian Sea.

Iran (Persia): Country in Southwest Asia. North borders on Caspian Sea, and south borders on Persian Gulf and Gulf of Oman.

Irana (Iranaparvata): Kingdom east of Nalanda in West Bengal. Identified with modern kingdom of Monghyr.

Issyk Kul: Lake 114 miles long in south-central Asia, in northeastern Kyrgyzstan.

Jade Gate (Yumenguan): Pass 50 miles northwest of Dunhuang. Formerly westernmost pass leading out of China.

Jalalabad (Nagarahara): Capital of Nigrahar province in Afghanistan.

Jalandhara: See Jullundur.

Jaxartes (Syr Darya): River 1,500 miles long. Flows from Tian Shan Mountains west and northwest into the Aral Sea.

Jiaohe (Yarkhoto): Ruined city 6 miles west of Turfan in Xinjiang.

Jingue: See Niya.

Jullundur (Jalandhara): City in northwestern India.

Jumna: See Yamuna.

Kabul: Capital of Afghanistan, on the Kabul River.

Kanauj: See Kanyakubja.

Kancipuram: City in north Tamil Nadu province, north of Madras.

Kansu: See Gansu.

Kanyakubja (Kanauj): Kingdom 50 miles northwest of Kanpur (Cawnpore), on the middle Ganges River.

Kao-ch'ang: See Gaochang.

Kapilavastu: Capital of Shakya Republic. Home state of the Historical Buddha. Its exact location on Indo-Nepal border is disputed.

Kapisa: Ancient kingdom in Afghanistan; its capital was Kapisi, which was the political capital and commercial center of the Kushan empire.

Kapitha: See Sankasya.

Glossary

Karashahr (Yanqi, Yen-ch'i): Archaeological site and seat of Yanqi region, between Turfan and Kucha, in Xinjiang.
Kasha: See Kashgar.
Kashgar (Kasha): City in far west China, in southwestern Xinjiang.
Kashgaria (Chinese Turkistan): Region in west China, in western and central Xinjiang.
Kashmir: Mountainous region in north India, west of Tibet and southwest of Xinjiang.
Kausambi (Kosam): Ancient capital on the Yamuna River, in Uttar Pradesh.
Khotan (Hotan, Hetian, Ho-tien): Oasis town in western China, southwest Xinjiang, at edge of Taklamakan Desert, at foot of Kunlun Mountains.
Khyber: Pass between Afghanistan and Pakistan, 33 miles long.
Kizil: Buddhist cave site 40 miles north of Kucha, in Xinjiang.
Kosala: Area of northeastern India. South Kosala (Maha Kosal), area in heart of Deccan, in India. Nagpur is modern capital.
Kosam: See Kausambi.
Kucha (Kuqa): Oasis on Northern Silk Road in Xinjiang province.
Kunduz (Huo): Kingdom east of Balkh in northern Afghanistan.
Kunlun (K'un-lun): Mountains in western China extending from the Pamir and Karakorum ranges east along northern edge of Tibetan plateau to southeast Tsinghai.
Kusinagara: Site in India on Gandak River, in Uttar Pradesh, where Buddha died.
Kyrgyzstan (Khirghizia, Khirgiz): Independent state, formerly republic of USSR in Central Asia, on Chinese border, northeast of Tajikistan.
Liangzhou: See Wuwei.
Longmen (Lung-men): Near present-day Luoyang; site of numerous Buddhist cave temples.
Loulan (Lou-lan): Important caravan trading center, west of Lop Nor, in Xinjiang, China.
Loyang: See Luoyang.
Lumbini: Site of Buddha's birth, in south Nepal close to India border.
Luoyang (Loyang): City in eastern China, in northwestern Henan province.
Magadha: Ancient state in north India. Included Bihar, where many events in Buddha's life took place, and Bodh Gaya, where he achieved enlightenment.
Maharashtra (Maharatta): Region in west-central India, bordering on Arabian Sea. Bombay is chief city.
Malva (Malava): Area north of Maharashtra, in India, now in Madhya Pradesh.
Mathura: City in north India, in Uttar Pradesh, 90 miles south of Delhi.
Matipura: Buddhist site in the present district of Bignor, on Ganges River, in north India.
Miran: Archaeological site in China in Xinjiang, near Charkhlik.
Mongolia: Region in East Asia, west of Khingan Mountains and east of Altai Mountains. Includes Gobi Desert.
Multan: City in northeast Pakistan southwest of Lahore.
Muztagh-Ata (Muztagata): Mountain (24,388 feet) in Pamirs, west of Kashgar.
Nagapattinam: City in Palar Valley, Tamil Nadu province, southwest of Madras.

Nagarahara: See Jalalabad.
Nalanda: Famous Buddhist monastery in Bihar state, near Rajgir, India.
Nasik: Cave site and center in western India north of Bombay, near Western Ghats. Former capital of King Pulaskesin II, in Maharashtra.
Nepal: Country in Asia on northeast border of India and in the Himalayas.
Niya (Jingjue): Famous archaeological site east of Khotan, in Xinjiang, China.
Oxus: See Amu Darya.
Pakistan: Country in Asia, formerly part of British India.
Pamir: Mountain region in Asia in Republic of Tajikistan; borders on Xinjiang, Kashmir, and Afghanistan; from this region radiate the Tian Shan, Kunlun, Karakorum, and Hindu Kush ranges. Many peaks over 20,000 feet.
Parvata: City near Chandrigarh in north India.
Pataliputra: See Patna.
Patna (Pataliputra): City in northeastern India on the Ganges River.
Persia: See Iran.
Peshawar (Purushapura): City situated near Khyber Pass, now capital of Northwest Frontier province in Pakistan.
Prayaga: See Allahabad.
Punjab: Region in Pakistan and northwest India occupying the valley of the Indus and its five tributaries.
Qiemo: See Cherchen.
Rajagriha (Rajgir): Capital of Magadha at the time of the Buddha. In Bihar, northeastern India.
Rajgir: Modern city on site of Rajagriha.
Ruoqiang: See Charkhlik.
Samarkand (Sam-o-kan): One of oldest cities in the world; ancient capital of Sogdiana. Now in Uzbekistan.
Samatata: Country in the delta of the Ganges River.
Sankasya (Kapitha): Former Buddhist center on Ganges River, in Uttar Pradesh, northern India.
Sarnath: Site where Buddha preached his first sermon, 6 miles north of Varanasi, in India.
Shache: See Yarkand.
Shahbaz Garhi: Archaeological site in Northwest Frontier province of Pakistan, 8 miles east of Mardan.
Sialkot (Sakala): City in northeastern Pakistan, 67 miles northeast of Lahore.
Sian: See Xi'an.
Sichuan (Szechwan): Province in southwestern China. Chengdu capital.
Simhala: Xuanzang's term for Sinhala. See Sri Lanka.
Sindhu (Sindh): Region in southern Pakistan in lower Indus valley.
South Kosala: See Kosala.
Sravasti: Buddhist site in Sahet Mahet district, in Uttar Pradesh, near Nepal border.
Sri Lanka (Simhala): Island at tip of Indian subcontinent. Formerly called Ceylon.
Srinagar: Historical capital of Kashmir in India on Jhelum River.
Srughna: Country on the upper reaches of the Yamuna River.
Swat: Mountainous area 95 miles north of Peshawar in northwest corner of Pakistan.

Syr Darya: See Jaxartes.
Szechwan: See Sichuan.
Tajikistan: Formerly autonomous republic within Soviet Central Asia bordering on China and Afghanistan; now independent state. Capital is Dushanbe.
Taklamakan (Takla Makan): One of world's largest sand deserts, about 105,000 sq. miles. Bounded on three sides by Tian Shan, Pamir, and Kunlun Mountains, in Xinjiang China.
Tamrallipti (Tamluk): Ancient city 40 miles south of Calcutta, in India.
Tarim: Basin, or arid plain, dominating the Taklamakan Desert.
Tashkent (Che-shih): Capital of Uzbekistan, in former Soviet Central Asia, east of Syr Darya River.
Tashkurghan: The name of two different cities, one in northern Afghanistan, and the other 162 miles west of Kashgar.
Taxila (Taksasila): Famous archaeological site 20 miles northwest of Peshawar, in Pakistan.
Tengri Khan: Mountain (23,620 feet) on border between Kyrgyzstan and Xinjiang.
Thailand (Siam): Country in Southeast Asia on the Gulf of Siam.
Tian Shan (T'ien Shan): Mountain range that branches east by northeast from the Pamirs for about 1,800 miles, north of the Taklamakan Desert.
Tibet: Region adjoining southwestern China on high plateau, north of Himalayas. Average altitude, 16,000 feet.
Tokharistan: Ancient area in Central Asia occupied by Tokharians.
Tokmak: City on north side of Lake Issyk Kul, in Kyrgyzstan.
Tun-huang: See Dunhuang.
Turfan (Turpan): Oasis in west China, in east Xinjiang, in northeast part of Tarim Basin.
Turkistan: Area of Central Asia between Iran and Siberia, divided among independent states that were formerly in the USSR, China, and Afghanistan.
Udyana (Uddiyana, Uddyana): Country located in Swat Valley in northwestern Pakistan. (The king of Kausambi was Udayana, from whom the Udayana image takes its name.)
Uzbekistan (Uzbek): Independent state in west-central Asia, east of the Amu Darya, formerly part of USSR.
Vaisali: City north of Patna in Bihar state, in northeastern India.
Varanasi (Benares): City on Ganges River, in southeast Uttar Pradesh, India.
Victoria (Sarikul Nahradda): Great Dragon Lake in the Pamir Mountains.
Wuwei (Liangzhou, Liang-chou): Political and commercial center of Gansu, in Gansu province, in western China.
Xi'an (Sian): Ancient Chinese capital city known in Tang dynasty as Chang'an, located on Wei River plain in Shaanxi province. Served as eastern terminus of Silk Road.
Xinjiang (Sinkiang): Province in northwest China between Kunlun and Altai Mountains. Urumchi capital.
Yamuna (Jumna): River 860 miles long in north India flowing from the Himalayas south and southeast into the Ganges River.
Yarkand (Shache): City in western China in southwest Xinjiang, at oasis on Yarkand River.
Yumenguan: See Jade Gate.
Yungang (Yun-kang): Buddhist cave site near Datong in north China.

Notes on Illustrations

Chapter 1

Fig. 1.1 Portrait of the Emperor Taizong. Album of twenty-four portraits of Chinese emperors, leaf j. Ch'ien Lung period: 1736–1795. Colors on silk. 60 × 21.8 × 27.8 cm; 24 × 8.75 × 11.13 in. Metropolitan Museum of Art, New York.

The brilliant Li Shih-min, who ruled from 623 to 649 C.E., was given the title Emperor Taizong (the Grand Ancestor) posthumously. His reign was one of the most successful in China's history. A heroic warrior, he eliminated military opposition to the Tang dynasty and conquered Central Asia, but his attempt to conquer Korea failed. He was a great consolidator and improved the institutional structures he inherited. With the expansion of his empire, the Tang capital, Chang'an, became the most cosmopolitan city in the world. The prestige and glory of his reign increased with the passage of time, and he came to be thought of as an ideal Confucian ruler who combined exemplary civil government and military power.

Fig. 1.2 Relief from the tomb of the Emperor Taizong, Xi'an, China. 637 C.E. Gray limestone. 5.66 × 6.75 ft. University of Pennsylvania Museum, Philadelphia, Pennsylvania.

The Emperor Taizong, a dashing and successful military commander, was a great horseman. Six of his favorite horses are preserved on stone reliefs from the emperor's tomb; two, in the University of Pennsylvania Museum in Philadelphia; the others, in the Shanxi Provincial Museum in Xi'an. They are sturdy creatures, more solid than the famous prancing terra-cotta Tang horses in so many museums in the West. In this relief one of Taizong's generals is pulling an arrow from the horse's chest.

Fig. 1.3 Traditional fourteenth-century portrait of Xuanzang. Rubbing from the stele at the Temple of Flourishing Teaching, outside Xi'an. Presumed copy of Song painting. 1935? Photo: Abe Dulberg.

This alleged portrait of Xuanzang (602–664 C.E.) with a modern-looking frame pack filled with the scriptures he brought with him from India may also be found at the Big Wild Goose Pagoda in Xi'an, China. Its source is a rubbing from a stele at his burial place, the Temple of Flourishing Teaching, near Xi'an. In his right hand Xuanzang carries a fan, symbol of authority for Buddhist priests even now, and in his left, a single scroll. However, the sutras Xuanzang brought back from India would have been in the form of flat, oblong *ola* leaves, not the Chinese scrolls that are in this portrayal. It is a relatively late representation, presumably from a Song (Sung) painting. Xuanzang's clothes do not correspond to the description of his contemporary biographer ("He liked to wear ample garments and a broad belt which gave him the appearance of a

Notes on Illustrations

scholar"). They also do not correspond to a newly discovered wall painting of Xuanzang from Yulin, 100 miles from Dunhuang.

Fig. 1.4 Wall painting and sculpture, with Bodhisattva as center figure. Cave #275, Dunhuang Caves, Gansu, China. Fifth century C.E. Lucy Lo Archive, Princeton University, Princeton, New Jersey.

These paintings and sculpture on the north wall of Cave #275, one of the earliest of the Dunhuang Caves, help us to understand the fervor and sincerity of a pilgrim such as Xuanzang. Xuanzang often prayed to Bodhisattvas, or Maitreyas (Buddhas of the Future), beings who postpone their own salvation so they may help others. The two chief ideas of Mahayana Buddhism, emptiness, signifying the object of wisdom, and Bodhisattva, signifying compassion, are here translated into the world of forms. The Bodhisattva ideal was best expressed by a Buddhist poet named Santideva: "May I become an unfailing store for the wretched, and the first to supply them with the manifold things of their need. My own self, my pleasures, all my righteousness, past, present, and future, I sacrifice without regard in order to achieve the welfare of all beings."

Fig. 1.5 Scroll containing the *Heart of the Perfection of Wisdom Sutra, Prajnaparamitahridaya-sutra*, in Chinese. Found in Dunhuang Cave, Gansu, China. Ninth century. Ink on paper. 42 × 22 cm; 16.4 × 8.7 in. British Library, London.

A copy of the *Heart of the Perfection of Wisdom Sutra*, usually called the *Heart Sutra*, translated by Xuanzang, was found in the Dunhuang Caves and is now in the British Library. This brief sutra can be written on a single sheet of paper, shown here in the diagrammatic form of a stupa or a pagoda. Xuanzang's translation is smooth and fluent, revealing his mastery of both Sanskrit and Chinese. This Hridaya mantra is usually thought of as opening the mind to enlightenment rather than used for personal safety, as Xuanzang did. The final words of the sutra: "Gone, gone, gone beyond, gone altogether beyond. O, what an Awakening! All hail!"

Chapter 2

Fig. 2.1 King and Queen of Kucha. Painted mural. Grotto of Maya, III Anlage, Kizil. Xinjiang, China. 600–650 C.E. Source: *L'Asie Centrale: Histoire et Civilisation* (Paris: l'Imprimerie Nationale, 1977), p. 32.

Authentic portraits of the king and queen of Kucha, dating from the first half of the seventh century, were among the frescoes in the Grotto of Maya at Kizil, near Kucha. The royal pair who greeted Xuanzang in 630 C.E. probably looked something like this. Despite the destruction of these portraits in Berlin during World War II, photographs still exist that reveal a man with light skin, like most of his subjects, and reddish brown hair parted in the middle. He is as elegantly dressed as his beautiful queen, who stands next to him, wearing a light green jacket that fits tightly at the waist and widens at the hips. Her large lapels are of navy blue and are bordered in brown dotted with white and gold. Beneath her sleeves, in almost a layered look, are long undersleeves striped in blue, brown, and tan. Her very wide skirt, with its delicate pattern of blue and brown flowers, looks as if it could be worn by a modern woman.

Chapter 3

Fig. 3.1 A small reliquary in the shape of a stupa. From Manikyala, Pakistan. First century C.E. Steatite. H. 21.5 cm; 8.4 in. British Museum, London.

This small model of a stupa, used as a reliquary as was the custom, has a molded base and a bell-shaped cylinder. There are four parasols on the *harmika*, the base of the shaft. Found in the relic chamber at the base of a large stupa, this reliquary contained an even smaller crystal reliquary. In the same relic chamber was a coin of the Kusha King Kujula Kadphises, dating from the early first century C.E.

Fig. 3.2 Ground Plan of rock-hewn chapels at Bamiyan, which form a semicircle around the 175-foot-high figure of the Buddha. Afghanistan. Source: Dietrich Seckel, *The Art of Buddhism*, trans. Anne E. Keep (New York: Crown, 1964), p. 140, fig. 34.

Outlines of the feet of the 175-foot-high Buddha are shown here framed by a semicircle of caves and grottoes. In Grotto IV there is a representation of arched squinches, making the transition from the square of the chamber to the circle of the cupola. Another feature found at Bamiyan is the *lantern roof*, as in Cave V. Instead of a cupola, the center panel is filled with squares laid diagonally across the corner and diminishing in size toward the top. These lantern roofs were copied extensively by the builders of rock caves in Central Asia and China. They are one of Bamiyan's most important contributions to art.

Fig. 3.3 Carved glass vase showing the Lighthouse of Alexandria. From Begram, Afghanistan. Fourth century (?) C.E. Carved glass. H. 18 cm; 7.08 in. Kabul Museum. Photograph, Musée Guimet, Paris. Photo: Delegation Archéologique Française en Afghanistan.

A symbol of the far-flung trade of the Kushan dynasties, this carved-glass vase found by French archaeologists is from the most landlocked country of Asia. This nautical treasure was part of the Begram hoard, collected in the palace of a Kushan ruler in Kapisa. On the vase is a representation of the Pharos (Lighthouse) of Alexandria, one of the seven wonders of the ancient world. Standing on the lighthouse tower is Poseidon, Greek god of the sea, flanked by two tritons. On the reverse side a galley with a bank of oars, a merchant ship with a sail, and a small fishing boat are depicted. This flotilla is similar to those in harbor views occasionally found on Roman sarcophagi or in harbor scenes on Roman wall paintings.

Fig. 3.4 Fragment of the Dipankara Buddha. Shotorak Monastery, Afghanistan. Third century C.E. Schist relief fragment. 35 × 21 cm; 13.7 × 8.2 in. Musée Guimet, Paris. Cliché des Musées Nationaux, Paris.

The story of Sakyamuni in a former existence meeting Dipankara, a former Buddha, is illustrated on this fragment. Surpassing the courtesy of Sir Walter Raleigh, who was said to have spread his cloak on the ground for Queen Eliza-

Notes on Illustrations 211

beth, the Buddha-to-be, in this version of the story, lay down his cloak and even knelt down and put his long hair on the deerskin cloak for the greater comfort of the Dipankara Buddha.

Chapter 4

Fig. 4.1 The Bimaran reliquary. From Bimaran stupa, Jalalabad, Afghanistan. Second–third century C.E. Gold repoussé decorated with jewels. H. 7 cm; 2.75 in. British Museum, London.

This tiny Bimaran reliquary, made of gold with rubies, is without a lid. The Buddha and the gods Indra and Brahma, framed by arcades formed with pointed arches, are shown twice, separated by a worshipper whose headdress, earrings, and armlets suggest a Bodhisattva. The repetition of figures in arched niches, called *homme arcade*, is often found on Christian sarcophagi in Asia Minor. The arches are in Indian style, and the flying eagles between them are Western in inspiration. The iconography of the Buddha figure is Indian. The Buddha has wide open eyes, a mustache, a high *usina*, a mound of wisdom, and a small halo with a double rim around it. His full robe is Western. In short, it is what art historians call a composite style.

Fig. 4.2 Reliquary of King Kanishka. Shah-ji-ki-Dheri, near Peshawar, Pakistan. First–second century C.E. Metal. H. 19.6 cm; 7.75 in. Original, Archaeological Museum, Peshawar, Pakistan; copy, British Museum, London.

This extraordinary piece was discovered in 1908 by D. B. Spooner. There is a very mutilated inscription, sometimes translated as referring to the first year of Kanishka's reign. More certain is the reading of the dedication by the Sarvastivadin (a Buddhist sect) and the name of the maker, Agisela, perhaps a craftsman of Greek origin. On the lid the Buddha is seated on a lotus pedestal. He makes the *Abhaya*, or "fear not," gesture with his hand. His hairstyle and robe conform to early Gandharan patterns. He is worshipped by Brahma and Indra. The top of the lid is incised with a lotus design, and around the edges is a frieze of flying geese. On the body of the casket is a Kushan monarch, probably intended to be King Kanishka himself, flanked by sun and moon gods, which indicate Iranian influence. On the sides are a Buddha image similar to the one on the lid and a royal figure worshipping him. The four scenes are held together by a garland supported by cherubs, a clear borrowing from the West.

Fig. 4.3 Gold coin with King Kanishka and the Buddha. From near Jalalabad, Afghanistan. First–second century C.E. Gold. British Museum, London.

The gold *BODDO* coin, with its standing Buddha on one side and Kanishka on the other, is deservedly famous, for it is among the first representations of the Buddha in human form, and its portrayal of King Kanishka in his long-skirted coat and boots is exactly like the one on the Kanishka reliquary, other coins, and the sculpture of Kanishka at Mathura. The Buddha is clearly identified by the Greek legend, *BODDO*. The right hand is raised in the "fear not" gesture and the left hand clasps the edge of his robe. The style of the standing Buddha, wearing a monastic robe, with its drapery folds and high wisdom mound, is Gandharan.

Fig. 4.4 Part of a frieze of the Tiger Jataka (tale of a previous incarnation of the Buddha). Cave #428, Dunhuang Caves, Gansu, China. c. 520–530 C.E. Lucy Lo Archive, Princeton University, Princeton, New Jersey.

The Mahasattva (the great being) Jataka. According to the story, three brothers who are out hunting see a starving tigress in a ravine. Mahasattva persuades them to leave and he stays behind. The next two scenes show him offering himself to a starving tigress. When she is too weak to respond, he flings his body hard on the rocks and dives from the precipice. His mutilated body, seen in this part of the frieze, is devoured by the tigress and her six or seven cubs. The brothers find out what has happened, report it to their father, and they erect a stupa to commemorate him. Finally Mahasattva appears as the perfect Buddha. This story illustrates the progress of one of the early incarnations of Sakyamuni, the Historical Buddha. By his wisdom and boundless self-sacrifice, Sakyamuni acquires such a good Karma that during his final incarnation he may become the Buddha.

Fig. 4.5 Sikri Stupa. Restored. H. approx. 5.1 m; 20 ft. Lahore Museum, Pakistan. Photo: Aallam Almakky.

The sixteen scenes depicted on the reconstructed Sikri stupa are (1) the Dipankara Buddha, (2) Buddha in Tushita Heaven, (3) the First Meditation, (4) the Conversion of Two Nagas, (5) Grass-cutter's present, (6) offering of the Four Bowls, (7) Indra and Brahma requesting Buddha to preach, (8) Buddha meditating among his monks, (9) Buddha's sermon to the thirty-three gods, (10) Amrapali's present of the Mango grove, (11) Indra's visit to the Indrasala Cave, and (12) Conversion of Alkavari. On the harmika (shaft rising from bell-shaped form) are (1) the offering of the honey bowl by monkey, (2) the birth of the Gautama Buddha, (3) the attack of Mara, and (4) the Mahaparininirvana of the Buddha.

Fig. 4.6 Buddhist Trinity. From Sahri Bahlol area (?), Pakistan. 182 C.E., fifth year of the Kanishka II era. Gray schist. 62 cm × 60 cm; 24.2 × 23.4 in. Collection of Claude de Marteau, Brussels, Belgium.

This very fine Gandharan relief sculpture contains a dated inscription of great importance in the history of Buddhist art. According to the inscription, the image was dedicated in the year 5 C.E. by Buddhananda, who was learned in the scriptures and wished to honor his parents. It is the fifth known dated image from Gandhara, upon which the chronology of the entire school rests. The Buddha is seated on a lotus. His hands show one of the earliest appearances of the teaching *mudra* gesture in Gandharan sculpture. His audience is a divine one—the Buddha of the Future, or Maitreya, so important to Xuanzang, on his right, and Avalokitesvara (originally a male deity who became Guanyin, a female deity in China) on the left, identified by the Buddha image in his crown. In the background are the Indian gods Brahma and Indra. It should be noted that the Maitreya figures in the Dunhuang Caves in China shown in Fig. 1.4 are very different from the Maitreya figures of Gandharan art.

Chapter 5

Fig. 5.1 Headless statue of Kanishka. From Mathura, Uttar Pradesh, India. c. 100 C.E. Red sandstone. H. 1.63 m; 64 in. Government Museum, Mathura.

A strong feeling of authority and power emanate from this giant statue. Although representation of donors does occur in Gandharan reliefs, the portrait-statues of the standing Kanishka and his father in the Mathura Museum are the sole examples of human portrait sculpture in ancient India. Statuary was usually reserved for images of deities. King Kanishka's clothes—the padded boots and long-skirted, heavy tunic covering the body—were suitable for a cold climate and nomadic life, not for Mathura, his southern capital. Similar Scythian-type costumes are often seen in Chinese paintings of the barbarians of Central Asia.

Fig. 5.2 Seated Buddha. From Katra Mound, Mathura, Uttar Pradesh, India. Second century C.E. Sikri sandstone. H. 69 cm; 27.25 in. Government Museum, Mathura.

This famous Buddha from the Katra Mound is an archetypal India sage with crossed legs in yogic meditation. He is seated on a lion throne—the Buddha was called the "lion of the Sakyas"—under a Bodhi tree, with a round halo behind him. Two attendants, identified by some as Indra and Brahma, and two celestial beings complete this stele. The Buddha's right hand is held up and turned sideways in a gesture that will evolve into the "fear not" gesture. His left hand is held lightly on his thigh, emphasizing the sheer physical strength and exuberance of the torso. In canonical accounts, the Buddha is said to have been born with the marks of the World Ruler, which included the spoked wheels on his feet. The wheel is an emblem of the Universal King. Other marks of supernatural perfection include the wisdom mound—in this case, a snail-like protuberance—and a tuft of hair between his eyebrows.

Fig. 5.3 King Udayana presenting Buddha image to the Buddha. Pakistan. n.d. British Museum photograph from Peshawar Museum, Pakistan.

According to the legend of the Udayana image, during the time the Buddha was in the Heaven of the Thirty-Three Gods preaching to his mother, King Udayana of Kausambi became so distraught that he sent an artist to heaven to create an exact image of him. When the Buddha returned to earth, King Udayana went to greet him and took the small sandalwood statue of a seated Buddha with him, as in this portrayal. The tale of the Udayana image continues in Central Asia with the legendary transporting of it to Kucha by an Indian ascetic reported to be Kumarajiva's father. (The ascetic carried the statue by day, and the statue carried him by night.) The authentic Udayana image has a long history, although no one knows why the seated figure, depicted here, later became a standing one.

Chapter 6

Fig. 6.1 Queen Maya's Dream. From Takht-ti-Bahi, Pakistan. Second century C.E. Schist. H. 20.5 cm; 8.11 in. British Museum, London.

Queen Maya, in a dream, saw the four divine kings arrive, lift her couch, and bear it to a gold mansion on a silver hill. There they anointed her with perfumes and clothed her in divine garments. Then a glorious elephant appeared and entered her right side. In this portrayal the Bodhisattva as elephant is haloed. A young female guard watches over the sleeping queen. There are famous depictions of the miraculous conception at Bharut and Amaravati as well as the one here.

Fig. 6.2 Sarnath plan of excavations, Uttar Pradesh, India. 1980. Director General, Archaeological Survey of India, New Delhi, India.

The various monuments on the ancient site of Sarnath, excavated in the nineteenth and early twentieth centuries, may be divided into four rows. Row 1 contains Monastery VII, Monastery V, and a modern Jain temple. Row 2 consists of the Dharmarajika stupa (Mauryan period), destroyed in 1794, as well as the Dhamekh stupa, which was originally Mauryan and later restored during the Gupta period. Row 3 contains the Apsidal chapel, the Asoka pillar, the main shrine, with a courtyard consisting of a large number of cells, miniature stupas, and subsidiary buildings. Row 4 consists of Monastery II, a *vihara* (temple) of the twelfth century, and Monasteries III and IV.

Fig. 6.3 Lion capital, Asoka Column. From Sarnath, Uttar Pradesh, India. c. third century B.C.E. Polished Chunar sandstone. H. 213 cm; 84 in. Sarnath Museum. Photo: American Institute of Indian Studies.

The cream-colored Asoka pillar from which this capital was taken, like many of Asoka's other pillars, was of considerable size, originally about 50 feet high. The edict engraved near the base makes a plea for unity within the monastic community. These highly polished pillars were crowned by animals, recalling pillars of the Persian Empire of Darius and Xerxes. Above the bell-shaped base (of upside-down lotus flowers) are an elephant, a bull, a horse, and a lion, separated from one another by wheels. Above these are four much larger lions, standing back to back. Their eyes once contained jewels, and their manes half cover their bodies. Not only is the lion the symbol of divine power and regal authority, but it was also the symbol of the Sakyas, the Buddha's clan, so the lions may refer to them as well. The pillar was originally crowned by a large *chakra*, or wheel of truth, some of whose spokes are in the Sarnath Museum.

Fig. 6.4 Buddha Preaching the First Sermon. From Sarnath, Uttar Pradesh, India. 475 C.E. Chunar sandstone. H. 1.57 m; 63 in. Sarnath Museum. Photo: American Institute of Indian Studies.

This justly famous and much copied Gupta Buddha is represented in a yoga posture with his feet turned up. His hands are in the Turning the Wheel of the Law pose. On the plinth below are the Buddha's earliest followers. Between them is the wheel, the symbol of preaching, and two deer, to suggest the Deer Park setting. Behind the head is a large halo, the Sun Wheel, with its center at the point between the Buddha's eyebrows, indicating the universal characteristic of the deity. On either side, as in a Renaissance painting, are two flying angels. The face of the Buddha is a perfect oval. The eyebrows follow the tensile curve of an Indian bow. The eyes are lotiform. The body is a combination of various allegories of great strength and beauty from Indian religious literature, drama, and poetry. It shows the Mahayana point of view, the eternal aspect of Turning the Wheel, typified by the Teaching gesture, rather than an actual episode in his teaching career. This eloquent image combines a circle and a triangle in perfect symmetry; both countenance and form convey the Mahayana paradox of great calm and great energy.

Notes on Illustrations

Fig. 6.5 Site Plan of Mahabodhi Temple at Bodh Gaya. Bihar, India. Source: Alistair Shearer, *The Traveler's Key to Northern India* (New York: Knopf, 1983), p. 440, fig. B.

The site plan of Bodh Gaya shows where the Buddha remained for seven weeks after the great enlightenment, while he enjoyed the bliss of nirvana and was trying to decide whether he should teach mankind. The Buddha spent the first week under the Bodhi tree, a pipal tree (*Ficus religiosa*). The second week he was so absorbed in bliss that he spent the time gazing at the Bodhi tree, transfixed, *unblinking*, commemorated by the Unblinking Shrine. The Jeweled Walk commemorates the place where he walked back and forth, for the third week. The fourth week he meditated northwest of the Bodhi tree; the Rainbow Shrine is presumed to mark the spot. The fifth week is associated with the Goatherd's tree, where Sujata offered him milk rice. The site of the sixth week of meditation is marked by the broken Asoka column, near the Muchalinda lake. Here Mara tried to disturb him. The serpent King Muchalinda rose out of the lake and spread his seven hoods over the Master's head to protect him from a storm. The seventh week is associated with a Rajata tree, where he made his first converts. Although a site is indicated on the site plan, the tree's location has not been verified.

Fig. 6.6 Mahabodhi temple and Bodhi tree at Bodh Gaya. Bihar, India. Fifth or sixth century C.E. Restored many times since then. Photo: American Institute of Indian Studies.

The Mahabodhi temple, the largest of the surviving early Buddhist temples and the first to be described by a historical person, Xuanzang, is preeminent among world religious monuments because of the antiquity of its associated event—the enlightenment of the Buddha in 530–520 B.C.E. A shrine next to the Bodhi tree was erected on the site by King Asoka when he visited Bodh Gaya c. third century B.C.E. The foundations of the present structure are linked to the Kushan dynasty. The temple was much changed during numerous restorations, especially a major one in the 1880s carried out by the Burmese. The 160-foot-high temple, which is on a platform 26.5 feet high, is accessible via two vaulted staircases, which lead to a circumambulating passage. There are four chapels and a central sanctuary. On the walls are story upon story of niches containing Buddha images. Four spires, one at each of the four corners, miniature replicas of the main spire, are a later addition.

Chapter 7

Fig. 7.1 Survey plan of excavated remains at Nalanda. Early twentieth century. Archaeological Survey of India.

The Nalanda Monastery flourished from c. 450 to 1100 C.E. Gupta period (320–480 C.E.) monasteries were laid out in the traditional pattern of the earlier Kushan age—a large square courtyard flanked on all sides with a running verandah, with the monks' cells at the back. All the remains bear indications of having been rebuilt again and again without any major deviation from the original plan. Site 1, depicted here, indicates as many as nine occupational levels.

Fig. 7.2 Fragment of hand holding a book. From Nalanda Monastery. Bihar, India. Stone. n.d. H. 8.5 in. Nalanda Museum. Photo: Archaeological Survey of India.

This fragment of a beautiful hand holding a book comes from Nalanda Monastery, at which, according to Yijing, who visited Nalanda after Xuanzang, there were eight large reading halls. Copyists, who reproduced manuscripts either on durable parchment or on palm leaves, seem to have been employed. Very likely students also made their own copies. Later Tibetan sources indicate that there were three libraries housed in monumental buildings in a special area known as the Treasury of Religion. Xuanzang must have had the opportunity to have his manuscripts prepared there for his eventual return to China.

Fig. 7.3 View of Stupa 3, the remains of the great temple. Nalanda Monastery, Bihar, India. Greatly restored in the seventh century. Photo: Archaeological Survey of India.

Stupa 3, a huge, solid structure, dominates the site of Nalanda today just as it must have during the seventh century when it was enlarged and beautifully embellished. Its final form is said to be the result of seven successive stages of building. One of the four towers at each corner can be seen here. The arrangement of a central stupa with four corner towers recalls that of the Mahabodhi Temple at Bodh Gaya, where there are four much smaller towers at the corners of that towering temple. Two of the towers, as well as the stepped walls flanking the great flight of stairs to the summit, are adorned with stucco figures of Buddhas and Bodhisattvas. The similarity of these carvings to the style of Sarnath is striking.

Fig. 7.4 Site map of old and new Rajgir. Bihar, India. 1975. Archaeological Survey of India.

Rajagriha, governed by King Bimbisara (c. 544–493 B.C.E.), was an important center of Buddhism. Bimbisara, who was a powerful northern Indian king, was a great admirer of the Buddha. Rajagriha was the site of the miracle of the taming of the mad elephant Nalagiri. The site plan shows the Bimbisara Road on Chhatha Hill and Vulture Peak (Gridhrakuta), where the Buddha loved to preach. It also shows Venuvana, the site of the Bamboo Grove, and Saptaparni Cave, presumed to be the site of the First Buddhist Council.

Fig. 7.5 Taming of the elephant Nalagiri. Chadigahr, India. c. second or third century C.E. Blue schist. Chadigahr Museum. Photo: American Institute of Indian Studies.

The encounter with the mad elephant at Rajagriha epitomizes the Buddha's protracted rivalry with his jealous cousin Devadatta, who released the elephant in an attempt to kill the Buddha. The elephant, here depicted as about the size of a large dog, suddenly became calm upon seeing the Buddha. According to other interpretations, the legend shows the Buddha overcoming evil or relates to the Asian tradition of conquering "the wild elephant" in us all.

Chapter 8

Fig. 8.1 Temple of the Tooth, Kandy, Sri Lanka. Building begun, sixteenth century; later additions. Photo: H. Wriggins.

Notes on Illustrations

The Temple of the Tooth is surrounded by the city of Kandy. Its roof was regilded in the twentieth century, for it is still revered as a place of great sanctity and power. The present temple was constructed mainly during the reign of the Kandy kings, 1687–1707 and 1741–1782. The octagonal tower seen in the photograph houses an important collection of *ola*, or palm leaf, manuscripts. The tooth of the Buddha is said to have been brought to Sri Lanka in the fourth century C.E. in the hair of a princess from Orissa. The relic is kept in a large, gold, bell-shaped stupa, inside of which are six smaller stupas, the sacred tooth being in the innermost one.

Fig. 8.2 Ajanta Cave #1, interior shrine door and Buddha. Ajanta, Maharashtra, India. c. late fifth century C.E. Archives of Asian Art, University of Michigan, Ann Arbor, Michigan. Photo: Walter Spink.

The Ajanta Caves were hollowed out of a 250-foot perpendicular cliff. The site contains both Hinayana and Mahayana Buddhist temples and monasteries from the mid-second century B.C.E. to the late fifth century C.E. The walls of Cave #1, a late-fifth-century cave, are adorned with impressive murals, and the doors of the shrine are elaborately carved. The colossal image of the Buddha is seated in a preaching attitude. At the top corners of his halo are two flying figures holding garlands. On the base, deer and a wheel in profile, recalling the wheel of the Buddha's first sermon, are worshipped by his first disciples. The heavy Buddha figure is typical of images at Ajanta, of which the majority are Buddhas. However lifeless they seem, compared to the Buddhas at Sarnath, in the dim religious light of the shrines, these large Buddhas are inspiring.

Fig. 8.3 Exterior view and entrance to sanctuary of rock-cut cave at Bhaja. Maharashtra, India. c. late second–early first century B.C.E. Photo: Roy C. Craven.

The earliest cave settlement in the Western Ghats is that of Bhaja. The entrance to the open *chaitra* (sanctuary) hall has a projecting vault that is framed by high towers, balconies, and dormer windows going along with two-story monks' cells. The large hall consists of a nave separated by rows of columns from smaller aisles. A semicircular apse contains the principal symbol of worship—a bell-shaped stupa. The pillars in the central nave are unadorned, emphasizing the severe spirituality of early Buddhism.

Fig. 8.4 The Bodhisattva of the Blue Lotus. Wall painting from Cave #1, Ajanta. Maharashtra, India. Second half of the fifth century C.E. Archives of Asian Art, University of Michigan, Ann Arbor, Michigan. Photo: Walter Spink.

The most famous surviving Buddhist paintings in India are in Ajanta Cave #1. On the left-hand wall is a large figure of a Bodhisattva with a blue lotus in a landscape teeming with smaller forms, loving couples, dwarflike creatures, apes, peacocks, and so on. The figure was composed according to a system of canonical proportions, probably nine *thalams* (hands), to the height of the figure. As an example of metaphorical composition, it has few equals. The parts of the face and body are drawn with reference to certain ideal forms that are presumed to create the imagined superior and eternal aspect of a god. The face has the perfect oval of an egg, the brows curve as an Indian bow, the eyes are lotiform, the body is "like a lion." Most beautiful of all, the hand suggests the pliant growth of the lotus flower it holds. The whole has a lyric quality in which physical beauty is fused with spiritual beauty. The Bodhisattva is the very embodiment of elegance and compassion.

Chapter 9

Fig. 9.1 View of the Pamirs. Afghanistan. Morden Clark Expedition of the Museum of Natural History, 1926. New York.

The name of the Pamir mountain chain derives from Persian "pai-mir" or "at the foot of the peaks," an apt description of their configuration. The chain contains high, bleak plateaus and many mountains over 20,000 feet and gives travelers, including Stein and Marco Polo, the feeling of "being in the highest place in the world." The Pamirs constitute a mountainous knot from which three other major ranges extend—the Hindu Kush to the west, the Karakorums to the east, and the Tian Shan to the north. A very strong wind blows up the valleys by day throughout the year. There is much snow in the valley bottoms, but the ridges are snow-free and without glaciers.

Fig. 9.2 Tangitar gorge, in the Pamirs between Tashkurghan and Kashgar. Source: Aurel Stein, *Serendia*, vol. 1 (Oxford: Clarendon Press, 1921), plate 29.

Stein surmised that Xuanzang lost his elephant in the Tangitar gorge, below Tar Bashi. "For over two miles it [the gorge] leads in the streambed itself between high frowning rocks, cliffs overhanging in a few places, which in case of a sudden rush of flood water would leave escape impossible." "Tangi-tar," i.e, "the narrow gorge," is the winter route. At a confined point in the gorge, large, well-cut holes on either side, evidently intended for a bridge, which Stein remarked on, are visible in the photograph. Kirghiz riding yaks are in the foreground. This was in all probability the narrow defile where Xuanzang's precious elephant, brought all the way from India, got lost in the water in the confusion caused by an attack of robbers.

Fig. 9.3 Mauri-tim stupa, outside Kashgar. Photo: S. Wriggins.

In the ancient village of Hanoi, which had been a thriving Buddhist settlement in Tang times, the Mauri-tim stupa, built of large sun-dried bricks, was 38 feet high at the time Aurel Stein saw it. The stupa has round niches occupied by Buddha images. A small shaft 2 feet by 8 inches square, which runs vertically through the center of the stupa dome and drum, was originally designed to hold a relic deposit. Many stupa robbers have been there since.

Fig. 9.4 Silk Princess. c. fifth or sixth century C.E. Dandan Oiluq, Khotan. Detail wooden votive tablet. 19 × 11.7 cm; 7.5 × 4.6 in. British Museum, London.

The votive tablet showing the Silk Princess's headdress was found in the ruins of a Buddhist monastery 75 miles northeast of Khotan, along with manuscripts, coins, sculpture, and paintings on wood and clay. Besides the princess, who, according to the legend, had brought the secrets of silk-making from China to Khotan, on the left of the long, horizontal panel is an attendant figure who points with an accusing figure to the princess's headdress. The divine personage on the right has four arms and has two of the attributes of the Iranian Bodhisattva, a cup and a knife with a short triangular blade. The line drawing appears to have some relation to Chinese technique, but the figures are the same combination of Indian and Iranian forms so frequent in Khotan.

Fig. 9.5 Nagini, or water spirit, and statue of Vaisravana. c. fifth or sixth century C.E. Dandan Oiluq, Khotan. Source: C. F. Andrews, *Wall Painting from*

Notes on Illustrations

Ancient Shrines in Central Asia (London: Oxford University Press, 1948), plate 32.

An unusual painting discovered by Stein at the site of Dandan Oiluq, near Rawak, of a voluptuous woman, accompanied by a small boy, standing in a lotus tank. It has been suggested that the woman is a water spirit, or Nagini, and that the picture refers to the legend recounted by Xuanzang of a nobleman who sacrificed his life by marrying a Nagini. In so doing he appeased the water dragon who had cut off the river water; the waters returned. The Nagini has a strong suggestion of an Indian style. This is probably the farthest eastward extension of the nude female, a subject that has never appealed to the Chinese or Japanese except in casual sketches or illustrations for pornographic literature. In the upper left portion of this painting are figures of a Buddhist teacher holding a sacred text and his monk companion. Visible also is a stucco image of Vaisravana dressed in scale armor. A demon lies under the feet of the deity.

Chapter 10

Fig. 10.1 Xuanzang returning from India. Cave #103, Dunhuang Caves. Gansu, China. Wall painting. 713–762 C.E. Lucy Lo Archive, Princeton University, Princeton, New Jersey.

The wall painting depicts a mahout, an elephant driver, walking in front of a huge white elephant, and a man on a horse, with two attendants. It represents Xuanzang's caravan before the loss of the elephant given to him by King Harsha. In another part of the frieze (not illustrated in Fig. 10.1), after the travelers have traversed a plain surrounded by a range of mountains, they emerge from a narrow pass in the foreground; Xuanzang has dismounted by the side of a waterfall by a pool. He is shown clasping his hands in gratitude for a safe journey. Behind him are King Harsha's royal elephant, horse, and attendants.

Fig. 10.2 Itinerant monk. Dunhuang Caves, Gansu, China. Ninth century C.E. Painting on silk. Musée Guimet, Paris.

The air of mystery in this ninth-century silk banner is palpable. The pilgrim's staff is topped by a dragon's head. He carries a little pot suspended on a stick that might carry incense or serve for cooking. The fly whisk, a symbol of authority, is carried by Zen monks even today. On the pilgrim's back are numerous little gourds for medicine and many vials hanging from a modern-looking frame pack. The tiger, which so often accompanies the prototype of the pilgrim traveler, is a symbol of the west or the beasts in the desert.

Fig. 10.3 Photograph of Paul Pelliot in Cave #17, Dunhuang Caves. Gansu, China. Pelliot Archives, Musée Guimet, Paris.

Paul Pelliot, who knew Chinese (which Stein did not know), photographed among the thousands of manuscripts and paintings on silk and paper found in Cave #17 at Dunhuang. The manuscripts are in Chinese, Uighur, Sogdian, Tibetan, and Sanskrit. The 50,000 items include religious texts, documents on history, customs, literature, art, mathematics, medicine, and economics. By the light of a single candle, Pelliot studied a thousand documents a day and selected the most valuable, which are housed in the Musée Guimet, Paris.

Fig. 10.4 Sakyamuni Buddha. North India. Late sixth century C.E. Bronze. H. 41.5 cm; 19.4 in. Asia House Gallery, New York. Collection Mr. and Mrs. John D. Rockefeller 3rd. Photo: Lynton Gardiner.

This large bronze Buddha standing with his right hand raised in the "fear not" gesture must have inspired countless worshippers. This image is regarded as one of the finest surviving bronzes of the Gupta dynasty (c. 320–480 C.E.). Though the statue resembles a typical Sarnath Buddha, the broad, almost square shoulders call to mind a Mathura Buddha. If, as has been speculated, some of the images Xuanzang brought back looked like this one, they probably exerted considerable artistic influence because of the eminence of Xuanzang. Clearly, Chinese artists' approach to sculptured form changed radically between the fifth and seventh centuries.

Fig. 10.5 Big Wild Goose Pagoda. Xi'an, China. 652 C.E. Restored in 1580. H. 73 cm; 190 feet. Photo: Dr. Glen Dudbridge.

The Big Wild Goose Pagoda was built in 652 C.E. by the Emperor Gaozong for Xuanzang after his pilgrimage to India. The 240-foot-high renovated pagoda has seven stories. Each story has openings on each of the four sides with vaulted passages. A large wooden staircase in the center of the pagoda leads to the top. On the south side are two monuments inscribed with prefaces to Xuanzang's translations provided by the Emperor Taizong and the Crown Prince.

Afterword

Fig. A.1 Udayana Image of Sakyamuni. Tenth century C.E. Bronze. Seiryoji Temple, Kyoto, Japan.

One of the most famous Buddha images in Japan is this statue of the Sakyamuni Buddha at the Seiryoji Temple in the outskirts of Kyoto. It was presumed to be a copy of the sandalwood image of King Udayana brought to Japan in 987 C.E. All such copies of this legendary statue were regarded as veritable material facsimiles of Sakyamuni, only slightly less potent than the Buddha's earthly manifestation. Chonen afforded it sanctity by depositing in the holy relic pictures, sutras, documents, and votive offerings. Its provenance is well documented. The well-preserved statue is an example of an image becoming a cult instrument and of an authentic, sanctified model being transmitted from one part of Asia to another.

Fig. A.2 Tang monk traveling, with sutras. Cave #3 near Yulin. Anxi, China. 1038–1127 C.E.. Source: *Weng Wen* 7-12 (July-Oct. 1980), p. 8.

The wall painting of a pilgrim with a monkey and a white horse and carrying what appears to be scriptures with numinous rays of light emanating from them was recently discovered in a cave at Yulin, 100 miles from Dunhuang. Scenes by a river like this one figure prominently in early versions of *Journey to the West*. Among the murals in existence today on this subject, this is the oldest authentic one, unlike the celebrated portraits that show Xuanzang carrying a backpack of scrolls.

Fig. A.3 Frontispiece of the *Perfection of Wisdom* sutra. Kofukuji Temple, Nara, Japan. Japanese woodblock edition of *Mahaprajnaparamita-sutra*. 1 fold-

Notes on Illustrations

ing vol. Ink on a mixture of *gampi* and mulberry paper. 29 × 9.6 cm; 11.4 × 3.8 in. British Library, London.

From the Nara period on, the *Perfection of Wisdom* sutra was thought to possess the power of protecting Japan from natural and human disasters. Each *maki* (volume) of this edition, bearing a handwritten date of Eitoku 3 (1383 C.E.), has a large frontispiece depicting Xuanzang meeting the Buddha to receive the *Tripitaka*. The Buddha is surrounded by deities, and he commands them to protect Xuanzang on his return from India to China.

Color Plates

Color Plate 1 Exterior of Dunhuang Caves, Gansu, China. Fourth–fourteenth century C.E. Photo: Paddy Booz.

Cave temples were first built in India in such places as Ajanta; the idea traveled to northwest China by way of Bamiyan, in Afghanistan. Dunhuang was founded in 366 C.E. by the monk Lo Tsun. Until the Yuan dynasty period (1271–1368), it was a center for Buddhist pilgrims; many caves were carved from the gravel conglomerate of the Dunhuang escarpment. During the Tang dynasty there were more than one thousand caves. Many of the early ones have narrow corridors leading into a simple rectangular sanctuary, with a recess in the western end for the major cult figures; others have a central stupa pillar decorated with sculptured Buddhas. There was space around the stupa to permit the rite of circumambulation. The caves have a skillful blend of paintings and sculpture covering every inch of their walls and ceiling.

Color Plate 2 General view of Bezeklik Monastery from the south. Xinjiang, China. Photo: S. Wriggins.

Bezeklik, which means "a decorated house" in Uighur, has sixty-seven (some say fifty-seven) caves, dating from the fourth century to the fourteenth. They are of diverse sizes; some are hewn out of the rock face, and others are constructed of sun-dried bricks. Many of the caves are carved deep into the cliff, an unusual feature. Most have barrel vaulting. The cells and chapels were decorated with sculpture and with paintings in tempera executed on walls covered with plaster. The living quarters were grouped together, with corridors, interior stairways, and narrow passages to link the different parts.

Color Plate 3 An Indian goddess and celestial musician. Wall painting, Cave of Frescoed Floor, Kizil. Xinjiang, China. 600–800 C.E. W. 134.5 cm; 53 in. Museum of Indian Art, Berlin.

In this wall painting a goddess and a celestial musician stand against a background of falling flowers, with a vague suggestion of fruit and petals, a kind of abstract decoration that might evoke thoughts of Matisse. The goddess wears an elaborate crown with three jeweled disks from which hang serpentine ribbons. Long, intertwined scarves, a *torgue*, or necklace of metal, and various pendant necklaces decorate the body. The musician at the right has a dark complexion, perhaps to suggest someone of Indian rather than Iranian nationality. The folds of his blue skirt are indicated by parallel, stringlike loops, as in many examples of Gandharan sculpture. The delicate and graceful curves of the scarves, the bow-shaped harp, and the bodies of the figures not only are very beautiful but also serve to express the idea of heavenly harmonies.

Color Plate 4 The mountains and Buddhas of Bamiyan. Afghanistan. Photo: Lee Coldren.

Because the two colossal Buddhas in the valley of Bamiyan are more than half a mile apart, only one of the niches in which they stand appears in this long-distance shot. Between them and for a considerable distance east and west, the cliff is honeycombed with vast complexes of cave chapels, assembly halls, sanctuaries, and monastic cells. Some of the caves are connected by grottoes within and along the front of the precipice. Both colossal Buddhas were designed with a system of stairways that gave access to the summit.

Around the smaller Buddha there is a gallery that makes it possible to circumambulate the image and that provides a view of the soffit of the niche. On the soffit is a gigantic painting of a Sun God and his chariot, pulled through the sky by snow-white horses, and attended by winged angels. He is wearing a long coat (an example of Iranian style as it developed under the Sassanians), with a sword attached to the belt, and he carries a scepter. There are many other paintings decorating the interior walls.

Color Plate 5 Buddha coming down the staircase from heaven. Burma. Early nineteenth century. Illustrated paper book in 70 folds, with Burmese text. 48 × 19 cm; 18.8 × 7.4 in. British Library, London.

The story of the Historical Buddha leaving earth for the Heaven of the Thirty-Three Gods and spending the months of retreat expounding the Four Noble Truths to his mother, followed by the drama of his glorious descent to earth, has stirred the imagination of artists in India, as well as in Tibet, Sri Lanka, Thailand, and Burma. In this colorful Burmese book illustration we see Indra sheltering the Buddha with an elegant jeweled parasol, on the Buddha's right, and Brahma with a whisk, on his left. The Buddha is descending a flight of ruby stairs—a slight variation of the usual iconography—and the other gods are on steps of gold and silver. Disciples kneel at the foot of this dramatically inclined staircase, and the Buddha is shown with his feet resting on a lotus, the symbol of purity.

Color Plate 6 General view of Sarnath. Uttar Pradesh, India. Photo: S. Hixon.

Five miles from Benares is the Deer Park at Sarnath, where Sakyamuni preached his first sermon and converted his first five disciples. Ruins on this site date back to the time of Asoka in the third century B.C.E. The Dhamekh stupa, whose vast silhouette is visible in the center, stands out in a setting where most of the ruins are little more than knee-high.

Color Plate 7 Overall view of Nalanda Monastery from Stupa 3. Bihar, India. Photo: S. Wriggins.

If one looks down from Stupa 3, one can see the outline of one of the monastic courtyards. In Xuanzang's time, along with the large preaching halls, there seem to have been six or seven courtyards flanked on all sides by a running veranda, with the monks' cells behind it. The cells were more spacious than usually found in monastic ruins, and there was an adjacent cell, perhaps for the keeping of manuscripts. A few of these courtyards and their verandas, with

Notes on Illustrations

remains of supporting pillars, can still be seen. Sometimes there was a shrine for a holy image with a dais in front at a lower level. It was in the courtyards, it seems, that many of the lectures and discourses to smaller audiences used to be delivered.

Color Plate 8 *Return of Xuanzang with the Buddhist Scriptures.* Dunhuang Caves, Gansu, China. n.d. Silk scroll. Fujita Art Museum, Osaka, Japan.

Xuanzang arrived in Chang'an laden with hundreds of precious relics, statues, and books, Mahayana and Hinayana scriptures as well as general works on logic and grammar. On this silk scroll from Dunhuang, horses carrying these books are led into the temple, followed by men bearing gifts. The street is lined with priests and officials, and at the right are people prostrating themselves in reverence. The stylized clouds at the top of the scroll might be the "colored cloud in the sky that seemed to float over the scriptures and the ... images as if it were welcoming the holy objects," about which Xuanzang reported.

Notes

Chapter 1

1. Nancy Elizabeth Boulton, "Early Chinese Buddhist Travel Records as a Literary Genre" (Ph.D. diss., University of Michigan, 1982), p. 281: "Xuanzang estimated that he had journeyed more than 50,000 *li*." That would equal 10,000 miles, according to Watters's and others' calculation of Xuanzang's *li* as one-fifth of a mile. Aurel Stein also believed that 5 *li* to the mile was generally correct. See his "The Desert Crossing of Hsuan-Tsang 630 A.D.," *Indian Antiquary* 50 (1921), pp. 15–25. *The Cambridge Encyclopedia of China*, ed. A. B. Hook (Cambridge: Cambridge University Press, 1982), states that a *li* equals one-third of a mile, which seems to be the most common modern interpretation. Xuanzang's achievement would become all the more remarkable, with his traveling at least 16,500 miles. I come back to Stein's view, because he followed Xuanzang so closely across the desert and located so many sites on the basis of a *li* equaling one-fifth of a mile. We are thus left with the question of what a *li* was regarded as in Tang times.

2. J. Schwartzberg, ed. *A Historical Atlas of South Asia* (Chicago: University of Chicago Press, 1978), p. 184.

3. D. Twitchett and J. Fairbank, *The Cambridge History of China*, vol. 3 (Cambridge: Cambridge University Press, 1979), pp. 191 and 240: "His style of government was esteemed not merely because of its success but because it approached the Confucian ideal of firm rule based upon responsiveness to the advice and opinion of ministers and concern for the welfare of the people, and because it showed real human empathy and intimate interplay between the ruler and his advisors."

4. A. F. Wright and D. Twitchett, *Perspectives on the T'ang* (New Haven: Yale University Press, 1973), p. 255. In general, Buddhist sources have tended to overestimate Xuanzang's influence and secular sources have tended to play it down. Buddhists have emphasized how often he was summoned to the palace, Taizong's authorizing fresh monastic ordinations, the completion of a new monastery for Xuanzang, and so on. The emperor also became interested in Buddhist translations and invited Xuanzang to live with him on various occasions. Wright attributed Taizong's Buddhist activities to his "astute political sense" and concluded that the emperor was primarily motivated by considerations of advantages to the dynasty and to the state. See also Kenneth Ch'en, *The Chinese Transformation of Buddhism* (Princeton: Princeton University Press, 1973), pp. 140ff; and Stanley Weinstein, *Buddhism Under the T'ang* (Cambridge: Cambridge University Press, 1987), pp. 26ff, which describes the great changes in the emperor's attitude toward Buddhism and how Xuanzang became his spiritual mentor in the last year of the emperor's life.

Notes to pp. 8–11

5. Wright and Twitchett, *Perspectives on the T'ang*, p. 14: "But its intellectual vitality had waned and in only a few circles were Confucian ideas seriously discussed. A violent age, an age of military domination made an inhospitable climate for Confucian studies."

6. S. Beal, trans., *The Life of Hiuen-Tsiang*, trans. from the Chinese of Shaman Hwui li (London, 1911; 2nd ed., Delhi: Munshiram Manoharlal, 1973), p. 3. Hereafter referred to as Beal, *Life*.

7. Beal, *Life*, p. 4.

8. Edward Conze, *Buddhism: Its Essence and Development* (Oxford, 1951; rpt. New York: Harper and Row, 1975), p. 125: "The two key words which occur on almost each page of Mahayana writings are the words Bodhisattva and emptiness."

9. Twitchett and Fairbank, *Cambridge*, vol. 3, p. 160. This time of disorder is confirmed by the following quote: "More than two hundred rebel organizations were involved in the fighting at the end of the Sui and during the early T'ang, although only about ten of these had any chance of establishing a stable regime and conquering the empire."

10. Li Yongshi, trans., *The Life of Hsuan-Tsang*, by Huili (Peking: Chinese Buddhist Association, 1959), p. 8. Hereafter referred to as Li Yongshi, *Life*.

11. As reported by Hans Biehlenstein in a lecture at Columbia University. See also A. Wright, "Changan," in *Cities of Destiny*, ed. A. Toynbee (New York: McGraw-Hill, 1967), p. 143: "The outer walls of the city ran ... 5.92 miles east and west and 5.27 miles north and south."

12. P. Hopkirk, *Foreign Devils on the Silk Road* (London: John Murray, 1980), p. 28: "In the year 742 its population was close on two million (according to the census of 754, China had a total population of fifty-two million, and contained some twenty-five cities with over half a million inhabitants). Chang-an ... had grown into a metropolis measuring six miles by five. ... Foreigners were welcome, and some five thousand of them lived there."

13. Beal, *Life*, p. 10.

14. Boulton, "Early Chinese Travel," p. 84: "The sophisticated ideas of Asanga and Vasubandhu came into vogue in China during the sixth century C.E. The *Sampari graha Sastra* (Collection of Mahayana writings) had been translated by Buddhasanta in 531, and again by Paramartha, in 563. ... Hsuantsang's brother was well known for preaching on this work. Hsuan-tsang also heard several famous Buddhist scholars lecture on it when he was at Ch'eng-du [Chengdu]. ... During this period, Hsuan-tsang also read Vasubandhu's lengthy *Abhidharma-kosa Sastra* [Treatise on the treasury of Buddhist philosophy], and later lectured on it. His profound comprehension of the inner significance of these texts never failed to astonish his teachers."

15. Edward Conze, *Buddhist Wisdom Books, the Diamond Sutra and the Heart Sutra* (1958; rpt. London: Allen and Unwin, 1980), p. 68. Conze used the phrase "So should one view what is conditioned" in the last line, which is very jarring to Western ears. Because he also said, "The characteristics of all conditioned things or of all the elements of *Samsara* (the world of birth and death) should be considered like the stars, a fault of vision ... ," I have taken the liberty of changing the last line.

16. Conze, *Buddhism* (1951 ed.), p. 168.

17. Zhu Qi (Chu Ch'i), *Xuanzang Xiyouji* (Xuanzang's journey to the West) (Hong Kong: Chan Chin Ta-yuan Shutien, 1957). This Chinese source, which is in the form of a novel, says that Xuanzang met an Indian scholar from Nalanda Monastery, the most famous Buddhist institution in the medieval world. This man said that there was a scholar there who understood the very doctrine that Xuanzang wished to study at Nalanda in India.

18. See Beal, *Life*, p. 11; and Li Yongshi, *Life*, p. 12.

19. Li Yongshi, *Life*, p. 270.

20. Arthur Waley, *The Real Tripitaka* (London: Allen and Unwin, 1952), p. 17.

21. See Beal, *Life*, p. 17; and Li Yongshi, *Life*, p. 18.

22. Beal, *Life*, p. 18.

23. Ibid., p. 18.

24. Conze, *Buddhist Wisdom Books* (1958 ed.), p. 103. Usually this sutra, called the *Hridaya* mantra, is not used for personal safety in the way Xuanzang used it. "The wondrous effect of the *Hridaya* lies in that it opens the mind to Enlightenment."

25. See Beal, *Life*, pp. 22ff.; and Li Yongshi, *Life*, p. 24.

26. Stein, "Desert Crossing," pp. 15–25.

27. J. Campbell, *The Hero with a Thousand Faces* (Princeton: Princeton University Press, 1968); and Esther Harding, *Journey into Self* (London: Longmans Green, 1956).

28. Waley, *Tripitaka*, p. 130.

Chapter 2

1. In the east the Tian Shan range divides Xinjiang into two great basins, the Tarim Basin to the south and the Dzungaria Basin to the north. At the western end of the mountains the Tian Shan range follows the boundary of China with the former Soviet Union.

2. When Xuanzang wrote his account of the western regions in 646 C.E., Turfan was no longer an independent kingdom. Since it was already part of the Tang empire, he began his narrative with the oasis of Karashahr. One has to rely on his biographer, Huili, for the record of his travels up to this point.

3. See Beal, *Life*, p. 26; and Li Yongshi, *Life*, p. 27.

4. Beal, *Life*, p. 30.

5. R. Grousset, *In the Footsteps of the Buddha*, trans. Mariette Leon (1932; rpt. London: Routledge and Kegan Paul, 1971), p. 50.

6. Li Yongshi, *Life*, p. 34. The Heavenly Ladder is a reference to the Buddha's descending from heaven after preaching to his mother, which is supposed to have taken place at Sankasya. The Bodhi tree is the tree under which the Buddha attained enlightenment.

7. T. Watters, trans., *On Yuan Chwang's [Xuanzang's] Travels in India* (London, 1904–1905; rpt. Delhi: Munshiram Manoharlal, 1961), vol. 1, p. 48.

8. Ibid., vol. 1, pp. 58, 59.

9. Grousset, *In the Footsteps*, p. 54.

10. Watters, *Travels in India*, vol. 1, p. 62.

Notes to pp. 30–38

11. Beal, *Life*, p. 41.
12. S. Beal, trans., *Si-yu-ki: Buddhist Records of the Western World*, by Hiuen Tsiang [Xuanzang] (London, 1884; rpt. Delhi: Oriental Books Reprint Corp., 1969), vol. 1, p. 26. Hereafter referred to as Beal, *Records*.
13. Beal, *Life*, p. 42.
14. Ibid.
15. Irene Frank and David Brownstone, *The Silk Road: A History* (New York: Facts on File, 1986), p. 176: "Hsüan-tsang's [Xuanzang's] view of this great nomadic assembly has a special interest for us in retrospect, because, following the pattern of steppe empires, the Turks were about to lose the always-fragile unity of the steppe peoples, fragmenting into several main branches that would make their name in the world." A few months after Xuanzang's departure, the Great Khan was killed by an assassin. After his death the ten tribes of the Western Turks were greatly weakened and divided into two khanates.
16. R. Grousset, *The Empire of the Steppes: A History of Central Asia*, trans. Naomi Walford (New Brunswick, N.J.: Rutgers University Press, 1970), p. 94.
17. B. A. Litvinsky, *Outline History of Buddhism in Central Asia*, Papers of UNESCO Conference on History, Archaeology and Culture in Central Asia (Calcutta: Kushan Studies in the USSR, 1970), p. 102. Many sites that reveal large quantities of Buddhist sculpture, paintings, and documents point to the presence of Buddhist along with Zoroastrian and Manichaean beliefs. In the early Middle Ages Buddhism was widespread in both Semirechye and Ferghana, judging from the archaeological material. See also D. Snellgrove, ed., *The Image of the Buddha* (London: Serindia; Paris: UNESCO; Tokyo: Kodansha International, 1978), p. 195.
18. Hans Bidder, *Carpets from Eastern Turkestan* (Accokeek, Md.: Washington International Associates, 1979), p. 18. To be sure, this is negative evidence, but Xuanzang's attention to detail was such that what he omitted was sometimes as important as what he included.
19. Beal, *Records*, vol. 1, p. 32.
20. J. Flecker, *The Golden Journey to Samarkand* (London: Max Goshen, 1913), p. 7.

Chapter 3

1. The ancient city where Xuanzang stayed lay further to the south than present-day Samarkand, close to the Zarasfshan River, where the excavations and cemetery of *Afrosiab* are now located. The pilgrim estimated its circumference to be 20 *li* or 5 to 7 miles.
2. Yasushi Inoue, *Journey Beyond Samarkand* (Tokyo: Kodansha International, 1971), p. 63: "It seems reasonable to suppose that these *Sui Chronicles* ... were based on reports made by Wei Chieh [Wei Jie] who says 'The people have deep-set eyes, high noses, and full beards. They are good at business and the city is always filled with foreign traders.'"
3. Beal, *Records*, vol. 1, p. 36.
4. S. Gaulier, R. Jera-Bezard, and M. Maillard, *Buddhism in Afghanistan and Central Asia* (Leiden: Brill, 1976), vol. 1, p. 2. The number of monks is of

considerable interest, for according to Chinese sources the first great translators of the Chinese canon came from Bactria and Sogdiana (Russia). See also Litvinsky, *Outline History*, pp. 64ff.

5. Litvinsky, *Outline History*, pp. 77, 73, 111. Kara-Tepe, a Buddhist cave monastery, has been excavated in the northwest corner of Old Termez. The distinctive feature of this first- to third-century C.E. monastic complex is that it was made up of caves hewn out of rock, an Indian characteristic quite exceptional in this area. Eight miles upstream from Termez is the astonishing site of Airtam, which was formerly a Buddhist settlement. The exquisitely carved limestone frieze showing male and female musicians is now in the Hermitage Museum in St. Petersburg. Finally, the reports of Xuanzang and a later pilgrim, Huichao (Hui-chi'ao), describing the spread of Buddhism in this area between Samarkand and Balkh, were brilliantly confirmed by the diggings at Zang-tepe, 30 kilometers from Termez. Fragments of birch-bark manuscripts with seventh- to eighth-century Buddhist texts consisting of rules of conduct for monks, nuns, and the Buddhist laity have been found.

6. J. Auboyer and others, *Buddha: A Pictorial History of His Life and Legacy*, trans. Anne E. Keep (New York: Crossroad Pub., 1983), p. 254.

7. The feeling of its ancient battlements is well described by the famous nineteenth-century traveler, R. Byron, in *The Road to Oxiana* (London: Jonathan Cape, 1937), p. 283: "After Akcha the colour of the landscape changed from lead to aluminium, pallid and deathly, as if the sun had been sucking away its gaiety for thousands and thousands of years; for this now was the plain of Balkh, and Balkh they say is the oldest city in the world."

8. B. Rowland, *The Art and Architecture of India: Buddhist, Hindu, Jain* (Baltimore: Penguin Books, 1953), p. 77: "The dates of Kanishka's reign have been the subject of considerable dispute among scholars. Although the years 78 and 128 C.E. have been suggested for the beginning of his reign, the most recent evidence seems to point to the year 144 as the date of his accession." For an authoritative discussion see also S. J. Czuma, *Kushan Sculpture: Images from Early India* (Cleveland: Cleveland Museum of Art, 1985), p. 40.

9. H. Bechert and R. Gombrich, *The World of Buddhism* (New York: Facts on File, 1984), p. 102. In addition to the economic and religious factors mentioned, Nancy Dupree told me that she felt that the possibility of flooding in the area was important.

10. Watters, *Travels in India*, vol. 1, p. 112.

11. Ibid., p. 102; and Frank and Brownstone, *Silk Road*, p. 135.

12. J. Majupurias, *Holy Places of Buddhism in Nepal and India* (Bangkok: Tecpress Service, 1989), p. 71.

13. D. Seckel, *The Art of Buddhism*, trans. Anne Keep (New York: Crown, 1964), p. 182.

14. Watters, *Travels in India*, vol. 1, p. 108.

15. Ibid., p. 115.

16. Waley, *Tripitaka*, p. 25. The sect was the Lokottara (Transcendental) school, which "came near to the Great Vehicle in that they did not accept the world ordinarily presented to our senses as real.... But there are transcendental realities, such as those achieved in the phases of consciousness called the Destruction of sorrow (*nirodna*) and the Road (*marga*) that leads to that de-

struction." See also S. Huntington and J. Huntington, *The Art of Ancient India* (New York: Weatherhill, 1985), p. 206. The Huntingtons thought that the cult of the Gigantic Buddhas might relate to Vairocana, the Buddha in whom the totality of the universe was personified.

17. Watters, *Travels in India*, vol. 1, p. 118.

18. B. Rowland, *Evolution of the Buddha Image* (New York: Asia Society, 1976), p. 10.

19. N. Dupree, *An Historical Guide to Afghanistan* (1970; rpt. Kabul: Afghan Tourist Association, 1977), p. 116.

20. Beal, *Records*, vol. 1, p. 55.

21. B. Rowland, *Art in Afghanistan: Objects from the Kabul Museum* (London: Allen Lane/Penguin Press, 1971), p. 24: "In Gandhara the translation of Buddhist iconography into ready-made foreign patterns is essentially the same process that took place in the formation of Early Christian art, so that it is not surprising in the earliest Gandhara Buddhas to find Sakyamuni with the head of a Greek Apollo, and arrayed in a pallium or toga. In exactly the same way the earliest representations of Christ show him with the head of a Greek sun god, and dressed in the garb of the teachers of the ancient world."

22. Watters, *Travels in India*, vol. 1, p. 124. Some versions indicate that there were several hostages, not just one. The Chinese hostage was apparently the son of a ruler of one of the Chinese dependencies.

23. Beal, *Life*, p. 55; and Beal, *Records*, vol. 1, p. 59.

24. See *Encyclopedia of Asian History*, ed. Ainslie Embree (New York: Scribner, 1988), p. 56.

25. Beal, *Records*, vol. 1, p. 90.

Chapter 4

1. A. Foucher, "Notes sur l'itineraire de Hiuan-Tsang en Afghanistan," *Etudes Asiatique pour le 25 Anniversaire de l'Ecole Française d'Extreme Orient* (Paris, 1925), p. 274. H. Wriggins translated the "Notes" for my use.

2. Watters, *Travels in India*, vol. 1, p. 140.

3. Ibid., pp. 131–178, for his general description of India.

4. J. B. Saint-Hilaire, *Hiouen Thsang in India*, trans. Laura Ensor (Calcutta: Susil Gupta, 1952), p. 62: "The peculiar talent of exposition of Chinese authors is a very curious phenomenon in the 7th century of our era. At this epoch, no one in Europe would have been capable of writing such books, and it is well to call attention again to this singular quality of Chinese writers, which has hitherto generally been ignored."

5. The grotto was located by A. Foucher, who followed the pilgrim mile by mile through both Afghanistan and Pakistan.

6. See Beal, *Life*, p. 60; and Li Yongshi, *Life*, p. 60. See also H. Giles, *The Travels of Fa-hsien (399–414 A.D.)* (Cambridge, 1923; rpt. London: Routledge and Kegan Paul, 1959), p. 18. Faxian, who had been there more than two centuries earlier, reported that it was like the Buddha's actual self with his golden complexion, his thirty-two greater and eighty lesser characteristic marks, all

brightly visible. He also said that the kings of various countries had sent skilled artists to sketch, but they had not been able to do so.

7. Alexander C. Soper, "Aspects of Light Symbolism in Gandharan Sculpture," *Artibus Asiae* 12, no. 3 (1949). Soper continued: "Of these, the first two, in spite of miraculous circumstances, might still be imagined as the work of human hands in common materials. The shadow alone was an essential part of the Buddha's person, not imitated" (p. 281). See also A. Soper, *Literary Evidence for Early Buddhist Art in China* (Ascona: Artibus Asiae, 1959), p. 141, and Appendix, "The Best Known Buddha Images," p. 259.

8. More than 1,000 stupas have been identified by French and Japanese archaeologists and the former Afghan Institute of Archaeology at nearby Hadda, one of the most exciting being the excavations at Tap-i-Shotor uncovered since 1965. Hellenistic figures were adapted. Zeus became Sarka (Indra) and Apollo was transformed into a Buddha. The Greek Heracles became Vajrapani, the thunder bearer.

9. Beal, *Records*, vol. 1, p. 91.

10. The boundaries of Gandhara are variously defined according to the period and subject of reference. Usually Gandhara refers to eastern Afghanistan and Pakistan.

11. Watters, *Travels in India*, vol. 1, p. 203.

12. Seckel, *Art of Buddhism*, p. 31. He modified this judgment somewhat on p. 116.

13. Beal, *Life*, p. 63; and H. Goetz, *The Art of India* (Baden-Baden, 1959; rpt. New York: Greystone Press, 1964), pp. 80ff. Another pilgrim, Songyun (Sungyun), who visited the site in 620 C.E., judged the height of the main building to be 400 feet; above this he saw an iron pillar 300 feet high supporting thirteen tiers of gilt disks, so that the total height comes to 700 feet. Goetz said that the whole monument was 638 feet tall, almost three times the height of the famous Qutb-Minar in New Delhi. The site in modern times seems to be buried under the modern city of Peshawar.

14. See Czuma, *Kushan Sculpture*, pp. 26ff, for a detailed discussion of the Buddha Image and Kushan chronology.

15. The gift of the Buddha's head, one of the most popular of the Buddhist legends, is portrayed in Miran on the Southern Silk Road, at the Dunhuang Caves in China, in many places in India, especially at Bharut, as well as in Tibet, present-day Pakistan, and Thailand.

16. Beal, *Records*, vol. 1, p. 113.

17. Nancy Dupree, "Gandhara: An Instant Guide to Pakistan's Heritage," Pakistan Tourism Development Corp., Karachi, n.d.

18. Geoffrey Ashe, *The Landscape of King Arthur* (New York: Henry Holt, 1987), p. 25.

19. Watters, *Travels in India*, vol. 1, p. 226.

20. Waley, *Tripitaka*, p. 29: "The strongly emotional side of his religion and his devout cult of the Buddhas and Bodhisattvas is constantly apparent throughout his career." See also Christine Guth Kanda, "The Silk Route and the Diamond Path," *Orientations*, May 1983. Also Pratapaditya Pal, *The Light of Asia: Buddha Sakyamuni in Asian Art* (Los Angeles: Los Angeles County

Museum, 1984), p. 256. The cult of the Healing Buddha gained special popularity in China after the translation of the *Bhaishajyagurusutra* (Healing Buddha sutra) by Xuanzang.

21. A. Foucher, *Notes on the Ancient Geography of Gandhara*, trans. H. Hargraves (Calcutta: Superintendent, Hindu and Buddhist Monuments Northern Circle, Government Printing Office, 1952), p. 39.

22. Giles, *Travels*, p. 9. Faxian described the territory vividly: "the side of the mountain being like a stone wall ten thousand feet in height. On nearing the edge, the eye becomes confused; and wishing to advance, the foot finds no resting place."

23. J. Mirsky, *Sir Aurel Stein* (Chicago: University of Chicago Press, 1977), p. 358. Stein, in one of his expeditions to Upper Swat, reported that the site of the Great Maitreya was still worshipped in "a Muhammadan guise."

24. Watters, *Travels in India*, vol. 1, p. 239.

25. Seckel, *Art of Buddhism*, p. 143.

26. See Huntington and Huntington, *Art of Ancient India*, p. 123, for a different interpretation of this early period in the development of Buddhist art.

27. Snellgrove, *The Image of the Buddha*, p. 46.

28. Ibid., p. 75: "The Christian gospels were compiled from earlier traditional materials and produced in Greek for Greek-speaking converts, who perhaps similarly wanted to know more of the person of this Christ Jesus, to whose teachings they had turned. . . . Similarly, the foreign converts of the far north-west of the Indian subcontinent would pose the question: 'What is a Buddha?'"

29. Beal, *Life*, p. 67.

30. Jean Fairley, *The Lion River: The Indus* (London: Allen Lane, 1975), p. 134.

31. Watters, *Travels in India*, vol. 1, p. 240.

32. J. Murray, *Handbook for Travellers in India, Pakistan, Burma and Ceylon* (London: John Murray, 1955), p. 501.

33. Isobel Shaw, *An Illustrated Guide to Pakistan* (Hong Kong: Hong Kong Guidebook Co., 1988), p. 126.

34. Watters, *Travels in India*, vol. 1, p. 250.

35. D. Klimburg-Salter, *The Silk Route and the Diamond Path* (Los Angeles: Los Angeles Art Council, 1982), p. 37.

36. A. Stein thought he recognized in the modern inhabitants the same characteristics that Xuanzang described. The pilgrim's brief sketch of Kashmir, Stein said, is the earliest ethnographic account of the region.

37. Beal, *Life*, p. 70.

38. Watters, *Travels in India*, vol. 1, p. 270.

39. Boulton, "Early Chinese Travel," p. 366. Apparently there are few details about it in later books. Buddhist schools differ in the councils they recognize. Only the first two are recognized by all schools. See Bechert and Gombrich, *World of Buddhism*, p. 78.

40. Waley, *Tripitaka*, p. 33.

41. Ibid., p. 32.

Chapter 5

1. See Beal, *Life*, p. 73; and Li Yongshi, *Life*, p. 73.
2. Beal *Life*, p. 74.
3. Waley, *Tripitaka*, p. 36.
4. Edward Conze, *Buddhist Scriptures* (1959; rpt. Harmondsworth: Penguin Books, 1984), p. 148.
5. Ibid., p. 150. Boulton, "Early Chinese Travel," p. 448. Karma: The Buddha took over the doctrines of *Karma* and *Samsara*, or Rebirth, which "were already present in India before his birth. Karma simply means deeds. A man's karma is the sum of his past and present actions which determine his future destiny.... Good deeds are rewarded and bad deeds punished either in present or future lives." A living being continues in the cycle of existence in which a being can be reborn as a deity, man, animal, hungry ghost, or denizen of hell. The goal of religion is to escape this cycle of rebirth.
6. Watters, *Travels in India*, vol. 1, p. 301.
7. Liu Xinru, *Ancient India and Ancient China* (Delhi: Oxford University Press, 1988). The larger bowls replaced the begging bowls of individual monks for donations during the Kushan period. The donations might have been money or valuable items.
8. R. C. Sharma, *Buddhist Art of Mathura* (Delhi: Agan Kala Prakashan, 1984), p. 47. Sharma believes that Xuanzang's account of Mathura may be the result of hearsay and tradition rather than firsthand observation.
9. S. Dutt, *Buddhist Monks and Monasteries in India* (London, 1962; rpt. Delhi: Motilal Banarsidass, 1988), p. 24. Also Bechert and Gombrich, *World of Buddhism*, p. 81.
10. Watters, *Travels in India*, vol. 1, p. 319.
11. See Beal, *Life*, p. 78: "So the common folk, men and women, are always congregating on the banks of the river. But this is merely the heretical belief of the district, and is not true."
12. Sarvepalli Gopal, *Jawaharlal Nehru: A Biography* (1989; abridged ed. Delhi: Oxford Indian Paperback, 1993), p. 453.
13. Ibid., p. 453.
14. Pal, *Light of Asia*, pp. 47ff, has an interesting discussion of why the Eight Miracles came to be associated with certain places. See also J. Huntington, "Sowing the Seeds of the Lotus: A Journey to the Great Pilgrimage Sites of Buddhism," *Orientations*, Nov. 1985, p. 46. The Scripture that is most often cited is the *Mahaparinibbana-sutta*, vv. 16-22: "There are four places, Ananda, which the believing man should visit with feelings of reverence and awe. What are the four? The place at which ... the Tathagata was born ... the place at which ... the Tathagata attained enlightenment, the place at which the Tathagata set up the Aryan kingdom ..., the place at which the Tathagata passed away."
15. Huntington, "Sowing the Seeds," p. 48. This is the first of a five-part series of articles in *Orientations* magazine: "Sowing the Seeds of the Lotus: A Journey to the Great Pilgrimage Sites of Buddhism." Part 1 discusses Asoka's archetypal pilgrimage, Lumbini and Kapilavastu, and Bodh Gaya and its environs; Part 2 (Feb. 1986, pp. 28-44), Varanasi and Sarnath; Part 3 (March 1986, pp.

32–47), Sravasti and the Jetavana Monastery and Sankasya; Part 4 (July 1986, pp. 28–41), Vaisali and Rajagriha; and Part 5 (Sept. 1986, pp. 46–59), Kusinagara, the Division of Relics, and the Eight *Mahastupas*, Asoka's division of relics, an alternative site for Kapilvastu, and the *Piprahwa Reliquary Inscription*.

16. Watters, *Travels in India*, vol. 1, p. 334.

17. In 1892 Alexander Cunningham identified the elephant capital as he followed in Xuanzang's footsteps in reconstructing his *The Ancient Geography of India* (1871; rpt. Delhi: Varnasi, Indological Book House, 1979). Cunningham was named the first head of the Archaeological Survey of India in 1861. The English translation of Faxian in 1836 and Xuanzang in 1858 opened whole new vistas for Indian archaeology, providing the possibility of finding lost buildings, Buddhist sites, and what Cunningham was proudest of doing, identifying the most famous cities in medieval India. See also Roy Sourindranath, *The Story of Indian Archaeology, 1784–1947* (Delhi: Indian Archaeological Survey, 1961), p. 38, where he quotes Cunningham: "In describing the ancient geography of India . . . the Elder Pliny, for the sake of clearness, follows the footsteps of Alexander the Great. For a similar reason I would follow in the footsteps of the Chinese pilgrim Hwen-Thsang." See also A. Imam, *Sir Alexander Cunningham and the Beginnings of Indian Archaeology* (Dacca: Asiatic Society of Pakistan, 1966), p. 213. Cunningham learned India by walking it. For the *Ancient Geography of India*, he chose the Buddhist period because of the favorable opportunities for local investigation that he enjoyed during his long and distinguished Indian career. To this Indian experience he added his knowledge of Burma. Thus the representation of clay seals found at Sravasti depicting bells hanging from stupas reminded him of still nights in Rangoon when the air was filled with the pleasing tinkling of bells from innumerable pagodas.

18. S. R. Goyal, *Harsha and Buddhism* (Meerut, India: Kusumanjali Prakashan, 1986). The thesis of this book is that Xuanzang's account of King Harsha's relation to Buddhism was misleading, that King Harsha never adopted Buddhism "as his personal religion," and that he remained devoted to Lord Siva, although he was extremely tolerant in his religious outlook. Goyal criticized Xuanzang for his "egotism and religious prejudices," completely overlooking the fact that it was his biographer who eulogized Xuanzang. The pilgrim is usually regarded as being unusually modest.

19. Beal, *Records*, vol. 1, p. 210.

20. Watters, *Travels in India*, vol. 1, p. 343.

21. D. Devahuti, *Harsha: A Political Study* (1970; rpt. Delhi: Oxford University Press, 1983), p. 179. King Harsha was also a poet and dramatist. One of his plays, the *Naga-ananda*, was set to music and performed as an opera. It was later taken to China and then to Japan, where it survives today as the world's oldest opera that is still being performed.

22. Devahuti, *Harsha*, p. 249, has a discussion of the dates of Xuanzang's two visits and the sending of an envoy to China by King Harsha, which she believed occurred before Xuanzang's second visit. That would explain how it was that on their first meeting King Harsha asked about the songs and dance celebrating Emperor Taizong.

23. Waley, *Tripitaka*, p. 38: "To begin with, the sort of Mahayana texts he was most interested in were to a considerable extent polemics against the

Hinayana, and it was essential to understand the doctrines that they were attacking."

24. Grousset, *In the Footsteps*, p. 131. This incident is reported in Beal, *Records*, p. 228, a little less romantically: "The disciple of Asanga was reposing outside the open window (*of Vasubandhu*) when in the after part of the night be began to quote the *Dasabhumi Sutra*. Vasubandhu, having heard it, understood its meaning and was deeply grieved that this profound and excellent doctrine had not come to his ears in times past and he laid the blame on his tongue as the origin of his sin of calumniating (*The Great Vehicle*) and so, said he, 'I will cut it out.'"

25. Grousset, *In the Footsteps*, p. 301.

26. Ibid. The effort to offer some insight into the Idealist school owes a great deal to Grousset's chapter on "The Flight of Mahayana Buddhism" and to Conze's *Buddhism* and his *Buddhist Scriptures*.

27. D. Ikeda, *The Flower of Chinese Buddhism*, trans. Burton Watson (New York: Weatherhill, 1986), p. 125.

28. See Beal, *Life*, p. 86; and Li Yongshi, *Life*, p. 85.

29. Watters, *Travels in India*, vol. 1, p. 368. Emphasis added.

30. Rowland, *Art and Architecture of India*, p. 143.

31. Soper, *Literary Evidence*, p. xiii.

32. Waley, *Tripitaka*, p. 127.

Chapter 6

1. Cf. *Mahaparinibbana-sutta, The Sutra of the Glorious Decease*, verses 16–22. Huntington, "Sowing the Seeds of the Lotus," part 1, p. 46. See also Boulton, "Early Chinese Travel," p. 85. It may be that Xuanzang was reading the later Mahayana version of the Great Decease, the *Mahaparinirvana-sutra*, not the earlier Pali text. It is certain that he was passionate in his devotion to Buddhism at an early age.

2. Snellgrove, *Image of the Buddha*. The four stages of his progress, birth, enlightenment, teaching, and final nirvana, and the four special miracles all became important places of pilgrimage. "It is quite possible that a deliberate collection of the stories and legends connected with these places provided the first incentive toward the production of a full-scale biography of Sakyamuni" (p. 45). See also A. Foucher, *The Life of the Buddha According to Ancient Texts and Monuments of India*, trans. S. B. Boas (Middletown, Conn.: Wesleyan University Press, 1963).

3. The holy land of Buddhism includes southern Nepal, the provinces of Uttar Pradesh, and southern Bihar.

4. Watters, *Travels in India*, vol. 1, p. 384. This scene is portrayed on reliefs in many places, such as Bharut, Amaravati, and Bodh Gaya.

5. Auboyer, *Buddha*, pp. 153ff, has a description of the miracle at Sravasti and says that Xuanzang went to where it was supposed to have happened and listened to the story of the miracle with tears in his eyes. See also Pal, *Light of Asia*, p. 48. Of the secondary miracles, the miracle of Sravasti is the most complex. Not only are there diverse textual traditions describing the event; it ap-

pears that there were actually several miracles performed on this occasion. The Buddha is said to have grown into an enormous tree from a mango stone, to have walked in the air in various attitudes, while alternately emitting flames and waves from the upper and lower parts of his body, and finally to have multiple images of himself in all directions. It is generally the multiplication and the teaching that are emphasized in artistic representations. See also A. Foucher, *The Beginnings of Buddhist Art*, trans. A. Thomas and F. W. Thomas (London: H. Milford, 1917), p. 183: "We are so accustomed to utilizing the archaeological information of the Chinese pilgrims in India, that we no longer think of being grateful to them for it; in order to measure the value of their help, we have to be once without it. That is the case in this occasion. . . . Fahien [Faxian] and Hiuan-tsang [Xuanzang], so explicit as regards the three other episodes, scarcely mention the one which interests us here," i.e., Sravasti.

6. Huntington, "Sowing the Seeds of the Lotus," pt. 3, p. 41.

7. Scholars are still debating the exact site of Kapilavastu. Xuanzang seems to have visited Tilurakot and Faxian Piprahwa.

8. Beal, *Records*, vol. 2, p. 19.

9. Xuanzang's description of Lumbini is quoted extensively in D. Mitra, *Buddhist Monuments* (1971; rpt. Calcutta: Sahitya Samad, 1980). See p. 58.

10. Beal, *Records*, vol. 2, p. 24.

11. Ibid., p. 25.

12. Watters, *Travels in India*, vol. 2, p. 44.

13. The usual account is of twin Sal trees, not four, as in Xuanzang's record.

14. Huntington, "Sowing the Seeds of the Lotus," pt. 5, p. 50. In connection with the Mauryan pillar commemorating the Buddha's nirvana reported by Xuanzang, Huntington said that it had "yet to be definitely identified at the site." He thought that it was possible that the remains could be under the surviving plinth of the temple, "but so far as this author is aware, no effort has been made to determine this."

15. Beal, *Records*, vol. 2, p. 7.

16. Watters, *Travels in India*, vol. 2, p. 42.

17. Ibid., p. 47.

18. Huntington, "Sowing the Seeds of the Lotus," pt. 2, p. 35.

19. A. Shearer, *The Traveler's Key to Northern India* (New York: Knopf, 1983), p. 429. Unfortunately the stupa was pulled down by Jagat Singh, the prime minister of the maharaja of Benares in 1794, but there were several excavations in the area (1904–1907), which unearthed both the famous Bala image and the Preaching Buddha. Public opinion was so enraged by the destruction of the stupa and the throwing of some of its relics into the river that when it was discovered, a new interest in Sarnath developed. See also D. C. Ahir, *Buddhist Shrines in India* (Delhi: B. R. Publishing, 1986), p. 23.

20. Shearer, *Traveler's Key*, pp. 432ff. The purpose of Indian art is to serve as a springboard from which the mind can ascend from the concrete world to the abstract realm of the spirit. In a series of diagrams Shearer showed the image as *Centered Energy, Potential Energy, Manifest Energy, Impersonal Energy*, and *Pure Energy*. These configurations resembling mandalas show that what began as a piece of figurative form of the highest quality dissolved into pure form of the diamond thunderbolt (*Vajra*), a comprehensive symbol of the *Dharma*

much beloved of Mahayanist iconographers. See also H. Zimmer's profound discussion of the spiritual message of sacred images. Zimmer contrasted the roving eye of normal vision with seeing a picture in its totality and keeping it all in focus, which relates to Indian ways of seeing images. H. Zimmer, *Artistic Form and Yoga in the Sacred Images of India*, trans. Gerald Chapple and James B. Lawson (Princeton: Princeton University Press, 1984), p. 197.

21. Ahir, *Buddhist Shrines*, p. 23. See also F. L. Woodward, ed. and trans., *Some Sayings of the Buddha* (1925; rpt. London: Oxford University Press, 1955), p. 7, which has a more complete rendering of the First Sermon.

22. Boulton, "Early Chinese Travel," p. 314.

23. Pal, *Light of Asia*, p. 48: "Curiously the miracle of the Monkey Giving an Offering of Honey to the Buddha is not given in any of the known biographical texts; it is, however, briefly described in the *Dhammapada Commentary* and by Xuanzang. Between these two sources, the story states that once a monkey offered honey to the Buddha and thereafter danced with joy, in his ecstasy fell into a well and died. It is curious that such an incident should have taken place in an urban environment; this seems to reveal the rather contrived association of the episode with the important city of Vaisali. Furthermore one would have expected an incident of this nature to have occurred during the Enlightenment Cycle when the Buddha would have need of nourishment."

24. Watters, *Travels in India*, vol. 2, p. 75.

25. E. J. Thomas, *The History of Buddhist Thought* (1933; rpt. Santa Fe, N.M.: Sun Publishing, 1981), p. 33. This council is not mentioned outside of Sri Lankan chronicles, which claim it sent missions throughout historic India and beyond. See also W. Zwalf, *Buddhism: Art and Faith* (London: British Museum Publications, 1985), p. 78, for a general discussion of Buddhist councils.

26. Watters, *Travels in India*, vol. 2, p. 113. Xuanzang's description is also cited in Mitra, *Buddhist Monuments*, p. 62, for as Mitra said, it is largely applicable even to the present remains.

27. Usually the text indicates that there was only one maiden.

28. Shearer, *Traveler's Key*, p. 439.

29. D. K. Barua, *Bodh Gaya Temple: Its History* (Bihar: Bodh Gaya Temple Management Co., 1981), p. 40.

30. The Tibetan practice of worshippers' prostrating themselves is very impressive. They slide forward, usually on a piece of wood. Their hands are protected with a wooden block. Then they pull themselves up again. I met one Tibetan who said he had performed this act 2,800 times that day and would continue to do that every day for a month.

31. Beal, *Life*, p. 104; and Watters, *Travels in India*, vol. 2, p. 115.

32. Beal, *Life*, p. 105. See also Li Yongshi, *Life*, p. 101: Xuanzang concluded his wailing with, "I can only have reached this place during the Image Period—How evil my deeds must have been." Buddhism is supposed to exist for three periods, i.e., the Right Dharma period of 500 years, the Resemblance period of 1,000 years, and the final period of 3,000 years. "Image" in this case refers to the Image Period, or what D. Ikeda called the Middle Period of the Law. See also Ikeda, *Chinese Buddhism*, p. 130.

Chapter 7

1. C. S. Upasak, *Nalanda: Past and Present* (Bihar: Nava Nalanda Mahavihara, 1977), p. 13. Today the Nalanda tradition is being revived. An institute of postgraduate Pali and Buddhist studies, established at Nalanda in 1951, has a fine library of Buddhist literature in Pali, Sanskrit, and other languages. In 1957, the Chinese government, in a gesture of friendship between China and India, provided a Xuanzang Memorial Hall to commemorate the stay of the Chinese monk at Nalanda. It has not yet been furnished.

2. There is little agreement on the duration of Xuanzang's stay at Nalanda. Vincent Smith, "The Itinerary of Yuan-Chwang," p. 329 (appendix), in Watters, *Travels in India*, said that he was at Nalanda in 637 C.E. and that he stayed for a while, returned, and then studied for fifteen months. Counting his subsequent visit at the end of 642 C.E., his total residence amounted to about two years. That seems very likely in view of his subsequent travels in India. He was in the south of India at 639 and in Nasik in 641 C.E. Waley, Saint-Hilaire, and others indicated that he was there for five years.

3. Beal, *Life*, pp. 105ff, and Li Yongshi, *Life*, pp. 102ff. Had he not been coached so carefully, as indicated in this story, we might think he was carrying out the Chinese practice of kowtowing on his hands and knees, not an Indian usage. But Xuanzang was familiar with forms of salutation in India. In his survey of India he enumerated the nine degrees of etiquette in showing respect: (1) greeting with a kind inquiry; (2) reverentially bowing the head; (3) raising hands to the head with an inclination of the body; (4) bowing with the hands folded on the breast; (5) bending a knee; (6) bowing down on both knees; (7) going down on the ground with hands and knees; (8) bowing down with knees, elbows, and forehead to the ground; (9) prostrating oneself on the earth. The performance of these nine acts from the lowest to the highest is only one act of reverence. Cf. Watters, *Travels in India*, vol. 1, p. 173.

4. Beal, *Life*, p. 107, and Li Yongshi, *Life*, p. 103. Xuanzang had been traveling now from 629 to 637 C.E., a full eight years.

5. Watters, *Travels in India*, vol. 2, p. 109.

6. Beal, *Life*, p. 111.

7. The Archaeological Survey of India lists eleven monastic sites and five temples. Xuanzang mentioned eight lecture halls, but it isn't clear what precisely the grounds included. "It is not possible to identify with any certainty any of the structures mentioned by Hieun-tsang or others like the Dharmaganja Library, the stupas of Sariputra or Buddha; Sakraditya's monastery, the Vihara of Harsha with its colossal bronze statue of the Buddha, or the Baladitya temple" (Upasak, *Nalanda*, p. 67).

8. F. Asher, *The Art of Eastern India 300 to 800* (Minneapolis: Oxford University Press and University of Minnesota, 1980), p. 46.

9. Upasak, *Nalanda*, p. 39: "If the last two strokes were already sounded, the inmates did not eat, and if anybody transgressed it, he was expelled in accordance with the rules." No explanation for this strict rule is given.

10. L. M. Joshi, *Studies in the Buddhist Culture of India During the Seventh and Eighth Centuries* (1967; 2d ed. Delhi: Motilal Banarsidass, 1971), p. 105.

11. L. Lahiri, trans., *Chinese Monks in India*, by Yijing (I Ching) (Delhi: Motilal Banarsidass, 1986), p. 56.

12. Dutt, *Buddhist Monks and Monasteries*, p. 340. Dutt thought the figure of above 10,000 monks was a gross exaggeration, "for I Ching [Yijing] who came to Nalanda only about three decades after Hsuan-tsang, puts the numbers 'upwards of 3,000' in his Record and 3,500 in his Memoirs." See also Beal, *Life*, p. 112.

13. Watters, *Travels in India*, vol. 1, p. 162. In his general discussion of India, Xuanzang said: "Wherever there is a community of brethren it makes [its own] rules of gradation. The Brother who expounds orally one treatise ... in the Buddhist Canon is exempted from serving under the Prior; he who expounds two is invested with the outfit of a Superior; he who expounds three has Brethren deputed to assist him; he who expounds four has lay servants assigned to him; he who expounds five rides an elephant; he who expounds six rides an elephant and has a surrounding retinue. Where the spiritual attainments are high, the distinctions conferred are extraordinary."

14. Beal, *Records*, vol. 2, p. 150.

15. Ibid., p. 153.

16. Ibid.

17. Li Yongshi, *Life*, p. 112. Ananda was excluded at first from this council because he was not free from "binding ties." Apparently Ananda tended to fall in love. He was finally allowed to participate because of a legendary miracle, which Xuanzang described very well. This incident is also mentioned in Kogen Mizuno, *Buddhist Sutras: Origin, Development and Transmission*, multiple translators (Tokyo: Kosei Publishing, 1982), p. 19.

18. Devahuti, *Harsha*, p. 284. Devahuti provided the first critical study of the correspondence between Indian monks and Xuanzang, both in the Chinese and Uigur-Turkish versions.

19. Li Yongshi, *Life*, p. 117, gives a detailed description of the lectures on various sastras that Xuanzang attended.

20. Waley, *Tripitaka*, p. 47.

21. What is perhaps of greater interest is that Xuanzang mentioned Panini, whose analytical study of grammar was founded in the fourth century B.C.E. in India. Xuanzang noted that Panini's work was "the one [which is] at present used in India" (Beal, *Life*, p. 122). Just as Xuanzang was interested in Indian logic, he may have wanted to introduce the complex inflections of the Sanskrit language to the Chinese as well in order to point out the sophistication of Indian grammar. See also J. Norman, *The Chinese* (New York: Cambridge University Press, 1988), p. 152: "As we have seen, China has a very rich tradition in phonological study; the study of grammar, on the other hand, is a rather recent development, ... Ma Jianzhong (1845–1900) was the first person to write a systematic grammar of Chinese."

22. Li Yongshi, *Life*, p. 119.

23. S. Beal, *Records*, vol. 2, p. 170.

24. See K. L. Hazra, *Buddhism in India as Described by the Chinese Pilgrims* (Delhi: Munshiram Manoharlal, 1983), p. 38, for a somewhat more detailed description of the curriculum.

25. Li Yongshi, *Life*, p. 155.

26. Ibid., p. 165.

27. Devahuti, *Harsha*, p. 283. She included a second letter from Xuanzang that contained some new material on both the use of cotton and a reference to the *Rig Veda*. It also showed a less generous Xuanzang who deplored the fact that one of the Indian monks with whom he had engaged in debate at Kanyakubja continued to hold to his Hinayana beliefs when he could so easily have saved himself and become a Mahayana Buddhist.

Chapter 8

1. Li Yongshi, *Life*, p. 121.

2. Ikeda, *Chinese Buddhism*, p. 134. See also Wright and Twitchett, *Perspectives on the T'ang*, p. 296.

3. D. T. Suzuki, *On Indian Mahayana Buddhism* (New York: Harper and Row, 1968), p. 101.

4. See Schwartzberg, *Historical Atlas*, p. 184: "Despite the fullness of his descriptions, the reconstruction of his itineraries is not free from controversy.... Hence his route like other Chinese pilgrims on our map is at best an approximation."

5. According to Robert Thurman, there is a tradition in Indian philosophy of knowing your opponent's philosophy and being able to elaborate it as convincingly as you can. This technique means that you push your own doubt to its strongest point, which enables you to give a more powerful argument for your own beliefs.

6. In the twentieth century the Sunderabends, with their dense jungle at the delta of the Ganges River, in Bangladesh, is still the home of the famed Bengal tigers.

7. Watters, *Travels in India*, vol. 2, p. 185.

8. Ibid., p. 191.

9. Beal, *Life*, p. 134.

10. Watters, *Travels in India*, vol. 2, p. 200.

11. Seckel, *Art of Buddhism*, p. 39: "It now became possible to render without hesitation the things of this world, and even the Buddha; but this had to be done in such a way that it did not set out to be a valid definition of a true reality, but only something temporary and makeshift, a mere reflection of ultimately valid truth—in other words, of the indefinable, invisible and unrepresentable 'Void' which at the same time means both 'yes' and 'no,' 'neither' and 'nor,' and whose apparently negative character actually implied the supreme positive. This development of Mahayanist philosophy—one of the most important for Buddhist art in general—was thus accomplished as early as the second century."

12. P. Williams, *Mahayana Buddhism: The Doctrinal Foundation* (London: Routledge, 1989), p. 56: "Modern scholars favor the theory that there were at least two Nagarjunas, distinguishing between the philosopher Nagarjuna, who was probably from the southern or Andhra region, ... and a later Nagarjuna who was a Tantric alchemist and yogin. In addition it is possible that works have been attributed by the Buddhist tradition to Nagarjuna simply because of

his doctrinal importance, so that the name Nagarjuna now refers to a composite being of myth rather than a historical figure."

13. Watters, *Travels in India*, vol. 2, p. 207, has a long footnote about this so-called Pigeon Monastery, which may be the Black Bee Mountain. Beal, in the preface to the *Life*, p. xx, suggested that after the Buddhists had established themselves in this monastery, the Brahmins, by a strategy, took possession of it and changed its name. Cunningham, *Ancient Geography of India*, pp. 440ff, also discussed the cave and its possible origin.

14. Beal, *Records*, vol. 2, p. 215.

15. J. Harle, *The Art and Architecture of the Indian Subcontinent* (Harmondsworth: Penguin Books, 1986), p. 45: "More than this," as Harle pointed out, "the concept of the cave with its elemental, uncreated (*svayambhu*) nature strikes one of the fundamental chords of Indian spirituality."

16. Zhu Qi (Chu Ch'i), *Xuanzang Xiyouji*. The novel was the only safe commemoration that could be made in the political climate of the time. "In Chu Chi's little book . . . there is some interest just in his conception of how to tell the tale for Chinese at a point of time in their history [1956] when scholars, tradition, history, and the sense of cultural values all were being battered about. That Chu Chi cast his book in the form and borrowing the tone of the traditional Chinese adventure novel, must have had a layer of meaning for him in that situation that is not immediately apparent" (Letter from Dr. Frederick W. Mote, November 30, 1983).

17. Grousset, *In the Footsteps*, p. 178. "It is really the Calukyan state of Vengipura that is mentioned by Hsuan-tsang under the name of the Andhra kingdom. The south-east of ancient Andhra, with Bezvada and Amaravati, towns situated on the two banks of the lower Krishna, formed in the seventh century the separate kingdom of Dhanakataka."

18. Xuanzang mentioned two rock-cut monasteries, which cannot be construed as the great Amaravati stupa standing in the middle of the plain. And yet his biographer said, "And so becoming bound together in mind they all went in company to pay reverence to the sacred traces of the region." It is possible that he saw Amaravati, but it there is no real evidence that he did.

19. Wei Tat, *Ch'eng Wei-Shih Lun* (The doctrine of mere consciousness) (Hong Kong: Ch'eng Wei-Shih Lun Publication Committee, 1973), pp. xlixff. The book includes an English translation of *Thirty Verses* and Xuanzang's commentary.

20. Li Yongshi, *Life*, p. 142.

21. Beal, *Records*, vol. 2, p. 256.

22. Watters, *Travels in India*, vol. 2, p. 239. It is interesting that D. Mitra regarded Xuanzang's description of Ajanta as being particularly vivid. See Mitra, *Buddhist Monuments*, p. 150. This description is included in the Archaeological Survey of India's pamphlet on Ajanta. Vincent Smith, *The Oxford History of India* (London, 1958; rpt. Oxford: Oxford University Press, 1967), regarded Xuanzang's description "brief and indistinct" but thought that he seemed to have gone there. Walter Spink, the authority on Ajanta, speculated that since he did not list the number of monks at Ajanta (although he did for the region of Maharashtra) or mention that the cave was deserted—which it may have been at the time—he may not have visited Ajanta.

Notes to pp. 139–151

23. Beal, *Records*, vol. 2, p. 278.

24. Xuanzang reported that the country had no male children, and a neighboring king sent men every year to cohabit with the women. Whatever male children were born were not reared there.

25. Xuanzang may have gone around northern India, back to Ujjain, and returned to the west coast. He then probably explored the delta region of the Indus River in present-day Pakistan. He traveled through Sindh and reported that the government held sway over four outlying provinces. It is difficult, according to Jean Fairley, *Lion River*, p. 233, who wrote about the Indus River, to identify the places he mentioned except for Multan.

26. Beal, *Records*, vol. 2, p. 274.

27. Xuanzang used the term *Five Indias* inconsistently. Sometimes he applied it to King Harsha's exploits in northern India. He also applied it to the whole continent. Other Chinese travelers observed that India had five main divisions: north, east, west, central, and south. Apparently they followed the notion then prevalent in India. Quote from Cunningham, *Ancient Geography of India*, p. 197, who confirmed Xuanzang's impression that the sun temple at Multan was widely known at the time. Later it was called the Golden Temple by the Arabs.

28. See Rowland, *Art and Architecture of India*, p. 61.

29. Fairley, *Lion River*, p. 182.

30. Snellgrove, *Image of the Buddha*, p. 86: "The greatest change in the history of Buddhist thought was occasioned by the general shift in Indian philosophical and cosmic theory, noticeable from about the beginning of the Christian era, perhaps about five hundred years after Sakyamuni's Final Nirvana. All Indian religious and philosophical schools were affected by it, and it could be argued that Buddhists initiated it. Its most famous representative is Nagarjuna, certainly an historical person who probably lived about the first century C.E. although the accounts of his life appear to be entirely legendary."

31. Beal, *Life*, p. 154.

32. Suzuki, *Indian Mahayana Buddhism*, p. 101.

33. Smith *Oxford History*, p. 183: "It is impossible to say exactly what happened in most of the provinces for a considerable time after his disappearance from the scene. . . . The partial unity of Indian history vanished with Harsha, and is not restored in any considerable measure until the closing years of the twelfth century."

34. Li Yongshi, *Life*, p. 161.

35. Ibid., p. 163.

36. R. Murphy, *A History of Asia* (New York: HarperCollins, 1992), p. 77.

37. Yin and Yang refer to the active masculine principle and the passive feminine principle in Chinese cosmology. Quote from Li Yongshi, *Life*, p. 163.

38. Beal, *Life*, p. 169.

Chapter 9

1. Waley, *Tripitaka*, p. 60. See also Rowland, *Evolution of the Buddha Image*, p. 8: "The *Dharmakaya* is the Buddha *logos*, an invisible force permeating the universe as the spiritual essence of the ultimate and absolute Buddha;

the *Sambhogakaya* or Body of Bliss is that transfigured Body of Splendor which the eternal Buddha reveals only to Bodhisattvas; and the *Nirmanakaya* is the noumenal earthly shape in which the cosmic Buddha reveals himself as an illusion for the benefit of mortals." See also Conze, *Buddhism* (1975 ed.), p. 38: "Wherever the word Buddha is used in the Buddhist tradition, one has this three-fold aspect of the Buddha in view. To the Christian and agnostic historian, only the human Buddha is real, and the spiritual and magical are nothing to him but fictions. The perspective of the believer is quite different. The Buddha-nature of the Buddha's 'glorious body' stands out most clearly, and the Buddha's human body and historical experience appear like a few rags thrown over this spiritual glory."

2. Devahuti, *Harsha*, p. 180: "King Harsha was always bestowing gifts on the pious and the learned. The "Life" records an offer by him of the revenue of eighty large towns to a versatile scholar named Jayasena and to Xuanzang a present of 10,000 gold pieces, three times as much silver, and other things."

3. Li Yongshi, *Life*, p. 170.

4. Ibid.

5. Beal, *Life*, p. 175.

6. Boulton, "Early Chinese Travel," p. 97: "He had a fine and sonorous voice and always spoke distinctly and elegantly so that his listeners never felt tired in his presence." See also Beal, *Life*, p. 177; and Li Yongshi, *Life*, p. 172.

7. Suzuki, *Indian Mahayana Buddhism*, p. 101.

8. Devahuti, *Harsha*, p. 282. Letter of Xuanzang to Prajnadeva, dated second month 654 C.E. The staging of public debates on Buddhist doctrine and philosophy is still practiced by Buddhist monks in Tibet; the participants lunge forward, clap their hands loudly, and are very aggressive as they try to break down the weakness of their opponents. (This was corroborated by Robert Thurman, Lecture, Columbia University, March 1989.)

9. Beal, *Life*, p. 188.

10. J. Mirsky, *The Great Chinese Travellers* (Chicago: University of Chicago Press, 1964), p. 105.

11. This well-known happening, which filled Xuanzang with such anguish, was echoed in the Ming novel *Journey to the West* and is part of temple lore even now in China. In Kunming there are fish drums in a Buddhist temple, so called because one may fill their mouths with paper money "to pay for new scriptures to replace those lost by the Buddhist pilgrim in the river." See also Waley, *Tripitaka*, p. 71: "Rare treasures and Buddha relics, we are told have the same effect. A similar disaster befell Sir George Scott Robertson, some 200 miles higher up on the Indus in 1890. Owing to the swamping of a boat, he lost 'all my toys and books, journals and diaries for three years besides a quantity of small valuables.'" See also Beal, *Life*, p. 191; and Li Yongshi, *Life*, p. 187.

12. Beal, *Records*, vol. 2, p. 286.

13. Sir Henry Yule, "Essay on the Geography of the Valley of the Oxus," in *Journey to the Source of the River Oxus*, by J. Wood (London, 1872; rpt. Karachi: Oxford University Press, 1976), p. xxvii: "When the Chinese pilgrim, Hwen Thsang, passed through the Oxus valley on his way to India in 630, and on his return in 644, he found the former empire of the Haiathalah [White Huns] broken into a great number of small states, of which he enumerates 27,

all acknowledging the supremacy of the Turkish Khakan [Khan]. . . . In studying the brief but tolerably precise notes of Xuanzang it is not a little remarkable how many of the political divisions, and even of the names are substantially identical with those which still exist. In fact this is the case with so large a proportion of these states, that we feel, in reading this part of Xuanzang's memoirs, that we have already opened the chapter of modern geography."

14. Waley, *Tripitaka*, p. 73. He described a spectacular headdress worn by the women, a wooden horn with two branches in front, one above the other; the upper branch represented the woman's father-in-law and the lower her mother-in-law. When both of the parents were dead, the horn headdress could be laid aside; when either in-law died, they removed a branch.

15. G. E. Wheeler, preface to *Journey*, by Wood, p. xii: "When proceeding along these a foot-passenger, in the words of a Russian writer, feels himself as precariously poised as a tear on an eyelash."

16. A. Stein, *On Ancient Central Asian Tracks* (Chicago: University of Chicago Press, 1964), p. 268. Stein, whose heroes were the Chinese pilgrim and the Venetian explorer, also visited Lake Victoria in 1913. He found the clearness, fresh taste, and dark blue color of the lake to be just as Xuanzang had described them. What the Kirghiz told him about the shore swarming with aquatic birds in spring and autumn proved to be true and agreed with Xuanzang's account.

17. Waley, *Tripitaka*, p. 74.

18. A. Stein, *Ancient Khotan* (Oxford: Clarendon Press, 1907), vol. 1, p. 31.

19. Watters, *Travels in India*, vol. 2, p. 286.

20. A. Stein, *Ruins of Desert Cathay* (London, 1912; rpt. New York: Dover, 1987), vol. 1, p. 93: "[I] felt not a little pleased to think that here, at the very first point where I had touched his Central-Asian route, archaeological evidence on the spot confirmed afresh the often-proved trustworthiness of my Chinese Patron Saint."

21. H. W. Tilman, *The Seven Mountain Travel Book* (London and Seattle: Diadem Books, 1983), p. 620, quotes Xuanzang's description of the Chickiklik plateau at some length.

22. Watters, *Travels in India*, vol. 2, p. 289.

23. Grousset, *In the Footsteps*, p. 230.

24. Watters, *Travels in India*, vol. 2, p. 293.

25. Ibid., p. 295.

26. Ibid., p. 297; and *Encyclopedia Britannica*, 1964 ed., vol. 20, p. 662. The essentials of silk making were taken from Khotan to Byzantium secretly.

27. Klimburg-Salter, *The Silk Route*, p. 89. See also Stein, *Ancient Khotan*, vol. 1, p. 154, which has an extensive discussion of the Indian element in Khotan.

28. Snellgrove, *Image of the Buddha*, p. 204. Snellgrove repeated the story of the Buddha flying to Pima as illustrating the importance of reproductions of the so-called Famous Images: Three hundred li east of Khotan "is a figure of the Buddha in a standing position, made of sandalwood. The figure is about 20 feet high. It works many miracles and reflects constantly a bright light. Those who have any disease, according to the part affected, cover the corresponding place on the statue with gold-leaf, and forthwith they are healed. People who address

prayers to it with a sincere heart mostly obtain their wishes. This is what the natives say: This image in old days when the Buddha was alive, was made by Udayana, king of Kausambi. When Buddha left the world it mounted of its own accord into the air and came to the north of this kingdom."

29. B. Rowland, *The Art of Central Asia* (New York: Crown, 1974), p. 127. See also J. Williams, "Iconography of Khotanese Painting," *East and West* 23 (1973).

30. Stein, *On Ancient Central Asian Tracks*, p. 56.

31. Waley, *Tripitaka*, p. 76. Waley explained on p. 70 that the *Abhidharma*, the one with the unimaginably long name, *Mahayana-abhidharmasamuccaya-vyakhya*, the Chinese abbreviate to two syllables: *Tui-fa* (i.e., *Abhidharma*).

32. Beal, *Records*, vol. 2, p. 325.

33. A. C. Moule and Paul Pelliot, eds., *Marco Polo: The Description of the World* (London: Routledge, 1938), p. 150.

34. J. Bonavia, *An Illustrated Guide to the Silk Route* London: Collins, 1988), p. 92.

35. Stein, *Ruins of Desert Cathay*, p. 517. At Miran Stein unearthed a Buddhist stupa with frescoes of youthful angels and a frieze telling the familiar story of Prince Visvantara, the Indian king who gave away all his possessions. Xuanzang had first encountered this story fourteen years earlier on his outward journey.

36. Watters, *Travels in India*, vol. 2, p. 305.

Chapter 10

1. Beal, *Life*, p. 209.
2. Li Yongshi, *Life*, p. 204.
3. A. De Silva, *The Art of Chinese Landscape Painting in the Caves of Tunhuang* (New York: Crown, 1964), p. 136. Some art historians think this represents an illustration to the parable of the Conjured-up City from the Lotus Sutra. See T. Akiyama and S. Matsubara, *Arts of China: Buddhist Cave Temples, New Researches*, trans. A. Soper (1969; rpt. Tokyo: Kodansha International, 1972), p. 72.
4. Li Yongshi, *Life*, p. 209.
5. Boulton, "Early Chinese Travel," p. 202. I have followed Boulton and Li Yongshi (p. 208) more closely than Beal, *Life*.
6. Pratapaditya Pal, *The Ideal Image: The Gupta Sculptural Tradition and Its Influence* (New York: Asia Society/Weatherhill, 1978), p. 49. See also Pal, *Light of Asia*, p. 171.
7. "They also received the scriptures which the Master had obtained in the western countries, namely 224 books of Mahayana sutras; 192 books of Mahayana sastras; 15 books of the *Tripitaka* of the Sthavira School; 15 books of the *Tripitaka* of the Sammatiya School; 22 Books of the *Tripitaka* of the Mahisasaka School; 17 books of the *Tripitaka* of the Kasyapiya School; 42 books of the *Tripitaka* of the Dharmagupta School; 67 books of the *Tripitaka* of the Sarvastivadin School; 36 books concerning the *Hetuvidya Sastra* and 13

Notes to pp. 179–181

books concerning the *Sabdavidya* Sastra; making a total number of 657 books, bound in 520 cases and loaded on 20 horses" (Li Yongshi, *Life*, p. 208).

8. Ibid., p. 210.

9. Ibid., p. 211.

10. Waley, *Tripitaka*, p. 83. See also Weinstein, *Buddhism Under the T'ang*, pp. 24ff.

11. Li Yongshi, *Life*, p. 213.

12. Ibid., p. 214.

13. Watters, *Travels in India*, vol. 1, p. 154.

14. Saint-Hilaire, *Xuanzang in India*, p. 52: "We must therefore conclude that in the seventh century after Christ, at the time when the Chinese pilgrim travelled over India, there were to be found in Sanskrit literature works which described more or less faithfully the history, statistics and geography of the country; none of them have come down to us . . . sometimes he calls them *Ancient Descriptions*, sometimes *Historical Memoirs*, sometimes *Collection of Annals* and *Royal Edicts*; at other times *Secular Histories* or simply *India Books* on such and such a country or *Memoirs of India*."

15. Murphy, *Asia*, p. 64: "Han writers set a high standard for historical scholarship that many Western scholars feel was not equalled elsewhere until the eighteenth century in the West." See also F. W. Mote, *Intellectual Foundations of China* (New York: Knopf, 1971 ed.), pp. 50ff.

16. Boulton, "Early Chinese Travel," p. 363. Boulton referred to Joseph Needham's "Time and Knowledge in China and the West," in *Voices in Time*, ed. J. T. Fraser (New York: Braziller, 1966), pp. 128–351.

17. Devahuti, who has written a political biography of King Harsha, noted, "It was natural for the Chinese pilgrim to try to establish the importance of 'filial piety' in Indian society because it was one of the highest virtues according to the Chinese way of life" (*Harsha*, p. 5).

18. Ibid., p. 8: "The criticism often levelled against Hsuan-tsang that he gives a biased picture of his Indian patron—not only because of the latter's munificence towards him, but also because of Harsha's marked inclination towards Buddhism—rests rather on presumption than on positive evidence. Although Xuanzang is enthusiastic when writing about his co-religionists and lacks zeal when describing Hindu or Hinayana kings, he repeatedly gives evidence of his sense of balance." She cited his treatment of Pulakesin II, King Harsha's great rival.

19. A. Embree, *Imagining India: Essays on Indian History* (New York: Oxford University Press, 1989), p. 49.

20. P. Spear, *India* (Ann Arbor: University of Michigan Press, 1961), p. 80. See also Vincent Smith, who was the scholar who traced Xuanzang's journey to and from China in great detail, research that caused him to write in *Oxford History of India*: "The memory of the Master of the Law . . . is still as fresh in Buddhist lands as it was 1200 years ago." He also remarked that "it is impossible to overestimate the debt which the history of India owes to Hieun Tsang." p. 182. In the same work, Smith cited Xuanzang as a source in such varied instances as the organization of the Indian army in general and King Harsha's army in particular, the existence of Brahmin rajas, conditions in Assam, and kingdoms in the Deccan and in the south.

21. Weinstein, *Buddhism Under the T'ang*, pp. 25ff.
22. Li Yongshi, *Life*, p. 231.

Afterword

1. Cunningham, *Ancient Geography of India*, p. viii.
2. Foucher, *Life of Buddha*, p. 216.
3. Mirsky, *Sir Aurel Stein*, p. 94.
4. Seckel, *Art of Buddhism*, p. 63.
5. Rowland, *Art and Architecture of India*, p. 99.
6. Snellgrove, *Image of the Buddha*, p. 105: "The testimony of Hsuan-tsang is important, for not only does it confute the easy way in which Buddhist art is often labeled Hinayanist when it appears relatively simple and Mahayanist when the decoration and symbolism appear more complex, usually with complete disregard of what may be known as the Buddhism of the area from other sources, but it also confirms the flourishing state, at least in some districts of the Gandharan style even after the Hun invasions."
7. Bechert and Gombrich, *World of Buddhism*, p. 84: "The nearest thing we have to a census of monks and monasteries in ancient India is the record compiled by Xuanzang between 630 and 644 C.E. He listed them by area. India for him included Sri Lanka, what is now Bangladesh, much of what is now Pakistan and Afghanistan, and a bit of modern Nepal. If we exclude Sri Lanka (with 20,000 monks), his totals come to about 115,000 Hinayana and about 120,000 Mahayana monks; however, about half of the latter also studied Hinayana. . . . The Hinayana had about 2,000 monasteries and the Mahayana had about 2,500." See also E. Lamotte, *History of Indian Buddhism* (Louvain-La-Neuve: Institute Orientaliste de Universite Catholique, 1988), pp. 539–545, for a detailed and informative discussion of sects.
8. An additional study has been made by S. Sinberg, "Introduction to the Data Base on Yuan Chwang's Travels in India: Its Material Culture/Religious Affiliations," New York (unpublished), 1984. In a preliminary paper she gave the total number of monasteries listed by Xuanzang in her statistical study as 6,150, all of which were divided into four categories: 480 Hinayana institutions, 1,820 Mahayana monasteries; 850 structures ascribed to both "Vehicles," and over 3,000 edifices simply termed "Buddhist." Outside India, along the northern route from China to India, Xuanzang designated 260 monasteries as Hinayana and approximately 100 to the Mahayana, and 50 were nondesignated. On his journey back to China along the southern route, the opposite situation occurred. Mahayana institutions numbered over 300, Hinayana about 220, and approximately 25 were nondesignated.
9. Seckel, *Art of Buddhism*, p. 157. In another version the Udayama image was brought to Kucha in Central Asia, and it was taken from there to China. See Pal, *Light of Asia*, p. 171.
10. P. Swann, *Chinese Monumental Art* (London: Thames and Hudson, 1963), p. 109. The historian René Grousset also saw a new plasticity in Tang art, especially in the grottos of T'ien-lung-shan (Tianlongshan) in northern Shansi (Shanxi) province; he attributed these changes partially to the example

of Indian Gupta models brought back by pilgrims such as Xuanzang. See Grousset, *The Rise and Splendour of the Chinese Empire*, trans. A. Watson-Gandy and T. Gordon (Berkeley: University of California Press, 1953), p. 142; and Pal, *Ideal Image*, pp. 49ff. Pal was content to say, "One would imagine that such images brought back by so eminent a teacher would have exerted considerable artistic influence." See also Rowland, *Evolution of the Buddha Image*, p. 24: "Of great import to the transmission of Indian types to China are the itemized lists of actual replicas of famous Indian statues collected by those visitors to the Western Countries; for example, Hsuan-tsang had copied the famous sandalwood image of King Udayana and other famous icons."

11. Anthony C. Yu, trans., *Journey to the West* (Chicago: University of Chicago Press, 1977), vol. 1, p. 11; also Glen Dudbridge, *The Hsi-yu-Chi: A Study of the Antecedents to the Sixteenth Century Chinese Novel* (Cambridge: Cambridge University Press, 1970), pp. 164ff; and V. Mair, "Suen Wu-king = Hanumat? The Progress of a Scholarly Debate," Proceedings of the Second International Conference on Sinology (Taipei: Academic Sinica, 1989), pp. 659–752.

12. *The Pilgrim's Progress* has been compared to the typical hero's journey by Esther Harding. See her *Journey into Self* (London: Longmans Green, 1956), and it has been translated into Jungian concepts of growth and integration of the psyche. Similarly, *Journey to the West* has been thought of as a manual of Buddhist, Daoist, or Confucian self-cultivation. See A. Plaks, *Four Masterworks of the Ming Novel* (Princeton: Princeton University Press, 1987), a sophisticated analysis of its themes.

13. See Mark Salzman, *The Laughing Sutra* (New York: Random House, 1991); and Maxine Hong Kingston, *The Tripmaster Monkey* (New York: Knopf, 1989).

14. The question of the authentic portrait of Xuanzang is complicated. Until the discovery of this representation in 1990 in Yulin, various portraits had been thought to be the Chinese pilgrim or the prototype of a Chinese pilgrim. See Victor Mair, "The Origins of an Iconographical Form of the Pilgrim Hsuan-tsang," *Tang Studies*, no. 4 (1986), which shows that the pilgrim traveler sometimes thought to be Xuanzang may be an itinerant monk or a "transformation performer."

15. Mizuno, *Buddhist Sutras*, p. 77. Ikeda, *Chinese Buddhism*, p. 17, lists Puk'ung rather than Amoghavajra.

16. Xuanzang's rendering of this sutra became the standard translation in Asia. Most Far Eastern Buddhists, especially Zen practitioners, know it by heart.

17. In 1973 a complete English translation of the *Thirty Verses* and its commentaries, including the Chinese original, *Ch'eng Wei-Shih Lun*, was made by Wei Tat in Hong Kong, suggesting a revival of interests there.

18. Wright and Twitchett, *Perspectives on the T'ang*, p. 296, considers some of the limitations of the school.

19. Ikeda, *Chinese Buddhism*, p. 133. Ikeda felt that the teachings that Xuanzang exposed represented "a doctrinal regression in the overall development of Chinese Buddhism in China," that his translations "were of a highly philosophical and abstruse nature . . . lacking in the true Mahayana spirit with its

concern for the salvation of all humankind." (This might be partisan, sectarian criticism.)

20. Pal, *Light of Asia*, p. 256. See also R. Birnbaum, *The Healing Buddha* (Boulder, Colo.: Shambala, 1979), p. 59: "Though popular before the seventh century it was by virtue of Hsuan-tsang's excellent translation that the *sutra* was truly disseminated throughout East Asia."

21. Waley, *Tripitaka*, p. 31.

22. Ibid.

23. "In reality . . . it was indeed the entire heritage of Indian thought which was made accessible to the subjects of the T'ang dynasty." See Grousset, *Rise and Splendour of the Chinese Empire*, p. 141. Also Rowland, *Evolution of the Buddha Image*, p. 23: "An inventory of the sutras translated by the Master of the Law at Ch'ang-an reveals how the first real conception of the faith of the Great Vehicle was due entirely to his enterprise. The contribution of Hsuan-tsang is comparable to the discoveries and influence of Renaissance humanists on the later development of classic learning in the West."

24. Only Ibn Batuta traveled more widely than Xuanzang. See Ibn Batuta, *Travels in Asia–Africa, 1325–1354*, trans. and ed. H.A.R. Gibb (London, 1929; rpt. New York: Kelley, 1969).

Selected Bibliography

Xuanzang, Buddhism, Buddhist Art

Auboyer, J., and others. *Buddha: A Pictorial History of His Life and Legacy.* Trans. Anne E. Keep. New York: Crossroad Pub., 1983.

Beal, Samuel, trans. *The Life of Hiuen-Tsiang.* Trans. from the Chinese of Shaman Hwui li. London, 1911; 2d ed. Delhi: Munshiram Manoharlal, 1973.

Beal, Samuel, trans. *Si-yu-ki, Buddhist Records of the Western World,* by Hiuen Tsiang. 2 vols. London, 1884; rpt. Delhi: Oriental Books Reprint Corp., 1969.

Bechert, H., and Gombrich, R. *The World of Buddhism.* New York: Facts on File, 1984.

Birnbaum, R. *The Healing Buddha.* Boulder, Colo.: Shambhala, 1979.

Boulting, William. *Four Pilgrims.* London: Kegan Paul/Trench, Trubner, n.d.

Boulton, Nancy Elizabeth. "Early Chinese Buddhist Travel Records as a Literary Genre." Ph.D. diss. University of Michigan, 1982.

Chau Bhikshu Thich Minh. *Hsuan tsang—The Pilgrim and Scholar.* Nha-Trang, Vietnam: Vietnam Buddhist Institute, Kalika Press, 1963.

Conze, Edward. *Buddhism: Its Essence and Development.* Oxford, 1951; rpt. New York: Harper and Row, 1975.

Conze, Edward. *Buddhist Scriptures.* 1959; rpt. Harmondsworth: Penguin Books, 1984.

Conze, Edward. *Buddhist Thought in India: Three Phases of Buddhist Philosophy.* London, 1962; rpt. Ann Arbor: University of Michigan Press, 1987.

Conze, Edward. *Buddhist Wisdom Books, the Diamond Sutra and the Heart Sutra.* 1958; rpt. London: Allen and Unwin, 1980.

Cummings, Mary. *The Lives of the Buddha in the Art and Literature of Asia.* Michigan Papers on South and Southeast Asia. Ann Arbor: University of Michigan Press, 1982.

Dudbridge, Glen. *The Hsi-yu chi: A Study of Antecedents to the Sixteenth Century Chinese Novel.* Cambridge: Cambridge University Press, 1970.

Fischer-Schreiber, I., Ehrhard, F., and Diener, M. *The Shambhala Dictionary of Buddhism and Zen.* Trans. Michael H. Kohn. Boston: Shambhala, 1991.

Foucher, A. *The Beginnings of Buddhist Art and Other Essays.* Trans. L. A. Thomas and F. W. Thomas. London: H. Milford, 1917.

Foucher, A. *The Life of the Buddha According to Ancient Texts and Monuments of India.* Abridged trans. Simone Brangier Boas. Middletown, Conn.: Wesleyan University Press, 1963.

Grousset, René. *In the Footsteps of the Buddha.* Trans. Mariette Leon. 1932; rpt. London: Routledge and Kegan Paul, 1971.

Kanda Christine Guth, "The Silk Route and the Diamond Path: Esoteric Buddhist Art on the Trans-Himalayan Trade Routes." *Orientations*, May 1983, pp. 29–36.

Li Yongshi, trans. *The Life of Hsuan-Tsang*, by Huili. Peking: Chinese Buddhist Association, 1959.

Mair, Victor H. "The Origins of an Iconographical Form of the Pilgrim Hsuan-tsang." *Tang Studies*, no. 4 (1986), pp. 29–41.

Mirsky, Jeannette. *The Great Chinese Travellers.* Chicago: University of Chicago Press, 1964.

Mizuno, Kogen. *The Beginnings of Buddhism.* Multiple trans. Tokyo: Kosei Publishing, 1980.

Mizuno, Kogen. *Buddhist Sutras: Origin, Development, and Transmission.* Multiple trans. Tokyo: Kosei Publishing, 1982.

Pal, Pratapaditya. *The Ideal Image: The Gupta Sculptural Tradition and Its Influence.* New York: Asia Society/John Weatherhill, 1978.

Pal, Pratapaditya. *The Light of Asia: Buddha Sakyamuni in Asian Art.* Los Angeles: Los Angeles County Museum, 1984.

Paul, Diana Y. *Philosophy of Mind in Sixth Century China: Paramatha's "Evolution of Consciousness."* Stanford: Stanford University Press, 1984.

Rowland, B. *The Evolution of the Buddha Image.* New York: Asia Society, 1976.

Rowland, B. "Indian Images in Chinese Sculpture." *Artibus Asiae* 10 (1947), pp. 5–20.

Saint-Hilaire, J. Barthelemy. *Hiouen Thsang in India.* Trans. Laura Ensor. Calcutta: Susil Gupta, 1952.

Seckel, Dietrich. *The Art of Buddhism.* Trans. Anne E. Keep. New York: Crown, 1964.

Sehrai, F. "The Buddha Story in the Peshawar Museum." Peshawar: F. Sehrai, 1985.

Sehrai, F. "A Guide to Takht-i-Bahi." Peshawar: F. Sehrai, 1986.

Sinberg, S. "Introduction to the Data Base on Yuan Chwang's Travels in India: Its Material Culture/Its Religious Affiliation." Unpublished. 1984.

Snellgrove, David L., ed. *The Image of the Buddha.* London: Serindia; Paris: UNESCO; Tokyo: Kodansha International, 1978.

Soper, A. "Aspects of Light Symbolism in Gandharan Sculpture." *Artibus Asiae* 12, no. 3 (1949), pt. 1, pp. 252–283; 12, no. 4, pt. 2, pp. 314–330; 13, no. 1 (1950), pt. 3, pp. 63–85.

Soper, A. "Representations of Famous Images at Tunhuang." *Artibus Asiae* 27, no. 4 (1965), pp. 349–364.

Suzuki, D. T. *On Indian Mahayana Buddhism.* New York: Harper and Row, 1968.

Thomas, E. J. *The History of Buddhist Thought.* 1933; rpt. Santa Fe, N.M.: Sun Publishing, 1981.

Waley, Arthur. *The Real Tripitaka.* London: Allen and Unwin, 1952.

Wang Jingru. "Western Xia Murals from Mogao Caves in Dunhuang and Yulin Caves in Anxi." *Wen Wu*, 9th issue, 1980, pp. 49–53.

Watters, Thomas, trans. *On Yuan Chwang's Travels in India.* 2 vols. London, 1904–1905; rpt. Delhi: Munshiram Manoharlal, 1961.

Wei Tat. *Ch'eng Wei-Shih Lun* (The doctrine of mere consciousness). Hong Kong: Ch'eng Wei-Shih Lun Publication Committee, 1973.
Whitfield, R. "The Monk Liu Sahe and the Dunhuang Paintings." *Orientations*, March 1989, pp. 64–71.
Williams, J. "The Iconography of Khotanese Painting." *East and West* 23 (1973), pp. 109–164.
Williams, Paul. *Mahayana Buddhism: The Doctrinal Foundation*. London: Routledge, 1989.
Woodward, F. L., ed. and trans. *Some Sayings of the Buddha*. 1925; rpt. London: Oxford University Press, 1955.
Yu, Anthony C., trans. *Journey to the West*. 4 vols. Chicago: University of Chicago Press, 1977–1983.
Zhu Qi (Chu Ch'i), *Xuanzang Xiyouji* (Xuanzang's journey to the west). Hong Kong: Chan Chin Ta-yuan Shutien, 1957. (Translated onto tapes for me from the Chinese by Kathy Swatek.)
Zimmer, H. *The Art of Indian Asia*. 2 vols. New York: Pantheon, 1955.
Zimmer, H. *Artistic Form and Yoga in the Sacred Images of India*. Trans. Gerald Chapple and James B. Lawson. Princeton: Princeton University Press, 1984.
Zurcher, E. *Buddhism: Its Origin and Spread in Words, Maps, and Pictures*. London: Routledge and Kegan Paul, 1962.
Zwalf, W. *Buddhism: Art and Faith*. London: British Museum Publications, 1985.

Pilgrimage and the Silk Route

Along the Ancient Silk Routes. New York: Berlin State Museum and Metropolitan Museum of Art, 1982.
Andrews, F. H. *Wall Paintings from Ancient Shrines in Central Asia Recovered by Sir Aurel Stein*. London: Oxford University Press, 1948.
Ashe, Geoffrey. *The Landscape of King Arthur*. New York: Henry Holt, 1987.
Association for Silk Road Exposition. *The Grand Exhibition of Silk Route Civilizations*. 3 vols. Nara, Japan: National Museum, Association for Silk Road Exposition, 1988.
Beal, S., trans. *Travels of Fa-hian and Sung-yun*. 1869; rpt. London: Susil Gupta, 1964.
Blunt, W. *The Golden Road to Samarkand*. London: Hamish Hamilton, 1973.
Bonavia, Judy. *An Illustrated Guide to the Silk Route*. London: Collins, 1988.
Boulnois, L. *The Silk Road*. Trans. Dennis Chamberlin. London: Allen and Unwin, 1966.
Byron, Robert. *The Road to Oxiana*. London: Jonathan Cape, 1937.
Cable, M., and French, F. *The Gobi Desert*. London: Hodder and Stoughton, 1942.
Campbell, J. *The Hero with a Thousand Faces*. Princeton: Princeton University Press, 1968.
Drege, J. P., and Buhrer, E. M. *The Silk Route Saga*. New York: Facts on File, 1989.

Flecker, James. *The Golden Journey to Samarkand.* London: Max Goshen, 1913.
Frank, Irene M., and Brownstone, David M. *The Silk Road: A History.* New York: Facts on File, 1986.
Giles, H. A. *The Travels of Fa-hsien (399–414 A.D.).* Cambridge, 1923; rpt. London: Routledge and Kegan Paul, 1959.
Harding, Esther. *Journey into Self.* London: Longmans Green, 1956.
Hedin, Sven. *The Silk Road.* Trans. F. H. Lyon. New York: Dutton, 1938.
Hirayama, Ikuo. *Sur la Route de la Soie.* Paris: Musée National des Arts Asiatiques—Guimet; Tokyo: Kodansha, 1991.
Hopkirk, Peter. *Foreign Devils on the Silk Road.* London: John Murray, 1980.
Huc, M. *Travels in Tartary, Thibet and China.* 2 vols. London: Office of the National Illustrated Library, n.d.
Huntington, John. "Pilgrimage as Image: The Cult of the Astamahapratiharya." *Orientations,* April 1987, pt. 1 (pp. 55–64); Aug. 1987, pt. 2 (pp. 56–69).
Huntington, John, "Sowing the Seeds of the Lotus: A Journey to the Great Pilgrimage Sites of Buddhism." *Orientations,* Nov. 1985, pt. 1 (pp. 46–62); Feb. 1986, pt. 2 (pp. 28–44); March 1986, pt. 3 (pp. 32–47); July 1986, pt. 4 (pp. 28–41); Sept. 1986, pt. 5 (pp. 46–59).
Ibn Batuta. *Travels in Asia–Africa (1325–1354).* Trans. and ed. H.A.R. Gibb. London, 1929; rpt. New York: Augustus M. Kelley, 1969.
Inoue, Yasushi. *Journey Beyond Samarkand.* Tokyo: Kodansha International, 1971.
Japan Broadcasting Company (NHK), ed. *The Silk Road.* 3 vols. Tokyo: Japan Broadcasting Company, 1981.
Kingston, Maxine Hong. *The Tripmaster Monkey.* New York: Knopf, 1989.
Klimburg-Salter, Deborah E. *The Silk Route and the Diamond Path.* Los Angeles: Los Angeles Art Council, 1982.
Le Coq, Albert von. *Buried Treasures of Chinese Turkestan.* Trans. Anna Barwell. New York: Longmans and Green, 1929.
Mirsky, Jeannette. *Sir Aurel Stein.* Chicago: University of Chicago Press, 1977.
Moule, A. C., and Pelliot, Paul, eds. *Marco Polo: The Description of the World.* 2 vols. London: Routledge, 1938.
Munro, E. *On Glory Roads: A Pilgrim's Book About Pilgrimage.* New York: Thames and Hudson, 1987.
Reischauer, E. *Ennin's Travels in T'ang China.* New York: Ronald Press, 1955.
Salzman, Mark. *The Laughing Sutra.* New York: Random House, 1991.
Scherman, Kay, *The Flowering of Ireland.* New York: Little, Brown, 1981.
Statler, O. *Japanese Pilgrimage.* New York: Morrow, 1983.
Stein, Aurel. *Ancient Khotan: Detailed Report of Archeological Explorations in Chinese Turkestan.* 2 vols. Oxford: Clarendon Press, 1907.
Stein, Aurel. "The Desert Crossing of Hsuan Tsang 630 A.D." *Indian Antiquary* 50 (1921), pp. 15–25.
Stein, Aurel. *On Ancient Central Asian Tracks.* Chicago: University of Chicago Press, 1964.
Stein, Aurel. *Ruins of Desert Cathay.* 2 vols. London, 1912; rpt. New York: Dover, 1987.

Bibliography

Stein, Aurel. *Serendia: Detailed Report of Exploration in Central Asia and Westernmost China.* 4 vols. Oxford: Clarendon Press, 1921.
Sykes, Sir Percy. *The Quest for Cathay.* London: A. and C. Black, 1936.
Tilman, H. W. *The Seven Mountain Travel Book.* London and Seattle: Diadem Books, 1983.
Vollmer, J., et al. *Silk Roads, China Ships.* Toronto: Royal Ontario Museum, 1983.
Wood, John. *Journey to the Source of the River Oxus.* London, 1872; rpt. Karachi: Oxford University Press, 1976.
Yang, Han-Sung, et al. *The Hye Ch'o Diary: Memoir of the Pilgrimage to the Five Regions of India.* Seoul, Korea: Asian Humanities Press/Po Chin Chai Ltd., n.d.
Younghusband, F. E. *The Heart of the Continent.* London, 1896; rpt. Hong Kong: Oxford University Press, 1984.
Yule, H., trans. *Cathay and the Way Thither.* 4 vols. London, 1915; rpt. Taipei: Ch'eng Wen Publishing, 1966.

The Indian Subcontinent, Central Asia, China, and Asia

Agrawala, V. S. "Sarnath." 3rd ed. Delhi: Director General, Archaeological Survey of India, 1980.
Ahir, D. C. *Buddhist Shrines in India.* Delhi: B. R. Publishing., 1986.
Akiyama, T., and Matsubara, S. *Arts of China: Buddhist Cave Temples, New Researches.* Trans. A. Soper. 1969; rpt. Tokyo: Kodansha International, 1972.
Asher, Frederick M. *The Art of Eastern India 300 to 800.* Minneapolis: Oxford University Press and University of Minnesota Press, 1980.
Bagchi, P. Ch. *India and China: A Thousand Years of Cultural Relations.* Bombay, 1950; rpt. Westport, Conn.: Greenwood Press, 1971.
Barua, D. K. *Bodh Gaya Temple: Its History.* Bihar: Bodh Gaya Temple Management Co., 1981.
Barua, D. K. *Viharas in Ancient India: A Survey of Buddhist Monasteries.* Calcutta: Indian Publications, 1969.
Bidder, Hans. *Carpets from Eastern Turkestan.* Accokeek, Md.: Washington International Associates, 1979.
Brown, Percy. *Indian Architecture.* Bombay: D. P. Taraporevala Sons, 1943.
Bussagli, Mario. *Central Asian Painting.* New York: Rizzoli International Pub., 1979.
Ch'en, K. *Buddhism in China: A Historical Survey.* Princeton: Princeton University Press, 1973.
Ch'en, K. *The Chinese Transformation of Buddhism.* Princeton: Princeton University Press, 1973.
Coomaraswamy, A. *History of Indian and Indonesian Art.* 1927; rpt. Delhi: Munshiram Manoharlal, 1972.
Craven, Roy C. *Indian Art: A Concise History.* 1976; rpt. London: Thames and Hudson, 1986.

Cunningham, Alexander. *The Ancient Geography of India.* 1871; rpt. Delhi: Varanasi, Indological Book House, 1979.

Czuma, S. J. *Kushan Sculpture: Images from Early India.* Cleveland: Cleveland Museum of Art, 1985.

De Silva, A. *The Art of Chinese Landscape Painting in the Caves of Tun-huang.* New York: Crown, 1964.

Devahuti, D. *Harsha: A Political Study.* 1970; rpt. Delhi: Oxford University Press, 1983.

Dobbins, J. Walton. *The Stupa and Vihara of Kanishka.* Calcutta: Asiatic Society, 1971.

Dupree, Nancy. "Gandhara: An Instant Guide to Pakistan's Heritage." Pakistan Tourism Development Corp., Karachi, n.d.

Dupree, Nancy. *An Historical Guide to Afghanistan.* 1970; rpt. Kabul: Afghan Tourist Association, 1977.

Dutt, S. *Buddhist Monks and Monasteries in India: Their History and Contribution to Indian Culture.* London, 1962: rpt. Delhi: Motilal Banarsidass, 1988.

Embree, Ainslie. *Imagining India: Essays on Indian History.* New York: Oxford University Press, 1989.

Embree, Ainslie, ed. *Encyclopedia of Asian History.* 4 vols. New York: C. Scribner and Sons, 1988.

Fairley, Jean. *The Lion River: The Indus.* London: Allen Lane, 1975.

Foucher, A. *Notes on the Ancient Geography of Gandhara.* Trans. H. Hargraves. Calcutta: Superintendent, Hindu and Buddhist Monuments Northern Circle, Government Printing Office, 1952.

Foucher, A. "Notes sur l'itineraire de Hiuan Tsang en Afghanistan." *Etudes Asiatique pour le 25 Anniversaire de L'Ecole Française d'Extreme Orient* Trans. H. Wriggins. Paris, 1925; pp. 257–284.

Gaulier, S., Jera-Bezard, R., and Maillard, M. *Buddhism in Afghanistan and Central Asia.* 2 vols. Leiden: Brill, 1976.

Ghosh, A. "Nalanda." 4th ed. Delhi: Director General, Archaeological Survey of India, 1959.

Ghosh, A. "Rajgir." Rpt. rev. 1958 ed. Delhi: Director General, Archaeological Survey of India, 1975.

Goetz, H. *The Art of India.* Baden-Baden, 1959; rpt. New York: Greystone Press, 1964.

Gopal, Sarvepalli. *Jawaharlal Nehru: A Biography.* 1989; abr. ed. Delhi: Oxford India Paperbacks, 1993.

Goyal, S. R. *Harsha and Buddhism.* Meerut, India: Kusumanjali Prakashan, 1986.

Grousset, René. *The Empire of the Steppes: A History of Central Asia.* Trans. Naomi Walford. New Brunswick, N.J.: Rutgers University Press, 1970.

Grousset, René. *The Rise and Splendour of the Chinese Empire.* Trans. A. Watson-Gandy and T. Gordon. Berkeley: University of California Press, 1953.

Hallade, M. *Gandharan Art of Northern India and the Graeco-Buddhist Tradition in India, Persia and Central Asia.* Trans. Diana Imber. New York: Abrams, 1968.

Bibliography

Hambis, M. Louis, et al. *L'Asie Centrale: Histoire et civilisation.* Paris: l'Imprimerie Nationale, 1977.

Harle, J. *The Art and Architecture of the Indian Subcontinent.* Harmondsworth: Penguin Books, 1986.

Hazra, K. L. *Buddhism in India as Described by the Chinese Pilgrims.* Delhi: Munshiram Manoharlal, 1983.

Herrmann, A. *A Historical Atlas of China.* Cambridge, 1935; rev. ed. Chicago: Aldine Pub., 1966.

Hook, B., ed. *The Cambridge Encyclopedia of China.* Cambridge and New York: Cambridge University Press, 1982.

Huntington, Susan, and Huntington, John. *The Art of Ancient India.* Tokyo: Weatherhill, 1985.

Ikeda, Daisaku. *The Flower of Chinese Buddhism.* Trans. Burton Watson. New York: Weatherhill, 1986.

Imam, A. *Sir Alexander Cunningham and the Beginnings of Indian Archeology.* Dacca: Asiatic Society of Pakistan, 1966.

Joshi, L. M. *Studies in the Buddhistic Culture of India During the Seventh and Eighth Centuries,* 2d ed. Delhi: Motilal Banarsidass, 1967.

Knoblock, E. *Beyond the Oxus: Archeology, Art and Architecture of Central Asia.* London: Ernest Benn, 1972.

Lahiri, Latika, trans. *Chinese Monks in India: Biography of Eminent Monks Who Went to the Western World in Search of the Law During the Great T'ang Dynasty,* A.D. *1–600,* by I Ching. Delhi: Motilal Banarsidass, 1986.

Lamotte, E. *History of Indian Buddhism.* trans. from the French by Sara Webb-Boin under the supervision of Jean Dantinne. Louvain-La-Neuve, Belgium: Institute Orientaliste de Universite Catholique de Louvain, 1988.

Litvinsky, B. A. *Outline History of Buddhism in Central Asia.* Papers of UNESCO Conference on History, Archeology and Culture of Central Asia. Calcutta: Kushan Studies in the USSR, 1970.

Liu Xinru. *Ancient India and Ancient China: Trade and Religious Exchanges.* Delhi: Oxford University Press, 1988.

Mair, Victor H. "Suen Wu-kung = Hanumat? The Progress of a Scholarly Debate." Proceedings of the Second International Conference on Sinology. Taipei: Academica Sinica, 1989; pp. 659–752.

Majupurias, J. *Holy Places of Buddhism in Nepal and India.* Bangkok: Tecpress Service, 1989.

Mitra, D. "Ajanta." 5th ed. Delhi: Director General, Archaeological Survey of India, 1986.

Mitra, D. *Buddhist Monuments.* 1971; rpt. Calcutta: Sahitya Samsad, 1980.

Mitra, R. C. *Decline of Buddhism in India.* Calcutta: Santiniketan Visvabharati, 1954.

Mote, Frederick W. *Intellectual Foundations of China.* New York, 1971; 2d ed. rev. New York: Knopf, 1989.

Murphy, R. *A History of Asia.* New York: HarperCollins, 1992.

Murray, John. *Handbook for Travellers in India, Pakistan, Burma and Ceylon.* London: John Murray, 1955.

Norman, Jerry. *The Chinese.* New York: Cambridge University Press, 1988.

Plaks, Andrew. *Four Masterworks of the Ming Novel.* Princeton: Princeton University Press, 1987.
Rice, Tamara Talbot. *Ancient Arts of Central Asia.* New York: Praeger, 1965.
Rowland, B. *The Art and Architecture of India: Buddhist, Hindu, Jain.* Baltimore: Penguin Books, 1953.
Rowland, B. *Art in Afghanistan: Objects from the Kabul Museum.* London: Allen Lane/Penguin Press, 1971.
Rowland, B. *The Art of Central Asia.* New York: Crown, 1974.
Roy, Sourindranath. *The Story of Indian Archaeology, 1784–1947.* Delhi: Archaeological Survey of India, 1961.
Sankalia, H. D. *The University of Nalanda.* Delhi: Oriental Publishers, 1972.
Schafer, Edward H. *The Golden Peaches of Samarkand: A Study of T'ang Exotics.* Berkeley: University of California Press, 1963.
Schwartzberg, J., ed. *A Historical Atlas of South Asia.* Chicago and London: University of Chicago Press, 1978.
Sharma, R. C. *Buddhist Art of Mathura.* Delhi: Agam Kala Prakashan, 1984.
Shaw, Isobel. *An Illustrated Guide to Pakistan.* Hong Kong: Hong Kong Guidebook Co., 1988.
Shearer, Alistair. *The Traveler's Key to Northern India.* New York: Knopf, 1983.
Sickman, L., and Soper, A. *The Art and Architecture of China.* 1956; rpt. Harmondsworth: Penguin Books, 1974.
Smith, Vincent. *The Oxford History of India.* London, 1958; rpt. Oxford: Oxford University Press, 1967.
Soper, A. *Literary Evidence for Early Buddhist Art in China.* Ascona, Switzerland: Artibus Asiae, 1959.
Spear, Percival. *India.* Ann Arbor: University of Michigan Press, 1961.
Swann, P. *Chinese Monumental Art.* London: Thames and Hudson, 1963.
Tulku, Tarthang. *Holy Places of the Buddha.* Berkeley: Dharma Publishing, 1994.
Twitchett, D., and Fairbank, J. *The Cambridge History of China.* vol. 3. Cambridge: Cambridge University Press, 1979.
Upasak, C. S. *Nalanda: Past and Present.* Bihar: Nava Nalanda Mahavihara, 1977.
Weinstein, Stanley. *Buddhism Under the T'ang.* Cambridge: Cambridge University Press, 1987.
Wright, Arthur. *Buddhism in Chinese History.* 1959; rpt. Stanford: Stanford University Press, 1971.
Wright, Arthur. "Changan." *Cities of Destiny.* Ed. Arnold Toynbee. New York: McGraw-Hill, 1967, pp. 138–150.
Wright, Arthur F., and Twitchett, D. *Perspectives on the T'ang.* New Haven: Yale University Press, 1973.

About the Book and Author

The saga of the seventh-century Chinese monk Xuanzang, who completed an epic sixteen-year journey to discover the heart of Buddhism at its source in India, is a splendid story of human struggle and triumph. One of China's great heroes, Xuanzang is introduced here for the first time to Western readers in this richly illustrated book.

Sally Hovey Wriggins, who journeyed in Xuanzang's footsteps, brings to life a man who transcended common experience. Eight centuries before Columbus, this intrepid pilgrim—against the wishes of his emperor—travelled on the Silk Road through Central Asia on his way to India. Before his journey ended, he had met most of Asia's important leaders and traversed 10,000 miles in search of Buddhist scriptures. He was both a mountain climber who scaled three of Asia's highest mountain ranges and a desert survivor who nearly died of thirst on the brutal flats; a philosopher and metaphysician; a diplomat who established China's ties to Central Asian and Indian kings; and above all a devout and courageous Buddhist who personally nurtured the growth of Buddhism in China by disseminating the nearly 600 scriptures he carried back from India.

Wriggins gives us vivid descriptions of the perils Xuanzang faced, the monasteries he visited (many still standing today), and the eight places of Buddhist pilgrimage in India. Detailed maps and color photographs provide striking evidence of the vast distances involved and the appalling dangers Xuanzang endured; reproductions of Buddhist art from museums around the world capture the glories of this world religion while revealing a cosmopolitan era in which pilgrims were both adventurers and ambassadors of goodwill.

An engaging introduction to Buddhism and Buddhist art, this unique book takes the reader on a rousing adventure that also gives a compelling view of Asian history and civilization.

Sally Hovey Wriggins is a writer and lecturer who has lived in Sri Lanka twice, most recently as the wife of the American ambassador. While there, she studied Buddhism with the Venerable Kheminda Thero. Her interest in Xuanzang dates back to 1977 when *White Monkey King* was published. Since then she has written of Xuanzang's extensive Asian travels in *Archeology* and *Orientations*.

Index

Abhidharma. See Tripitaka
Account of Western Lands of the Great Tang Dynasty. See Xuanzang Original Works, Record of the Western Regions, 152, 180
Adzhina-tepe Monastery, 38
Afghanistan, 84, 186. See also Kushan Empire
Ajanta
   cave, 1, 140
   monastery, 135, 138–139, 143
   See also Architecture
Aksu, 29
Alexander the Great, 40, 46, 53, 67, 186
Almsgiving. See Buddhism, Customs and Ceremonies
Amoghavajra, 191
Amu Darya. See Rivers, Oxus
Ananda, 124
Andhra, Kingdom of, 136. See also Dignaga
Angkor Wat, 173
Apsaras, playing music at Kizil, 28, Color Plate 3
Aral Sea, 159
Archaeological Site Maps
   Bodh Gaya, 107
   Nalanda, 114
   Old and new Rajagriha, 122
   Sarnath, 101
   Trade routes, caves W. India, 141
   Turfan, 23
Archaeological Sites
   Adzhina-tepe, 38
   Ak Beshim, 30
   Begram, 46
   Dunhuang, 172, 186
   Jalalabad, 55
   Khotan, 165–166
   Lumbini, 97
   Miran, 168
   Peshawar, 59
   Taxila, 68
Archaeology, 38, 79
   Archaeological survey of India, 185
   Dunhuang Caves, 172, 186
   Nalanda Monastery, 187

   See also Cunningham, Sir Alexander; Stein, Sir Aurel
Architecture, 46, 53, 59, 77, 100, 106, 108, 135, 138–139
Asanga, 11, 71, 76, 85–86, 125, 131, 145
Ascetics, 100
Asoka, 41, 67, 131
   as builder, 54, 60–61, 68, 82, 87, 97, 99, 101–102, 108, 187
Assam, 132
Atman, 85
Avalokitesvara, 66
Ayodhya (Oudh), 84. See also Mahayana Buddhism

Badakhshan, kingdom at, 158, 188
Balkh, 39
Bamiyan, 43, 45–46, 144, 155, 187, Color Plate 4
Bana, 152
Bandha, 13
Bangladesh, 132
Banner of Famous Indian Images, 188. See also Dunhuang caves
Barula Gorge, 69
Begram, 46–47
Bezeklik, 24, Color Plate 2
Bhaja Caves, 139, 141
Bharukaccha (Broach), 139
Bimaran Reliquary, 55–56
Bimbisara, King, 121–122
Bimbisara Road, 122–123
BODDO coin, 59–60
Bodh Gaya, 68, 82, 105–107, 110
   temple, 108, 144. See also Pilgrimage
Bodhisattvas, 9, 65–66
   Bodhisattva of Blue Lotus, 139, 143
   compassionate Bodhisattvas, 184
   key concept in Mahayana, 8
   See also Buddha Images
Bodhisattva Avalokitesvara (sandalwood statue), 131
Bodhisattva Guanyin. See Guanyin
Bodhisattva Maitreya. See Maitreya
Bodhisattva of Wisdom. See Manjusri
Bodhi Tree (Bo Tree), 107, 110
Bombay, 137, 139

Brahma, 55–56, 66, 82, 153
Brahmins, 53, 79, 154. See also Castes
Buddha. See Sakyamuni
Buddha, Historical. See Sakyamuni
Buddha Images, 44, 46, 119, 165, 187
   Bimaran Reliquary Buddha at Jalalabad, 56
   Buddha Image at Seiryoji, 188
   Buddha Multiplying Himself at Sravasti, 94
   Buddha of the Future at Darel, 64
   Colossal Images at Yungang, 64
   Dated Buddha Image from Sahri Bahlol, 66
   Dipankara Buddha from Shotorak, 48
   Great Buddhas at Bamiyan, 43, Color Plate 4
   Mathura Buddha from Katra Mound, 80
   Parinirvana Buddha at Adzhina-tepe, 38
   Starving Buddha at Bodh Gaya, 108
   Turning Wheel of Law from Sarnath, 100, 103, 104
   Udayana Buddha at Kausambi, 38
   See also Gandharan Art; Gupta Images; Xuanzang's Replicas
Buddha Legends, 87, 95, 98–99, 103, 154
   Dragon Gopala, 54
   Dream of Maya, 97
   84,000 Stupas, 41
   First Disciples, 108
   Four-fold Rim, 108
   How to Make Stupa, 40
   Temptation of Mara, 109
   See also Jataka Tales
Buddha of the Future. See Maitreya
Buddhism, 10, 181–182
   in India, 79
   "The Buddha Legend," 194
Buddhism, Customs and Ceremonies, 48, 54
   almsgiving, 84, 154
   circumambulating, 109
   display of king's poverty, 44, 155
   procession of images, 28, 103

Index

Buddhism, Schools of
  Fa-xiang, 193
  Hinayana, 84, 132, 136, 153, 162
  Madhyamika, 134
  Realist, 59, 70
  Tantric, 193
  Zen, 40, 192
  See also Hinayana Buddhism; Mahayana Buddhism
Buddhist Art
  first human representations, 64
  Gupta images, 7, 9
  influence of emptiness doctrine, 135
  Kushan Images, 79
  Xuangzang's record, 187–188
  See also Buddha Images; Gandharan Art; Painting; Xuanzang's Replicas
Buddhist Councils
  First Council, 124
  Fourth Council, 70–71
  Second Council, 105
  Third Council, 106
Buddhist Doctrine
  doctrine of emptiness, 8, 135, 192
  doctrine of the Middle Way, 100, 103, 108, 140
  emperor's interest in, 182
  four noble truths, 103, 111
  noble eightfold path, 103, 111
  See also Buddha Images

Calukya Dynasty, 138
Caravan, 12–13, 37, 141, 171
  crossing desert, 167–168
  Hindu Kush, 43, 157
  at Jalandhara, 155
  in the Pamirs, 158
  Tian Shan, 30
  Trapusa and Bhallika, 40
Carpets, Xuanzang describes, 32, 139, 162
Castes, 54
  Brahmins, 54
  Kshatriyas, 54
  Sudras, 54
  Vaisyas, 54
Caves, 24, 105, 135
  at Ajanta, 135, 138–140
  A Thousand Buddhas, 172
  Bamiyan Monastery, 40
  at Bezeklik, 24
  at Bhaja, 139, 142
  Cave of Three Immortals at Kashgar, 162
  at Dunhuang, 172
  at Ellora, 135
  at Jalalabad (Shadow Cave), 54
  at Karashahr, 25
  at Kizil, 28
  at South Kosala, 135
  at Subashi, 28
Central Asia. *See* Turkestan
Chang'an (Xian), 8, 12, 37, 46, 176, 182, 185
  as cultural center, 10
  as Tang capital, 3, 172
Charkhlik (Ruoqiang), 168
Charsadda, 59
Chengdu, 8, 166
Cherchen (Qiemo), 168, 171
Chickiklik plateau, 160
China, 3, 147, 162, 168, 171, 193
Chinabhukti (Firozpur), 75
Chonen, 188
Christianity, 65
City of Light. *See* Varanasi
Conception of Buddha, 97
Confucianism, 147, 181
  Xuanzang as Confucian, 5, 8
Cult of the Healing Buddha, 193. *See also* Buddhism, Schools of
Cunningham, Sir Alexander, 6, 185

Dandan Oilik. *See* Archaeological Sites, Khotan
Daoism, 181
Deserts, 15, 32, 166
Destruction of Heresy. See Xuanzang Original Works
Devadatta, 95, 121
Dharmapala, 125, 131, 136. *See also* Xuanzang Intellectual Influences
Dharmasimba, 39
Diamond Sutra, 11, 173
Diamond Throne, 109
Dignaga, 71, 125, 131, 136, 138, 193. *See also* New Logic
Dipankara, 48, 54. *See also* Buddha Images; Sakyamuni
Dravida, 136–137
Dunhuang Caves (Tunhuang), 9, 15–16, 58, 61, 168, 175–176, 188, Color Plate 8
  juncture of north and south Silk routes, 14, 158, Color Plate 1
  opening up in 1906–08, 172
  See also Stein, Sir Aurel

Eightfold Path. *See under* Buddhist Doctrine
Elephants, 123
  Harsha's gift, 153–154, 160
  painting at Dunhuang, 172
  for use at Nalanda, 120
  use in war, 84, 138
  See also Sakyamuni, Eight Main Events

Ellora Monastery, 135
Enlightenment. *See* Sakyamuni, Eight Main Events

Faizabad, 158
Faxian, 64, 79, 93, 106, 133, 135, 137, 177, 181, 187–188
Fa-xiang (Fa-hsiang). *See* Buddhism, Schools of
Flecker, James, 33
Foucher, Alfred, 63, 186
Four Noble Truths. *See under* Buddhist Doctrine
Fuhrer, A., 97

Gandhara, 40, 57
Gandharan Art, 46, 56, 61, 64–65, 186. *See also* Buddha Images
Ganges River, 132, 151
Gansu, 12
Gaochang, 23, 26
Gaozong, Emperor, 182, 184–185
Gauhati, 151
Ghats, 139
Great Debate, 153
Great Decease. *See* Parinirvana
Great Dragon Lake, 158
Greater Vehicle. *See* Mahayana
Great Khan of Western Turks, 3, 25, 37, 179
  Buddhism, 31
  greets Xuanzang, 30–31
  murder, 4
  summer at Tashkent, 4
Great Miracle, 94
Guanyin, 14–15, 17
Gupta Images, 79, 178, 188

Hackin, Joseph, 46
Hadda, 55, 57
Hami, 14–15, 17
Han Dynasty, 180
Hariti, the Mother Goddess, 119
Harsha, 54, 71, 138, 145, 147, 151–153, 155, 179
  as builder at Nalanda, 118
  capitol at Kanyakubja, 83
  Emperor sends envoys to, 5
  uniter of North India, 3
  Xuanzang participates in religious debate, 84, 154
Heart Sutra, 16, 120, 192
Hinayana Buddhism, 85, 106, 132, 136, 152, 166. *See also* Buddhism, Schools of
Hindu, 50, 79, 151, 153
  ascetics, 100, 146
  at Great Debate, 153

Index

Xuanzang as Art Collector, 48
  Buddha descending from heaven, 82
  influence in introducing Indian art into Far East, 88
  records of Buddhist art, 188
Xuanzang Calamities, 15
  attack by pirates on Ganges River, 86
  beset by robbers at Kucha, 29; at Kapisa, 54; Qoltag, 56
  beset by robbers at Sakala, 75
  boat capsizes on Indus River, 67, 157
  loses elephant, 160
  loses scriptures, 160
Xuanzang as Debater, 126
  Great Debate, 84, 151, 154
  with Hindu Brahmin, 145–146
Xuanzang as Diplomat, 7, 179
Xuanzang Dreams, 15, 145
  of Mount Sumeru, 12, 182
Xuanzang Early Life, 5, 9
Xuanzang Friendships
  Prajnakara, 43
  Silabhadra, 127
Xuanzang Intellectual Influence
  Asanga, 11, 71, 85–86, 125, 131, 136, 145, 166
  Confucian classics, 181
  Dharmapala, 136
  Vasabandhu, 11, 58, 85, 125, 131, 136, 145, 166
  Venerable One, Silabhadra, 125, 136
  Yogacara Buddhism, 11, 76, 85–86, 125, 136, 144–145, 192–193
Xuanzang as Influencer, 184, 188
  in archaeology, 185–186
  in art history, 89, 187–190
  in Chinese Buddhism, 63, 191–194
  in literature, 190–191
Xuanzang Language Studies, 11
  at Chang'an, 10–12
  at Chengdu, 9
  at Kashmir, 71
  language abilities: Sanskrit, Tokharian, 10
Xuanzang Letters
  from the Emperor, 171
  to Emperor Taizong, 172
  of introduction, 39
  "Memorial" to the emperor that he was coming home, 165
  to Venerable One's pupil, 127
Xuanzang as Metaphysician, 105, 132, 146, 153
Xuanzang as Monk, 9, 179
  as master of the law, 44
  as monk at Monastery of Hostages, 48
  as student at Nalanda, 125
Xuanzang Omens, 131, 133
  Jain fortune teller, 146, 151
Xuanzang Original Works, 67
  Commentaries on Thirty Verses, 136–137
  Destruction of Heresy, 146, 153
  On the Harmony of Principles, 145
  Record of the Western Regions, 152, 180
  Three Persons of the Buddha, 151
  Treatise on the Harmony of Teaching, 126
Xuanzang as Preacher
  at Kashmir, 69
  at Khotan, 166
  at Nalanda, 126
  at Samarkand, 38
Xuanzang as Pilgrim, 94, 96, 98, 100, 103
  at sacred sites in Buddha's life, 93, 98, 106, 108, 111, 121
  Vulture Peak, 121
Xuanzang Predecessors, 10. *See also* Faxiang
Xuanzang Relations with Rulers, 24, 152
  Emperor Gaozong, 182
  Emperor Taizong, 7, 171, 177, 181
  Great Khan, 30
  Harsha, 84, 151, 155
  King of Assam, 151
  King of Bamiyan, 44, 46
  King of Kapisa, 48
  King of Kashmir, 69, 157
  King of Khotan, 162
  King of Samarkand, 38
  King of Turfan, 18
  meets with Taizong, 7, 177, 181
Xuanzang's Replicas, 176–177
  Golden Buddha teaching on Vulture Peak, 123–124
  Golden Buddha at Praghbodhi Mountain, 124
  Sandalwood Buddha in his work of conversion at Vaisali, 106
  Sandalwood replica from the Shadow Cave at Nagahara, 54, 87
  Sandalwood Turning the Wheel of the Law at Sarnath, 103
  Sandalwood Udayana Image at Kausambi, 87
  Silver Buddha descending at Sankasya, 82, 87
Xuanzang Returns to China, 180, 184
  asks Emperor to excuse him from accompanying him, 180
  in triumph, 176
  within China, ends his record, 168
Xuanzang as Translator, 11, 191
  Heart Sutra, 16, 120, 192
  Lotus Sutra, 121, 177
  Master of Lapis Lazuli Radiance, 193
  New Logic, 71, 93
  Perfection of Wisdom, 193
  Sutra of Eleven-Faced Avolokitesvara, 63
  Treasury of Buddhist Philosophy, 166
  Treatise of Yoga Practice, 86, 166
  Treatise on Thirty Verses on Consciousness Only, 192
  Vimalakirti Sutra, 105
Xuanzang as Trekker, 11, 17, 29, 38, 43–44, 50, 63, 76, 131

Yarkand (Soche), 158
Yijing, 120, 133
Yogacara (Idealism), 11, 70, 76, 85–86, 124–125, 136, 144–145, 192–193
Yu, Anthony, 191
Yungang (Yunkang) torsos, 190

Zhiyan (Chih-Yen), 10
Zoroastrianism, 10, 37

Index

Hinduism
  Samkhya, 146
  Vaiseshita, 146
Hormuz, 139
Huili, 75, 100, 168, 181
Hund, 67, 157

Images, seven famous. *See* Xuanzang's Replicas
Indra, 55–56, 64, 66, 82, 92, 105–106, 108
Indu (India), 145, 152, 155, 158, 172, 180, 186–187
Indus River, 67, 157
Islam, 10, 180
Issyk Kul, 30

Jade Gate, 3, 13, 17
Jains, 50, 79, 146, 153–154
Jalalabad, 53–57
Jalandhara (Jullundur), 155
Japan, 137
Jataka Tales, 63, 186
  friezes on reconstructed Sikri Stupa in Lahore Museum, 63
  gift of Buddha's Head, 59
  gift of eyes, 59
  Prince Visvantara, 58–59, 168
  sacrifice for dove, 59
  sacrifice for tiger, 59, 61
  tiger at Dunhuang, 61
  See also Buddha Legends
Jayasena, 144
Jesus Christ, 65, 96
Jetavana, 94
Jewel of the Empire. *See* Xuanzang
Journey to the West, 124, 190–191

Kalidasa, Sanskrit poet, 139
Kancipuram, 136–137
Kanishka, King, 46, 57, 70, 77, 187
  reliquary, 58
  reverse BODDO coin, 60
  statue, 78
Kanyakuba (Kannauj), 83, 153
Kapilvastu, 95
Kapisa, 45, 57
Kapisa, King of, 48, 153, 157
Kapota Monastery, 131
Karashahr (Yanqi), 25
Karez (wells), 21
Kashgar, 10, 158, 160. *See also* Oases
Kashmir, 57
Kashmir, Vale of, 75
Kasyapa, 99, 124
Kathiawar, 139
Kausambi, 75, 87, 165, 188
Kawak Pass, 157

Khotan (Kustana), 158, 164–165, 168, 171–172
Khyber Pass, 56
Kizil, 28, Color Plate 3
Krishna, 79
Kshatriyas. *See also* Castes
Kucha, 26, 160
  as center of Buddhism, 28
  music in, 27
  Xuanzang describes, 26
Kucha, King and Queen of, 27
Kulu Valley, 75
Kumara, King of Assam, 146–147, 151, 153
Kumarajiva, 191
  monastery association at Tashkurghan, 160
  translator of Lotus of the Law, 29
Kunala Stupa, 68, 165
Kunduz, 39, 158
Kushan Empire, 46
Kusinagara, 82, 93
  great decease, 98
  See also Pilgrimage Sites

Lake Lop Nor, 168
Lake Victoria. *See* Great Dragon Lake
Land of Gems. *See* Simhala
Land of the Western Women, 139
Lankavatara Sutra, 144
Le Coq, Albert von, 24, 29
Legends
  aquatic monsters, 158
  Buddha images fly to Khotan, 165
  buried treasure at Monastery of Hostages, 48
  desert evil spirits, 167
  founding of Simhala, 137
  Khotan colonized by Indian immigrants, 164, 165
  local, 48, 61, 135, 157
  Maiden's Castle, 160
  miraculous stupa on mountain summit, 160
  modern, 135
  Naga River, 166
  rat worship, 166
  spread of silk culture, 164
  Xuanzang at Shadow Cave, 54
Letters, 127, 155, 165, 171
Liangzhou (Wuwei), 12
Library of Truths, 152
Lighthouse of Alexandria Vase, 47
Lion Capitol of King Asoka, 102
Logic. *See* New Logic; Old Logic
Lotus Sutra, 121, 177
Loulan, 7, 168
Lumbini, 82, 93, 95

Luoyang, 8, 10
  Xuanzang meets with the Emperor, 177

Magadha, King of, 105, 117–118
  kingdom of, 115, 177, 121
Mahabodhi Temple, 107–110, 118
Maharashtra, 137
Mahayana Buddhism, 48, 85, 132, 136, 152–153, 160, 164, 166
  Ayodhya, home of Mahayana, 85
  Bodhisattvas; concepts of emptiness, 134
  establishment of school, 106
  fourth Buddhist council, 70–71
  sage at Kashmir, 70
  second Vaisali Council, 105
  Xuanzang's attraction to, 8, 85, 154
Mahendra, 137
Maitreya, 9, 64, 86, 131
Malva, 139
Manjusri, 105, 136, 145
Mara, 109
Masson, Charles, 55
Master of the Law. *See* Xuanzang as Metaphysician
Mathura, 77
Mauri-tim Stupa at Hanoi, 163
Maya, 96–97
Mind Only Philosophy. *See* Buddhism, Schools of
Miracles. *See* Sakyamuni
Miran, 168
Mirsky, Jeanette, 186
Monasteries, 8, 10, 21, 37–41, 44, 46, 76, 83, 158, 164, 176
  Ascharya at Subashi, 28
  Ayodha, 85
  Deer Park at Sarnath, 100
  Hushkara at Kashmir, 70
  Jaulian at Taxila, 67
  Karashahr, 26
  Nalanda, 84, 193, Color Plate 7
  Pigeon Monastery at South Kosala, 135
  Pure Land at Luoyang, 8
Monasteries, locations, 138–139, 182
Monastic Life, 8, 118, 119
Monkey. See Journey to the West
Monkeys, 105
Morasampuru, 141
Mountains, 159
  Hindu Kush, 157–159, Color Plate 4
  Karakorum, 159
  Kunlun, 162
  Pamir, 158
  Sumeru, 12, 17
  Tian Shan, 24, 28

Index

Multan, 141, 144
Muztagh-Ata Mountain, 160

Nagarjuna, 131, 134, 145
Nairanjana River, 108
Nalanda, 114–128, 144–145, 151
   monastery, 82, 100
   stupa, 3, 118, Color Plate 7
Nasik, 137, 139
Nehru, Jawajarlal, 81, 85
New Logic, 71, 75. *See also* Dignaga
Nirvana 103, 106
Niya (Jingjue), 166. *See also* Archaeology
Noble Eightfold Path. *See under* Buddhist Doctrine
Northern Wei Figures, 190
Novel, 135, 190
Nuns, community of, 94

Oases, 4
   Aksu, 29
   Dunhuang, 14
   Hami, 15, 21
   Karashahr, 25
   Kashgar, 160
   Khotan, 162
   Kucha, 26
   Samarkand, 37
   Turfan, 22
Old Logic, 71. *See also* Vasubandhu
On the Harmony of Principles, 145. *See* Xuanzang Original Works
Original Hall of Fragrance, 100
Orissa, 133

Pagoda, 41. *See also* Stupas
Paintings
   "Boddhisattva of the Blue Lotus," 139, 143
   Bodhisattva Wall Painting at Dunhuang, 9
   at Dandan Oilik, "Nagini," 166–167
   Dunhuang, silk scroll, procession of manuscripts, 177, Color Plate 8
   Dunhuang, Xuanzang as Pilgrim, 172–173
   King and Queen of Kucha at Kizil, 27
   legendary depiction of Xuanzang, 192
   prototype of Pilgrim from Dunhuang, 174
   "Rat worship," 166
   Silk Princess Headdress, 165
   Tiger Jataka at Dunhuang, 61
   Xuanzang giving thanks, 172
   Yulin rendering of Xuanzang, 191
Pakistan, 186
Palace of the Phoenix, 177
Palk Straits, 133

Pamirs, 4, 38, 158–159, 179
   Taghdumbash Range, 159
Paramartha, 166, 191
Parinirvana, 38, 98
Parthians, 10
Parvata, 144
Pataliputra (Patna), 105–106
Pelliot, Paul, 173, 175
Penj Valley, 158
Perfection of Wisdom, 134, 145, 154, 194. *See also under* Xuanzang as Translator
Persia (Sassanid Empire), 139
Persian Gulf, 139
Peshawar, 56–57, 59
Pigeon Monastery, 135
Pilgrimage Sites
   eight traditional places, 82, 121, 187, Color Plate 5, Color Plate 6
   See also Bodh Gaya; Kusinagara; Lumbini; Rajagriha; Sankasya; Sarnath; Sravasti; Vaisali
Pima. *See also* Buddha images
Polo, Marco, 158–159, 167–168
Pragbodhi Mountain, Dragon Cave, 177. *See also* Xuanzang's Replicas
Prajnakara, 43
Prajnaparamita, 145
Prasinajit, King, 94
Prayaga (Allahabad), 154–155, 157
Prince of Pilgrims. *See* Xuanzang
Pulakesin II, King, 137–138
Punjab, 76

Questions of Milinda, 76

Rain, 23
   digging up treasure at Monastery of Hostages, 48
   scant at Hami, 21
Rain Retreat, 48, 79, 95, 136
   at Dhanakaka, 136
   at Jalandhara, 76
   at Kancipuram, 136
   at Kanyakubja, 155
Rajagriha (Rajgir), 82, 121–123
Ramayana, 190
Record of the Western Regions, 152, 180. *See under* Xuanzang Original Works
Relics, 40–41, 182
Religions, 10, 190
Rivers
   Gandak, 98
   Ganges, 81, 85–87, 132–133
   Gez, 160
   Godavari, 136
   Indus, 64, 67, 155

   Jamur, 144
   Jaxartes (Syr Darya)
   Jhelum, 69
   Krishna, 136
   Oxus (Amu Darya), 37–38, 158
   Quiakmakh, 162
   Yamuna, 77, 81, 87
   Yarkand, 159
Roof of the World. *See* Pamirs
Rulers
   endowing monasteries, 118
   relationships: Great Khan of Western Turks; King Harsha and China, 5, 157

Saketa. *See* Ayodha
Sakyamuni, 44, 48, 54, 67, 88, 182, 187
   Eight Main Events
     Nativity, 95, 97, 144
     Enlightenment, 103, 108, 187, 193
     First Sermon at Sarnath, 93, 103–104, Color Plate 6
     Final Nirvana at Kushinagara, 99, 177
     Descent from Heaven, 95, Color Plate 5
     Great Miracle at Sravasti, 95
     Subduing Nalagiri, 121, 123
     Monkey's Offering, 105.
     See also Buddha Image, Dipankara
Samarkand, 37–38, 158
   culture. *See* Sassanian people
   language. *See* Sogdian language, people
   religion. *See* Zoroastrianism
Samatata (Dacca), 133
Sankasya, 82, 87, 93, 95, 176, Color Plate 5
Sanskrit, 10–11
   Buddhist canon written under Kanishka auspices, 71
   as Buddhist scriptural language, 9
   as monastic subject, 125
Sarikol people, 160
Sarnath, 62, 93, 101–102, 104, Color Plate 6
   Deer Park, 100
   image of Buddha, 176
   See also Asoka; Xuanzang's Replicas
Sassanian people, 37, 139
Sectarianism, 193
Seven Famous Images. *See* Xuanzang's Replicas
Shahbaz Garhi, 58
Shotorak, 49
Sichuan, China, 133
Sikri, 61
   reconstructed stupa, 62

Silabhadra (the Venerable One), 115, 125, 127, 131, 144, 148, 193
Silk culture, 164–165. *See also* Legends
Silk Road, 3, 46, 172, 188
  Chang'an as origin of, 10
  northern, 21
  southern, 158, 162
Simhala (Sri Lanka), 133–134, 136–137
Sindh (in Pakistan), 141
Sirkap, 68
Sirsukh 67–68
Siva, 100, 152, 154
Skepticism, 144
Sogdian language, people, 10, 37, 40, 162
South Kosala, 134–135
Sravasti, 82, 94
Sri Lanka. *See* Simhala
Srinigar, 69
Srughna, 79
Statue Hand Holding Leaf at Nalanda, 116
Stein, Sir Aurel, 17, 160, 166, 168, 172
Stupas, 41, 54–55, 59, 95–96, 99, 101–102, 105, 108, 118, 123, 162
  Balkh, 39
  Kunala Stupa, 68
  Manikyala Reliquary, 42
  Monkey's Gift, 105
  Sacrificial Head, 68
  Stupa #3 at Nalanda, 119, Color Plate 7
  Tooth of Buddha, 133, 137
  Tower Stupa of King Kanishka, 187
  Triple Stairs, 82
  See also Relics; Wild Goose Pagoda
Subashi, 28
Subhadra, 99
Suddahana, King (father of Buddha), 96
Sui Dynasty, 8
Surya (Sun God), 141, 144, 154, 160
Sutras, 16, 63, 71. *See also* Kunala Stupa
Sutra of the Glorious Decease, 93
Swat, 57, 59
Syr Darya. *See* Termez

Taizong, Emperor
  and Buddhism, 3, 181–182
  relationship with Xuanzang, 7, 12, 164, 171–181
  relationships with other rulers, 26, 38
  Xuanzang's eulogy at Nalanda, 147
Taklamakan Desert, 15, 158–159, 166
Tamils, 136
Tamrallipti (Tamluk), 133
Tang Empire, 3, 8, 10, 171–172, 181
  art, 188
  expansion of, 152
  prestige of, 179

Tangitar Gorge, 160–161
Tara, 119
Tardu, Prince, 39
Tashkent, 32
Tashkurghan, 160
Taxila, 58, 67–68, 155, 165
Temple of the Tooth, 134. *See also* Stupas, Tooth of Buddha
Temples, 87
  at Gupta, 87
  Mahabodhi at Bodh Gaya, 107, 110
  of Seiryoji, 188
Termez, 38
Thirty-Three Fallacies, 193
Three Persons of the Buddha. *See* Xuanzang Original Works
Tian Shan Mountains, 21, 24, 28–30
Tibet, 134, 162. *See also* Buddhism, schools of, Madhyamika
Trade, 13, 21, 141, 172
  India with Persia, 139
  at Samarkand, 37
Treasury of Buddhist Philosophy, 59, 70. *See also* Vasubandhu
Treatise on Logic, 136. *See also* Dignaga
Treatise on the Harmony of Teaching, 126. *See also* Xuanzang Original Works
Treatise on the Stages of Yoga Practice, 11, 86, 115, 125, 127, 137, 144, 181, 193
Treatise on Thirty Verses on Consciousness Only 76, 136, 192. *See also* Vasubandhu
Tripitaka, 70, 105, 194
  three baskets of, 71, 124, 166
"Triumph of the Prince of Qin," 152. *See also* Taizong, Emperor
Turfan, King of, 23, 31, 179
  as Buddhist, 22
  daughter's political intrigue, 39
  equipping Xuanzang, 24
  letter of thanks, 81
  relatives of, 25
Turfan Basin, 10, 172
Turkestan, 186
Turks, 4
  eastern, 4
  western, 4
Turning the Wheel of the Law, 100, 103, 104. *See also* Buddha Images
Tushita Heaven, 64, 86, 131

Udayana, King of Kausambi, 55, 157
Udayana Image, 88, 165, 176–177, 188–189. *See also* Xuanzang replicas

Ujjaini, 139
Upali, 124

Vairocana, 164. *See also* Buddhism, schools of, Tantric
Vaisali, 82, 105, 177, 186. *See also* Pilgrimage sites
Vaisravana, 164, 167
Vaisyas. *See also* Castes
Vajra, fortune teller, 146, 151
Valabhi, kingdom of, 139
Varanasi (Benares) (City of Light), 100
Vasubandhu, 11, 59, 85, 125, 131, 136, 145, 166
  logic of, 71, 76
  See also Treatise on Thirty Verses on Consciousness Only; Treasury of Buddhist Philosophy
Venerable One. *See* Silabhadra
Venuvana (Bamboo Grove), 124
Vimalakirti, 105, 147
Vinaya Pitaka. *See* Tripitaka
Vinitaprabha, 75
Visvantara, Prince, 58, 154. *See also* Jataka Tales
Vulture Peak, 121–124, 177

Wakhjir Pass (Great Divide of Central Asia), 159
Waley, Arthur, 166, 191, 193
Western Parallel Figures
  Abelard, Peter, 144
  Berkeley, George, 11
  Herodotus, 166
  Luther, Martin, 145
  Polo, Marco, 17, 158
Wheel of Buddhist Law, 65, 177
White Huns, 40, 57, 158, 166
Wild Goose Pagoda, 182–183, 185
Wisdom Sutras, 132, 145, 154, 184
Woods, John, 158
World King
  Indian concept of, 65
Wu Cheng'en, 190

Xuanzang
  as appreciator of nature, 69
  born, 7
  census taker, 63, 116, 126, 132, 136, 139, 162, 188
  as folk hero, 18, 190–191
  as historian, 181
  in modern portrait, ii
  studies at Pure Land Monastery at Luoyang, 8
  as superstitious, 13, 30, 43
  in traditional portrait, 6